Learning
Power Query

*Simplify data cleaning and analysis with
Excel's most powerful tool*

Adam Szczepan Kopeć

bpb

www.bpbonline.com

First Edition 2025

Copyright © BPB Publications, India

ISBN: 978-93-65891-539

LIMITS OF LIABILITY AND DISCLAIMER OF WARRANTY

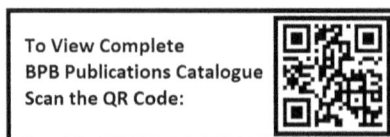

To View Complete
BPB Publications Catalogue
Scan the QR Code:

Dedicated to

My wife Agnieszka and children Hania i Wojtek

About the Author

Adam Szczepan Kopeć is a passionate user of Excel and Power Query. For many years, he has been utilizing these tools in his professional work and training others to help them better leverage the capabilities of these applications.

Since 2012, he has been running a Polish YouTube channel (Excel i Adam), where more than 1,000 public videos are available. These videos are watched approximately 3,000 times daily by over 20,000 subscribers. Since 2022, he also runs a channel in English.

His passion has led to the publication of three books on Excel in collaboration with the KomputerŚwiat editorial team and one written independently:

- Excel w przykładach. Zaawansowane funkcje krok po kroku
- Excel 50 najważniejszychfunkcji
- MistrzExcela w 20 dni (the first Excel book written as a dialogue)
- Excel SuperHero, czyli od zera do Bohatera w pracy (translated as: Excel SuperHero, or from zero to hero at work)

On May 1, 2017, he received the Microsoft Most Valuable Professional award. This award is granted to individuals who demonstrate expertise in Microsoft technologies (Excel) and contribute to the community by creating YouTube videos, writing books, or speaking at conferences.

He has over six years of experience as a trainer and holds the Microsoft Office Specialist Excel 2010 certification. However, he values the gratitude of those he has helped solve Excel-related problems far more than any formal credential.

He has trained individuals, including through the unique concept of writing a book about Excel as a dialogue (MistrzExcela), as well as small and medium-sized companies. For these companies, he has designed custom Excel spreadsheets to facilitate tasks such as summarizing sales data, creating price lists, and managing vehicle fleets or translators.

During his training sessions, he works directly with participants' files, enabling them to immediately apply the skills they learn.

About the Reviewers

❖ **Marco Primatesta** is a finance professional and technical reviewer with a strong passion and proven skills in financial controlling and accounting. He holds a master of science in finance from Hult Business School and an MBA from SAA – School of Management in Turin, developing deep expertise in financial management, business intelligence, and data visualization.

Marco's career spans established companies, innovative start-ups, and consulting roles, where he has specialized in implementing robust controlling systems and optimizing financial processes. He is dedicated to leveraging tools like Power Query and Power BI to automate workflows, enhance reporting accuracy, and support colleagues in ensuring reliable data elaboration. His hands-on experience includes leading projects that integrate advanced technologies to streamline calculations, improve management reporting, and strengthen accounting practices.

Fluent in English and Italian, with intermediate proficiency in Spanish, Marco is committed to fostering efficiency, precision, and a culture of continuous improvement across diverse industries, from automotive to premium labeling. His focus remains on reducing manual errors, maximizing business value, and advancing best practices in financial controlling and accounting.

❖ **Igor Oliveira** is a data analyst and internal solutions developer with strong expertise in Power Query (M) and Power BI, transforming raw data into automated, insightful dashboards. He specializes in creating scalable solutions through advanced DAX, SQL, and ETL pipelines using Talend, ensuring data consistency and availability across systems. With additional experience in Python, AI integration, and modern web technologies like Next.js, Igor bridges the gap between data analysis, automation, and internal tool development. His work combines deep technical skill with a strategic understanding of business needs, delivering end-to-end solutions that drive efficiency, intelligence, and informed decision-making.

Acknowledgement

I would like to sincerely thank my family for their patience and understanding during the many late evenings spent writing, testing, and rewriting. Your quiet support gave me the space to focus when I needed it most.

My appreciation also goes to the team at BPB Publications for their steady collaboration and openness to refining this book with care and technical accuracy. Working together across drafts made the content sharper and more relevant.

I am grateful to the many analysts, trainers, and Power Query users I have met during my career as a trainer. Conversations, questions, and feedback from the community have shaped not only this book but also how I approach data transformation as a discipline.

Lastly, to every reader who seeks more than just clicking through menus. This book is for those who want to truly understand what happens under the surface. Thank you for trusting it to guide your journey.

Preface

Power Query has become one of the most important tools in Excel for anyone working with data. As organizations collect and process more information than ever before, the ability to transform data directly within Excel is no longer optional. Power Query offers both simplicity through its interface and power through the M language, making it a critical skill for modern data professionals.

This book is organized to take readers from foundational transformations all the way to advanced scenarios. Early chapters introduce essential commands and logic, while later sections explore parameterization, error handling, performance, recursion, and custom functions. The material is structured to build confidence step by step, with each topic preparing the ground for the next.

Throughout the book, examples are grounded in practical use cases rather than abstract theory. Readers will see how Power Query can be applied to real business problems, and how writing M code directly can unlock flexibility and efficiency beyond what the interface offers. The goal is not just to follow steps, but to understand the why behind the transformations.

This book is written for Excel users who want to move beyond formulas and for analysts who need better ways to prepare and automate data transformation. It also supports trainers and professionals looking to learn more about Power Query and gain clarity in explaining its logic to others.

By the final chapter, readers will be able to design streamlined, automated query workflows with confidence. They will not only know how to use the GUI, but how to write and refactor M code, manage performance, and build transformations that scale.

General introduction to the book followed by,

Chapter 1: Getting Started with Power Query – Introduces Power Query as a core tool for importing, transforming, and automating data work in Excel. Covers how to access the interface, connect to sources like text files or websites, and apply basic transformations. Emphasizes the importance of proper data structure and shows how to begin building repeatable, efficient workflows.

Chapter 2: Advanced Data Connections and Imports – Shows how to connect Power Query to structured and semi-structured sources, including tables, named ranges, folders, and Access databases. Demonstrates techniques for handling inconsistent headers, filtering files and hidden elements, and dynamically importing content. Ends with practical guidance on setting up automatic refresh using both Power Query settings and VBA.

Chapter 3: Combining Data Queries – Covers the core techniques for combining datasets using Power Query. Readers learn the difference between appending rows and merging columns, along with various join types such as inner, outer, anti, and fuzzy merges. Practical use cases include importing multi-year sales data, building price lookups, aggregating invoice details, and matching fuzzy city names. The chapter also explores advanced operations like self-joins, list comparisons, and transformation tables.

Chapter 4: Grouping Data – Organize and summarize information using various grouping techniques in Power Query. From simple aggregations to dynamic product lists, rankings with ties, and local grouping, this chapter covers the full range of Group By operations. Explore how to apply functions like List.Modes and Table.Group with GroupKind.Local, while ensuring correct data types for reliable and efficient analysis.

Chapter 5: Pivot and Unpivot – Reshape complex, report-style tables into structured datasets ready for analysis. Follow practical examples that guide you through unpivoting irregular headers, turning repeated rows into columns, and adjusting fields to support consistent and automated transformations.

Chapter 6: Adding Columns – Perform transformations that enrich your data, such as calculating and rounding discounts, splitting fields by custom logic, and converting durations into time-based outputs. Use Column From Examples to define complex logic through patterns, creating structured and readable transformations grounded in real-world needs.

Chapter 7: Logical Operations and Conditional Columns – Explores the power of conditional logic in Power Query through real-world applications like calculating overtime, assigning bonuses, and grading student scores. Demonstrates how to use logical operators, nested ifs, and M functions to automate decisions and handle exceptions. Covers practical methods for comparing rows, managing errors, and analyzing absence periods using both interface tools and advanced M code.

Chapter 8: Parameters and Query Parameterization – Covers how to create and use parameters in Power Query to build dynamic and reusable queries. Step-by-step examples show how to extract values from cells, use drill down for precise data targeting, and replace hardcoded file paths. Practical guidance is given for managing parameters from lists, queries, or worksheet cells, and using M code for greater flexibility. Readers also explore how to avoid common issues with non-unique keys and privacy settings.

Chapter 9: Creating Custom Functions – Discover how to encapsulate and reuse transformations across multiple datasets using custom functions in Power Query. From understanding how Power Query generates functions during folder imports to building reusable logic from parameterized queries, this chapter provides hands-on techniques for modular design. It also demonstrates how to construct custom M functions from scratch, handle optional arguments, and standardize data formats effectively—laying the groundwork for scalable, automated workflows.

Chapter 10: Examples Using M Language – Presents advanced data transformation techniques that go beyond the graphical interface by leveraging the M language. Covers a wide range of real-life scenarios such as running totals, custom sorting, dynamic row and column removal, and pair generation. Demonstrates how recursion works through a factorial function and offers scripting and structural best practices to improve query flexibility and performance.

Chapter 11: Optimization and Extensions – Focuses on making Power Query workflows more efficient, readable, and maintainable. Introduces built-in view and statistics tools that help detect data quality issues and evaluate transformations. Highlights concrete strategies for improving query performance by removing unnecessary data early, reducing applied steps, using correct data types, and avoiding computationally expensive operations. Discusses techniques to measure execution time using Power Query, VBA, and Power BI diagnostics. Also explores Visual Studio Code as an alternative editor for better M code formatting and development.

Code Bundle and Coloured Images

Please follow the link to download the
Code Bundle and the *Coloured Images* of the book:

https://rebrand.ly/dc5315

The code bundle for the book is also hosted on GitHub at
https://github.com/bpbpublications/Learning-Power-Query.
In case there's an update to the code, it will be updated on the existing GitHub repository.

We have code bundles from our rich catalogue of books and videos available at https://github.com/bpbpublications. Check them out!

Errata

We take immense pride in our work at BPB Publications and follow best practices to ensure the accuracy of our content to provide with an indulging reading experience to our subscribers. Our readers are our mirrors, and we use their inputs to reflect and improve upon human errors, if any, that may have occurred during the publishing processes involved. To let us maintain the quality and help us reach out to any readers who might be having difficulties due to any unforeseen errors, please write to us at :

errata@bpbonline.com

Your support, suggestions and feedbacks are highly appreciated by the BPB Publications' Family.

> Did you know that BPB offers eBook versions of every book published, with PDF and ePub files available? You can upgrade to the eBook version at www.bpbonline.com and as a print book customer, you are entitled to a discount on the eBook copy. Get in touch with us at :
>
> business@bpbonline.com for more details.
>
> At www.bpbonline.com, you can also read a collection of free technical articles, sign up for a range of free newsletters, and receive exclusive discounts and offers on BPB books and eBooks.

Piracy

If you come across any illegal copies of our works in any form on the internet, we would be grateful if you would provide us with the location address or website name. Please contact us at business@bpbonline.com with a link to the material.

If you are interested in becoming an author

If there is a topic that you have expertise in, and you are interested in either writing or contributing to a book, please visit www.bpbonline.com. We have worked with thousands of developers and tech professionals, just like you, to help them share their insights with the global tech community. You can make a general application, apply for a specific hot topic that we are recruiting an author for, or submit your own idea.

Reviews

Please leave a review. Once you have read and used this book, why not leave a review on the site that you purchased it from? Potential readers can then see and use your unbiased opinion to make purchase decisions. We at BPB can understand what you think about our products, and our authors can see your feedback on their book. Thank you!

For more information about BPB, please visit www.bpbonline.com.

Join our Discord space

Join our Discord workspace for latest updates, offers, tech happenings around the world, new releases, and sessions with the authors:

https://discord.bpbonline.com

Table of Contents

CHAPTER 1
Getting Started with Power Query

Introduction

In this book, we will discuss the **extract, transform, and load** (**ETL**) tool known as **Power Query**. ETL means that Power Query allows users to retrieve data from various sources, merge it, transform it, and then load it primarily into Excel. This tool will be examined from the perspective of Excel, but it is also an integral part of Power BI Desktop.

In this chapter, we will begin exploring Power Query and its basic functionalities, such as retrieving data from text and **.csv** files and performing simple transformations. We will also learn what a proper data range is and why it simplifies further analysis.

Understanding Power Query will allow you to automate repetitive transformations and prepare data for reporting.

Structure

This chapter introduces Power Query and its core functionalities and covers the following topics:

- Introduction to Power Query
- Retrieving data from a webpage
- Retrieving data from a .txt file

Objectives

By the end of this chapter, you will be able to retrieve data from websites and text files (`.csv`, `.txt`). You will be able to perform basic text transformations, which will allow you to, among other things, remove unnecessary spaces, change letter case, or split text. You will learn simple mathematical operations that will, for example, allow you to calculate profit.

You will also understand what a proper data structure is, which will make it easier for you to prepare your data in a way that simplifies further processing and analysis.

Introduction to Power Query

Power Query is a powerful tool that allows you to retrieve and combine data from multiple sources, then transform it, and finally load it into Excel to facilitate further analysis or to create reports based on already transformed and cleaned data. The first step in working with Power Query is to retrieve data from at least one source.

Data retrieval

Power Query enables users to retrieve and connect to data from various source types. This is the first step in transforming data for further analysis. Whether the data is stored locally or online, structured or not. The most commonly used data sources are as follows:

- **Files:**
  - Text files (`.txt`, `.csv`, `.prn`)
  - Excel files (tables, sheets, ranges)
  - Folders, including subfolders
- **Databases:**
  - Access
  - SQL Server
  - Oracle
  - Other databases
- **Various other sources:**
  - Web pages
  - PDF files
  - SharePoint
  - Images

And many other sources.

The next step is transforming the data.

Data transformation

Power Query allows for numerous data transformations, including the following:

- Adding and removing rows and columns.
- Splitting a column based on delimiters or a specific number of characters.
- Filtering and sorting data.
- Replacing values in columns.
- Formatting text: converting to lowercase or uppercase, trimming spaces, and adding text.
- Performing operations on data: multiplication, division, and other mathematical calculations.
- Grouping data.
- Merging and appending data.
- Unpivoting columns.

The final step is loading the data.

Loading data

Power Query allows data to be loaded into Excel in the following ways:

- Into standard Excel tables.
- Into pivot tables.
- Into the data model (an option related to the Power Pivot add-in, which is not covered in this book).
- Loaded only to the Power Query editor, where it serves as a background query for other queries.

Advantages and disadvantages of Power Query

Power Query could be installed as an add-in for Excel 2010 and 2013. Since the 2016 version, it has become an integral part of Excel and is located on the **Data** tab. In this book, we will be working with Power Query available in Excel 365 in 2025.

Power Query is primarily represented by the **Get & Transform Data** group of commands (*Figure 1.1*), but it is also connected to commands from the **Queries & Connections** group.

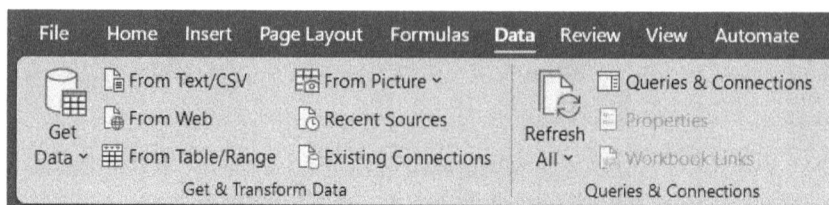

Figure 1.1: *Power Query commands on the Data tab*

Power Query allows for performing advanced transformations directly from the user interface, making it a tool that users can quickly benefit from with minimal learning effort. In more complex scenarios, however, the built-in tools may not be sufficient to achieve specific business objectives. In such cases, it becomes necessary to use M, the internal language of Power Query, which enables creating highly customized and flexible data transformations. Moreover, Power Query helps avoid repetitive and potentially error-prone manual data operations, making it a reliable and efficient solution for data preparation.

Advantages of Power Query

The following are the main advantages of Power Query:

- It is easy to use and quick to learn.

- It allows seamless integration of data from various sources, including multiple files within a specified folder.

- Once configured, a query can be reused multiple times.

- The original data remains unchanged, as a copy is created and transformed instead.

- It is integrated with Excel and Power BI, enabling further data analysis, reporting, and visualization.

Disadvantages of Power Query

The following are the main disadvantages of Power Query:

- The output data does not update automatically when the source data changes.

- With very large files and complex transformations, Power Query may run slowly.

- Lack of integration with **Visual Basic for Applications** (**VBA**) prevents more advanced automation of queries in Excel.

- Queries may be rigid and sensitive to changes in the structure or content of the source data, potentially causing errors if column names or formats are modified.

Correct data range

When transforming data, it is important to ensure that the source data closely resembles a proper data range (*Figure 1.2*). This can be understood as an Excel table. Such data is easier to analyze and further transform. Additionally, using tables helps ensure that data entry is performed correctly, minimizing structural errors. Unfortunately, much of the data we will work with will not have this structure.

For this reason, it is essential to understand what a correct data structure looks like, so we know how to transform the data initially. This will make subsequent transformations much simpler or even possible in the first place. The reason for encountering incorrect data ranges is that humans often find it more convenient to record data in formats that are not ideal for databases or other data analysis tools.

	A	B	C	D	E
1	Date	Merchant	Product	Income	Quantity
2	1/1/2023	Skipper	Gold coins	$250.00	25
3	1/1/2023	Julien	Pearls	$67.20	8
4	1/1/2023	Skipper	Gold bars	$999.60	4
5	1/1/2023	Melman	Gold bars	$749.70	3
	1/2/2023	Skipper	Iodeite	$12.00	1

Figure 1.2: *Example of a correct data range*

Characteristics of a correct data range

The following are the main characteristics of a correct data range:

- A header row that clearly defines the data contained in each column. It should include short descriptions of the data in individual columns. Column names should not be abbreviations and must be unique.

- A single column should contain only one type of data, meaning that merged data should not be present within a column.

- No empty rows or columns. This is especially important in Excel, as an empty column or row may indicate a different dataset.

- Avoid empty and merged cells. Missing data always complicates data analysis because it is unclear whether a cell should actually be empty or if it should contain repeated information from the cell above. In Excel, merged cells should also be avoided.

- Avoid category duplication in columns. For example, instead of having twelve columns named after months, there should be a single column where the names of the months are listed in separate rows.

Retrieving data from a webpage

In this chapter, data will be retrieved from sources outside of Excel, and the transformed results (queries) will be loaded into a blank Excel file. The first step will be to retrieve a simple dataset from a website[1] to perform basic transformations on it. The main objective is to become familiar with the Power Query editor.

This is a deliberately simplified example, as websites typically request user permission (e.g., through authentication or cookie dialogs), and identifying the correct table to import is not always straightforward. More complex websites may require additional configuration steps or do not expose data in an easily accessible tabular format.

To retrieve data from a website, the first step is to click the **From Web** command, which is located in the **Get & Transform Data** group on the **Data** tab (*Figure 1.1*). This will open the **Import Data from Web** window, as shown in *Figure 1.3*:

Figure 1.3: *Import data from the web window*

We remain on the **Basic** option, where it is sufficient to enter the correct URL and confirm it by clicking the **OK** button. If connecting to a given website for the first time, the **Access Web content** window should appear, as shown in *Figure 1.4*:

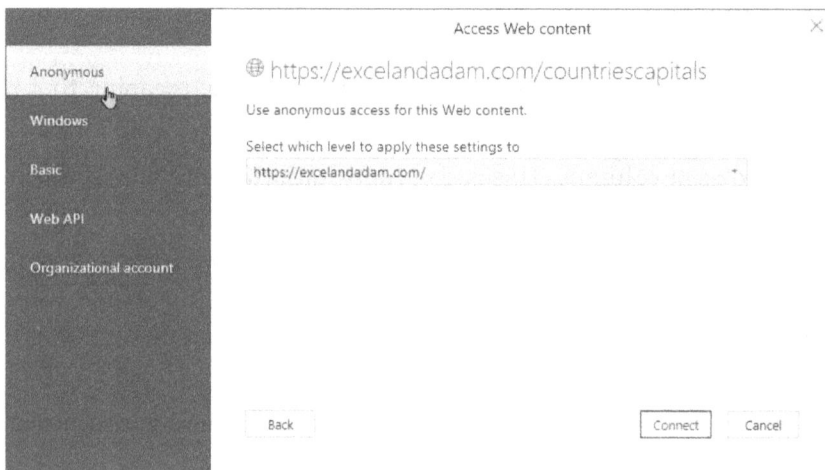

Figure 1.4: *Access Web content window*

---

1 **https://excelandadam.com/countriescapitals./**

The website does not require login credentials, so we can remain on the **Anonymous** tab and confirm the connection by clicking the **Connect** button. This will open the **Navigator** window, as shown in *Figure 1.5*:

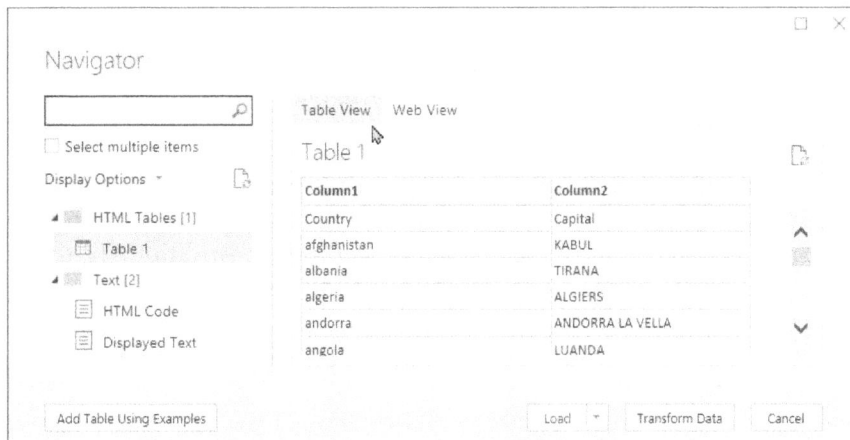

Figure 1.5: Navigator window

If Power Query detects a table structure in the HTML code of the specified website, the corresponding entries will appear in the list on the left side with default names assigned to them. When selecting one of these entries, a preview of the chosen table will be displayed on the right side. Theoretically, it is possible to switch from **Table View** to **Web View**, but Power Query is not a good web browser, and most websites are displayed in a way that is not user-friendly.

In addition to the detected tables, the latest version of Power Query should also recognize text objects. This section should contain the entire HTML code of the loaded page as well as the displayed text without any formatting. In most cases, these elements are very difficult to analyze because they contain all the text from the page (such as the top and side menus, bottom footer, etc.), as well as the entire HTML code, including the meta section, styles, and scripts.

Although there is a button in the lower-left corner labelled **Add Table Using Examples**, which facilitates searching for specific text, this method requires text to be located in distinct **Cascading Style Sheet** (**CSS**) selectors. Therefore, in most cases, the simplest approach is to extract tables from web pages.

In our example (*Figure 1.5*), we can see that our table contains only two columns. The first column contains country names, while the second column contains their capitals. It is noticeable that the data in both columns is not properly formatted. Therefore, it will be necessary to transform the data, which can be done by clicking the **Transform Data** button. Clicking the **Load** button would automatically load the data into Excel. Alternatively, expanding the **Load** button and selecting the **Load To** option would allow us to specify exactly where to import the data. However, in most cases, data should be transformed before loading it into Excel.

It is also worth mentioning the **Select multiple items** checkbox, which allows loading more than one table at a time from similar navigation windows into the Power Query Editor. However, it is important to remember that in such cases, each table will be loaded as a separate table.

In this example, only one table needs to be loaded, so it should be selected without changing the default options, followed by clicking the **Transform Data** button. This will open the **Power Query Editor**, with the selected table loaded as a query.

Since this is assumed to be the first time Power Query is being used, the **View** tab should be selected to ensure that the **Query Settings** option is highlighted. This setting is responsible for displaying the query steps on the right side of the window. Additionally, the **Formula Bar** checkbox should be selected so that the **M language code** for the active or selected query step appears above the data, as shown in *Figure 1.6*:

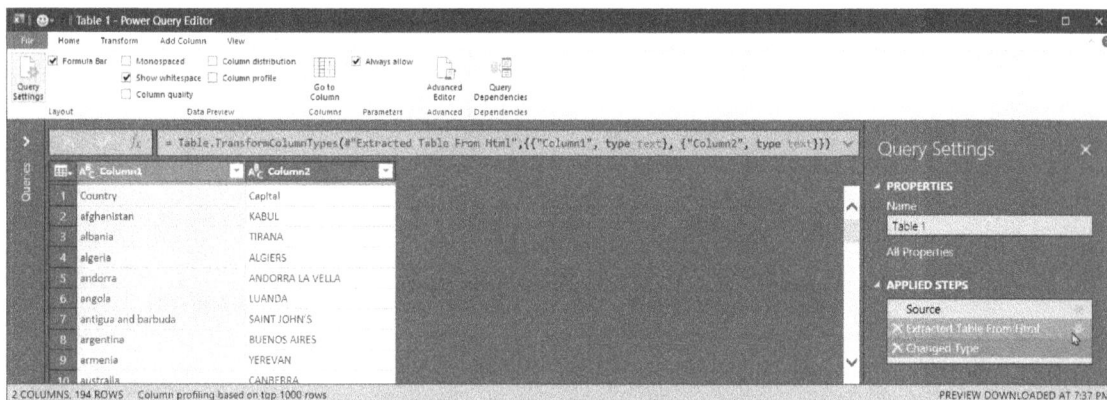

Figure 1.6: *First look at the Power Query editor and View tab*

Starting with Excel 2021, this **M language code** is also color-coded. The **Always allow** checkbox, related to **Parameters**, can also be enabled, as it will be useful in later examples.

Apart from these options, it is important to note that on the right side, in the **Query Settings** section, the default name of the newly created query can be found. By default, this name is taken from the loaded table or file. In this example, the default name does not indicate the content of the data, so it can be changed to something more descriptive, such as **Countries & Capitals**. To rename it, simply select the text in the **Name** field and enter the preferred name.

Below the query name, the **APPLIED STEPS** are listed, showing the transformations applied to the data from the moment it was loaded (the first step, **Source**). Clicking on each step will update the central view of the **Power Query Editor**, displaying how the data appears after that specific transformation. The **M language code** in the **Formula Bar** will also be updated accordingly.

At this stage, no modifications will be made to the **M language code**. Instead, the focus is on becoming familiar with its structure and recognizing keywords, which are usually highlighted in blue and greenish shades.

For some steps, a **gear icon** appears to the right of the step name. This indicates that the step can be modified using the **user interface**. Clicking the **gear icon** will open the appropriate settings window for that step. However, in this example, the applied steps will not be modified.

Fun fact: **Clicking the gear icon does not always open the same window that was used to create a specific step.**

To the left of the step name (except for the **Source** step), there is an **x** icon. Clicking it will remove the selected step.

Note: **Removing a query step cannot be undone using the Ctrl + Z shortcut. A deleted step can only be restored by repeating the transformation manually. At the beginning, it is recommended to delete only the last step, because removing a step in the middle of the query affects all subsequent steps. Without experience, it may be difficult to predict the consequences of such a change.**

Tip: **Double-clicking a step name is equivalent to clicking the gear icon. Pressing the F2 key while a step is active or selected allows renaming the step (except for the Source step).**

In the lower-left corner of the Power Query Editor, the number of columns and rows in the table resulting from the currently selected step is displayed. Next to this, the **Column profiling based on top 1000 rows** option can be found. Clicking it allows switching to **Column profiling based on the entire data set**. These options will be discussed later (*Figure 1.28*).

On the left side, the word **Queries** is displayed vertically along with a > symbol. Clicking this symbol expands or collapses (**changing to <**) the list of queries in the file. At this point, only one query exists, so there is no need to display the list. This list allows switching between queries and renaming a query by double-clicking on its name.

Similar to Excel, ribbon tabs with commands are visible at the top. These will be discussed in detail in various examples.

The most important sections of the Power Query Editor have been covered. Now, the focus shifts to analyzing the query steps in more detail as follows:

- **First step (source)**: Specifies the location from which the data is retrieved. In this example, it is a web page.

- **Second step (extracted table from HTML)**: Select a specific element or table from the website.

- **Third step (changed type)**: As the name suggests, this step modifies the data type. It should be added automatically based on Power Query's default settings. However, in this example, it does not contribute anything useful.

In both the second and third steps, column headers display **ABC icons**. These icons indicate that the text data type is assigned. Clicking the icon in a column header expands a **context menu** (*Figure 1.7*), allowing the selection of a different data type if Power Query has not assigned one (icon **123ABC**) or has chosen an incorrect type.

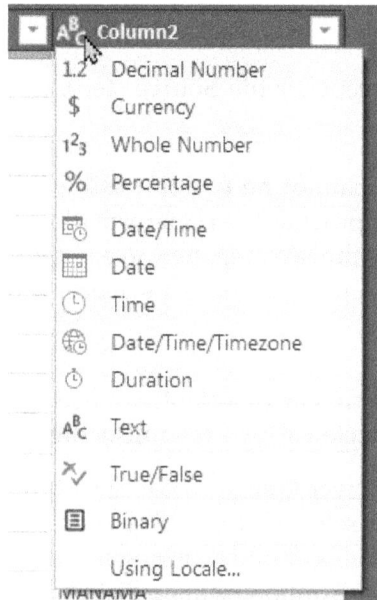

Figure 1.7: Context menu with a list of data types for a column

In this example, the correct data type has already been assigned to the columns in the second step, so the last step can be removed. Removing unnecessary steps is important when working with data that requires extensive transformations or contains a large amount of information.

By closely examining the data loaded into the editor (*Figure 1.5* and *Figure 1.6*), it becomes evident that the first row of data should be the header row.

To adjust this, the **table options context menu** (table icon) can be expanded. This icon is located just above the **row numbers** (*Figure 1.8*). From this menu, the **Use First Row as Headers** option should be selected.

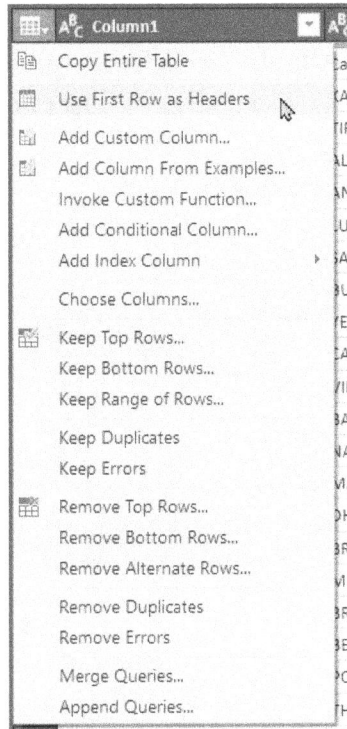

Figure 1.8: Context menu for table options

This option/command can also be found on the **Home** tab (*Figure 1.9*). Expanding it allows performing the reverse operation as well. However, in this example, the goal is to promote the first row as the column headers for this table.

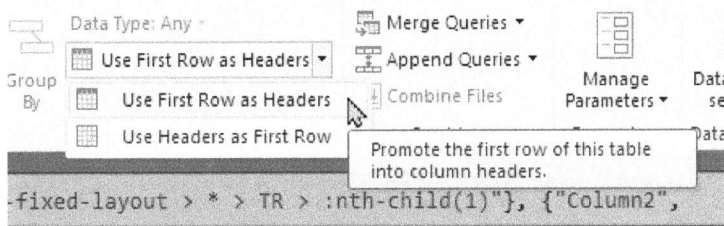

Figure 1.9: Use First Row as Headers command

Regardless of where the selected option is applied, Power Query will add the Promoted Headers step. Additionally, it will automatically insert another step called **Changed Type**.

Since this step is not needed in this example, it should be removed again.

If the automatic addition of this step is not desired, the following steps should be taken:

1. Click the **File** menu.
2. Expand **Options and settings** and select **Query options**.
3. In the window that appears, navigate to the **Data Load** tab under the **Global** section (*Figure 1.10*).
4. Modify the **Type Detection** setting.

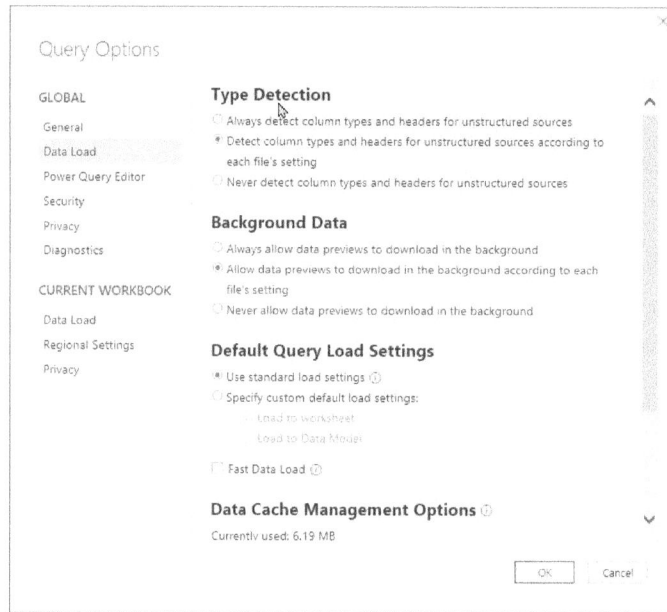

Figure 1.10: *Global data load options*

This option can also be changed only for the current Excel file (*Figure 1.11*) by unchecking the **Type Detection** checkbox.

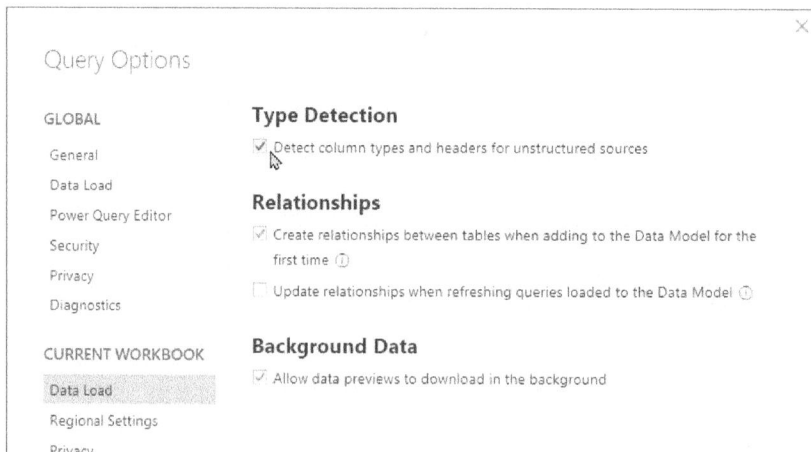

Figure 1.11: *Data Load options for Current Workbook*

It is generally advisable to keep this option enabled, as removing a single step from the query is easier than manually changing the data type for dozens of columns. In this example, the letter case for both the first and second columns (now named **Country** and **Capital**) should be changed so that each word starts with a capital letter.

This transformation can be performed in several ways as follows:

- Selecting both columns while holding the *Ctrl* key (for non-adjacent columns, similar to Excel).

- Holding the *Shift* key to select adjacent columns (from the first selected column to the last clicked column).

- Applying the transformation separately to each column.

  Power Query should recognize that the same transformation is being applied to multiple columns and merge them into a single step called **Capitalized Each Word**.

The transformation that needs to be applied can be found on the **Transform** tab by expanding the **Format** command (*Figure 1.12*).

Tip: **A similar command is also available on the Add Column tab. However, using it there would create a new column with the transformed data rather than modifying the existing column. Additionally, this option would only work for one column at a time.**

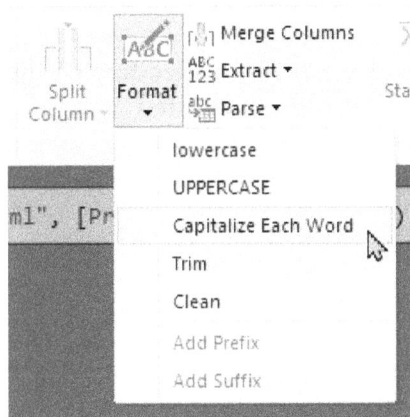

Figure 1.12: Commands related to text formatting

The last two transformations under the **Format** command, **Add Prefix** and **Add Suffix,** will only be active when a single column is selected.

Tip: **If you hover over a command and wait for a moment, a detailed description of its functionality should appear.**

Since this is the first example, no further transformations will be applied. The data will now be loaded into Excel.

To do this, on the **Home** tab, the **Close & Load** command should be expanded, and the **Close & Load To** option should be selected (*Figure 1.13*). This allows specifying the exact location for loading the query/table.

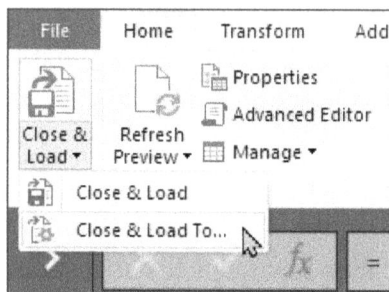

Figure 1.13: *Close & Load To command*

If we simply click **Close & Load** without expanding it, Power Query will load the data into a new worksheet as an Excel table, applying the default load settings. This is often convenient, but it does not allow for customized loading options, such as choosing between a table loaded into a specific location, PivotTable, or loading only to the data model.

The **Import Data** window (*Figure 1.14*) will assist in selecting the destination location for loading the query.

Tip: **In this book, the Default Query Load Settings (Figure 1.10) are not changed because different loading methods may be required depending on the situation. Additionally, it is easy to forget which default settings were selected for a specific computer.**

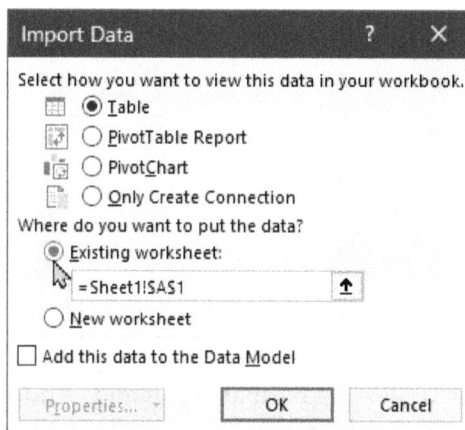

Figure 1.14: *Import Data window*

Since a table needs to be created, the first default option, **Table,** is selected. This table should be placed in an **existing worksheet**, not a new one. Therefore, the **Existing worksheet** option is selected.

By default, the field below this option should contain a reference to cell A1. If this has changed or the default location is not suitable, clicking inside the **cell reference field** and then selecting a **cell in the worksheet** will change the destination location for the table. Excel should automatically add the worksheet name before the cell reference. The selection is confirmed by clicking **OK**.

The checkbox **Add this data to the Data Model** is not selected because it is related to Power Pivot, which is not covered in this book.

Loading the query into Excel results in the creation of a new table, where the name is based on the query name. However, unlike Power Query, Excel table names cannot contain special characters such as spaces or ampersands. Therefore, similar characters will be replaced with underscores, and the newly created table will be named: `Countries___Capitals`.

When a cell within this table is selected, Excel will display two additional tabs: **Table Design** and **Query**, as shown in *Figure 1.15*:

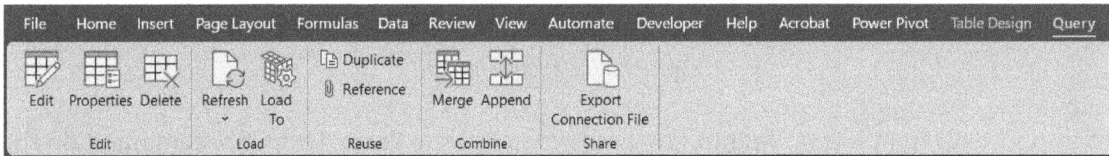

Figure 1.15: Query tab

In addition to loading the table, the **Queries** window should automatically open on the right side of Excel, as shown in *Figure 1.16*:

Figure 1.16: Queries window

This window is now integrated with the **Connections** window. If it does not open automatically, it can be manually opened by clicking the **Queries & Connections** command on the **Data** tab (*Figure 1.1*). The **Queries** window displays a list of queries along with a brief summary. In this example, the **Countries & Capitals** query/table contains 193 rows (the header row is not counted).

Tip: **The Queries window should be wide enough to leave some space after the row count summary. This is important because if errors appear in the query, they will also be displayed below the query name.**

Retrieving data from a .txt file

In this example, data about countries and their capitals will once again be imported, but this time from a text file (**Countries_and_capitals.txt**). The structure of this data differs from that found on the website (*Figure 1.17*). Most notably, it is not in a table, does not have a header row, and the column separation is indicated by an unusual delimiter.

Figure 1.17: Data in a text file

To import data from a text file into Power Query, click the **From Text/CSV** command on the **Data** tab (*Figure 1.1*). This will open the **Import Data** window (*Figure 1.18*), which allows browsing the disk to locate the file from which the data should be retrieved. In this case, the file **Countries_and_capitals.txt** should be selected from the folder containing the files for **Chapter 1**.

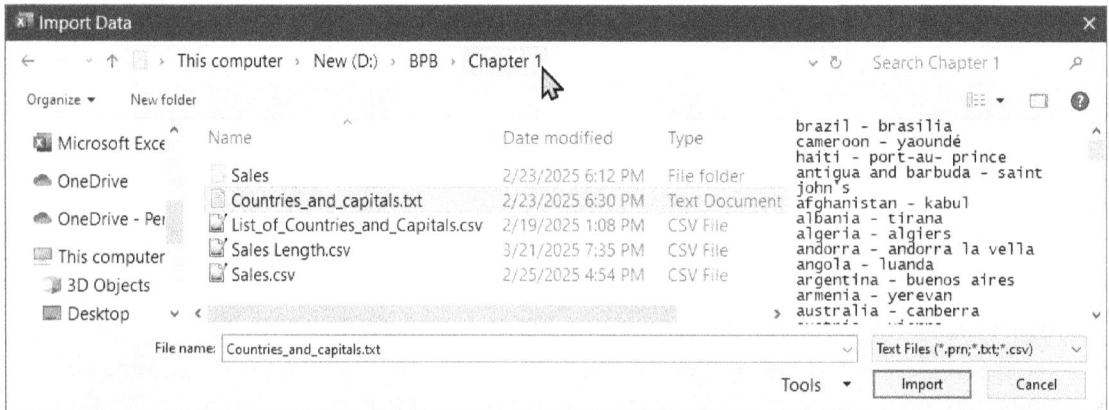

Figure 1.18: Explorer window

Tip: **If the folder containing the file to be imported into Power Query is already open, the path to that folder can be copied from the address bar and pasted into the data import window in Power Query (Figure 1.18).**

In this window, only one file can be selected at a time. The file can be opened by clicking the **Import** button or by double-clicking it. This action will open another window (*Figure 1.19*), where the file origin can be selected from the **File Origin** dropdown list, determining the encoding as follows:

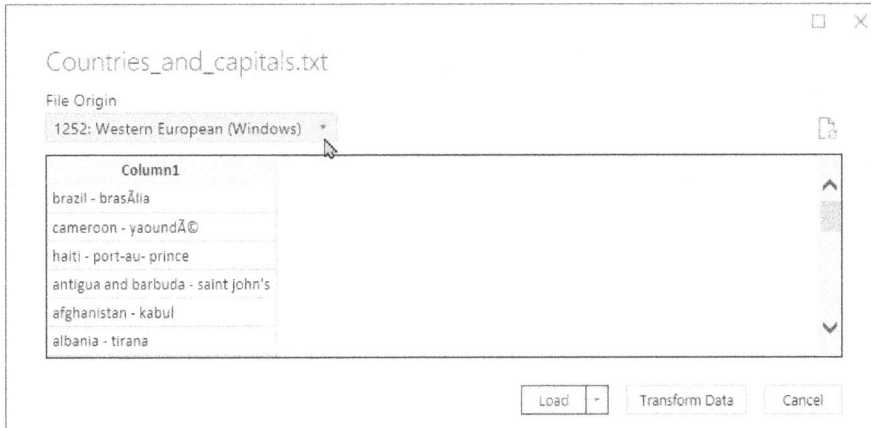

Figure 1.19: *File encoding selection window*

In most cases, Power Query should be able to correctly detect the file encoding, which primarily affects the proper display of special characters. In this example (*Figure 1.19*), the initial rows contain incorrect capital names. Therefore, the correct encoding must be selected manually from the list. In this case, the appropriate choice is **UTF-8**, as shown in *Figure 1.20*:

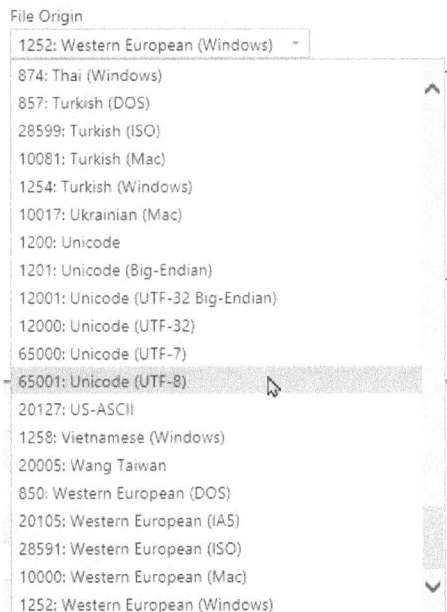

Figure 1.20: *Encoding list*

Now, further data transformations can be performed by clicking the **Transform Data** button (*Figure 1.19*). Only a single column with a default name will be imported into Power Query (*Figure 1.21*). This will be associated with only one step (**Source**) in the query.

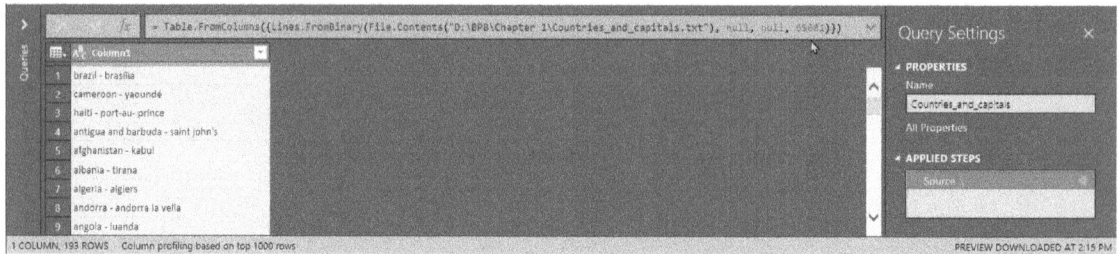

Figure 1.21: The imported text file in Power Query

The next step will be to split this column into two separate columns, one containing the country name and the other containing the capital name. To achieve this, ensure that the column is selected (it should be highlighted in green), then locate and expand the **Split Column** command from the **Home** tab (or the **Transform** tab) and select the **By Delimiter** option, as shown in *Figure 1.22*:

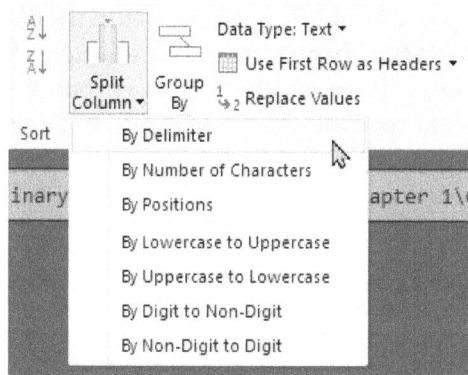

Figure 1.22: Options for the Split Column command

Most of the options visible in the preceding figure are self-explanatory, but two of them sound very similar, although there is an important difference between them as follows:

- **By Number of Characters**: Always splits after the same number of characters, meaning each column will have the same width.

- **By Positions**: Splits the column based on specified character positions from the beginning of the row, which allows creating columns of varying widths.

Choosing the **By Delimiter** option will open the **Split Column by Delimiter** window (*Figure 1.23*). In this window, Power Query will attempt to detect the delimiter used to split the data into columns. In this example, it correctly identified that a **custom delimiter** is being used, which is a hyphen. However, it did not recognize that a proper split also requires including the space before and after the delimiter. These spaces must be added manually.

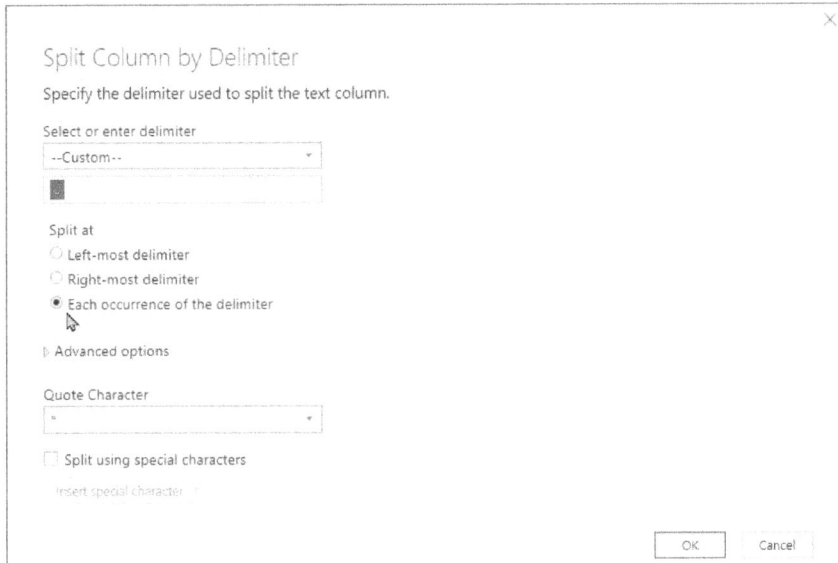

Figure 1.23: Split Column by Delimiter window

After entering the delimiter (which can be a sequence of characters), the selection must be made regarding how the split should occur as follows:

- Left-most delimiter (only at the first occurrence).
- Right-most delimiter (only at the last occurrence).
- Each occurrence of the delimiter (splitting at every instance).

In this example, the selection does not matter because the sequence *space-hyphen-space* appears only once in the data.

The **Quote Character** field remains unchanged. This option is useful when the data contains text that includes the specified delimiter, but the delimiter should not be considered for splitting. If the text is enclosed in double quotation marks, all characters within will be ignored during the split.

At the bottom of this window, the checkbox **Split using special characters** allows for the easy insertion of special character codes, such as a tab character or a non-breaking space.

After confirming the selected options by clicking **OK**, Power Query should add two steps: **Split Column by Delimiter** and **Changed Type**. The second step, as in the previous example, does not add value, so it can be removed.

After the transformation, two columns will appear in the query table (*Figure 1.24*). These columns will have numerical suffixes added to the previous column name (*Figure 1.21*).

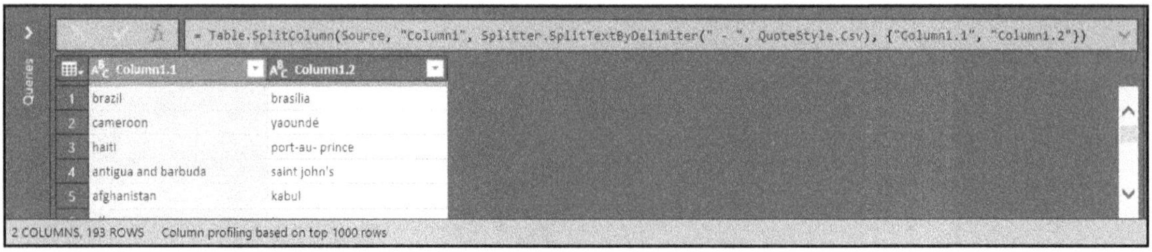

Figure 1.24: Data after splitting by delimiter

It should be evident that the column names need to be changed. This time, the first row of data does not contain correct column names, so renaming must be done manually by double-clicking the header, selecting the column, and pressing *F2*, or using the **Rename** command from the **Transform** tab. The column names should be changed to **Country** and **CAPITOL**.

After renaming the first column, a new step (**Renamed Columns**) will be added, while the second renaming action will be incorporated within the same step.

> Tip: **Column name changes should be performed together whenever possible. This ensures that they are executed within a single step. If another transformation is inserted between renaming actions, the next column name change will be recorded as a separate step, unnecessarily increasing the number of transformation steps.**

Now, the letter case of these columns should be adjusted. The text in the **Country** column should be formatted in proper case, while in **CAPITOL**, all letters should be uppercase. The appropriate options can be selected from the **Format** command on the **Transform** tab (*Figure 1.12*).

> Note: **The order of the last three steps does not matter until an attempt is made to rearrange them after they have been created. If the column names are changed first, the subsequent transformations will be applied to the new column names, and these names will be hardcoded in the M code. Therefore, moving these steps above the renaming step will result in an error, as Power Query will not be able to find columns by the specified names.**

In this example, two additional tasks need to be completed. The first is changing the column order. To do this, simply drag the **CAPITOL** column header and drop it onto the **Country** column while holding down the left mouse button. Alternatively, the **Move** command from the **Transform** tab can be used.

After making this change, it would be beneficial to rename the query accordingly. Instead of the default `Countries_and_capitals` (created based on the file name), it should be changed to `CAPITALS and Countries`.

After renaming, the data can be loaded into Excel using the **Close & Load To** command (*Figure 1.13*). In this example, a new worksheet has not been created for placing the new table, so in the **Import Data** window (*Figure 1.14*), the **Table** option, along with the **New worksheet**, should be selected. Excel will generate a new worksheet named after the query and insert the new table (query result) in cell **A1**.

Upon reviewing the query result in the third row of the table (*Figure 1.25*), a small data issue can be observed: a redundant space in the capital city's name, as follows:

	A	B
1	CAPITOL	Country
2	BRASÍLIA	Brazil
3	YAOUNDÉ	Cameroon
4	PORT-AU- PRINCE	Haiti
5	SAINT IOHN'S	Antigua And Barbuda

Figure 1.25: Query result

Similar errors should ideally be corrected directly in the source data. However, after making changes and saving the file, the query must be refreshed for the updates to appear in Power Query and, consequently, in Excel.

This can be done using one of the following three methods:

- Using or expanding the **Refresh All** command from the **Data** tab (*Figure 1.1*).
- Selecting the **Refresh** option from the context menu of the table by right-clicking any cell within the table.
- Selecting the **Refresh** option from the context menu of the query, by right-clicking the query in the **Queries & Connections** window, as shown in *Figure 1.26*:

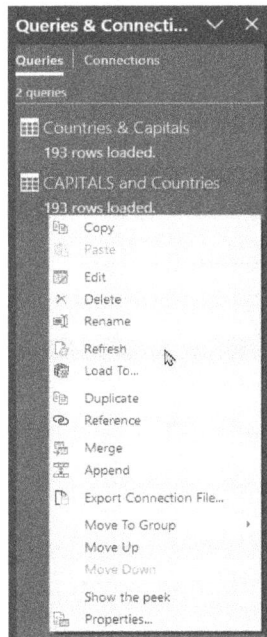

Figure 1.26: Query context menu

If additional transformations need to be applied to the query, meaning the query must be edited again, this can be done by selecting the **Edit** option from the query's context menu (*Figure 1.26*) or by clicking the **Edit** command on the **Query** tab (*Figure 1.15*).

Retrieving data from a .csv file

In this example, data is imported from a **`.csv`** file (Sales.csv), where columns are separated using a comma.

Fun fact: **In `.csv` files, a comma (,) is not always used as the delimiter for separating columns. This is the case, for example, in the United States, the United Kingdom, and Canada, but in countries like Poland, France, and Germany, a semicolon (;) is used instead.**

The specific file being used is **`Sales.csv`**, which contains sales data. However, it also includes additional rows at the beginning and end of the file that are not needed for analysis, as shown in *Figure 1.27*:

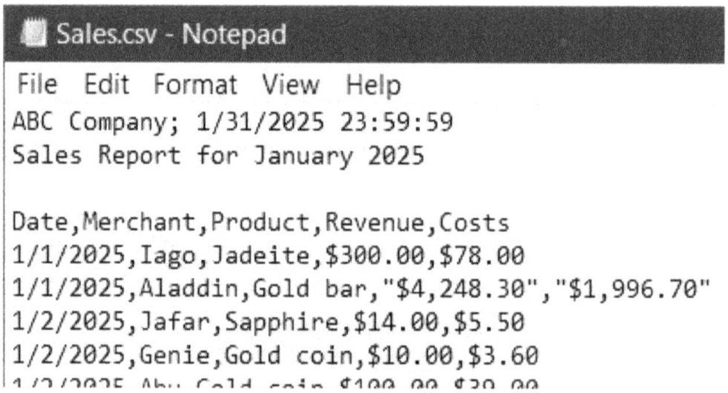

Sales.csv - Notepad

File Edit Format View Help

```
ABC Company; 1/31/2025 23:59:59
Sales Report for January 2025

Date,Merchant,Product,Revenue,Costs
1/1/2025,Iago,Jadeite,$300.00,$78.00
1/1/2025,Aladdin,Gold bar,"$4,248.30","$1,996.70"
1/2/2025,Jafar,Sapphire,$14.00,$5.50
1/2/2025,Genie,Gold coin,$10.00,$3.60
```

***Figure 1.27**: Data in a .csv*

Similar to the previous example, the **From Text/CSV** command from the **Data** tab (*Figure 1.1*) is used to locate and import the file from disk (*Figure 1.18*).

After selecting the file, the import window should appear slightly different compared to importing data from a text file. At the top of the window, the following options should be displayed:

- **File Origin**: Encoding of the file.
- **Delimiter**: Used to define column separation (*Comma* in this case).
- **Data type detection**: A dropdown list for automatic data type identification.

Since the file contains additional rows before the actual data, Power Query could not correctly identify the header row. As a result, default column names are assigned, as shown in *Figure 1.28*:

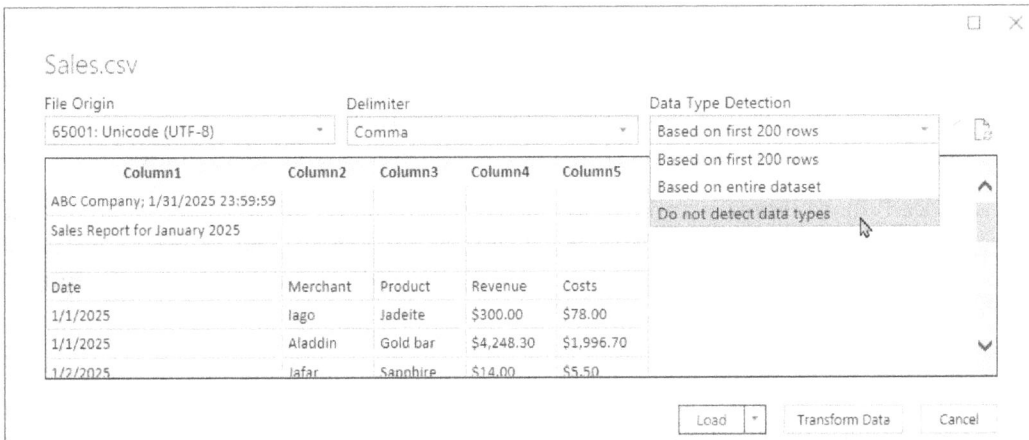

Figure 1.28: CSV file import window

For the same reason, data type detection can be skipped by selecting the **Do not detect data types** option (*Figure 1.28*). Since, in this example, the header row is in the fourth row of the dataset, Power Query would otherwise assign a text data type to each column. This is the default data type for text and **.csv** files.

Now, all settings should match our needs, so clicking the **Transform Data** button will proceed to the Power Query editor.

Even though the **Do not detect data types** option was selected (*Figure 1.28*), Power Query might still automatically apply **data type detection** based on its default settings (*Figure 1.10* and *Figure 1.11*). If this happens, the last step should be removed.

At this stage, the query should contain only the **Source** step and five text columns, as shown in *Figure 1.29*:

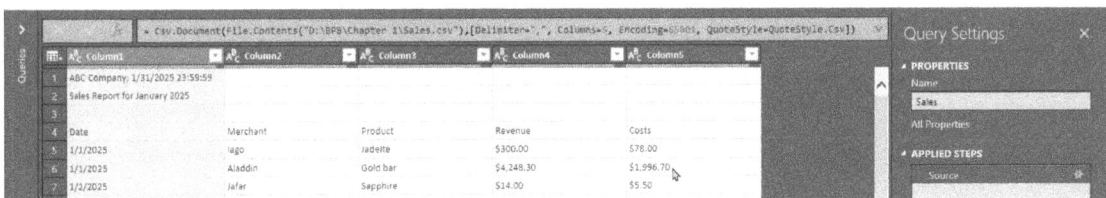

Figure 1.29: Data imported from the CSV file into the editor

It can be observed that in the **sixth row**, there are commas present, but Power Query did not split the data into separate columns at these points. This is because, in the **.csv** file, these numerical values were enclosed in double quotation marks (*Figure 1.27*). This signals Power Query to ignore any delimiters found inside double quotation marks as well as the quotation marks themselves. As a result, the data was placed into the appropriate columns.

Note: **This book follows American regional settings, where a period (.) is used as the decimal separator and a comma (,) is used as the thousands separator. These same numeric separators are used in countries such as the United Kingdom and Canada. However, this can lead to errors when importing numbers from .csv files. To prevent this, any numbers from one thousand and above should be enclosed in double quotation marks.**

Countries like Poland, France, and Germany use a comma as the decimal separator and a space as the thousands separator. Since these countries typically use a semicolon (;) as the column delimiter in .csv files, there is no need to enclose numbers in double quotation marks.

Now, unnecessary data needs to be removed. The extra rows at the beginning are easy to identify. However, the rows at the end may be harder to spot because the Power Query editor displays only the first 1,000 rows by default. To view additional rows, it would be necessary to scroll to the bottom of the visible data and drag the scroll bar to load more rows. However, this is a slow and impractical approach, especially for larger datasets.

It is important to remember that the Power Query editor is not designed to display all data but rather to facilitate efficient transformations. Therefore, the most essential rule when working with data is: *Know your data.*

In this example, three rows need to be removed from the beginning of the data and four rows from the end. To accomplish this, the **Remove Rows** command from the **Home** tab should be expanded, as shown in *Figure 1.30*:

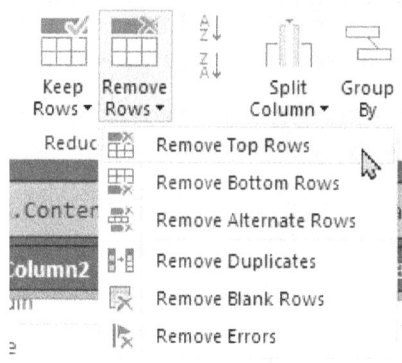

Figure 1.30: Remove Rows command

First, the **Remove Top Rows** command should be used. This will open a window where the number of rows to remove from the top of the table can be entered, as shown in *Figure 1.31*:

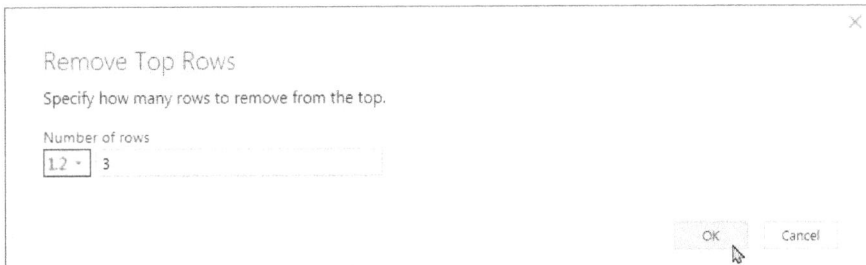

Figure 1.31: Remove Top Rows window

Similarly, the **Remove Bottom Rows** command should be used afterwards to remove the last four rows. The window that appears will be identical to the one used for removing the top rows.

Now, the first row can be used as headers (*Figure 1.8* or *Figure 1.9*). After this transformation, Power Query should automatically add the **Changed Type** step, which will detect data types for each column, as shown in *Figure 1.32*:

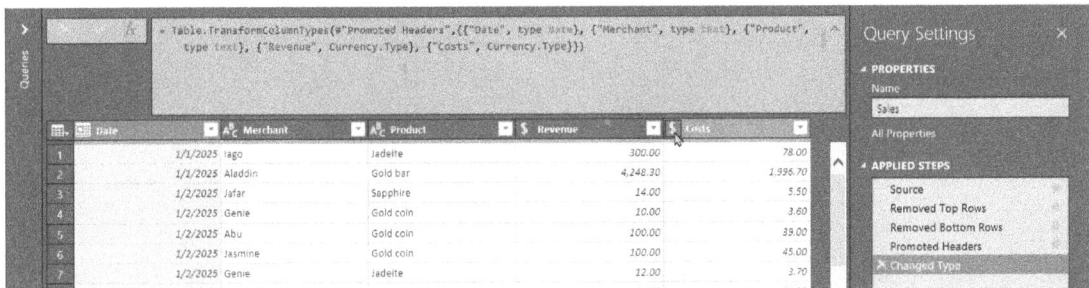

Figure 1.32: Changed Type step

The **Date** column should be assigned the **Date** data type. The **Merchant** and **Product** columns should have the **Text** data type, while the **Revenue** and **Costs** columns should have the **Currency** data type. It can be observed that for **Date** and **Currency** data types, values in the columns are right-aligned, which is the default alignment for numbers in Excel. Additionally, the **Currency** format removed the dollar symbol (**$**) from the data.

It is important to note that the **Currency** type, unlike in Excel, does not automatically add a currency symbol but rather sets the numerical precision. The four types of numeric formatting in Power Query are:

- **Whole number**: An integer without a decimal part.
- **Currency**: A decimal number with precision up to four decimal places.
- **Decimal number**: A decimal number with precision up to fifteen decimal places.
- **Percentage**: Displays a number as a percentage with a precision of two decimal places. It also shows the percentage sign. This formatting is not transferred to Excel.

In this example, an additional step is required to calculate the **Income** by subtracting the **Costs** column from the **Revenue** column.

To do this, follow these steps:

1. Select the **Revenue** column.

2. While holding the *Ctrl* key, click on the **Costs** column.

3. On the **Add Column** tab, expand the **Standard** command and select **Subtract,** as shown in *Figure 1.33*:

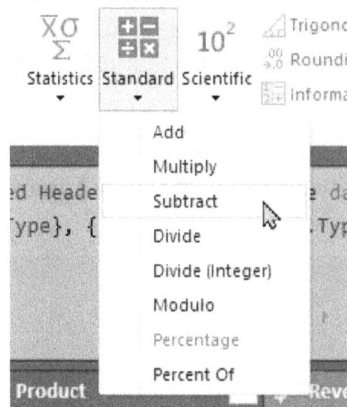

Figure 1.33: Standard command from the Add Column tab

Power Query will add a step (**Inserted Subtraction**), creating a column with the default name **Subtraction**, as shown in *Figure 1.34*:

#	Merchant	Product	Revenue	Costs	Subtraction
1	025 Iago	Jadeite	300.00	78.00	222.00
2	025 Aladdin	Gold bar	4,248.30	1,996.70	2,251.60
3	025 Jafar	Sapphire	14.00	5.50	8.50
4	025 Genie	Gold coin	10.00	3.60	6.40
5	025 Abu	Gold coin	100.00	39.00	61.00

Figure 1.34: Data after adding the subtraction column

This column name needs to be changed. To do this, we could double-click on the column header as done in previous examples, but this would add a new step. Whenever possible, it is best to limit the number of steps in queries. In this case, it is very simple. Since the formula bar has been enabled (*Figure 1.6*), the name of the new column appears highlighted in burgundy within double quotes. Simply replace the word with **Income** and confirm the change by pressing *Enter*.

Now, the data can be loaded into Excel using the **Close & Load To** command (*Figure 1.13*). The default query name can remain unchanged. As in the previous example, a new worksheet was not created for the new table. Therefore, in the **Import Data** window (*Figure 1.14*), select the **Table** option and **New worksheet**. Excel will create a new worksheet with the same name as the query and insert the new table in cell **A1**, as shown in *Figure 1.35*:

	A	B	C	D	E	F
1	Date ▾	Merchant ▾	Product ▾	Revenue ▾	Costs ▾	Income ▾
2	1/1/2025	Iago	Jadeite	300	78	222
3	1/1/2025	Aladdin	Gold bar	4248.3	1996.7	2251.6
4	1/2/2025	Jafar	Sapphire	14	5.5	8.5

Figure 1.35: Query result

It is worth emphasizing that the **Currency** data type from Power Query did not transfer as a currency number format in Excel. The values appear only as numbers with different precision levels. If the numbers in the Excel table must be displayed as currency, an appropriate number format can be applied. This formatting will persist in Excel even after refreshing the query.

Date values imported from Power Query into Excel retain their date format.

Importing fixed-width column data

In this example, the goal is to import data from a text file (**Sales Length.csv**) where column separation is determined by a fixed number of characters. It does not matter whether the file has a **.txt** or **.csv** extension. Power Query will correctly detect the file structure in both cases.

These are the same data as in the previous example; however, unlike the previous case, this file does not contain additional rows at the beginning or end. The file consists only of a header row, followed by data separated according to a fixed column width (*Figure 1.36*). If additional informational rows were present at the beginning of the file, they would prevent Power Query from correctly detecting the structure of the file.

Comparing the data in this example (*Figure 1.36*) to the previous example (*Figure 1.27*), it is noticeable that there is no need to enclose data in double quotation marks. Even though the data are imported from a **.csv** file, column separation is not determined by the appearance of a comma but by a specific number of characters (column width).

```
Sales Length.csv - Notepad
File  Edit  Format  View  Help
Date       Merchant  Product    Revenue    Costs
1/1/2025   Iago      Jadeite    $300.00    $78.00
1/1/2025   Aladdin   Gold bar   $4,248.30  $1,996.70
1/2/2025   Jafar     Sapphire   $14.00     $5.50
1/2/2025   Genie     Gold coin  $10.00     $3.60
1/2/2025   Abu       Gold coin  $100.00    $39.00
1/2/2025   Jasmine   Gold coin  $100.00    $45.00
```

Figure 1.36: Data in CSV file

Similarly, to the previous example, use the **From Text/CSV** command from the **Data** tab (*Figure 1.1*) and locate and import the file from the disk (*Figure 1.18*). The data import window will appear, similar to the previous one (*Figure 1.28*), but with a significant difference in the separator setting, as shown in *Figure 1.37*:

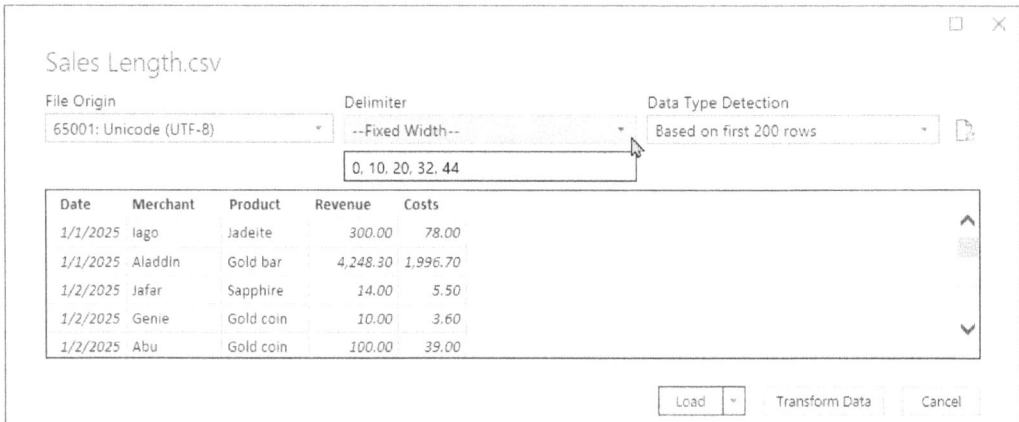

Figure 1.37: Import data window for a fixed-width column file

In the **Delimiter** list, Power Query should automatically select **Fixed Width** and display a sequence of numbers: `0, 10, 20, 32, 44`. Each number indicates a column break position from the beginning of the row. Zero means a split before the first character, and the second column starts after the 10th character. This means that the first column has a width of 10 characters. Similarly, the third column starts after the 20th character from the beginning of the row, meaning that the second column has a width of 10 characters (20 minus 10). From the remaining numbers, it follows that the third and fourth columns have a width of 12 characters each. However, based on this data alone, it is not possible to determine the width of the fifth column.

Important: **Power Query uses zero-based indexing by default. This means that, internally, the first character or row is numbered as zero.**

In the **Import Data** window (*Figure 1.37*), Power Query correctly identifies the first row as column headers. Based on the alignment of data in the **Date**, **Revenue**, and **Costs** columns, it becomes clear that these values have been recognized correctly as numbers. Now, click **Transform Data** to load the data into the Power Query editor.

In the editor, three steps should be visible: **Source**, **Promoted Headers**, and **Changed Type,** as shown in *Figure 1.38*:

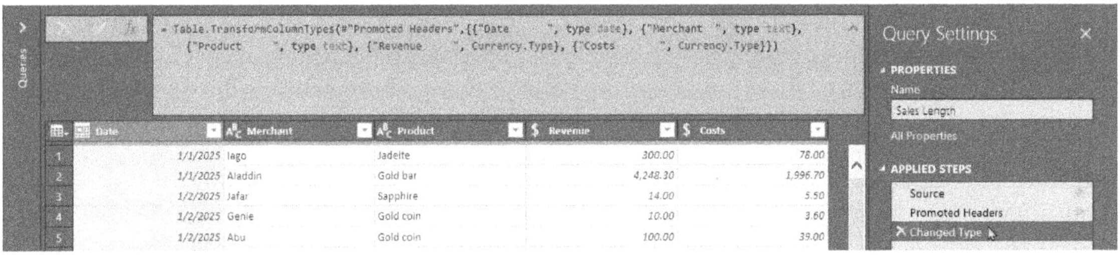

Figure 1.38: Data after the Changed Type step

The automatic **Changed Type** step in this example provides an additional advantage. It not only detects the correct data types for each column but also helps identify issues with column names. Since the **Formula Bar** was enabled earlier (*Figure 1.6*), it is now visible that the column names contain extra spaces at the end. This happens because, in fixed-width column files, spaces are inserted to maintain a uniform column width. Therefore, a manual correction is necessary to remove the unnecessary spaces from all column names.

The next step is to remove unnecessary spaces from text columns. If a single cell in the **Merchant** column is selected, its value appears below the table. By double-clicking on it, it becomes evident that extra spaces exist after the merchant's name, as shown in *Figure 1.39*:

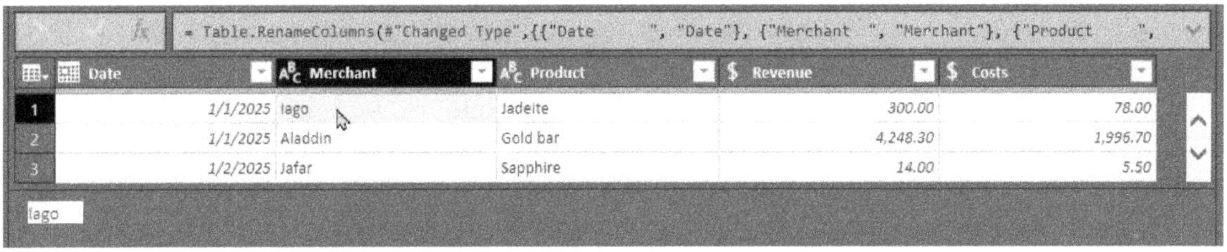

Figure 1.39: Extra spaces in text column cells

These spaces need to be removed. To do this, select the **Merchant** and **Product** columns, then go to the **Transform** tab, expand the **Format** command, and choose the **Trim** option, as shown in *Figure 1.40*:

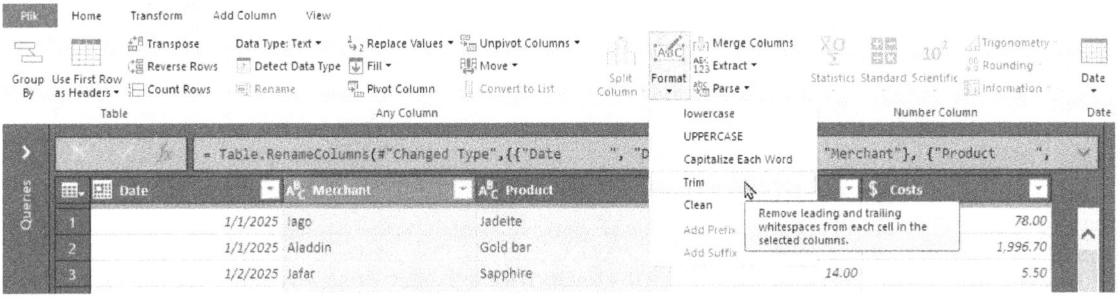

Figure 1.40: Trim option in Format command

It is worth noting that the **Trim** option differs from the `TRIM` function in Excel. The **Trim** option removes only extra spaces from the beginning and end of the text but leaves all spaces within the text, whereas the `TRIM` function keeps only single spaces between words or characters.

There is no need to remove extra spaces for the **Date**, **Revenue**, and **Costs** columns because the detected data type automatically removes unnecessary spaces from these columns. Additionally, due to regional settings, it also removed the dollar sign (\$) from the **Revenue** and **Costs** columns.

Now, similarly to the previous example (*Figure 1.33* and *Figure 1.34*), we can add the **Income** column. After this, we can proceed with loading our query as an Excel table in a new worksheet.

Tip: **If we had kept only the Source step and removed extra spaces from all columns in the second step, then by applying the Promoted Headers step (Figure 1.8), we would have already had the correct column names. This would have allowed us to avoid manually renaming columns and reduced the number of steps in the query.**

In this example, we also want to discuss moving a query, specifically, changing the location where it is loaded. If we only need to change the cell or worksheet where the table is loaded, we can simply select the entire table (e.g., using *Ctrl + A*), cut it (*Ctrl + X*), and then paste it in the new location (*Ctrl + V*).

However, if we want to keep only the query connection instead of loading it into an Excel table, meaning the query result remains only in the Power Query editor, we need to delete the table. To do this, select the table (*Ctrl + A*), then delete it (*Delete* key). Before completely deleting the table, we must confirm this action by clicking **Yes** in the confirmation window that appears, as shown in *Figure 1.41*:

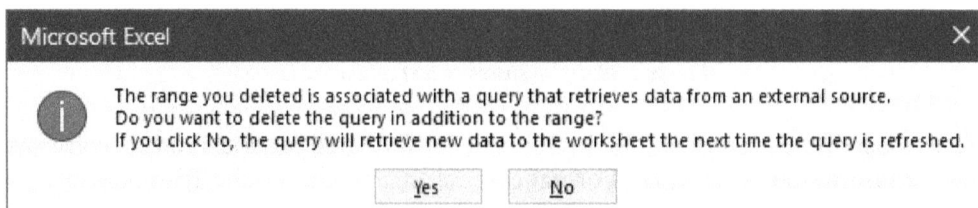

Figure 1.41: *Confirmation of table (query) deletion*

If a query is accidentally deleted when it was intended to be loaded into Excel, or if the **Only Create Connection** option was mistakenly selected in the **Import Data** window (*Figure 1.14*), it will not be possible to load the query into Excel using the **Close & Load** command (*Figure 1.13*). This is because the **Close & Load To** option becomes inactive when reopening the query for editing.

However, the query can still be loaded into Excel through the query context menu (*Figure 1.26*) by selecting the **Load To** option.

Conclusion

In this chapter, we introduced Power Query as an ETL tool for retrieving, transforming, and loading data into Excel. We covered importing data from text and .csv files, performing basic transformations, and understanding the importance of proper data structure for analysis.

By mastering these fundamentals, you can automate repetitive tasks and efficiently prepare data for reporting. In the next chapter, we will explore more advanced transformations and data manipulation techniques in Power Query.

Multiple choice questions

1. **What does ETL stand for in Power Query?**

    a. Extract, transfer, and load

    b. Extract, transform, and load

    c. Evaluate, transform, and load

    d. Extract, tabulate, and load

2. **Which Power Query function allows removing unnecessary spaces from text?**

    a. Clean

    b. Trim

    c. Format

    d. Substitute

3. **What is the main advantage of using Power Query for data retrieval? (Select all that apply)**

    a. Automates repetitive data transformations

    b. Allows integration of data from multiple sources

    c. Modifies the original data directly

    d. Provides a user-friendly interface for data transformation

4. **What is a key characteristic of a properly structured data range?**

    a. Each column contains only one type of data

    b. Merged cells are used for better readability

    c. Multiple column headers are allowed

    d. Empty rows separate different sections of data

5. **What is the purpose of the Use First Row as Headers option in Power Query?**

   a. To promote the first row of data as column headers

   b. To automatically rename all column headers

   c. To convert text data into numerical values

   d. To split a column into multiple rows

6. **What happens when a transformation step is deleted in Power Query?**

   a. Subsequent steps dependent on it may cause errors

   b. The original data source is modified

   c. The transformation is undone using Ctrl + Z

   d. It automatically recreates itself when the query refreshes

Answers

Question number	Answer option letter
1.	b.
2.	b.
3.	a., b., d.
4.	a.
5.	a.
6.	a.

Join our Discord space

Join our Discord workspace for latest updates, offers, tech happenings around the world, new releases, and sessions with the authors:

https://discord.bpbonline.com

CHAPTER 2

Advanced Data Connections and Imports

Introduction

In the previous chapter, we introduced Power Query, exploring its interface, basic data loading, and simple transformations. You learned how to connect to Excel tables, clean data, and apply foundational steps like filtering, renaming columns, and changing data types.

This chapter builds on that foundation by focusing on advanced data connections and import methods. You will learn how to retrieve data from named ranges, Excel workbooks, folders, and Access databases, and how to handle hidden objects, inconsistent structures, and multiple file imports.

We will also cover ways to automate query refresh, using both built-in settings and **Visual Basic for Applications** (**VBA**). These techniques will prepare you to work efficiently with more complex and dynamic data sources in real-world scenarios.

Structure

This chapter explores the following topics:

- Retrieving data from tables and named ranges
- Importing data from an Excel file
- Importing data from folders

- Importing data from Access
- Automatic query refresh

Objectives

By the end of this chapter, you will be able to import data from a variety of sources, including Excel tables, named ranges, folders, and Access databases. You will learn how to identify and manage hidden objects, resolve issues with inconsistent data structures, and handle default column names during the import process. The chapter will also guide you through cleaning and transforming imported data by filtering, expanding, and combining content from multiple files or sheets. In addition, you will apply proper data types and structure queries for use in reports and dashboards. Finally, you will discover how to automate query refresh using both Power Query settings and VBA, ensuring your data stays current with minimal manual effort.

Retrieving data from tables and named ranges

In this example, we work with and aim to retrieve data from a simple table (*Table1*) located in the file **TableAndRange.xlsx** (*Figure 2.1*). This file also contains a very similar data range on the **SheetRange** worksheet, which has also been named.

	A	B	C	D	E
1	Date	Merchant	Product	Quantity	Price
2	9/11/2024	Jafar	Gold coin	2	10
3	10/12/2024	Jafar	Copper coin	22	1
4	10/30/2024	Abu	Ruby	7	16
5	11/28/2024	Jafar	Diamond	3	19.9
6	11/15/2024	Jasmine	Silver coin	10	5

Figure 2.1: Table for data retrieval

Tip: **To assign a name to a range in Excel, simply select the range, type the desired name into the Name Box, and confirm by pressing Enter.**

The command used to import data from a table into Power Query: **From Table/Range** from the **Data** tab (*Figure 1.1*), also allows importing data from named ranges.

In the latest version of Excel, Power Query handles named ranges without issues. However, in older versions, Excel may sometimes prompt the user to convert the range into a table (this prompt always appears for unnamed ranges). In rare cases, attempting to import a named range directly using **From Table/Range** may result in an error.

To retrieve data from an Excel table within the current file, select any single cell inside the table and use the **From Table/Range** command. Since every table in Excel must have a header row, this row will automatically be used to name the columns when the data is loaded into Power Query, as shown in *Figure 2.2*:

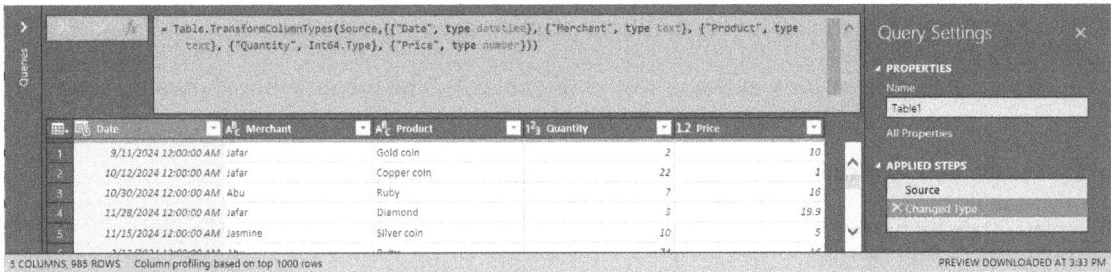

Figure 2.2: Data from the table loaded into the Power Query editor

As the table already includes a header row, there is no additional Promoted Headers step, as seen in some previous examples (e.g., *Figure 1.38*).

Right from the **Source** step in the Power Query editor, the columns are already named, as shown in *Figure 2.3*:

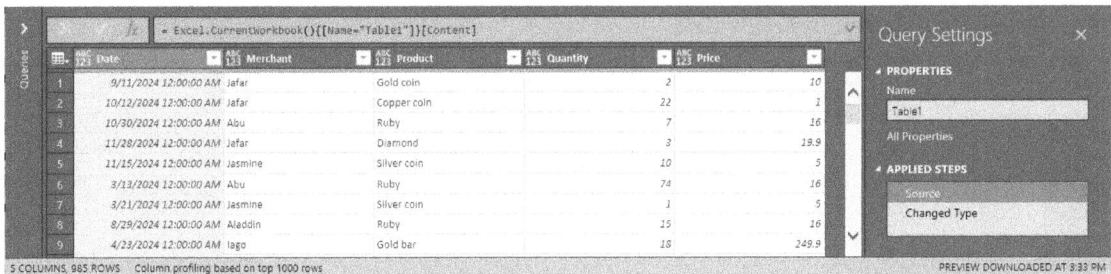

Figure 2.3: Source step with correct column names

Additionally, in the first step of the query, it can be observed that Power Query does not automatically determine the data types, which is why each column is assigned a **General** type (represented by the **ABC123** icon). It is only in the next step that the editor recognizes the appropriate data types for each column.

In both query steps (*Figure 2.2* and *Figure 2.3*), it is visible that when date data is imported from Excel, a time component is automatically appended to it.

It is also worth noting that Power Query recognized the Price column as a Decimal Number rather than Currency. This is because the column was not previously formatted as currency in Excel. As a result, Power Query applied the default data type for columns containing decimal numbers.

> Note: **Data types for columns are automatically detected based on the first 200 rows. If, for example, the first 200 rows contained only whole numbers and decimal numbers appeared later, Power Query would incorrectly detect the data type for that column, leading to potential data loss. This highlights the importance of the Know Your Data principle.**

Tip: **Choosing the correct data type helps optimize query performance.**

Now, let us take another look at the first step (*Figure 2.3*). The formula bar shows that the data is being retrieved from the current Excel file:

```
= Excel.CurrentWorkbook(){[Name="Table1"]}[Content]
```

It is also possible to identify the name of the data source element, which in this case is `Table1`.

In older versions of Power Query, when it was necessary to import data from a named range that could not be converted into a table, an alternative approach was used. Users could first load data from any table and then manually modify the data source name in the first step of the query.

To simulate this scenario in the current query, we modify the name inside the double quotation marks in the formula bar, changing `Table1` to `Range`.

Power Query does not encounter any issues with this adjustment. It successfully loads the named range, as shown in *Figure 2.4*:

Figure 2.4: Data retrieved from a named range

Unlike an Excel table, Power Query does not receive any information about the presence of a header row when importing data from a named range. As a result, the header row remains part of the data (appearing as the first row in the dataset).

This causes an error in the second step of the query, as shown in *Figure 2.5*:

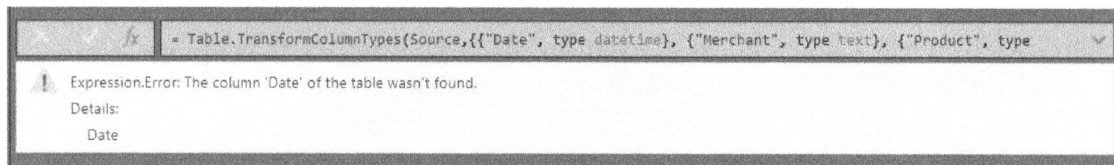

Figure 2.5: Error related to column names

Power Query cannot locate the Date column because, at this stage, the first column is still labeled as `Column1`, while the `Date` header is currently in the first row of data.

Tip: **When Power Query encounters an error in a query step, it only displays a message about the first detected issue. For example, Figure 2.5 only reports that the Date column is missing, even though other columns (for which we are changing data types) also do not exist. Power Query will only reveal the next error after correcting the first one, if any remain.**

To fix this query, the easiest approach is to:

1.   Remove the **Changed Type** step.
2.   Use the **Use First Row as Headers** option (*Figure 1.8*) for the **Source** step.

After applying this transformation, Power Query will automatically add back the **Changed Type** step, but this time, it will recognize the correct column names.

However, two columns will still have incorrect data types. To correct them:

1.   Change the Date column type to **Date**.
2.   Change the Price column type to **Currency**.

When modifying data types within the **Changed Type** step, Power Query displays a message asking whether to update the current step or add a new step, as shown in *Figure 2.6*:

Figure 2.6: Data type change notification

Wherever possible, efforts should be made to limit the number of steps in a query. Therefore, in this case, always click the **Replace current** button.

Now, the next step is to calculate Income. To achieve this, select both the **Quantity** and **Price** columns, then go to the **Add Column** tab, expand the **Standard** command, and choose **Multiply** (*Figure 1.33*).

As seen in similar examples from the previous chapter, this action adds a new column with the default name **Multiplication**, as shown in *Figure 2.7*:

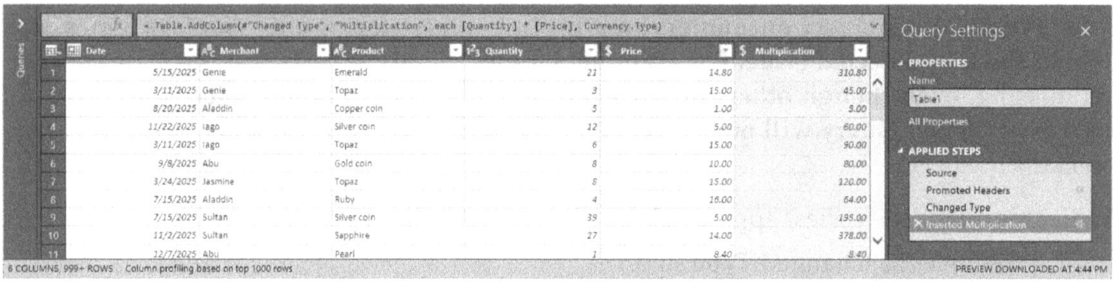

Figure 2.7: Multiplication result

The column name should be changed immediately in the formula bar to **Revenue**, so there is no need to add an extra step for renaming.

An important detail to note is that Power Query automatically assigns the **Currency** data type to this column. This selection is based on the data types of the columns used in the multiplication.

Now, the final step is to rename the query to, for example, `DataFromRange`, and then load the data into Excel as usual.

Tip: **A recommended best practice is to rename the query at the very beginning of the transformation process. However, in this book, the renaming step is intentionally performed at the end in most examples, as a finishing touch.**

Importing data from an Excel file

In this example, data will be imported from another Excel file named `SalesSheets.xlsx`. The goal is to select and merge specific data from chosen worksheets (a process similar to importing and combining data from selected tables). The merged data will then be loaded into a newly created Excel file named `AdvancedImports.xlsx`.

The key focus of this example is to understand the types of objects that exist within an Excel file and how they can be imported into Power Query. Additionally, it will highlight which objects are created automatically and under what circumstances. For this reason, the file contains more objects than usual, requiring proper filtering of unnecessary data.

To import data from another Excel file, go to the **Data** tab, expand **Get Data**, navigate to **From File**, and select **From Excel Workbook**, as shown in *Figure 2.8*:

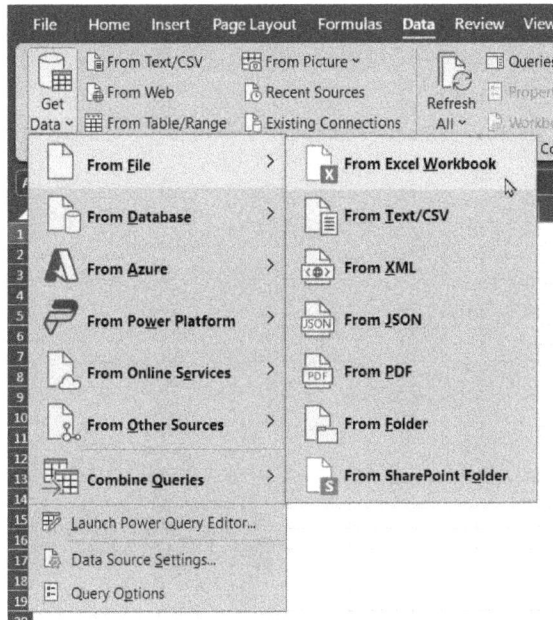

Figure 2.8: *Option for importing data from an Excel file*

Next, the file must be located on the disk and imported into Power Query, as shown in *Figure 2.9*:

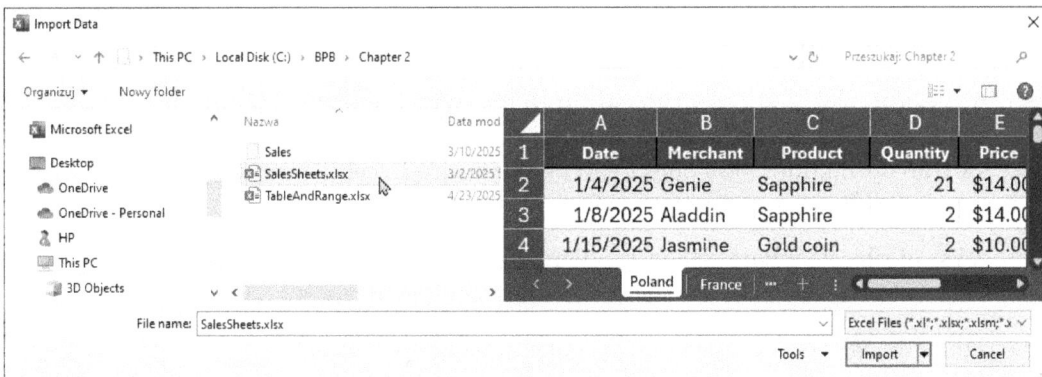

Figure 2.9: *Windows Explorer*

Clicking the **Import** button or double-clicking the selected file will open the **Navigator** window, where the data to be further transformed in Power Query must be selected, as shown in *Figure 2.10*:

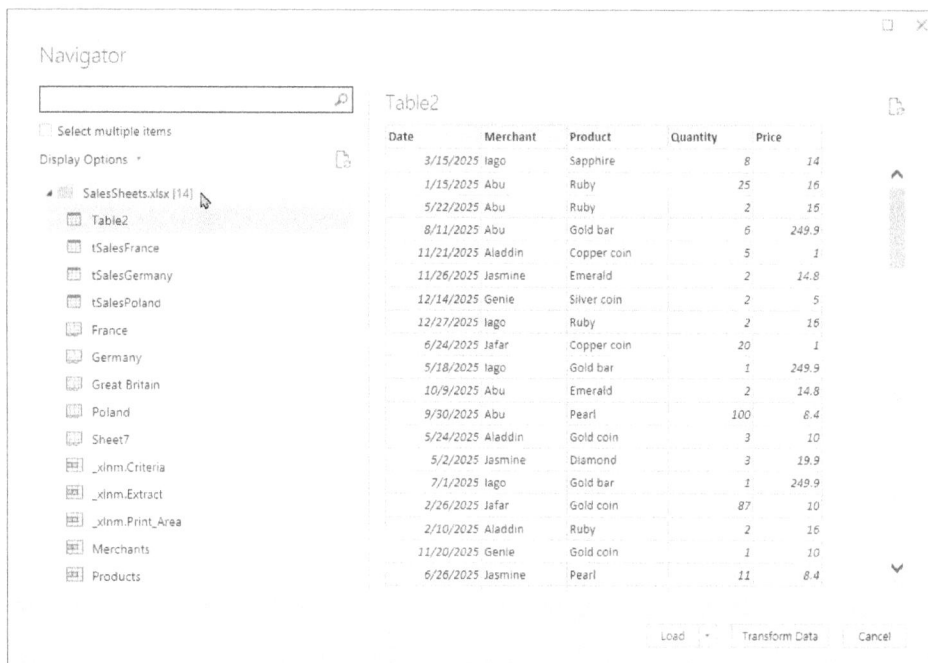

Figure 2.10: Navigator window

On the left side of this window, from the top, we have the following:

- A search field that allows filtering the list of items to display only those containing the entered text in their names.

- A checkbox labeled **Select multiple items**, which enables loading multiple objects/ tables simultaneously as separate queries. If unchecked, only one object can be selected for transformation. This object can be the entire Excel file, including all its contained objects (folder icon).

- A list of objects where tables are displayed first, followed by sheets, and then named ranges. Each type of object has a corresponding icon.

On the right side, we see a preview of the currently selected object.

To retrieve and combine data with the same structure from an Excel file, the simplest approach is to select the entire file (folder icon) and then apply transformations. We will be starting with filtering out unnecessary data.

After clicking **Transform Data**, the list of objects is loaded into the Power Query editor. Here, we can observe that the Power Query editor detects 17 objects, as shown in *Figure 2.11*, whereas the **Navigator** window displays only 14:

Figure 2.11: *List of objects loaded into Power Query*

The difference in the number of objects between the **Navigator** window and the Power Query editor occurs because the **Navigator** window does not display hidden elements, whereas the Power Query editor does. These hidden objects can be identified by the **Hidden** column, which has a Boolean data type (True/False). In this example, there are three hidden objects as follows:

- Sheet `Hidden`, which has been hidden from within Excel.

- Sheet `VeryHidden`, which has been hidden using VBA with the `VeryHidden` setting. This type of sheet cannot be unhidden or accessed from within Excel without using VBA.

- The named range `_xlmn._FilterDatabase`, is automatically assigned to a range filtered using **Advanced Filters**. Advanced Filters also generate the named ranges `_xlmn.Criteria` and `_xlmn.Extract`, but those are visible objects.

Since hidden information is not relevant in this example, these objects should be filtered out. From a user perspective, this process is similar to filtering tables in Excel. The filtering menu can be accessed by clicking the icon on the right side of the column header, where unwanted elements can be deselected, as shown in *Figure 2.12*:

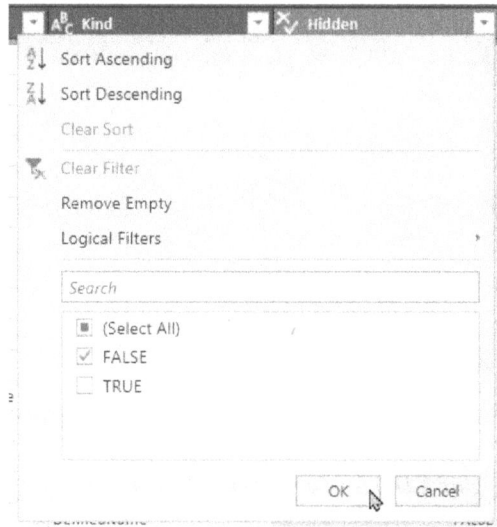

Figure 2.12: Filtering menu for the Hidden column

After confirming the filter selection by clicking **OK**, Power Query will add the **Filtered Rows** step, reducing the number of data rows to 14. This leaves only the objects that were visible in the **Navigator** window (*Figure 2.10*).

Upon further examination of the data, we can observe four additional columns as follows:

- **Kind column**: Stores text values indicating the type of object. Either **Sheet, Table,** or **DefinedName**.

- **Name column**: Stores the name of the object (text data type).

- **Item column**: Also stores the name of the object (text data type) but differs from the **Name** column only for named ranges assigned to a specific worksheet. In this example, this applies to ranges related to Advanced Filters and the Print Area (**_xlnm. Print_Area**). All these named ranges belong to **Sheet7**, so in the Item column, these objects have a prefix of the sheet name followed by an exclamation mark. This can be seen in *Figure 2.11*.

  Tip: **Named ranges such as Merchants and Products were manually named and are therefore available throughout the entire Excel file. As a result, their names do not contain references to specific sheets.**

- **Data column**: Stores data in the form of tables for each object. To view the data, simply click on a selected cell within this column. Below the table, the stored data will appear as a **Table** variable. This is shown in *Figure 2.13*:

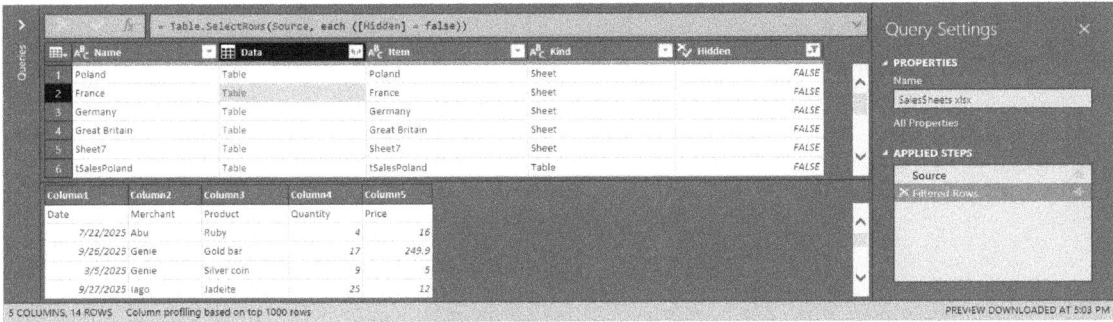

Figure 2.13: Viewing the Table variable

Tip:

- **The Table data type, as seen in the Data column in Figure 2.13, cannot be manually assigned. It is automatically determined based on the structure of the imported data.**

- **When importing data from an Excel file, each table will also appear as a Sheet object. If a sheet contained only a table, the only difference between these objects would be the header. Power Query automatically recognizes headers in tables, while in sheets, it assigns default column names.**

By carefully examining the data (Table variables in the Data column), it becomes evident that, in most cases, the data in tables matches the data from sheets. The exception is **Sheet7**, which means that importing both tables and sheets simultaneously is unnecessary. A decision must be made about the preferred source of data.

Named ranges are not relevant in this case, but choosing between tables and sheets is not always straightforward. Tables are generally the better choice because they must follow a structured format. However, in this example, one table has a different naming pattern from the other. Three tables start with **tSales**, but one table has the default name **Table2**. The assumption might be that this table should not be imported, but in this case, such an assumption would be incorrect.

For this example, we assume that the goal is to import data from all sheets that do not have default names (i.e., those that do not start with Sheet).

To achieve this, filtering must now be applied to the **Kind** column. This is done similarly to the filtering in the Hidden column, but this time, the **DefinedName** and **Table** options are unchecked, as shown in *Figure 2.14*:

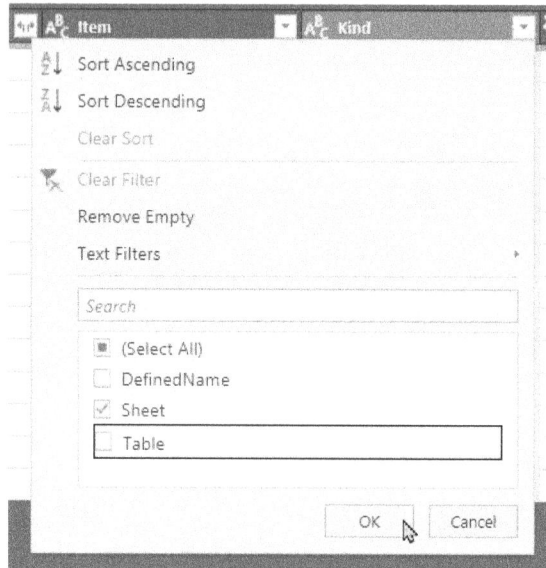

Figure 2.14: *Filtering menu for the Kind column*

After confirming the filter by clicking **OK**, the new filter condition should be added to the existing **Filtered Rows** step as an additional condition. This means that instead of:

```
= Table.SelectRows(Source, each ([Hidden] = false))
```

the formula bar will now display:

```
= Table.SelectRows(Source, each ([Hidden] = false) and ([Kind] = "Sheet"))
```

Tip: **Power Query attempts to write the shortest possible code. For example, in the filtering process (Figure 2.14), instead of specifying that the data should not equal DefinedName and Table, it simply states that the data must equal Sheet. This approach requires only one comparison operation instead of two.**

Now, all sheets that begin with the term **Sheet** must be filtered out. This is done in the same way as in Excel, by selecting **Text Filters** in the **Item** (or **Name**) column and choosing the **Does Not Begin With** option, as shown in *Figure 2.15*:

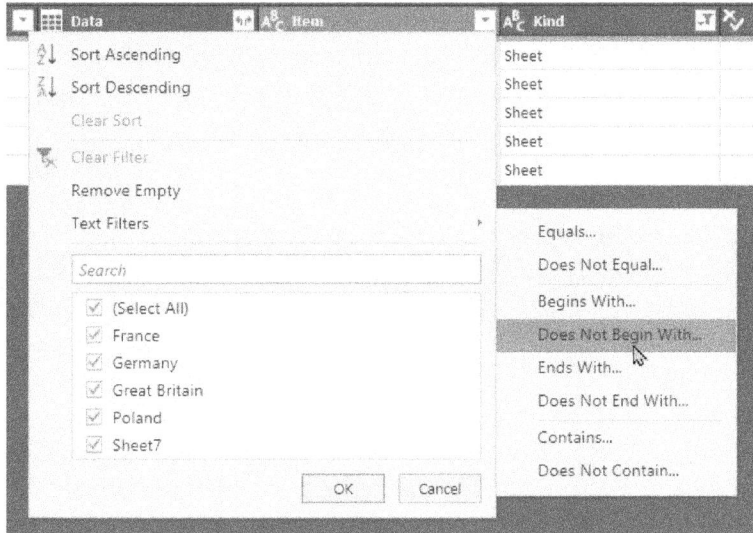

Figure 2.15: *Text filters for the Item column*

This action will open the **Filter Rows** window, where the **Basic** option allows the addition of up to two custom filters, which can be combined using either **And** or **Or** conditions. The **Advanced** option enables the application of multiple filters.

In this case, only one filter is needed, so the default settings remain unchanged. Simply enter **Sheet** in the field of the first row, as shown in *Figure 2.16*:

Figure 2.16: *Filter Rows window*

It is important to enter **Sheet** with an uppercase *S* because Power Query is case-sensitive, and the default names in the English version of Excel start with this phrase.

Additionally, note that the fields where the filter criteria are entered contain drop-down lists with all the unique values found in the selected column.

After confirming the new filter by clicking **OK**, a new step named **Filtered Rows1**, as shown in *Figure 2.17*, will be added, as a different type of filter is being applied:

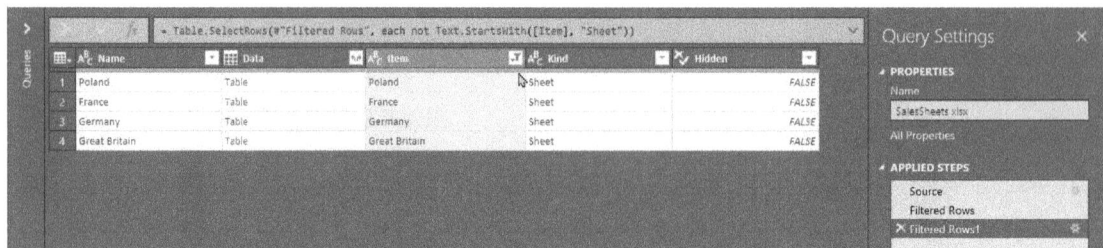

Figure 2.17: Data after applying text filter

Fun fact: **In the step related to filtering, a filter icon appears in the header of the filtered column (Figure 2.17 and Figure 2.13), but not in the headers of previously filtered columns.**

Now, we are close to performing the operation of combining data from the objects of interest by expanding the **Data** column. However, before doing so, we must determine whether any descriptive information about these objects will be needed.

By analyzing the data stored in the **Data** column (*Figure 2.13*) and using our knowledge of the dataset, we can conclude that the **Name** or **Item** column is necessary, as it contains the names of the countries where the products were sold.

We want to delete three columns (**Item**, **Kind**, and **Hidden**) while keeping the two columns, **Name** and **Data**. Since there are fewer columns to keep, we select those columns (for example, by holding down the *Ctrl* key and clicking on them), then right-click and choose **Remove Other Columns** from the context menu, as shown in *Figure 2.18*:

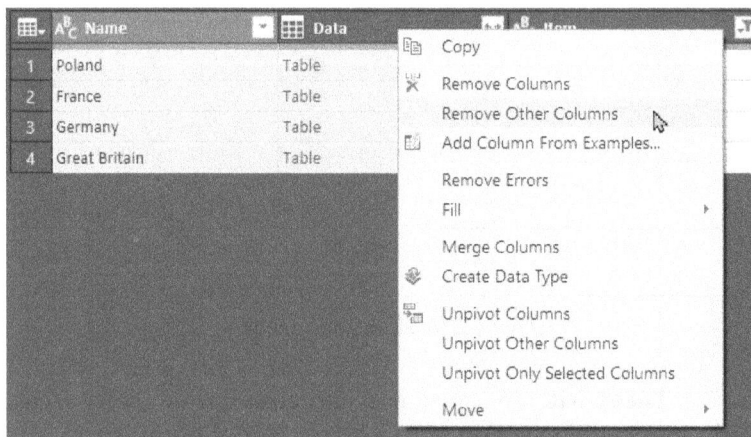

Figure 2.18: Remove Other Columns option

Fun fact: **The order in which columns are selected before choosing the Remove Other Columns option (Figure 2.18) matters. After removing other columns, the remaining columns will be arranged in the order in which they were selected before the removal process.**

Power Query will create a new step called **Removed Other Columns**, generating the following M code:

```
= Table.SelectColumns(#"Filtered Rows1",{"Name", "Data"})
```

If we had chosen to remove the unnecessary columns instead, Power Query would have created a step called **Removed Columns** with the following M code:

```
= Table.RemoveColumns(#"Filtered Rows1",{"Item", "Kind", "Hidden"})
```

In this example, the difference in the number of columns is small. However, in cases where this difference is significant, it is crucial to consider whether to remove the selected columns or those that were not selected.

After removing the unnecessary columns, we can expand the data stored in the **Data** column. To do this, click the expand icon (two arrows) in the column header. This will open the **Expand** window, as shown in *Figure 2.19*:

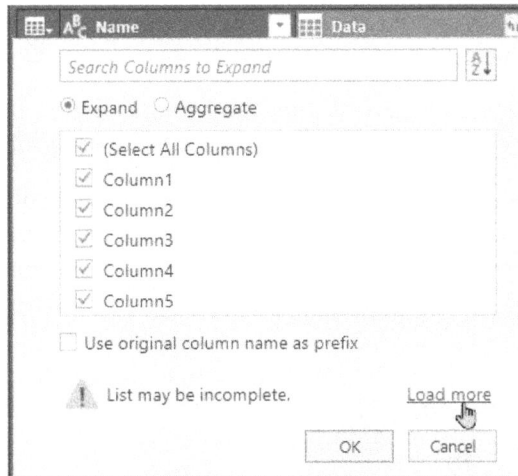

Figure 2.19: Expand column with data

In this window, we should only uncheck the **Use original column name as prefix** checkbox since we do not need the name of the currently expanded column as a prefix. Optionally, we can click the **Load more** link to ensure that Power Query has loaded all the available columns.

In our source data, there are only five columns, meaning that all columns have been detected. Unfortunately, they have default names because we are importing data from worksheets rather than tables.

As a result, after confirming the column expansion by clicking **OK**, we will get data where the header row is repeated. Specifically, for each row corresponding to sales from a given country, the name from the **Name** column will also be repeated, as shown in *Figure 2.20*:

Figure 2.20: Data after expanding the Data column

The process of preparing the table correctly and ensuring the data is properly structured involves the following steps:

1. Avoid using the **Use First Row as Headers** option (*Figure 1.8*), because the first row in the *Name* column contains a country name, not a column header.

2. Consider that if the layout of the source file changes, a different value might appear in the first row, which could lead to an error.

3. Rename the columns manually so that their names match the values in the first row, except for the first column, which should be renamed to *Country*.

4. Filter out the unnecessary rows that contain the repeated column headers by selecting any column other than *Country*. Use the search field in the filter menu to find and deselect the header value, similar to how filtering is performed in Excel.

5. Select all columns by pressing *Ctrl + A*.

6. On the **Transform** tab, click **Detect Data Type** to assign the correct data types to each column, as shown in *Figure 2.21*:

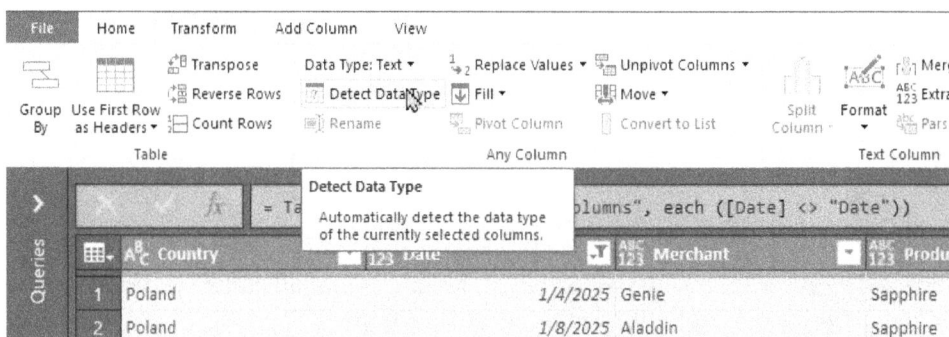

Figure 2.21: Detect Data Type command

Power Query quickly detects the data types for us. Although selecting the **Name** column was unnecessary since it was already recognized as text (*Figure 2.20*), its impact on data optimization is minimal. It is generally easier to select all columns at once rather than omitting just one.

Next, we can optionally calculate Revenue, following the same steps as in the previous example (*Figure 2.7*). After that, we can load the data into an Excel table, just as we did in the first chapter (*Figure 1.13* and *Figure 1.14*).

Before that, we should rename the query. By default, Power Query assigns the query name based on the source file name (*Figure 2.11*). To make it clearer, we simply remove the **.xlsx** extension from the query name.

Importing data from folders

In this example, we will import and combine data from **.csv** files located in a designated folder (**Sales**). Additionally, we want to retrieve data from a subfolder within the specified folder.

Before selecting the folder for data import, we first open the **Empty.xlsx** file and make any modifications without saving it. This action should generate a temporary file containing details about the unsaved changes.

The next step is to locate the **From Folder** option. The path to this option is the same as for importing data from an Excel file (*Figure 2.8*). On the **Data** tab, we expand **Get Data**, navigate to **From File**, and select **From Folder**.

This will open the **Browse** window, where we need to specify the folder from which we want to import data, as shown in *Figure 2.22*:

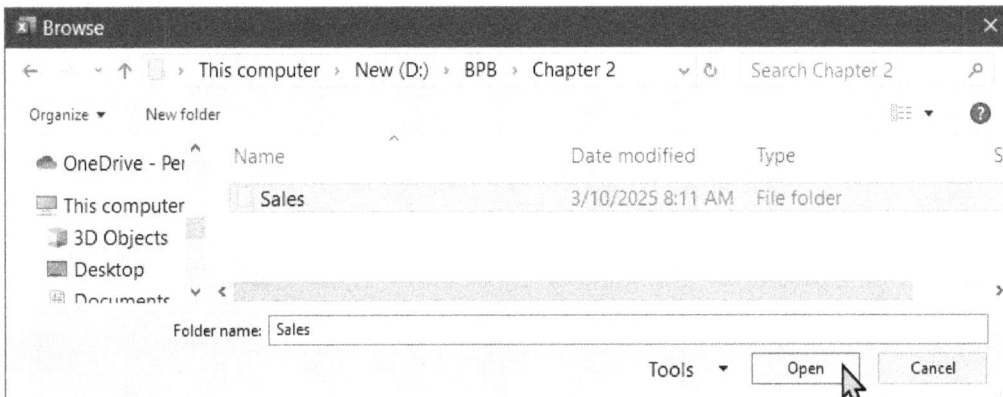

Figure 2.22: Folder selection for data import

In this window, no files will be visible. It is important to note that we are selecting only the folder itself, not navigating into it. To confirm the folder selection, we click the **Open** button.

This action will open the **Navigator** window, displaying a list of files located within the specified folder and its subfolders, as shown in *Figure 2.23*:

Content	Name	Extension	Date accessed	Date modified	Date created	Attributes	Folder Path
Binary	Empty.txt	.txt	3/5/2025 4:58:40 PM	3/5/2025 4:58:40 PM	3/5/2025 4:58:40 PM	Record	D:\BPB\Chapter 2\Sales\
Binary	Empty.xlsx	.xlsx	3/5/2025 5:03:01 PM	3/5/2025 5:03:01 PM	3/5/2025 5:01:59 PM	Record	D:\BPB\Chapter 2\Sales\
Binary	France.CSV	.CSV	3/5/2025 5:01:44 PM	2/19/2025 12:55:12 PM	3/4/2025 4:10:05 PM	Record	D:\BPB\Chapter 2\Sales\
Binary	Great Britain.csv	.csv	3/4/2025 4:10:05 PM	2/19/2025 12:59:07 PM	3/4/2025 4:10:05 PM	Record	D:\BPB\Chapter 2\Sales\
Binary	Poland.csv	.csv	3/4/2025 4:10:05 PM	2/19/2025 12:56:50 PM	3/4/2025 4:10:05 PM	Record	D:\BPB\Chapter 2\Sales\
Binary	~$Empty.xlsx	.xlsx	3/5/2025 5:02:08 PM	3/5/2025 5:02:08 PM	3/5/2025 5:02:08 PM	Record	D:\BPB\Chapter 2\Sales\
Binary	Germany.Csv	.Csv	3/5/2025 5:02:17 PM	2/19/2025 12:58:10 PM	3/4/2025 4:10:05 PM	Record	D:\BPB\Chapter 2\Sales\SubFolder\
Binary	picture.png	.png	3/5/2025 5:03:25 PM	3/5/2025 5:03:25 PM	3/5/2025 5:01:31 PM	Record	D:\BPB\Chapter 2\Sales\SubFolder\

Figure 2.23: Folder from which we retrieve data

At this point, we should see the temporary Excel file created by Windows when we opened the **Empty.xlsx** file and made modifications. This file may not have been visible in the standard Windows File Explorer, but Power Query detects it. It is the file that starts with a tilde (~) and a dollar sign ($), such as **~$Empty.xlsx**.

Unlike the previous **Navigator** windows we have seen, this window includes an additional **Combine** button. This option allows us to merge all files. However, we rarely want to use it because it is rare that our data does not require transformation before merging. Even the **Combine & Transform Data** option (*Figure 2.23*) does not effectively prevent errors or the inclusion of unnecessary files, such as temporary files or any other files we do not want to be part of the merging process.

The **Load** button, in this case, would only load the file list. Therefore, we usually proceed by clicking **Transform Data**, which moves the file list to the Power Query editor.

It is worth noting the **Attributes** column, which contains variables of the **Record** type, as shown in *Figure 2.24*:

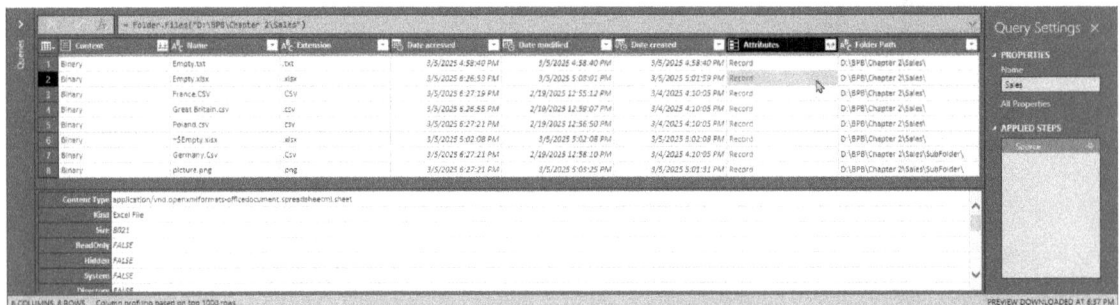

Figure 2.24: Details for Attributes column

This is simply a row containing additional information about the files. If we needed to include any of these additional file details, we could expand the **Attributes** column in the same way we expanded the **Data** column in the previous example (*Figure 2.19*). However, in this case, we are not interested in extra file information, so we will not expand this column.

Next, we need to remove temporary files from the list. This step is always worth performing, even if no temporary files appear in the current list. To do this, we need to filter out all the files that start with a tilde (~) and a dollar sign ($).

As in the previous example, we open the filter menu for the **Name** column, select **Text Filters**, and click **Does Not Begin With** (*Figure 2.15*). Then, in the **Filter Rows** window that opens (*Figure 2.16*), we enter the tilde (~) and dollar sign ($). At this point, we confirm the filter by clicking **OK**.

The next step is to filter out any files that are not in **.csv** format. It is important to remember that Power Query is case-sensitive, and different programs may generate file extensions with different capitalization styles. This is why, in this example, **.csv** files have been prepared with varying letter cases. This can be seen in the filter menu for the **Extension** column, as shown in *Figure 2.25*:

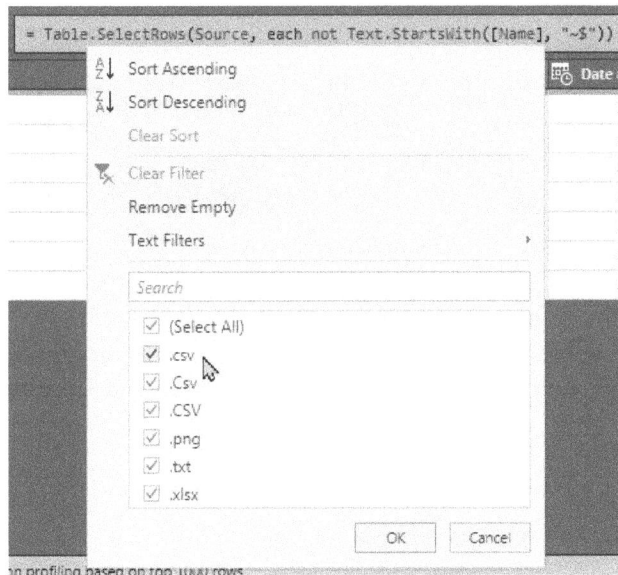

Figure 2.25: Folder from which we retrieve data

To ensure consistency in file extensions before filtering, we should apply text formatting to the **Extension** column, just as we did in the previous chapter. We begin by selecting the column, then navigating to the **Transform** tab, expanding the **Format** menu, and choosing one of the options: **lowercase**, **UPPERCASE**, or **Capitalize Each Word** (*Figure 1.12*). From Power Query's perspective, it does not matter which option we choose, as the goal is to make all extensions uniform in letter case. In this example, we assume we will use the **lowercase** option.

Now, we simply uncheck all extensions except **.csv** and confirm the filter by clicking **OK**.

> Tip: **When applying a filter in advance to a column that currently contains only one unique value, we cannot simply uncheck other values from the list because they do not exist yet. Instead, we must select Text Filters, choose Equals (Figure 2.15), and manually enter the desired value.**

In this example, we are retrieving data from both the selected folder and its subfolders. If we were not interested in data from subfolders, we would need to apply an additional filter to the **Folder Path** column.

The next step is expanding the data from the **Content** column. Instead of tables, we will see **Binary** variables in this column, which contain references to specific files, as shown in *Figure 2.26*:

Figure 2.26: Binary variable

To expand the files in the **Content** column, simply click the icon with two downward-pointing arrows located in the column header (*Figure 2.26*). After this operation, Power Query will generate multiple steps and queries, but first, it will open the **Combine Files** window, as shown in *Figure 2.27*:

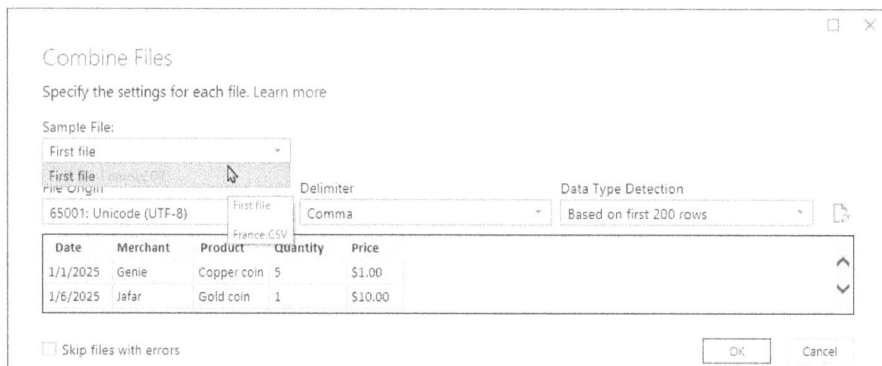

Figure 2.27: Combine Files window

This window resembles the **Import Data** window for a `.csv` file (*Figure 1.28*), but it additionally allows us to see which file will be used as the reference for transformations applied to all selected files (*Figure 2.26*). In this example, the first file is `France.CSV`. The default options selected by Power Query correctly detect the encoding and delimiter, so we can click the **OK** button to allow the editor to perform all necessary transformations to merge files from the folder.

First, expand the **Queries** pane on the left side of the editor to see the queries added by Power Query, as shown in *Figure 2.28*:

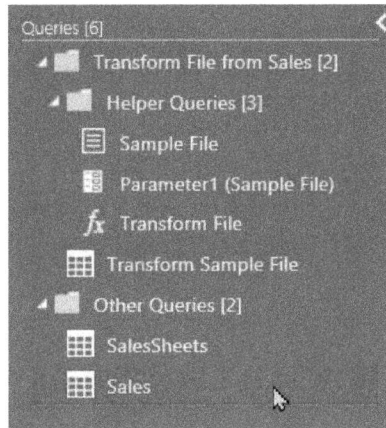

Figure 2.28: List of queries

Apart from the previously loaded query (**SalesSheets**) and the current query (**Sales**), there are four additional queries grouped into separate folders. For now, a basic understanding of their functions will suffice. From top to bottom, these are as follows:

- **Sample File**: The first data file selected from the **Sales** query (*Figure 2.26*), used as the reference for transformations.

- **Parameter1 (Sample File)**: A Binary file parameter, required as an argument for the function.

- **Transform File**: A function containing M code that transforms each selected file. It is based on the steps recorded in the sample query.

- **Transform Sample File**: A sample query storing all steps/transformations to be applied to each file in the folder before merging them. In this example, apart from loading data (**Source** step), Power Query has automatically added the step that promotes the first row as headers. If needed, we can add more steps here, and they will be automatically included in the function and applied to all files in the folder.

In later chapters, we will explore different types of queries in more detail. For now, let us note that depending on what a query returns, it is assigned a different icon next to its name. Until now, all queries have returned data tables, but now, looking from the top (*Figure 2.28*), we also see icons representing a file (Binary variable), a parameter, and a function.

Now, let us examine the steps that have been added to the main query, where we intend to merge the files from the folder, as shown in *Figure 2.29*:

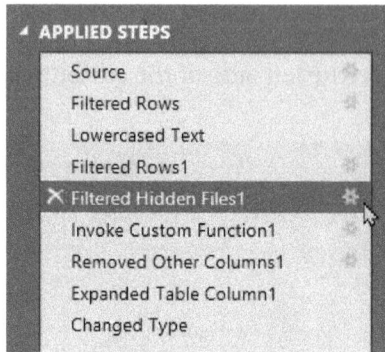

Figure 2.29: Query steps

A total of five steps have been added to the **Sales** query. These steps, in order, are as follows:

- **Filtered Hidden Files1**: An additional filter that removes hidden files based on values in the **Hidden** column, which is stored within the **Record** inside the **Attributes** column.

- **Invoke Custom Function1**: This step applies the **Transform File** function, which extracts and transforms data from individual files, returning tables. These tables are placed as cells in a newly created column (**Transform File**).

- **Removed Other Columns1**: In this step, Power Query removes all columns except for the one containing tables (**Transform File**).

- **Expanded Table Column1**: Here, Power Query expands the data from the tables inside the **Transform File** column. Since each file already had the **Promoted Headers** step applied, we do not need to worry about repeating header rows as part of the data table.

- **Changed Type**: The default step that detects data types for individual columns.

As a result, the query outputs five columns containing sales data, as shown in *Figure 2.30*:

▦	Date	A^B_C Merchant	A^B_C Product	1²₃ Quantity	$ Price
1	01.01.2025	Genie	Copper coin	5	1,00
2	06.01.2025	Jafar	Gold coin	1	10,00
3	16.01.2025	Genie	Gold coin	2	10,00
4	17.01.2025	Jasmine	Emerald	4	14,80
5	02.02.2025	Aladdin	Sapphire	25	14,00
6	04.02.2025	Genie	Jadeite	2	12,00

Figure 2.30: Result after merging files

The current output lacks an important piece of information, that is, the country name. This information was originally present in the **Name** column (as seen in *Figure 2.26*), but it was removed due to the default steps (specifically in the **Removed Other Columns1** step).

To correct this, there are two possible approaches. The simpler method is to click on the gear icon next to the **Removed Other Columns1** step. In the **Choose Columns** window that appears, select the **Name** column along with the **Transform File** column by checking the corresponding checkbox, as shown in *Figure 2.31*:

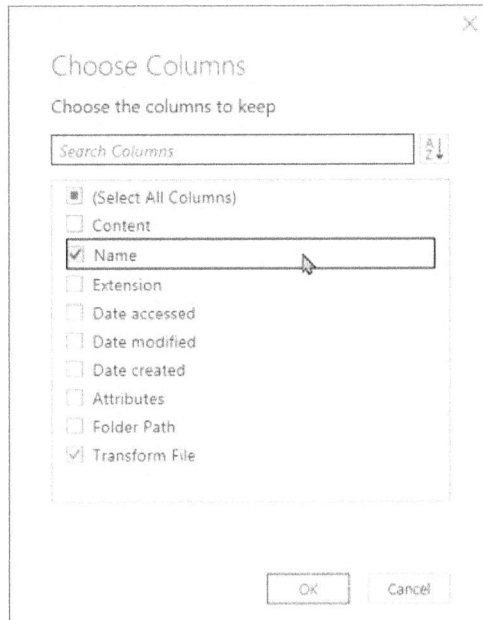

Figure 2.31: Choose Columns window

Another approach is to modify the M code in the formula bar for this step. The **Name** column needs to be added before the **Transform File** column, enclosed in double quotation marks and separated by a comma.

Instead of the following code:

```
= Table.SelectColumns(#"Invoke Custom Function1",{"Transform File"})
```

It should be modified to:

```
= Table.SelectColumns(#"Invoke Custom Function1",{"Name", "Transform File"})
```

This modification will not affect the subsequent steps. The **Changed Type** step does not need to modify the **Name** column's data type, as it was initially assigned a text data type.

However, the **Name** column contains the country name along with the file extension, which is not needed. To remove the extension, select the **Name** column, go to the **Transform** tab, expand the **Extract** command, and choose **Text Before Delimiter**, as shown in *Figure 2.32*:

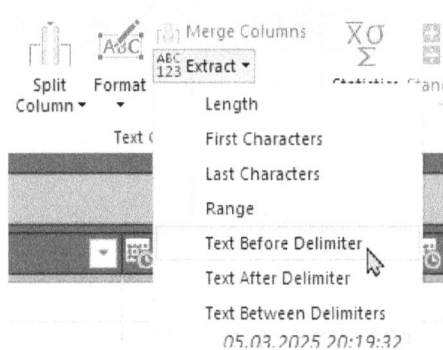

Figure 2.32: Extract command

This action will open the **Text Before Delimiter** window, as shown in *Figure 2.33*:

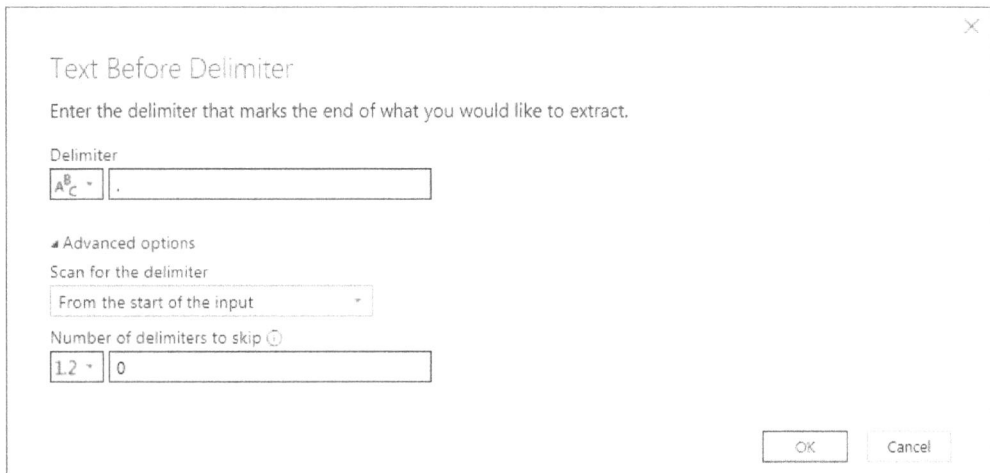

Figure 2.33: Text Before Delimiter window

In this window, enter a period (**.**) in the **Delimiter** field. Additionally, you can expand the advanced options to see that it is possible to choose whether to search for the delimiter from the beginning or the end of the text, as well as specify the number of delimiters to skip. For example, if the **From the start of the input** option is selected and **Number of delimiters to skip** is set to **1**, Power Query will extract the text from the beginning up to the character before the second occurrence of the specified delimiter. In this case, we need to extract the text before the first delimiter, so no changes are needed in the advanced options.

Now, we can optionally calculate Revenue in the same way as in the previous example (*Figure 2.7*) and then load the data into an Excel table, following the same process as in the first chapter (*Figure 1.13* and *Figure 1.14*). The default query name (**Sales**) can remain unchanged, as it was created based on the folder name from which the data was retrieved.

In this example, Power Query created additional queries, but they will all be loaded as a **connection only** (*Figure 2.34*). The load location is determined only for the **Sales** query, as shown in the following figure:

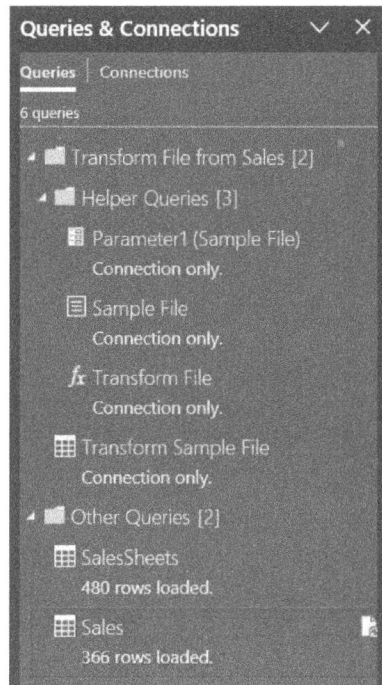

Figure 2.34: *Loaded queries into Excel*

Importing data from Access

In this example, data will be imported from an Access database file (**CitiesAndManagers.accdb**). The goal is to examine how relationships within a simple database influence query results.

The Access file contains three tables as follows:

- **Cities** {*Figure 2.35 (a)*}
- **CityManager** {*Figure 2.35 (b)*}
- **Managers** {*Figure 2.35 (c)*}

These tables are linked through relationships, which will be considered when performing transformations in Power Query.

Figure 2.35 (a): Cities table

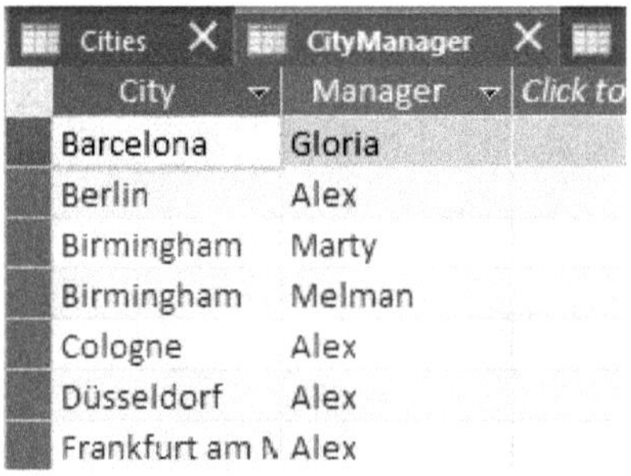

Figure 2.35 (b): CityManager table

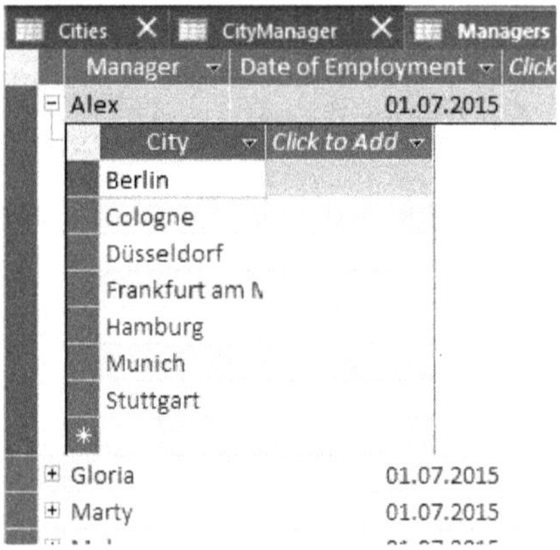

Figure 2.35 (c): Managers table

These tables store information about employed managers and the cities where they work. From a database perspective, it is essential to note that:

- A single manager can work in multiple cities {*Figure 2.35 (c)*}.
- Multiple managers can work in a single city {*Figure 2.35 (a)*}.

Since Access does not allow many-to-many relationships directly between tables, an intermediary table was created: **CityManager** {*Figure 2.35 (b)*}. This table enables the establishment of one-to-many relationships (*Figure 2.36*), correctly linking the **Managers** table with the **Cities** table, as shown in the following figure:

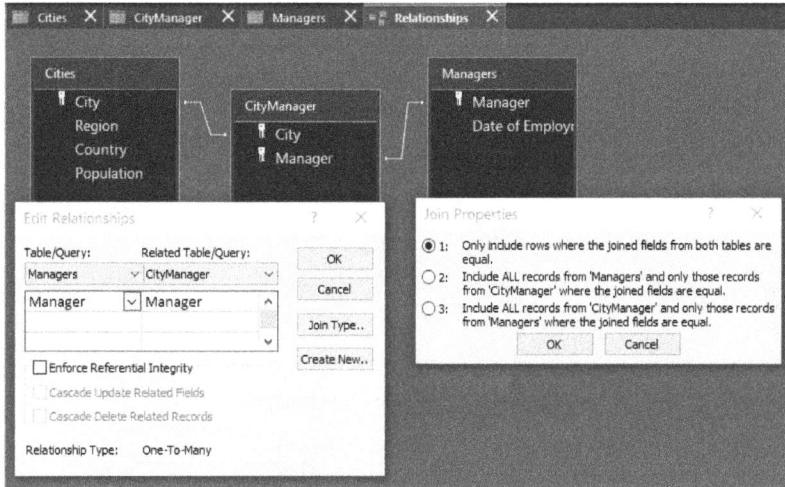

Figure 2.36: *Relationships in Access*

To retrieve data from Access, which is a database, navigate to the **Data** tab, expand the **Get Data** command, go to **From Database**, and select **From Microsoft Access Database**, as shown in *Figure 2.37*:

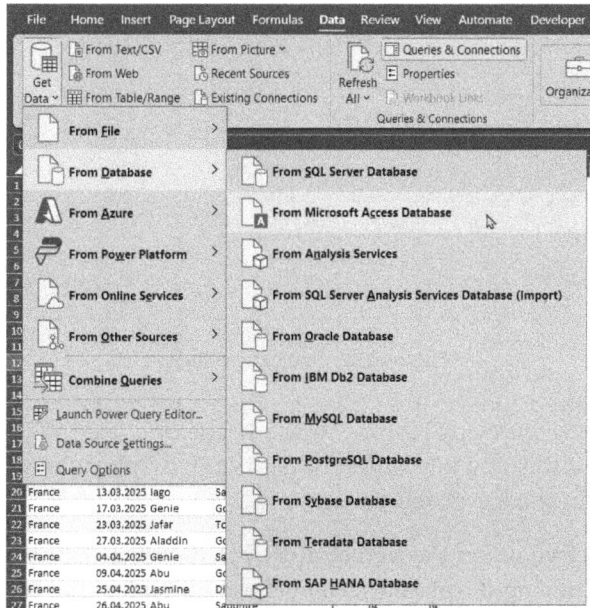

Figure 2.37: *Database data import options*

Selecting this option will open the **Import Data** window, where the required database file must be located and selected for import into Power Query, as shown in *Figure 2.38*:

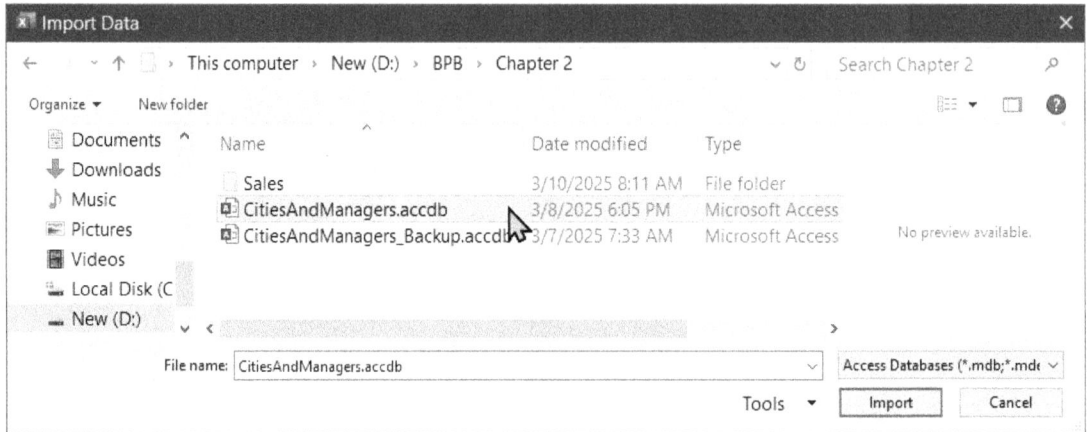

Figure 2.38: Import Data window

It is important to import data from the original file rather than a backup file that Access may create when editing the database. Clicking the **Import** button or double-clicking the file will open the **Navigator** window, as shown in *Figure 2.39*:

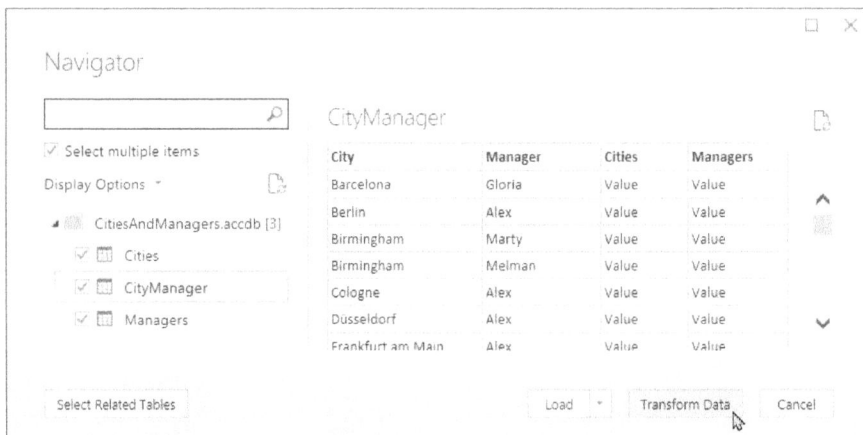

Figure 2.39: Navigator window

The **Navigator** window (*Figure 2.10*) looks similar to the one used when importing data from another Excel file, but with some key differences. It only displays tables, and there is a **Select Related Tables** button in the lower-left corner.

This button becomes active when the **Select multiple items** checkbox is selected and at least one table is checked. Clicking it automatically selects all tables that have direct relationships with the chosen tables.

In this example, all three tables (**Cities**, **CityManager**, and **Managers**) should be selected for import. After selecting them, clicking **Transform Data** will import them into Power Query as separate queries, as shown in *Figure 2.40*:

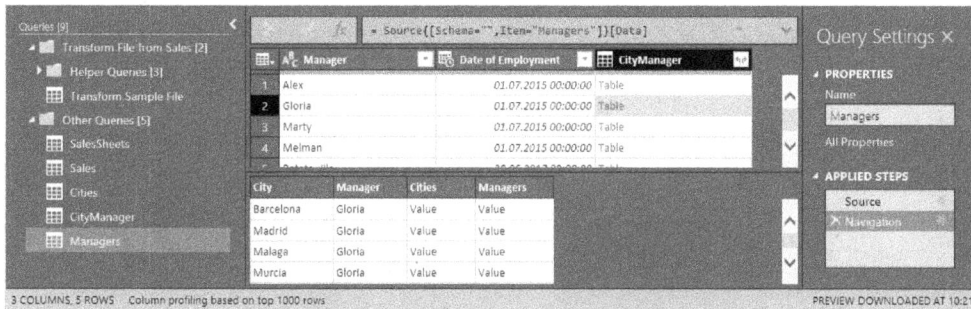

Figure 2.40: Queries loaded into Power Query

Tip: By default, queries in the list are arranged in the order they were imported into Power Query. The easiest way to change their order is by dragging a selected query up or down.

Each table imported from the database (*Figure 2.39* and *Figure 2.40*) has at least one additional column. These columns are linked to database relationships. If a table has relationships with two other tables, it will contain two additional columns. If it is linked to only one table, there will be just one additional column.

These extra columns contain Table or Value as their values as follows:

- Table appears when Power Query detects that more than one matching row exists in the related table.

- Value is used when there is always only one matching row. Technically, Power Query should display Record as the data type, but since it is not certain, it uses the more general Value type.

Once the data is loaded into Power Query, the goal is to enrich the **Managers** table with additional context by pulling in related information from the other tables. Specifically, the following:

- City information is stored in the **CityManager** and **Cities** tables.
- Region information is found in the **Cities** table.

The easiest way to achieve this is by expanding the necessary columns.

Before expanding the columns, the **Date of Employment** column should be adjusted. Power Query inherited the data type from Access as Date/Time, but since this column contains only date values, the data type should be changed to Date to optimize storage.

After this, the **CityManager** column should be expanded to include **City** and **Cities**, similar to the expansion process in the earlier example (*Figure 2.19*). Since managers work in multiple cities, expanding this column will result in additional rows for each manager, as shown in *Figure 2.41*:

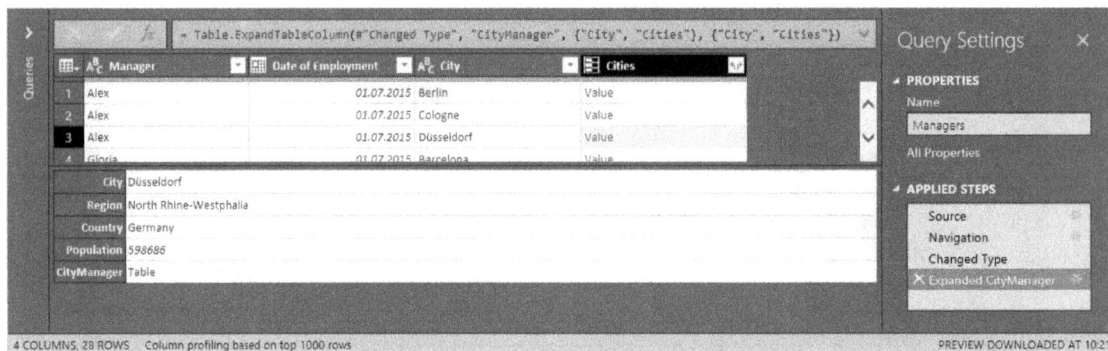

Figure 2.41: Result after expanding the first related column

Now, the **Cities** column can be expanded to extract information about the **Region** each city belongs to.

By expanding the **CityManager** and **Cities** tables, the **Managers** table now includes city and regional details (*Figure 2.42*). However, this was achieved without needing to import the **CityManager** and **Cities** tables fully into Power Query (*Figure 2.40*):

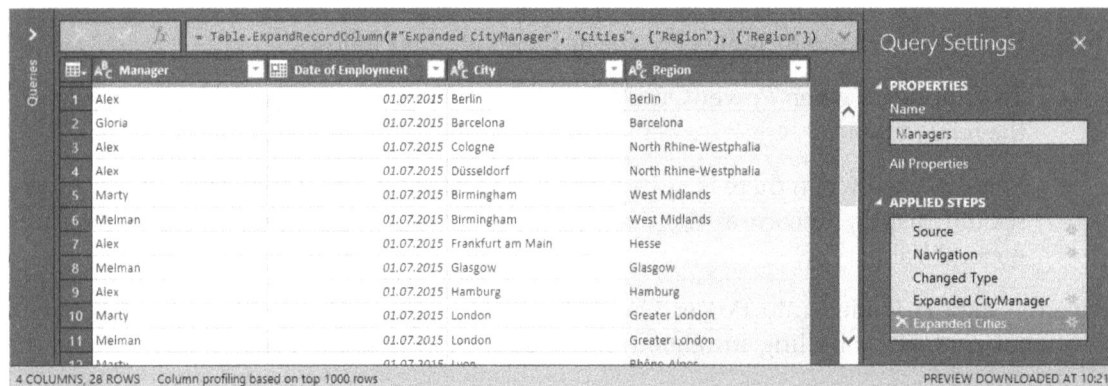

Figure 2.42: Result after expanding the second related column

Since the **CityManager** and **Cities** tables were only used to extract information and are no longer needed, it is a good practice to remove them from Power Query memory.

This is a simple task, following these steps:

1. Expand the **Queries** list.

2. Select the query to be deleted.

3. Click the **Delete** button.

4. Confirm the deletion action, as shown in *Figure 2.43*:

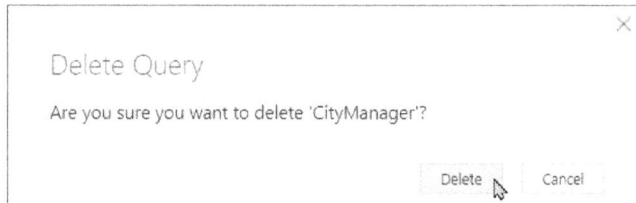

×

Delete Query

Are you sure you want to delete 'CityManager'?

Delete   Cancel

Figure 2.43: *Confirmation window for deleting a query*

Note: **Deleting a query, just like deleting a query step, cannot be undone using the Ctrl + Z shortcut. To restore a deleted query, it must be reloaded into Power Query, and all previously applied transformations must be re-executed.**

After deleting the **CityManager** and **Cities** queries, the **Managers** query can now be loaded into Excel as demonstrated in previous examples.

The created table could be used to answer questions such as how many managers work in each region. However, to analyze this data effectively, grouping operations are needed, which will be covered in *Chapter 4, Grouping Data*.

Automatic query refresh

By default, Power Query does not refresh data automatically (see *Figure 1.26*), which can lead to outdated results in your reports. To ensure your data stays current, you can set up automatic refresh using two main methods.

The first is to adjust query settings, such as enabling refresh on file open or setting timed intervals. The second method uses VBA macros to trigger refresh actions based on specific events or commands.

Both options help keep your queries up to date with minimal manual effort, especially when working with frequently changing data sources.

The first option is to change the query settings.

Changing query settings

One of the simplest ways to enable automatic refresh in Power Query is by adjusting the query properties directly in Excel. This allows the users to control when and how the data updates without writing any code.

This can be done by the following:

*   Right-clicking on the query (as shown in *Figure 1.26*) and selecting **Properties** from the context menu.

- Navigating to the **Query** tab and clicking on **Properties** (*Figure 1.15*).

This will open the **Query Properties** window (*Figure 2.44*), where specific refresh settings can be adjusted, as shown in the following figure:

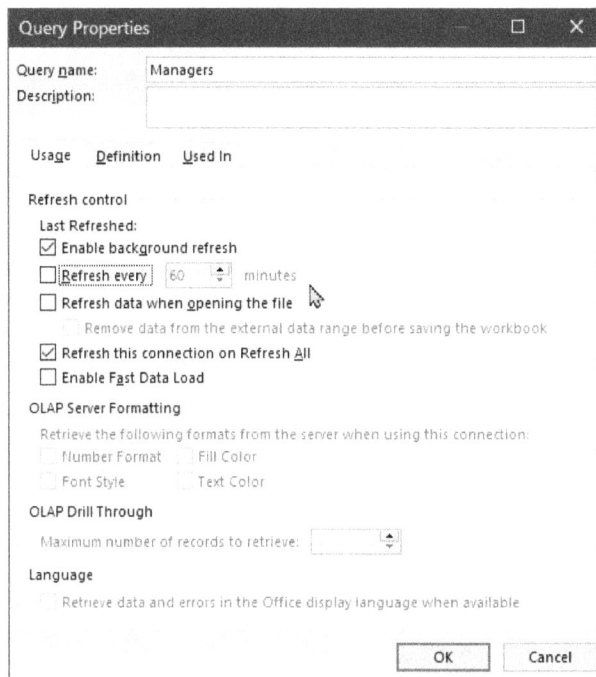

Figure 2.44: Query Properties window

In the context of query refresh, the **Usage** tab in the **Query Properties** window contains a group of checkboxes and options under **Refresh Control**. These options include the following:

- **Enable background refresh**: Power Query allows background query refresh by default, enabling users to continue working in Excel before the query completes. However, when refreshing queries via VBA, this option may need to be disabled. If left enabled, the VBA code might execute before the query has fully refreshed, potentially leading to incorrect results if the code depends on the updated data.

- **Refresh every [X] minutes**: Enables automatic query refresh at a specified interval. The default setting is 60 minutes, with a minimum of 1 minute. This option is disabled by default.

- **Refresh data when opening the file**: Enables automatic query refresh every time the Excel file is opened. This option is disabled by default.

- **Remove data from the external data range before saving this workbook**: Ensures that data retrieved from an external source is removed before saving the workbook. This option is only available after selecting the previous checkbox.

- **Refresh this connection on Refresh All**: Determines whether the query refreshes when the **Refresh All** command is used from the **Data** tab (*Figure 1.1*). This option is enabled by default.

- **Enable Fast Data Load**: Enables faster data loading, but at the cost of losing control over the loading process and potentially affecting the correct refresh of formulas. This option is disabled by default.

Tracking query usage

If it is unclear where a query is loaded or if the file is received from another user, the **Used in** tab can be useful. This tab provides the following:

- The exact range in Excel where the query results are inserted (*Figure 2.45a*).

- An indication that the query is only used as a connection (*Figure 2.45b*). This information can also be found in the **Queries & Connections** pane under the **query name** (*e.g.,* *Figure 2.34*):

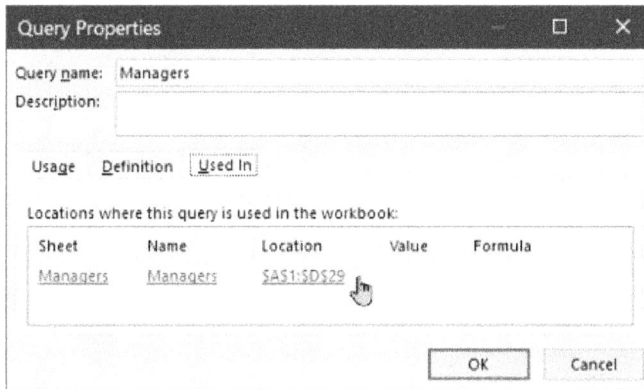

Figure 2.45a: Information on the query load range

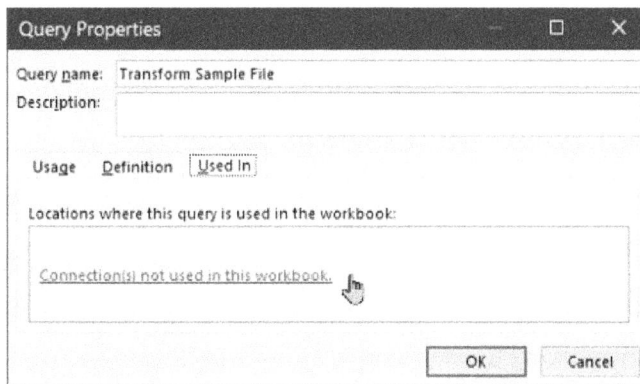

Figure 2.45b: Information that the query is not loaded into the Excel file

VBA auto refresh

Another way to automatically refresh a query is by using **VBA code**. In this book, we will only demonstrate how to record a single line of code that refreshes a query (or multiple queries) rather than writing the entire procedure.

To record a macro, the simplest way is to click the macro recording icon in the lower-left corner of Excel. If all other operations, such as writing formulas, have been completed, this icon should appear next to the **Ready** text, as shown in *Figure 2.46*:

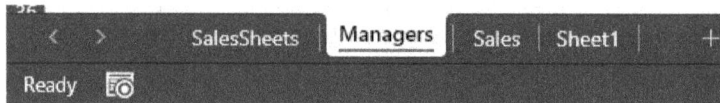

Figure 2.46: *Macro recording button*

Clicking this button will open the **Record Macro** window (*Figure 2.47*). From our perspective, the most relevant action here is renaming the macro. For example, to `Refresh_Query`, as shown in the following figure:

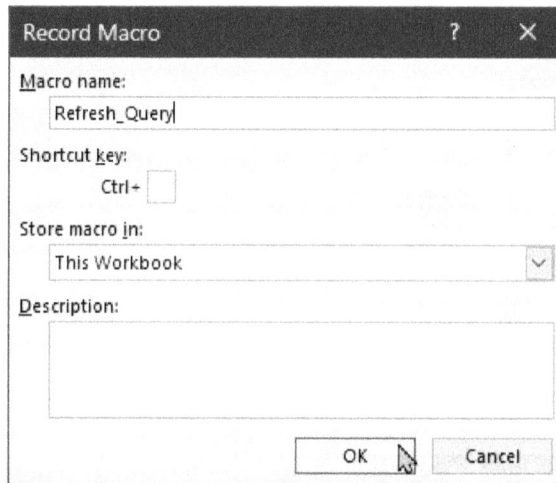

Figure 2.47: *Record Macro window*

After clicking **OK**, refresh the macro from three locations as follows:

- The context menu for the table.
- The **Refresh All** command on the **Data** tab (*Figure 1.1*).
- The context menu for the specific query in the **Queries & Connections** window (*Figure 1.26*).

Then, stop recording by clicking the **macro recording icon** (*Figure 2.46*), which will now appear as a stop button.

Now, open the **VBA Editor** using the shortcut *Alt + F11*. The recorded code should look similar to the following:

```
Sub Refresh_Query()
' Refresh_Query Macro
    Range("B7").Select
    Selection.ListObject.QueryTable.Refresh BackgroundQuery:=False
    ActiveWorkbook.RefreshAll
    ActiveWorkbook.Connections("Query - Managers").Refresh
End Sub
```

The first line containing the word **Sub** marks the beginning of the macro, while the last line with **End Sub** signifies its end.

Any lines beginning with a single apostrophe (') are simply default comments. When refreshing a query from the worksheet, the recorded macro might also capture the selection of a cell **Range("B7").Select** if a cell was clicked during recording.

Each line of the recorded code serves a specific function as follows:

- **Refreshing a query based on the current selection**: This line includes an option to disable background refreshing (**BackgroundQuery:=False**). If **True** were assigned instead, background refreshing would be enforced.

- Refreshing all queries, pivot tables, and other data sources.

- **Refreshing a query based on its internal name**: The internal name of a query differs from the one displayed in Power Query, at least by having the prefix **Query –** (which varies depending on the language settings). Other differences, such as a numerical suffix, might appear depending on how many times the same query has been loaded and deleted. When using this option, background refresh settings cannot be changed within VBA.

Depending on specific needs, choose the line that best fits the required query refresh method and any additional VBA code.

Conclusion

In this chapter, we explored advanced data connections and import methods in Power Query. We covered how to retrieve data from tables, named ranges, Excel files, folders, and databases, addressing common challenges such as filtering unnecessary data, expanding columns, and combining information. Additionally, we discussed methods to automate query refresh using built-in Power Query settings and VBA macros.

In the next chapter, we will take things further by learning how to merge and append queries. Those are essential techniques for integrating data from multiple sources into a single dataset ready for analysis.

Multiple choice questions

1. **What is the recommended way to import data from a named range in Excel?**
   a. Using the From Table/Range option in the Data tab
   b. Copying the data manually into Power Query
   c. Using the Import from Folder option
   d. Exporting the named range to a CSV file first

2. **Which statement about data types in Power Query is true? (Select all that apply)**
   a. Power Query detects data types based on the first 200 rows
   b. Incorrect data type detection may lead to data loss
   c. Power Query always assigns the correct data type automatically
   d. Data types must be manually assigned for all columns

3. **What happens when importing data from an Excel workbook with hidden sheets?**
   a. Hidden sheets are automatically included in the import
   b. Hidden sheets appear only in Power Query, not in the Navigator window
   c. Power Query does not support importing hidden sheets
   d. Only named ranges can be imported from hidden sheets

4. **How does Power Query handle merging data from multiple CSV files in a folder?**
   a. It merges files automatically without user intervention
   b. It requires selecting a reference file for transformation
   c. It applies the same transformations to all files before merging
   d. Only the most recent file in the folder is imported

5. **Which technique can be used to remove unnecessary columns in Power Query? (Select all that apply)**
   a. Manually selecting and deleting columns
   b. Using the Remove Other Columns option
   c. Power Query automatically removes unnecessary columns
   d. Using VBA scripts

6. **Which of the following options can be used to automate query refresh in Power Query? (Select all that apply)**

    a. Using query settings to refresh data on file open

    b. Scheduling periodic refresh intervals

    c. Writing a custom SQL script

    d. Using VBA to trigger a refresh

Answers

Question number	Answer option letter
1.	a.
2.	a., b.
3.	b.
4.	c.
5.	a., b.
6.	a., b., d.

Join our Discord space

Join our Discord workspace for latest updates, offers, tech happenings around the world, new releases, and sessions with the authors:

https://discord.bpbonline.com

CHAPTER 3
Combining Data Queries

Introduction

In Power Query, data is combined in two main ways: appending data and merging data. Appending adds new rows to an existing dataset, making it ideal for combining data from different periods or regions. Merging, on the other hand, adds new columns that provide additional attributes or descriptions to an existing column in a table. For example, it can be used to look up a product's price from a price list table, similar to Excel's VLOOKUP function. This chapter presents the key transformations and scenarios related to data combining, highlighting the difference between appending and merging. Understanding these operations will help prepare only the relevant data for further analysis.

Structure

This chapter covers the following topics:

- Appending data
- Merging data

Objectives

By the end of this chapter, you will be able to append data from multiple sources, even with small differences in structure. You will also be able to merge data with single or multiple conditions, aggregate merged data, compare lists, and perform self-joins.

Appending data

Appending involves adding data below the existing dataset, meaning new rows are added within the same columns. The most common use cases for appending data include merging datasets from different time periods or regions.

Appending data from three tables with different columns

In the following example, we want to merge data from three sales tables (these could just as well be three different *.csv* files or other data sources), all of which are located in the Excel file named **Append.xlsx**. Each table contains sales data for a single year, but their structures differ from one another {*Figure 3.1 (a), 3.1 (b), 3.1 (c)*}. Therefore, we cannot merge them all at once. The individual tables are named **Sales2023**, **Sales2024**, and **Sales2025**, respectively.

We need to load them individually (using the **From Table/Range** command on the **Data** tab) and then apply the necessary transformations to ensure that all tables have the same columns, are named identically (including case sensitivity), and store the same type of data.

◢	A	B	C	D	E
1	Date	Merchant	Product	Income	Quantity
2	1/1/2023	Skipper	Gold coins	$250.00	25
3	1/1/2023	Julien	Pearls	$67.20	8
4	1/1/2023	Skipper	Gold bars	$999.60	4
5	1/1/2023	Melman	Gold bars	$749.70	3
6	1/2/2023	Skipper	Jadeite	$12.00	1

Figure 3.1 (a): Sales table from the year 2023

◢	A	B	C	D	E	F	G
1	Date	Merchant	Product	Income	Quantity	Weight [g]	Weight [oz]
2	1/1/2024	Maurice	Emeralds	$103.60	7	12.60	0.49
3	1/1/2024	Julien	Jadeite	$108.00	9	45.00	1.62
4	1/1/2024	Mort	Copper coins	$32.00	32	3200.00	112.96
5	1/2/2024	Mort	Pearls	$168.00	20	240.00	8.6
6	1/3/2024	Mort	Sapphires	$14.00	1	1.50	0.06

Figure 3.1 (b): Sales table from the year 2024

	A	B	C	D	E	F
1	Date	Merchant	Product	Quantity	Price	Discount
2	1/1/2025	Maurice	Gold coins	17	10	15%
3	1/1/2025	Julien	Silver coins	9	5	20%
4	1/1/2025	Skipper	Rubies	4	16	8%
5	1/1/2025	Skipper	Jadeite	23	12	20%

***Figure 3.1 (c)**: Sales table from the year 2025*

We assume that the correct column structure is in the first table, i.e., the year 2023 {*Figure 3.1 (a)*}. Therefore, we need to bring all tables to the same format (ensuring they have the same columns). To achieve this, we must follow these steps:

1. Load the table into Power Query by selecting a single cell within the table and then clicking **From Table/Range** on the **Data** tab in Excel (*Figure 1.1*).
    a. Optionally, the data type of the first column can be changed from **Date/Time** to **Date**.
2. Use the **Close & Load To** command from the **Home** tab (*Figure 1.13*) to finish editing the query.
3. In the **Import Data** window (*Figure 1.14*), select the **Only Create Connection** option.

For now, we can do the same with the table for 2024 {*Figure 3.1 (b)*}. However, after loading the 2025 table {*Figure 3.1 (c)*} into Power Query, we want to append the remaining tables. To do this, we select the **Append Queries** command from the **Home** tab. Expanding this command gives us the option to append queries within the current query or create a new query (*Figure 3.2*).

Since we will still be making transformations in the 2025 sales query, creating a new query will be a more convenient and readable approach.

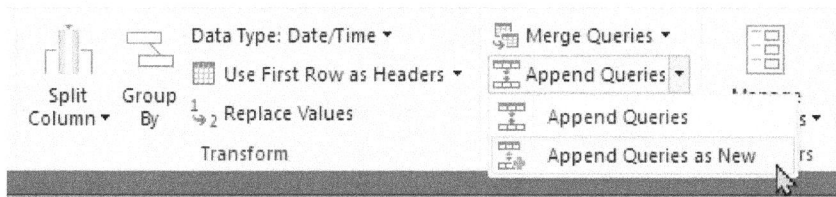

***Figure 3.2**: Append Queries command from the Home tab*

The **Append** window will open, where the default option is to merge two tables. However, in this example, we need to merge three tables, so we must switch to the **Three or more tables** option (*Figure 3.3*).

Here, we will sequentially select the tables we want to add from the left list and move them to the right list by clicking the **Add** button in the center of the window. To remove queries from the right list, simply select them and click the **X** icon next to them.

Fun fact: **A single query can be added more than once in the Append option.**

Once all queries have been added, we confirm our selection by clicking **OK**.

Tip: **We can also select multiple tables at once by using the Ctrl key to select non-adjacent tables or the Shift key to select adjacent tables. The selection order determines the order in which the columns appear on the right list after clicking the Add button.**

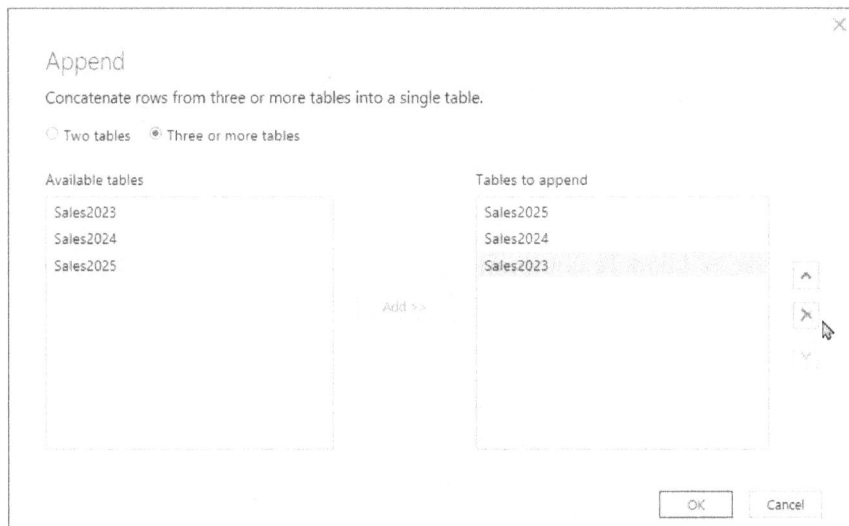

Figure 3.3: Append window: Three or more tables

After this step, we should have four queries in Power Query. The new query will be automatically named **Append1** (*Figure 3.4*).

If we change the data type of the date column to *Date* in all previous queries, the new query will also have the same data type. However, if even one of the queries retained the default *Date/Time* type when importing dates from Excel, the new query will also use the *Date/Time* type.

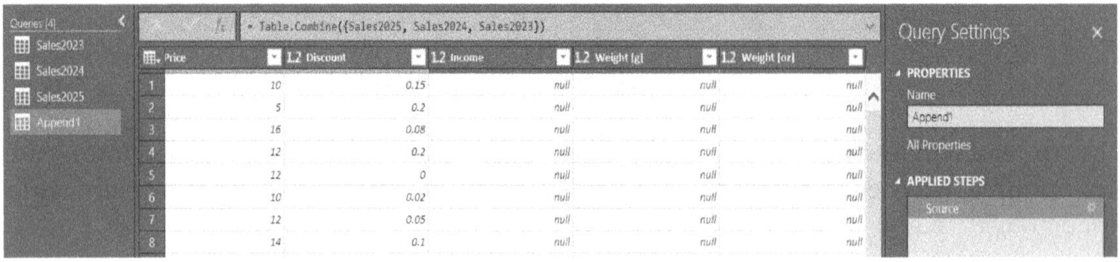

Figure 3.4: Appended data in a new query

In this example, the data type is not critically important, but in general, we should use a data type that takes up the least space while preserving the necessary information.

What is important here is that columns that were not present in all tables/queries are filled with **null** values for rows where this information was missing. For example, weight values are only available in the *Figure 3.1 (b)* dataset. In *Figure 3.1 (a)* and *Figure 3.1 (c)*, these columns will contain **null** values.

It would be a good idea to rename the query to *AllSales*.

Now, we can make adjustments to individual queries. The *Sales2023* query remains unchanged because it already has the exact column structure as needed.

In *Figure 3.1 (b)*, weight columns were added, but since they were determined as non-essential, they will simply be deleted. To do this, follow these steps:

1. Select both columns while holding *Ctrl* (for non-adjacent columns) or *Shift* (for adjacent columns).

2. Then, we can either press the *Delete* key or right-click and choose **Remove Columns** from the context menu, as shown in *Figure 3.5*:

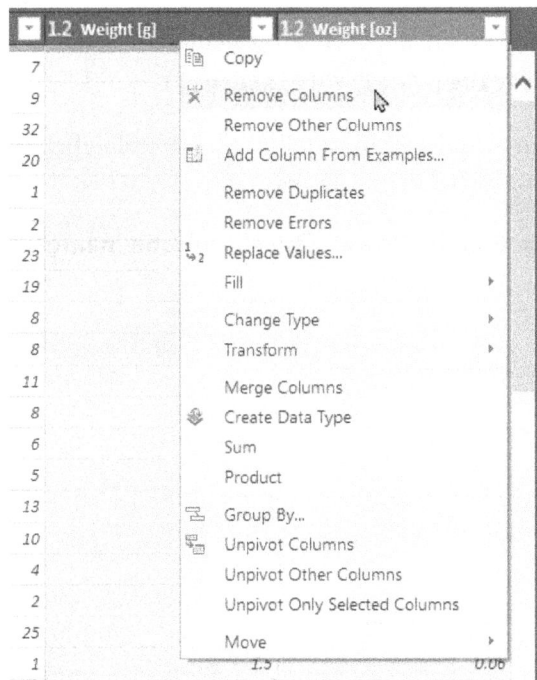

Figure 3.5: *Context menu for columns*

After removing the unnecessary columns from the *Figure 3.1 (b)* dataset and switching briefly to the merged query, we can observe that the weight columns are no longer present. This happens because queries are appended based on their last transformation step, which, in this case, occurs after deleting the unnecessary columns. We can verify this in the formula bar of the first step of the merged query (*Figure 3.4*). We have direct references to query names here.

Now, we can proceed to modify the *Figure 3.1 (c)* query. In this dataset, the **Income** column has been split into **Price** and **Discount** columns. Additionally, the **Quantity** column is crucial for correctly calculating the revenue.

To add a calculated **Income** column, we can follow these steps:

1. Click **Custom Column** on the **Add Column** tab, as shown in *Figure 3.6*:

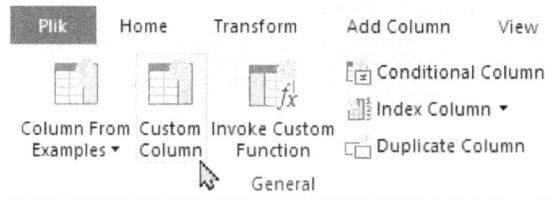

Figure 3.6: *Custom Column command*

2. The **Custom Column** window will open, where we need to change the default column name to **Income** and create a formula to calculate revenue (*Figure 3.7*):

```
= [Quantity] * [Price] * (1 - [Discount])
```

Column names can be entered manually or by double-clicking the column name from the list on the right side of the window.

Note: **Remember that in Power Query, column names are enclosed in square brackets.**

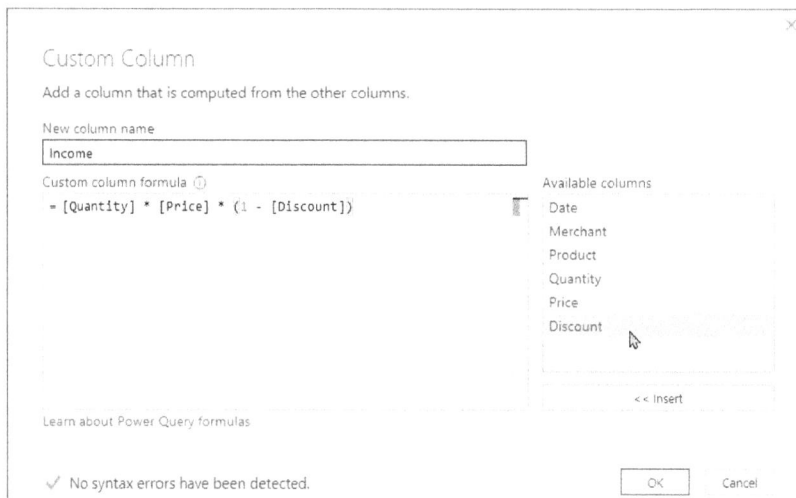

Figure 3.7: *Income custom column*

When we add the column using this method, Power Query will usually assign it a general (Any) data type. We should change it to a *Decimal Number*, as this should match the data type detected for the **Income** column in previous years.

3. We can change the data type by modifying the column directly, which will add another step in Power Query. Alternatively, we can modify the formula in the formula bar for the last step by adding a **type number** argument before the final parenthesis (remember to add a comma before the argument):

   = TableAddColumn(#"Changed Type", "Income", each [Quantity] * [Price] *
   (1 - [Discount]), type number)

4. After adding the **Income** column, we can delete the **Price** and **Discount** columns in the same way we removed the weight columns in *2024* (*Figure 3.4*).

5. Once this step is completed, we can load the data into Excel by selecting **Close & Load To** again. However, we need to remember that in this Power Query session, we created two queries:

   a. The sales data for 2025.

   b. The combined sales data.

   Due to this, we will not be able to choose a specific location for both the combined dataset and the 2025 sales data. Instead, both will be loaded onto new sheets or as connections only.

   We do not need to reload the 2025 sales data separately, but removing its newly created sheet is easier than changing the **Load To** settings for the combined data query.

Merging data

Merging adds data to the right of the existing dataset, meaning new columns with additional information are added. A typical example of merging is looking up a product's price in a price list table. From Excel's perspective, merging can be considered the equivalent of the **VLOOKUP** function. In this chapter, we are working with data from the **Merge.xlsx** file.

Finding the price for all products

In this example, we want to retrieve the product price (**Price** column from the **tLeftProduct** table) and, more specifically, merge it into the **tLeftSales** table located on the left worksheet, as shown in *Figure 3.8*:

Table name: **tLeftSales**

Date	Product	Quantity
1/1/2023	Rubies	25
1/1/2023	Silver coin	8
1/1/2023	Topazes	4
1/1/2023	Gold coin	3
1/2/2023	Gold coin	1
1/2/2023	Rubies	5

Table name: **tLeftProduct**

Product	Price
Gold coin	$10.00
Silver coin	$5.00
Rubies	$16.00
Topazes	$15.00

Figure 3.8: Sales table and price list table

To achieve this, we follow these steps:

1. First, import the **tLeftProduct** table into Power Query as a **connection only**.
2. Then, import the **tLeftSales** table and perform further transformations on it.

   The first transformation we need to perform is merging tables/queries. To do this, we follow these steps:

   a. Locate the **Merge Queries** command on the **Home** tab, as shown in *Figure 3.9*:

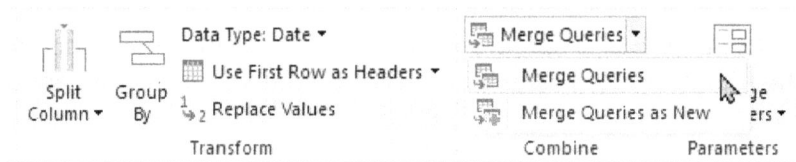

Figure 3.9: Merge Queries command

   b. Since we want to add a new column(s) to an existing query, we do not need to expand the command to look for other options. We can simply click the **Merge Queries** command directly on the **Home** tab.

   c. Clicking this will open the **Merge** window (*Figure 3.10*). At the top of this window, we will see the table from the active query. At the bottom, select the table we want to merge with.

   For now, this file contains only two tables, making it easy to choose the correct one. Additionally, one of the tables will have the (**Current**) label next to its name, indicating that it is the table displayed at the top of the window.

Note: **Reusing the same query during merging will be needed in a later example.**

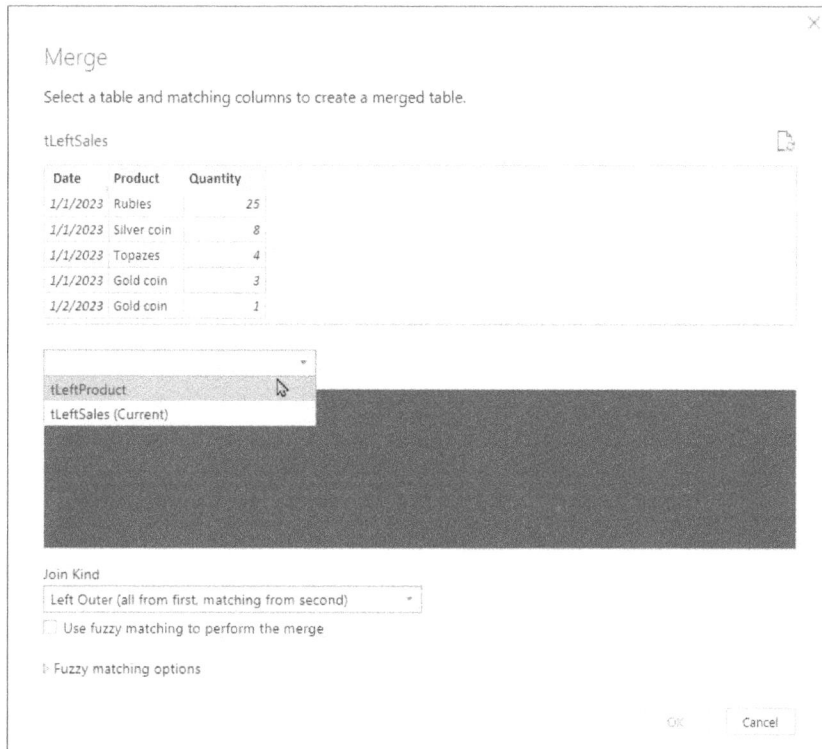

Figure 3.10: *Basics of the Merge window*

3. Once we have selected the queries to merge, we need to specify which column(s) Power Query should use for the merge. This is done by the following steps:

    a. Click on the corresponding column in both the top and bottom tables.

        If the selected columns contain matching values (including case sensitivity), Power Query will perform the mapping. We can see the results at the bottom of the Merge window, as shown in *Figure 3.11*.

    b. To confirm the merge settings, simply click **OK** (*Figure 3.11*). After merging, Power Query will add a new column containing **Tables** (*Figure 3.13*).

In our example, we can see that for all 11 rows in the top (left) table, a match was found in the bottom (right) table. This does not mean that both tables have the same number of rows, but rather, for every row in the top table, Power Query found at least one row in the bottom table with a matching value in the selected column.

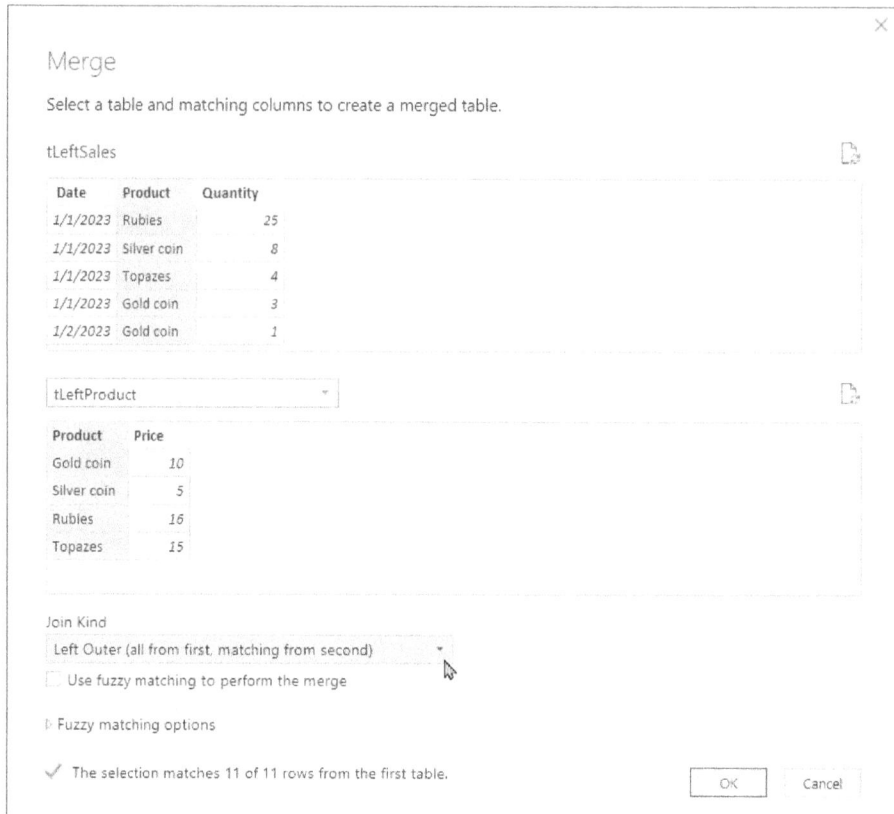

Figure 3.11: Merge window with selected columns for matching

An important option when merging queries is **Join Kind**. By default, Power Query selects **Left Outer** (all from the first, matching from the second).

This means that all rows from the top (left) table will be used, and only the matching rows from the bottom (right) table will be added.

In our example, every row found a match, but there may be cases where some rows in the top (left) table do not have corresponding matches in the bottom (right) table. In such cases, Power Query will display the number of unmatched rows at the bottom of the **Merge** window.

Since we are using a **Left Outer** join, we will not see if any rows from the bottom (right) table do not have a match. In this example, every row has a match, but even if some did not, it would not affect the goal of this example because the objective is to find prices for the products that exist in the top (left) table.

Apart from the **Left Outer** join, Power Query provides five other join types, as shown in *Figure 3.12*:

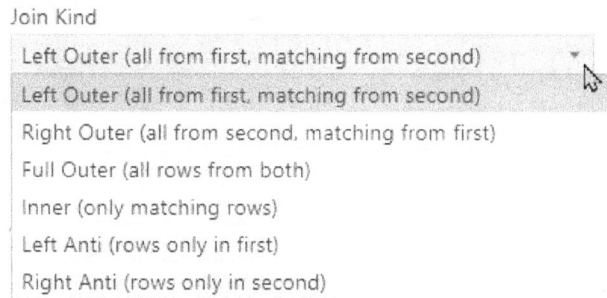

Figure 3.12: *Available join types*

The different types of joins in Power Query determine how data from two tables is combined based on matching values. The following is a summary of each join type and how it affects the resulting dataset:

- **Left Outer join**: Selects all rows from the top (left) table and matches them with corresponding rows from the bottom (right) table.

- **Right Outer join**: Selects all rows from the bottom (right) table and matches them with corresponding rows from the top (left) table.

- **Full Outer join**: Selects all rows from both tables. If a row has no match in the other table, it is merged with a row filled with **null** values on either the right or left side of the result table.

- **Inner join**: Selects only the matching rows from both the top and bottom tables. If a row has no match in the other table, it will not appear in the result table. The top table is the primary table in this join.

- **Left Anti join**: Keeps only the rows from the top (left) table that do not have a match in the bottom (right) table.

- **Right Anti join**: Keeps only the rows from the bottom (right) table that do not have a match in the top (left) table.

Tip: **In practice, using right joins is unnecessary because they are just reversed versions of left joins. Additionally, extracting relevant information is more challenging in the right joins, see the corresponding example.**

We will discuss each type of join in the following examples.

Fun fact: **The inserted column will have the same name as the query that was merged with the active query/table. In our example, it should match the name of the previously loaded Excel table. This name can be changed in the added step by modifying the formula in the formula bar as shown in Figure 3.13:**

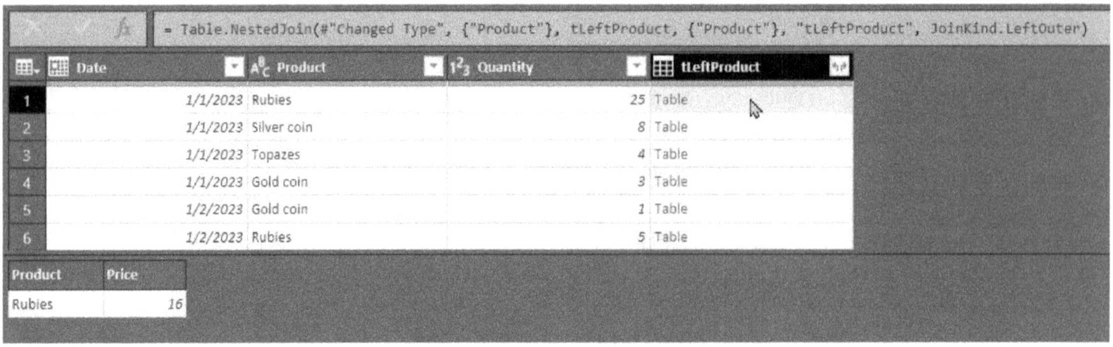

Figure 3.13: Table with an added column containing matched rows from the second table

Behind these tables are the matched rows from the bottom table (*bottom-left corner of Figure 3.11*).

In this example, each row in the top table (our current query) has exactly one matched row from the bottom table. However, we do not want to see it as a table within a row (since Excel cannot display such a column). Instead, we want to extract the relevant information, specifically, the **Price** column.

To do this, we follow these steps:

1. Click the expand icon (two outward arrows) in the column header containing the tables. This will display the column expansion options, as shown in *Figure 3.14*.

    By default:

    a. The **Expand** option is selected.

    b. All columns are checked.

    c. The checkbox **Use original column name as prefix** is enabled.

2. In this example, we only need information from a single column, the Price column; therefore:

    a. Select only **Price**.

    b. Uncheck the prefix option (since we do not need to add a prefix to the column name).

    c. Confirm by clicking **OK**.

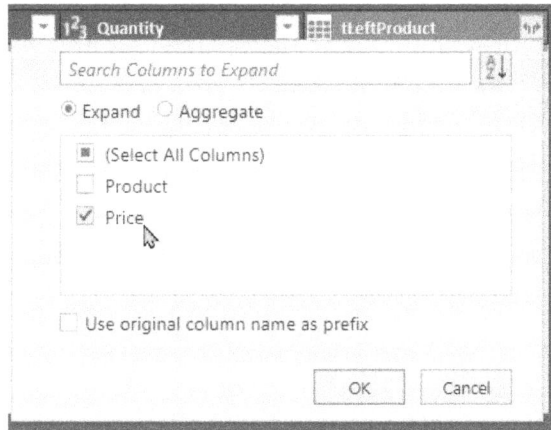

Figure 3.14: Column expand options

3. After expanding the merged column, we obtain a table with four columns, as shown in *Figure 3.15*:

    a. Three columns from the original query.

    b. One column containing the price from the related query.

This is exactly the result we were looking for, so we can now load it into Excel and move on to the next example.

Figure 3.15: Data after expanding the merged column

Merging with two criteria

In this example, we will retrieve data from the **Left2** sheet in the **Merge.xlsx** file. It is very similar to the previous one because, once again, we want to find the product price. However, this time, we want to do it based on two criteria: the product name and its short description, as shown in *Figure 3.16*:

◢	A	B	C	D	E	F	G	H
1	Table name: **tLeft2Sales**					Table name: **tLeft2Product**		
2	**Date**	**Product**	**Description**	**Quantity**		**Product**	**Description**	**Price**
3	1/1/2023	Diamond	Clear	25		Diamond	Clear	$24.90
4	1/1/2023	Pearl	Pink	8		Diamond	Flawless	$39.90
5	1/1/2023	Rubie	Sparkling	4		Rubie	Bright	$17.00
6	1/1/2023	Diamond	Flawless	3		Rubie	Sparkling	$19.00
7	1/2/2023	Rubie	Radiant	1		Rubie	Radiant	$21.00
8	1/2/2023	Diamond	Clear	5		Jadeite	Polished	$14.90
9	1/2/2023	Diamond	Flawless	3		Pearl	Pink	$12.40
	1/2/2022	Rubie	Radiant	3				

Figure 3.16: Sales table and Price List table

So once again, we follow these steps:

1. First, load the price list table (**tLeft2Product**) and then the sales table (**tLeft2Sales**).

2. The next step is to select the **tLeft2Sales** table/query and click **Merge Queries** (*Figure 3.9*). In the **Merge** window, we will see more queries available for selection in the lower table, but the general functionality of the window remains the same.

However, we need to change how we select the related columns. Clicking a single column is not enough. We must select two columns in both tables. To do this, follow these steps:

1. Hold down the *Ctrl* key, allowing us to select non-adjacent columns one by one. It is crucial to click the columns in the same order in both the upper and lower tables (*Figure 3.17*).

    On some monitors, the numbers in the headers of the selected columns may be difficult to see, but they are there.

Tip: While holding the Ctrl key, we can also deselect the incorrectly selected columns. Holding the Shift key allows us to select adjacent columns. The order in which the columns are selected remains crucial.

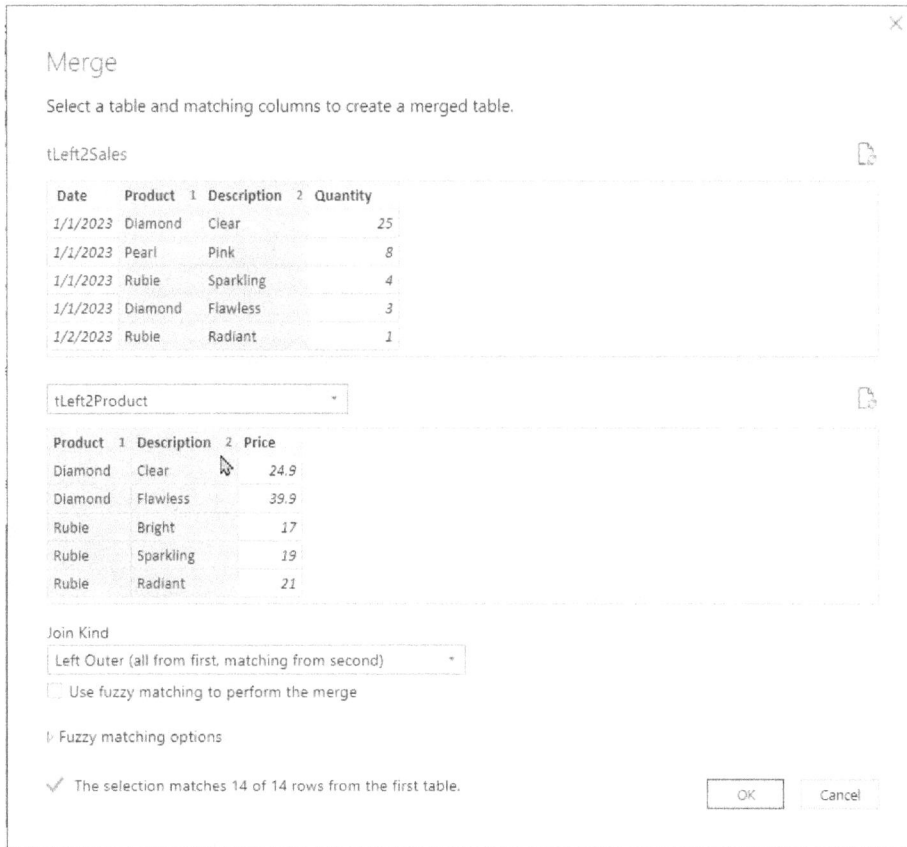

Figure 3.17: *Merging tables based on two criteria/columns*

2. After confirming the **merge** options, we will get a similar column to the one in the previous example (*Figure 3.13*). Similarly, we will need to expand it (*Figure 3.14*), but this time, we must deselect two columns, since we still want to add only the **Price** column and avoid any prefixes.

This will give us a sales table with the product price included, as shown in *Figure 3.18*. However, this time, we also want to add one more column, a column to calculate revenue.

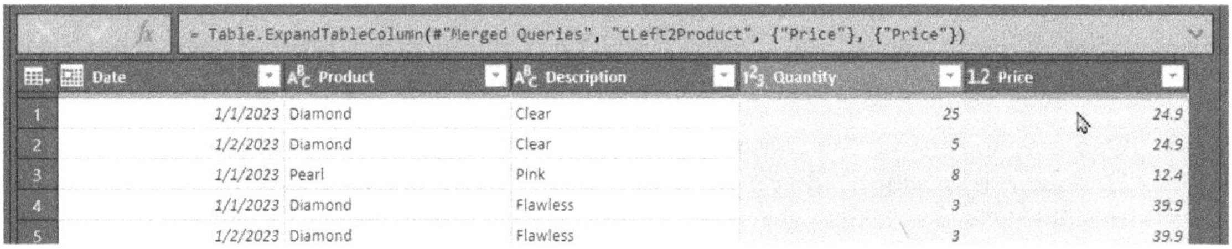

Figure 3.18: *Result after merging data*

3. To quickly add the revenue column, select the **Quantity** and **Price** columns (the selection order does not matter).

4. Then, go to the **Add Column** tab, expand the **Standard** command, and choose **Multiply**, as shown in *Figure 3.19*:

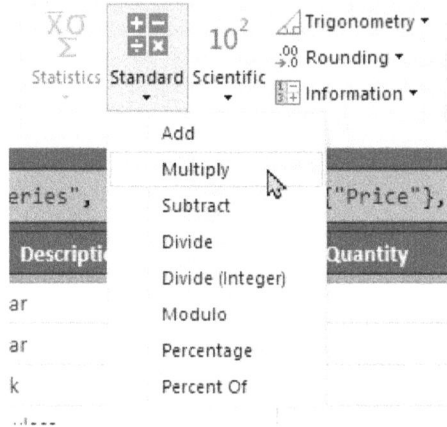

Figure 3.19: *Standard calculations on columns*

This will automatically add a new column with the result of multiplying the values from the **Quantity** and **Price** columns, as shown in *Figure 3.20*.

Since the order of factors does not matter in multiplication, the order in which we selected the columns earlier also did not matter.

Figure 3.20: *Multiplication result*

When Power Query adds a column using default calculations, it does not know what name we want, so it assigns a default name (for multiplication, this will be **Multiplication**). This default name is rarely useful, so we should change it.

5. One way to rename the column is to double-click the header and enter a new name. However, this action adds a new step, which may not be ideal for longer queries. While this is not a major issue in short queries like the ones we are discussing, it can become significant in more complex transformations.

Therefore, in this example, we will modify the formula in the formula bar, instead of adding a new step. We simply need to locate **Multiplication** in the formula (*Figure 3.20*) and replace it with a more suitable name, such as *Income*.

6.　After making this change, we can load the table into Excel.

Summarizing data in merges

In this example, we want to combine invoice details stored in two separate tables located on the *Left3* worksheet (*Figure 3.21*). Specifically:

- One table contains only the invoice number and customer name.

- The second table lists the invoice details.

For better readability, rows have been sorted by invoice number and color-coded, allowing us to see that each invoice has a different number of related rows.

In previous examples, each matching record corresponded to only one row. However, in this case, there will be multiple matching rows per invoice.

This time, instead of expanding the merged table with additional columns (*Figure 3.14*), we will aggregate the data.

	A	B	C	D	E	F	G
1	Table name: **tInvoices**			Table name: **tDetails**			
2	**Invoice Id**	**Client**		**Invoice Id**	**Item**	**Quantity**	**Unit Price**
3	IN2025/10/2	Wobbly Walrus Workshop		IN2025/10/2	Extra Slippery Soap	2	$7.99
4	IN2025/10/3	Sassy Snail Solutions		IN2025/10/2	Walrus-Sized Sunglasses	1	$12.50
5	IN2025/10/5	Bouncy Banana Bureau		IN2025/10/3	Speedy Slime Polish	2	$5.99
6				IN2025/10/3	Snail Shell Paint	4	$9.50
7				IN2025/10/3	Tiny Umbrellas	3	$3.99
8				IN2025/10/5	Banana-Proof Paper	5	$2.50
9				IN2025/10/5	Monkey Business Briefcase	1	$15.00
10				IN2025/10/5	Banana-Scented Ink	2	$4.99
11				IN2025/10/5	Peel-Resistant Notebooks	3	$8.25
12				IN2025/10/5	Extra Curved Rulers	5	$3.99

Figure 3.21: Tables with Invoice information

As usual, we follow these steps:

1.　Start by importing the second table (**tDetails**) into Power Query as a connection only.

2.　Then, import the first table (**tInvoices**) and merge it with the second one using a **Left Outer** join, as shown in *Figure 3.22*.

　　At the bottom of the **Merge** window, we can see a message indicating that each row from the upper table has found a match in the lower table (*3 of 3*). However, this message does not specify how many rows from the lower table have been matched to each row in the upper table.

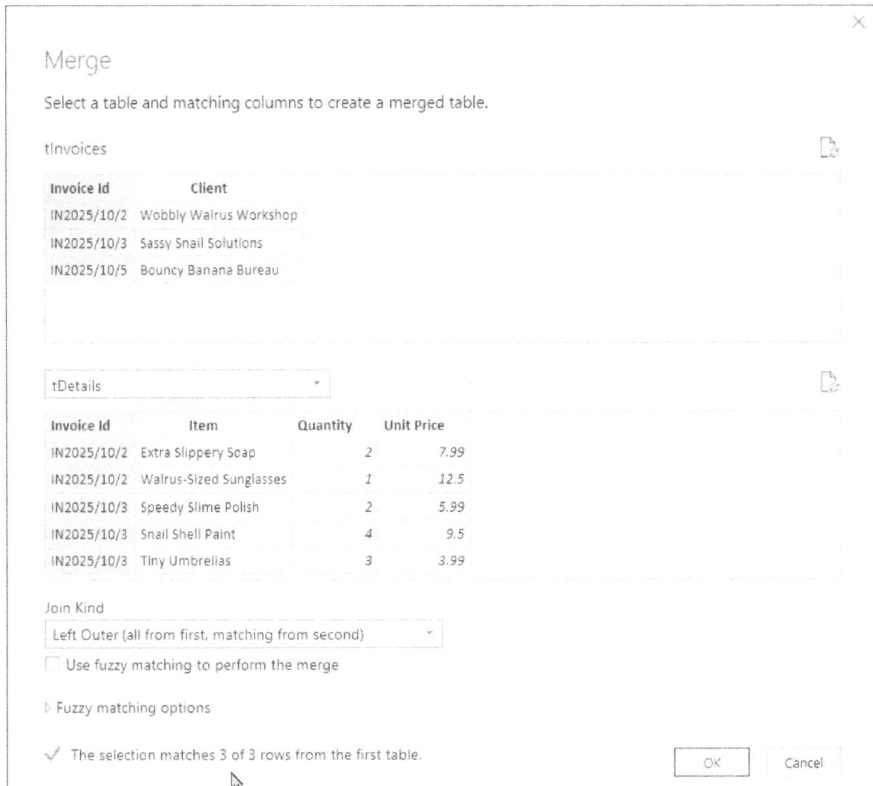

Figure 3.22: Merging with multiple matches

3. We can see this only after confirming the merge by clicking **OK** and then selecting a cell that contains the merged table, as shown in *Figure 3.23*:

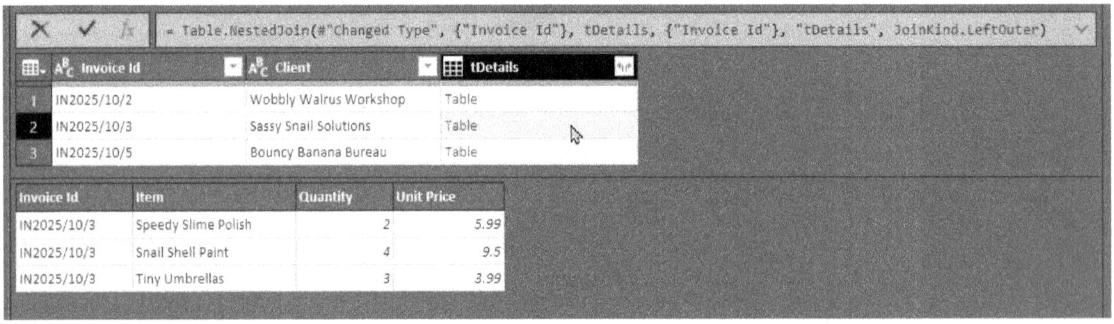

Figure 3.23: Merge results with multiple matching rows

For example, the invoice **IN2025/10/3** has three matching rows in the lower table.

If we were to expand the **tDetails** column now, the information from the upper table (left side) would be duplicated as many times as there are matching rows in the lower table. However, we do not want to repeat this data.

4. Instead, when expanding the **tDetails** column, we select the **Aggregate** option, as shown in *Figure 3.24*:

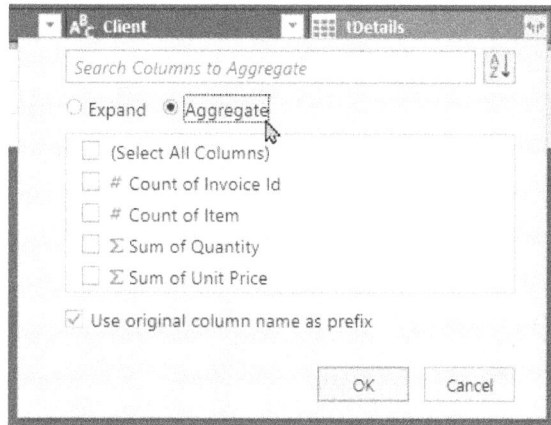

Figure 3.24: Aggregating data when expanding the tDetails column

We can observe that:

a. Text columns are automatically set to aggregate using **Count** (specifically, Count All).

b. Numeric columns are automatically set to aggregate using **Sum**.

c. The prefix checkbox is enabled by default, but in most cases, we want to uncheck it.

5. If these default aggregations are sufficient, we can simply check the appropriate boxes and confirm by clicking **OK**.

However, in this example, we want to calculate:

a. The average and median for the **Unit Price** column.

b. The number of items on the invoice (Count All from any column in the table).

6. To count the number of matching rows, we just need to check the box next to any column, such as **Invoice Id.**

To find the average and median, we need to expand the available options for the relevant column. To do this:

a. Hover over the desired column.

b. Click the small triangle that appears on the right side of the highlight to open the list of available aggregation options, as shown in *Figure 3.25*.

The available aggregation options will vary depending on the data type of the column.

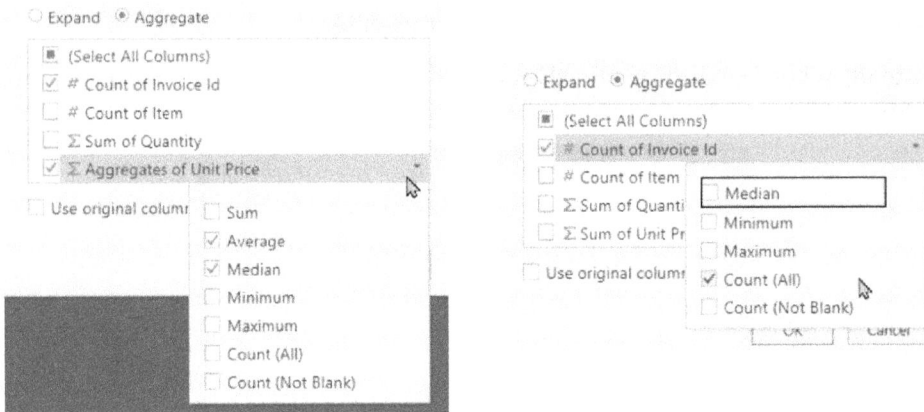

Figure 3.25: Available Aggregation options

> **Fun fact:** **If we select only one aggregation option, the outer aggregation method (Figure 3.24) will automatically adjust to reflect that choice. However, if we select two or more aggregation options for a single column, we will see the label Aggregates instead.**

7. After selecting the desired aggregation methods for the relevant columns (*Figure 3.25*) and clicking **OK**, we will see the results applied in the next step, as shown in *Figure 3.26*:

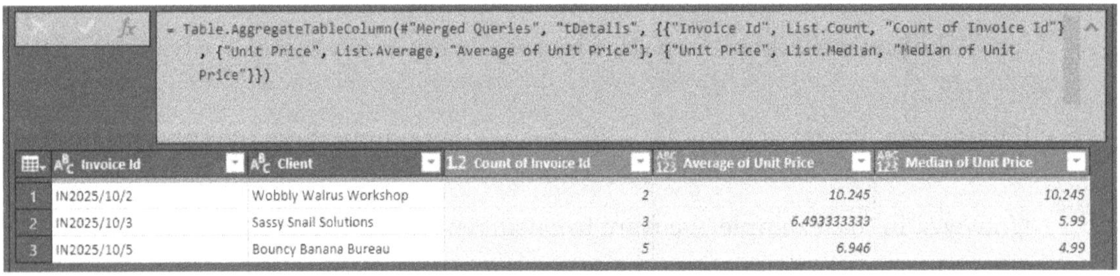

Figure 3.26: Aggregation results

As in the previous examples, the formula bar displays default names for the newly added columns, which include:

- The aggregation type.

- The column name on which the aggregation was performed.

If any of these names are not suitable, we can rename them. However, for this example, we will leave them as they are.

The formula bar also shows the exact function name used for each aggregation, such as **List.Count**.

8. Since we do not need any further transformations in this example, we can now load the table into Excel.

Right join and full join

We have already mentioned that in most cases, right joins are unnecessary because they are simply left joins with the table order reversed. However, it is worth exploring them at least once to understand how they work in practice.

In this example, we want to merge two tables located on the *Right* worksheet (*Figure 3.27*):

*   The first table (**tProducts**) contains information about the ordered product, its quantity, and the city/mine it originates from.

*   The second table (**tTownsMines**) includes city/mine names, their locations, and the number of employees.

In both tables, the last row has been highlighted because it does not have a match in the related table.

	A	B	C	D	E	F	G
1	Table name: **tProducts**				Table name: **tTownsMines**		
2	**Product**	**Town/Mine Name**	**Quantity**		**Town/Mine Name**	**Localization**	**# of Employees**
3	Gold coin	Moria	25		Azmarin	Pearl City of the Shimmeri	120
4	Silver coin	Moria	8		Moria	The Lord of the Rings	96,669
5	Ruby	The Mines of Mandaria	4		The Mines of Mandari	The Inheritance Cycle	4,500
6	Topaz	Ironforge	3		Ironforge	World of Warcraft	2,000
7	Jadeit	Ironforge	1		Blackreach	The Elder Scrolls V: Skyrim	300
8	Pearl	Azmarin	5				
9	Jadeit	Ironforge	3				
10	Pearl	Azmarin	12				
11	Ruby	Moria	13				
12	Diamond	Calaris	99				

Figure 3.27: Tables to merge

Similar to the previous examples, we follow these steps:

1. First, load the **tTownsMines** table as a connection only.

2. Then, load the **tProducts** table.

3. Next, we merge **tProducts** with the previously loaded table.

4. In the **Merge** window, instead of selecting the previously used **Left Outer** join, we choose **Right Outer**, as shown in *Figure 3.28*:

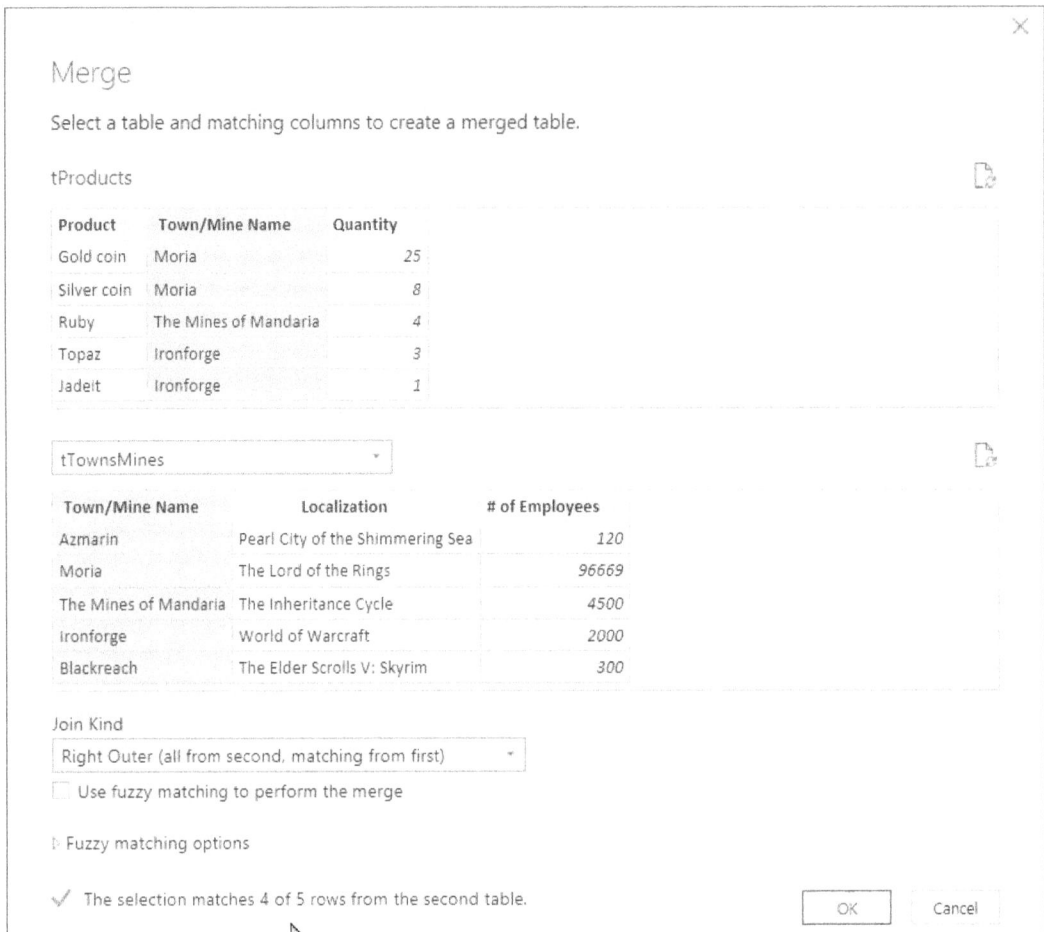

Figure 3.28: Right Outer join

At the bottom of the **Merge** window, we can see that Power Query found matches for 4 out of 5 rows in the second table (whereas in the **Left Outer** join, 9 out of 10 rows were matched).

5. Now, we confirm the merge by clicking **OK**. After this, we will see the resulting table (*Figure 3.29*), which contains nine rows from the **tProducts** table. The tenth row was not included because the selected join type, rows without a match in **tTownsMines** are excluded.

In contrast, the tenth row of the merged table is filled with **null** values, indicating missing data. This row corresponds to the last (unmatched) row from **tTownsMines**, which is stored under the **Table** variable. If there were more unmatched rows, they would all appear in this section.

```
= Table.NestedJoin(#"Changed Type", {"Town/Mine Name"}, tTownsMines, {"Town/Mine Name"},
  "tTownsMines", JoinKind.RightOuter)
```

	Product	Town/Mine Name	Quantity	tTownsMines
1	Gold coin	Moria	25	Table
2	Silver coin	Moria	8	Table
3	Pearl	Azmarin	5	Table
4	Ruby	The Mines of Mandaria	4	Table
5	Topaz	Ironforge	3	Table
6	Jadeit	Ironforge	1	Table
7	Jadeit	Ironforge	3	Table
8	Pearl	Azmarin	12	Table
9	Ruby	Moria	13	Table
10	null	null	null	Table

Figure 3.29: Result of Right Outer join

Just like in the previous example (*Figure 3.14*), we now want to expand the **tTownsMines** column. Our goal is to extract only the **Localization** column without prefixes.

After expanding, we will still have a ten-row table (*Figure 3.30*).

a. The last row will have **null** values on the left side (from the unmatched row in **tProducts**).

b. The **Localization** column (on the right side) will contain a value from the unmatched row in **tTownsMines**.

This confirms that in a Right Outer join, every row from the second table (**tTownsMines**) appears at least once in the result table.

```
= Table.ExpandTableColumn(#"Merged Queries", "tTownsMines", {"Localization"}, {"Localization"})
```

	Product	Town/Mine Name	Quantity	Localization
1	Gold coin	Moria	25	The Lord of the Rings
2	Silver coin	Moria	8	The Lord of the Rings
3	Pearl	Azmarin	5	Pearl City of the Shimmering Sea
4	Ruby	The Mines of Mandaria	4	The Inheritance Cycle
5	Topaz	Ironforge	3	World of Warcraft
6	Jadeit	Ironforge	1	World of Warcraft
7	Jadeit	Ironforge	3	World of Warcraft
8	Pearl	Azmarin	12	Pearl City of the Shimmering Sea
9	Ruby	Moria	13	The Lord of the Rings
10	null	null	null	The Elder Scrolls V: Skyrim

Figure 3.30: Result of the Right Outer join after expanding the Localization column

Now, we want to see how our result changes when we switch from a Right Outer join to a Full Outer join. To do this, we follow these steps:

1. Select the second-to-last step in the query (which should have the default name **Merged Queries**).

2. Then, click the gear icon next to it, as shown in *Figure 3.31*:

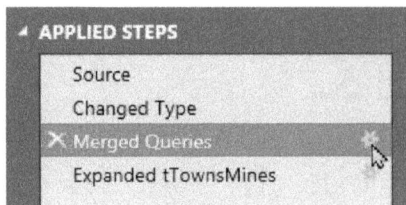

Figure 3.31: Query steps list

Clicking the gear icon will reopen the **Merge** window. When we change the join type, we will see a summary from the perspective of both merged tables, as shown in *Figure 3.32*:

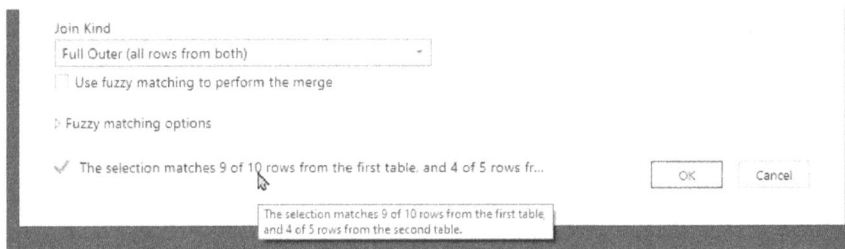

Figure 3.32: Full Outer join summarization

3. Now, we can confirm the join type change by clicking **OK** and proceeding to the last step of the query. At this stage, we will now see eleven rows in the result table, as shown in *Figure 3.33*:

Figure 3.33: Result of Full Outer join after expanding the Localization column

The additional row that appeared is the last row from the *tProducts* table, which did not have a match in *tTownsMines*. This is why the **Localization** column contains a **null** value.

A Full Outer join is useful when we want to retain all the information from both tables, including both matched and unmatched records.

Now, we could load this table into Excel, but before doing so, we want to perform one more operation in the Power Query Editor.

So far, we have created eight queries, and we will be adding even more. With so many queries, grouping them can be helpful for better organization.

To do this, follow these steps:

1. Expand the **Queries** list on the left side of the editor.

2. Select the queries you want to group (using *Ctrl* for non-adjacent queries or *Shift* for adjacent ones).

3. Right-click on any selected query.

4. In the **context menu**, choose **Move To Group**, as shown in *Figure 3.34*:

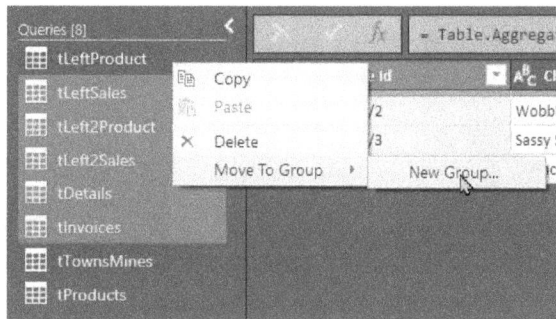

Figure 3.34: Creating a new query group

Since we have not created any groups yet, we need to create a new one first. After clicking **New Group**, the **New Group** window will open, as shown in *Figure 3.35*:

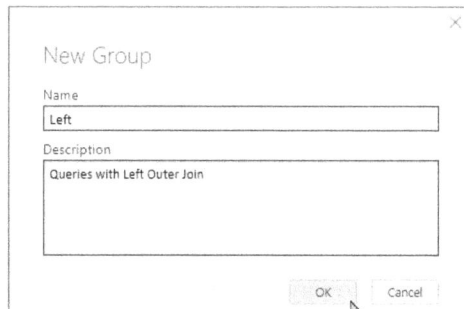

Figure 3.35: New query group window

5. In this window, enter a group name (essentially creating a folder) and optionally add a description. This description will be visible when hovering over the group name in the **Queries** list.

6. Similarly, create a **Full** group for the two queries from this example.

    Once the first group is created, we notice that all the remaining queries are placed in the default **Other Queries** group. Even after moving all queries into our custom groups, the **Other Queries** group will remain visible (*Figure 3.36*).

7. If we right-click on a query, we can choose, from other options, to move it to a different group. Alternatively, we can move queries using drag and drop.

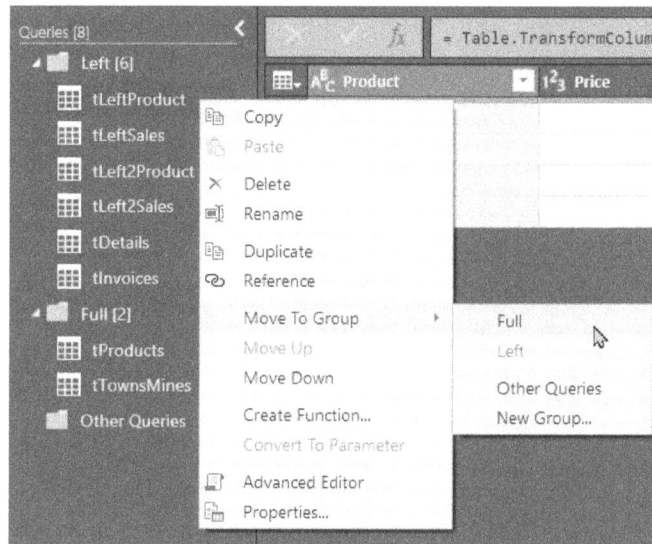

Figure 3.36: Popup menu for a single query

Once we have created all the necessary groups and moved the queries accordingly, we can collapse groups that are not relevant at the moment.

8. To do this, click the small triangle next to the folder icon for the group you want to collapse/expand.

    Next to the group name, we will see the number of queries contained within that group.

    Created groups are only visible in the **Queries** pane but will not appear in dropdown lists where queries are selected (e.g., for merging queries) (*Figure 3.10*).

    Fun fact: **By default, queries in the Queries pane are listed in the order they were loaded into Power Query. However, when selecting a query from a dropdown list (e.g., for merging), queries are displayed in alphabetical order.**

9. Now, we can load our query into Excel.

Finding common elements in lists

Sometimes, we need to extract a list of elements that appear on both lists, while other times, we may want to extract only the elements that appear on one list but not the other. The appropriate merge type can be used for both scenarios.

For example, we have a list of subscribers and a list of customers located on the *Lists* worksheet (*Figure 3.37*) as follows:

- A subscriber follows us on social media.
- A customer has made a purchase.

One person can be both a customer and a subscriber (these individuals are highlighted in the tables), but some may be only subscribers or only customers.

We want to create separate lists for each of these cases.

	A	B	C	D
1	Table name: **tSubscribers**		Table name: **tClients**	
2	**Subscribers**		**Clients**	
3	Alice		Juliet	
4	Beatrice		Beatrice	
5	Eleanor		Edward	
6	Henry		Alice	
7	Grace		Isaac	
8	Felix		Daniel	
9	Edward		Arthur	
10	Daisy		Grace	
11	Hazel		Eleanor	
12	James		George	
13	George			
14	Benjamin			

Figure 3.37: List of subscribers and customers

To do this, we follow these steps:

1. Start by loading the **tClients** table into Power Query as a connection only (since it is shorter).

2. Next, load the **tSubscribers** table and merge it with **tClients**. Alternatively, we can first move both queries into a new group (Lists) for better organization.

3. In the merge options, select **Inner** join (*Figure 3.38*), meaning we want to extract only the elements that appear on both lists.

   We can see that 6 elements match on both sides. Additionally, this is the first time in our examples that the columns have different headers before merging.

4. Now, confirm the merge.

    Note: **In Power Query, column names do not affect the merge process.**

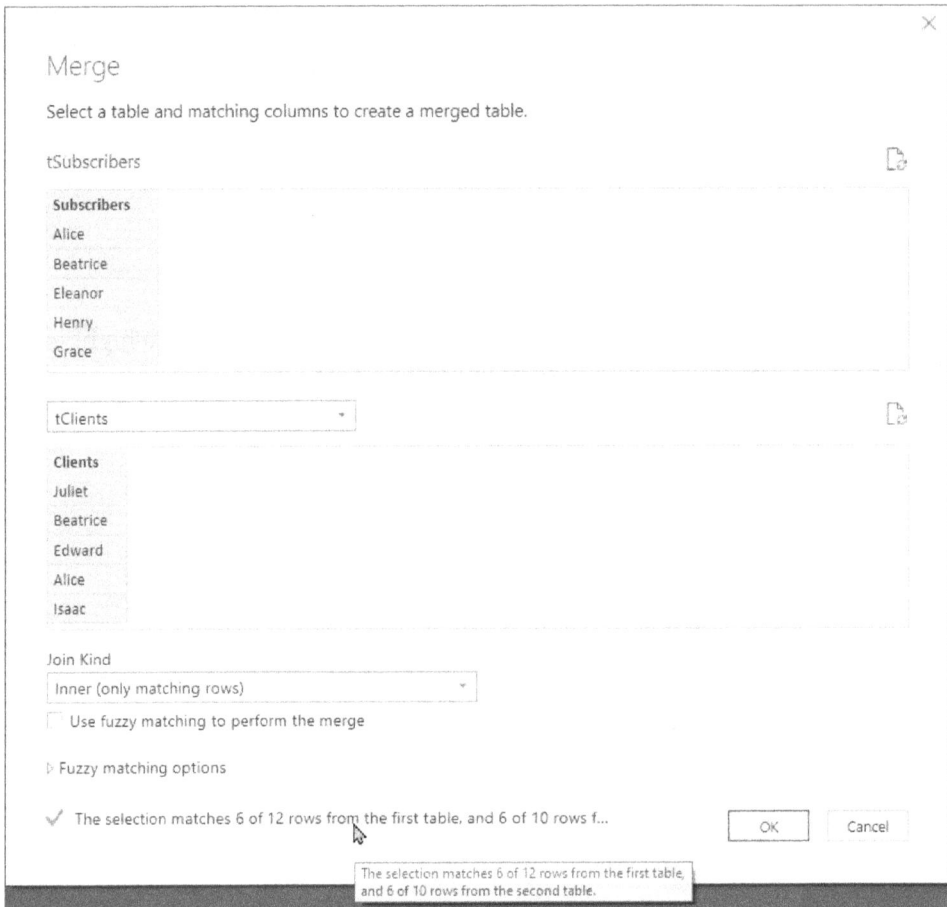

Figure 3.38: Inner join merge

As a result of the merge, we obtained a table with six rows (representing the number of elements that appear on both lists) and two columns (*Figure 3.39*).

a. The first column comes from the **tSubscribers** table.

b. The second column is a collapsed column from the **tClients** table.

Since each table contains only one column, and the second table holds identical information to the first, there is no need to expand the second table.

5. Instead, we can delete it by selecting the column and pressing the *Delete* key.

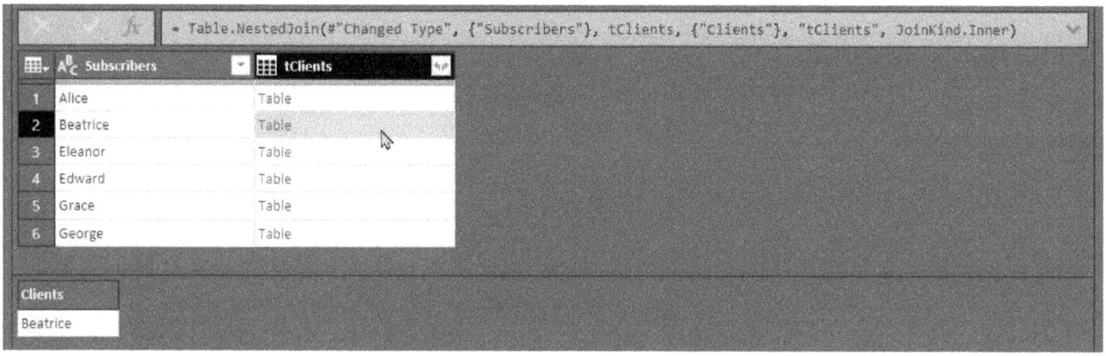

Figure 3.39: *Result of Inner join merge*

With this result, we have obtained a list of people who are both subscribers and customers.

Now, we also want to generate two additional lists:

    a.   People who are only subscribers.

    b.   People who are only customers.

6.   To create these lists, we need two more queries, which will look very similar to the current one. Instead of recreating them from scratch, we can simply duplicate the current query:

    a.   Right-click on the query.

    b.   Select **Duplicate** from the pop-up menu (*Figure 3.36*).

7.   Now, we rename the queries as follows:

    a.   Subscribers&Clients (no modifications needed, except optionally renaming the Subscribers column to Subscribers&Clients)

    b.   onlySubscribers

    c.   onlyClients

For the **onlySubscribers** query, we only need to change the join type, just as we did in the previous example (*Figure 3.31*).

8.   However, this time we select **Left Anti** join (*Figure 3.40*), which will return only the elements that exist in the *Subscribers* list but not in the Clients list.

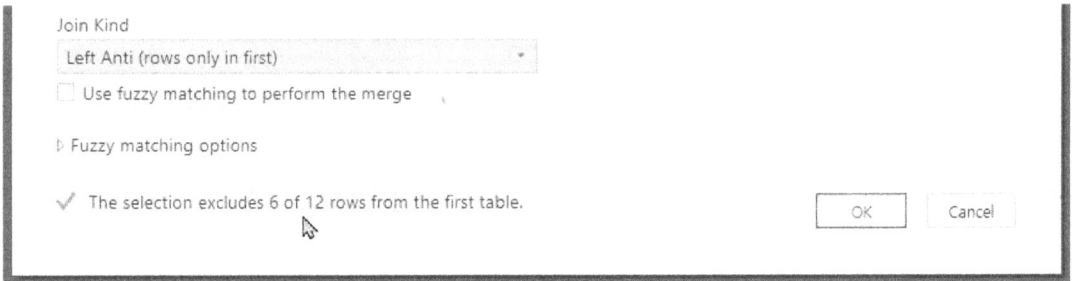

Join Kind

Left Anti (rows only in first) ▾

☐ Use fuzzy matching to perform the merge

▷ Fuzzy matching options

✓ The selection excludes 6 of 12 rows from the first table.

[OK] [Cancel]

Figure 3.40: Left Anti join

In the merge summary, we can see that 6 rows were removed from the first table, exactly the number of elements that appeared on both lists.

9. Now, we simply confirm this change by clicking **OK** and move on to modifying the `onlyClients` query.

    Note: **The last step of removing the column should remain unchanged.**

For the `onlyClients` query, we follow these steps:

1. Remove the last step where the column was deleted (click the small **X** to the left of the step name).

2. Change the join type to **Right Anti** join (*Figure 3.41*).

    This will return only the elements that exist in the Clients list but not in the Subscribers list.

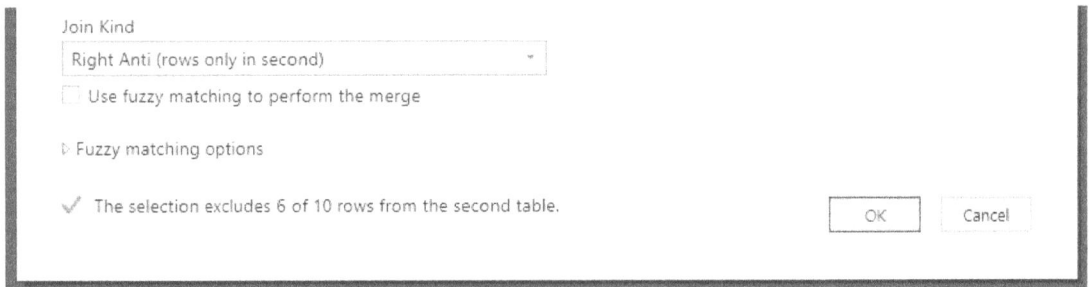

Join Kind

Right Anti (rows only in second) ▾

☐ Use fuzzy matching to perform the merge

▷ Fuzzy matching options

✓ The selection excludes 6 of 10 rows from the second table.

[OK] [Cancel]

Figure 3.41: Right Anti join

Again, we see a summary stating that 6 rows were removed. After confirming the merge, we now see only one row in the result (*Figure 3.42*). This happens because the Right Anti join keeps only the non-matching rows from the right (lower) table. This outcome highlights how the Right Anti join functions by filtering out matching rows and preserving only those without a counterpart in the left table. As a result:

a. There is no matching value on the left side, which is why we see **null** in that column.

b. All the relevant names are stored within the **Table** variable inside the **tClients** column.

3. To extract them, we expand the **tClients** column as usual, making sure to remove prefixes.

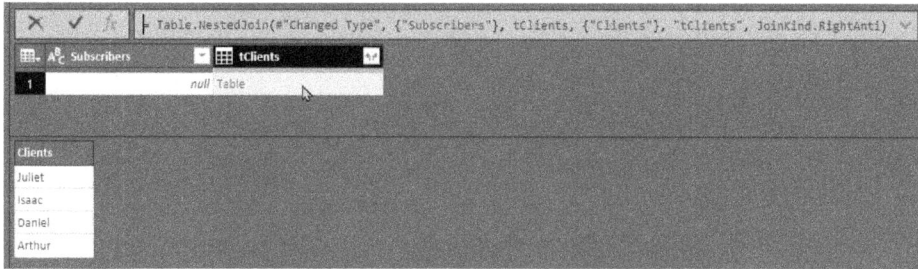

Figure 3.42: Result of Right Anti join merge

4. After expanding the **tClients** column, we get a table with four rows:

a. The **Subscribers** column will contain repeated **null** values.

b. The second column will display the list of customers who are not subscribers.

c. The **Subscribers** column can now be removed, as it no longer contains useful information.

At this point, we have finished transforming all three queries.

5. Now, load them into Excel as tables on new sheets (since when loading multiple queries at once, we cannot assign them to specific locations on an existing sheet).

However, we want all these tables to be placed on the *Lists* sheet. To do this, we follow these steps:

1. We need to select the tables.

2. Cut them (*Ctrl + X*).

3. Paste them (*Ctrl + V*) onto the *Lists* sheet.

4. Finally, delete any unnecessary (empty) sheets.

Fun fact: **Query names can include special characters like spaces or ampersands (&), but table names cannot. So, after loading the Subscribers&Clients query into Excel, the ampersand (&) will automatically be replaced with an underscore (_) in the table name (Subscribers_Clients).**

Merging a query with itself

In this example, we have a single table containing the employee data located on the *Lists* worksheet (*Figure 3.43*). The key columns for us are: **Employee ID** and **Supervisor ID**.

These columns define the relationship between employees and their supervisors.

For example, the first employee, *Tammy*, has a *Supervisor ID* of *1011*. Since this ID corresponds to another employee's ID, we can see that Tammy's supervisor is *Oscar*.

The goals are to:

- Find the supervisor's details for each employee (Some employees may not have a supervisor).

- Count the number of subordinates that each supervisor manages.

Employee ID	Name	Last Name	Position	Supervisor ID
1001	Tammy	TaterTot	HR	1011
1002	Lucy	Lollipop	HR	1011
1003	Gregory	Gherkin	Analyst	1013
1005	Harvey	Hotdog	Analyst	1013
1007	Bobby	Bubblewrap	Programmer	1019
1011	Oscar	Oatmeal	PM	
1013	Molly	Muffin	Tester	1023
1017	Felix	Fizzles	Tester	1023
1019	Cindy	Cupcake	Analyst	1001
1023	Nigel	Noodles	Director	
1029	Nina	Noodles	Programmer	1007
1031	Victor	Vanilla	Tester	1001
1037	Debbie	Dingleberry	Secretary	1023
1041	Lucy	Lumpkin	Manager	
1043	Peter	Potato	PM	1041
1047	Frank	Flapjack	PM	1041

Figure 3.43: tEmployee table

The steps are as follows:

1. The first step is to load the table into Power Query as usual. We can leave our query in the **Other Queries** group.

2. Next, merge the query with itself (Self join).

   Steps to merge the table with itself:

   a. Click **Merge Queries** (*Figure 3.9*).

   b. For the bottom table, select the current query (**tEmployee (Current)**) (*Figure 3.44*).

      i. This query is easy to recognize because Power Query automatically adds (**Current**) to indicate the same table.

  c. Keep the join type as **Left Outer**.

  d. Select the matching columns:

      i. **Top table**: **Supervisor ID** (since we are looking for the supervisor of each employee).

      ii. **Bottom table**: **Employee ID** (since we are matching it to find the supervisor's details).

This will allow us to find the supervisor for every employee who has a value in the **Supervisor ID** column.

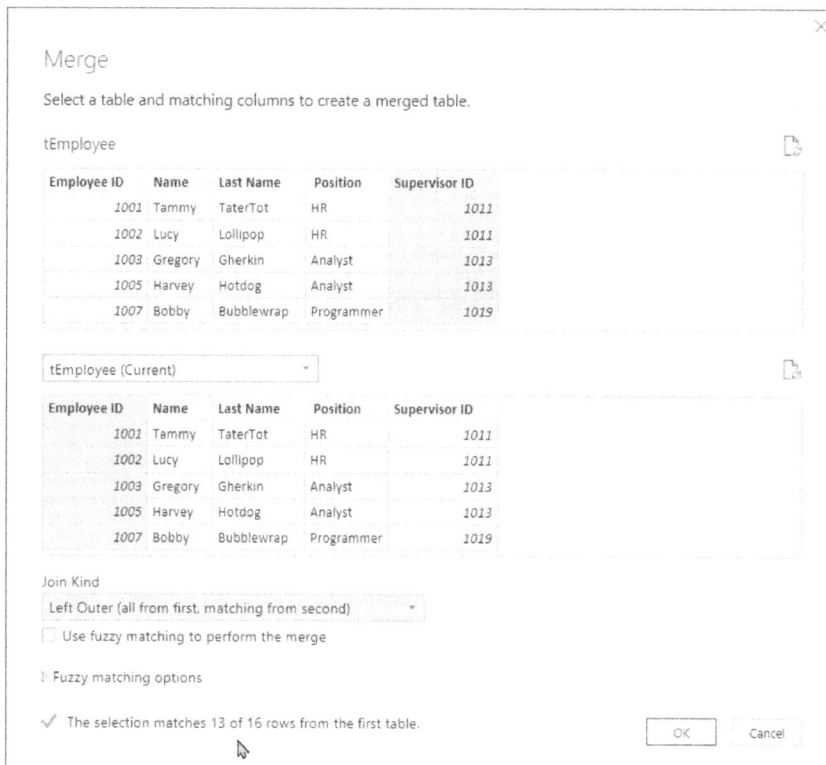

Figure 3.44: Merging the query with itself

3. Now, simply click **OK** to confirm the merge. In the result step, we can observe in the formula bar that the same table from the previous step (#*"Changed Type"*) is being merged with itself (*Figure 3.45*).

In previous examples, we merged the previous step with a different query (*Figure 3.13*). Here, however, we are joining the same query, creating a *self-join*.

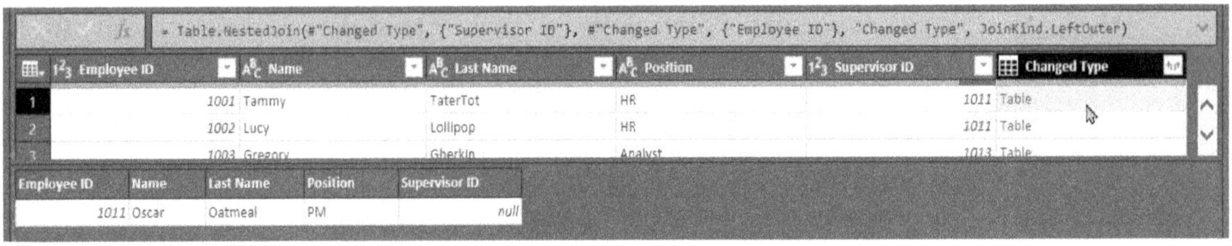

Figure 3.45: Result of merging the query with itself

We can now see that in the **Changed Type** column (the default column name, based on the previous step), the **Table** variables contain individual rows from our dataset.

For our needs, we only need to extract (expand) the **Name** column from this table (*Figure 3.46*). Expanding only the **Name** column allows us to highlight the following:

- There are two employees named **Lucy** in the dataset.

- From a database perspective and merging, these are not the same person, as one **Lucy** has the ID **1002**, while the other has the ID **1041**.

This distinction is crucial for understanding how Power Query handles merging and ensuring accurate results in our self-join.

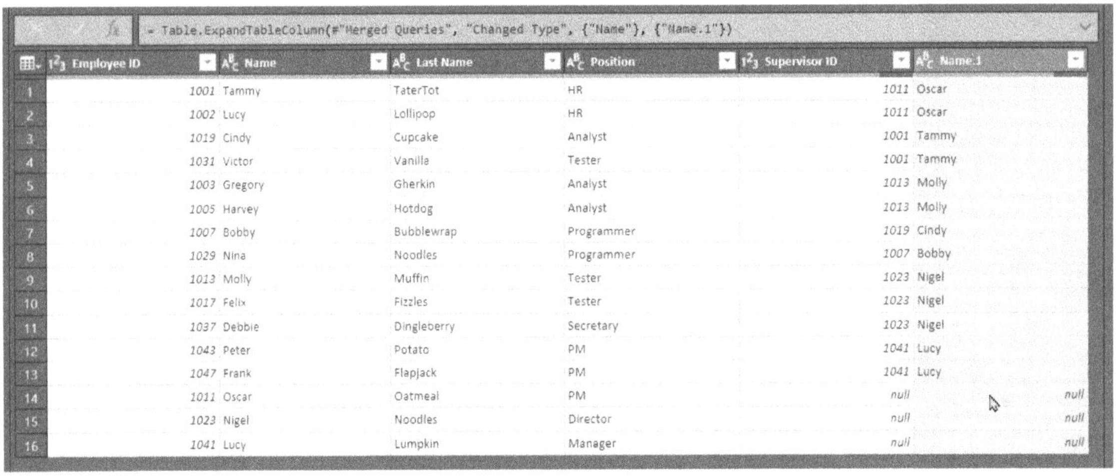

Figure 3.46: Table after expanding merged data

Since some rows did not have a match (i.e., their **Supervisor ID** was empty), those rows moved to the bottom of the table after expanding the **Changed Type** column.

Additionally, because our table already had a column named **Name**, Power Query automatically renamed the newly expanded column to **Name.1** to avoid duplicate column names.

Now we want to count subordinates. To do it, we follow these steps:

1. Merge the query with itself again, but this time:
    a. **Top table:** Select **Employee ID.**
    b. **Bottom table:** Select **Supervisor ID.**
2. In the merge summary, we should see 7 out of 16 matches.
    a. This means that only 7 out of 16 employees are also supervisors.
    b. However, this is not the information we are currently looking for, so we simply confirm the merge by clicking **OK.**
3. Expand the merged column with the aggregation option, just like we did in the previous example (*Figures 3.24 and 3.25*).
4. Count the number of rows in the merged results, but be careful:
    a. Do not use the standard **Count (All)** aggregation because it counts empty tables as 1, which would give incorrect results.
    b. Instead, choose **Count (Not Blank)** to exclude the empty tables from the count.
5. We can apply this aggregation to any column in the merged table.
    a. If there is a match between merged columns, then every cell in that row will contain data, so choosing any column will work correctly. For example, if we apply this aggregation to the **Employee ID** column, we will get the result shown in *Figure 3.47.*
6. If desired, we can rename the newly created column in the formula bar to something more meaningful, such as *Team Size.*
7. Finally, we can load the query into Excel.

#	Employee ID	Name	Last Name	Position	Supervisor ID	Name.1	Count (Not Blank) of Employee ID
1	1001 Tammy	TaterTot	HR	1011 Oscar		2
2	1002 Lucy	Lollipop	HR	1011 Oscar		0
3	1019 Cindy	Cupcake	Analyst	1001 Tammy		1
4	1031 Victor	Vanilla	Tester	1001 Tammy		0
5	1003 Gregory	Gherkin	Analyst	1013 Molly		0
6	1005 Harvey	Hotdog	Analyst	1013 Molly		0
7	1007 Bobby	Bubblewrap	Programmer	1019 Cindy		1
8	1029 Nina	Noodles	Programmer	1007 Bobby		0
9	1013 Molly	Muffin	Tester	1023 Nigel		0
10	1017 Felix	Fizzles	Tester	1023 Nigel		0
11	1037 Debbie	Dingleberry	Secretary	1023 Nigel		0
12	1043 Peter	Potato	PM	1041 Lucy		0
13	1047 Frank	Flapjack	PM	1041 Lucy		0
14	1011 Oscar	Oatmeal	PM	null	null	2
15	1023 Nigel	Noodles	Director	null	null	3
16	1041 Lucy	Lumpkin	Manager	null	null	2

Figure 3.47: Query with the number of subordinates

Fuzzy merge

In this example, we want to merge the **tSales** table with the **tCities** table, which are located on the Fuzzy worksheet, using the **City/City Name** columns.

However, we face a problem, standard merging requires an exact match, but in this case:

- There are errors in city names in the **City** column.
- Some entries use abbreviated city names instead of full names.

To handle these inconsistencies, we use **Fuzzy merge**.

Additionally, when using this option, a third table (**tFromTo**) may also be useful (*Figure 3.48*). This table contains manual mapping rules, allowing us to define specific corrections. For example, if Power Query finds **Minas T.**, we can explicitly tell it to match it with **Minas Tirith**. This helps improve matching accuracy when using fuzzy merge.

	A	B	C	D	E	F	G
1	Table name: **tSales**				Table name: **tCities**		
2	**Sele Id**	**Product**	**City**		**City Name**	**Universum**	**Population**
3	1	Elven Silk Cloaks	Minas Tirih		Minas Tirith	The Lord of the Rings	200,000
4	2	Dwarven Steel Ingots	Watedeep		Waterdeep	Forgotten Realms	130,000
5	3	Ankh-Morpork Coffee Beans	Ankh-Morp.		Ankh-Morpork	Discworld	1,000,000
6	4	Valyrian Steel Daggers	King's Landing		King's Landing	Game of Thrones	500,000
7	5	Plasmid Energy Vials	Raptur		Rapture	BioShock	25,000
8	6	Gondorian Warhorses	Minas T.				
9	7	Magical Spellbooks	Waterdipp		Table name: **tFromTo**		
10	8	Sausage-Inna-Bun Stands	Ankh Morpok		**From**	**To**	
11	9	Lannister Gold Coins	Kings Lnding		Minas T.	Minas Tirith	
12	10	Big Daddy Armor Plating	Rap		Water	Waterdeep	
13	11	Barrels of Dorwinion Wine	Minaz Tirith		Ank-Mork	Ankh-Morpork	
14	12	Dragonhide Boots	Wtrdeep		Rap	Rapture	
15	13	Dis-organizer Mk. II	Ankh-Morpork				
16	14	Ravens for Message Delivery	Kings Landing				
17	15	Gene Tonics	Raptyr				

Figure 3.48: Tables for fuzzy merge

Load the tables using the following steps:

1. Load **tCities** and **tFromTo** as connections only.
2. Import **tSales** as a query.
3. Move all the loaded tables into a new group named **Fuzzy** for better organization.

Perform the fuzzy merge using the following steps:

1. Click **Merge Queries** on the **Home** tab.
2. Merge **tSales** with **tCities**, using a **Left Outer** join (default).
3. Select the **City** column in **tSales** and the **City Name** column in **tCities** as the matching fields.

Before enabling fuzzy matching, we see that only 2 out of 15 rows have matched (*Figure 3.49*). This is because standard merging requires exact matches, and our dataset contains inconsistencies.

Now, let us enable fuzzy merge to allow for similarity-based matching.

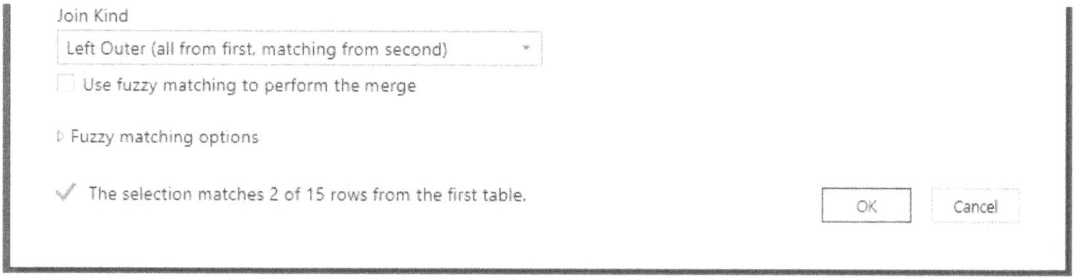

Figure 3.49: Merge summary without fuzzy matching enabled

After checking the **Use fuzzy matching to perform the merge** option, we immediately see much better results, 12 out of 15 rows are now matched (*Figure 3.50*).

This demonstrates how fuzzy merge helps identify similar values, even when they contain spelling errors, abbreviations, or formatting differences.

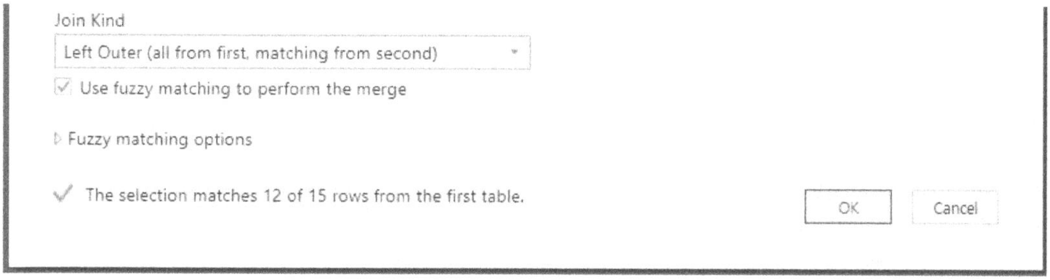

Figure 3.50: Merge summary with default fuzzy matching

These results are much better, but we need to expand the fuzzy matching options to see what customization options are available, as shown in *Figure 3.51*:

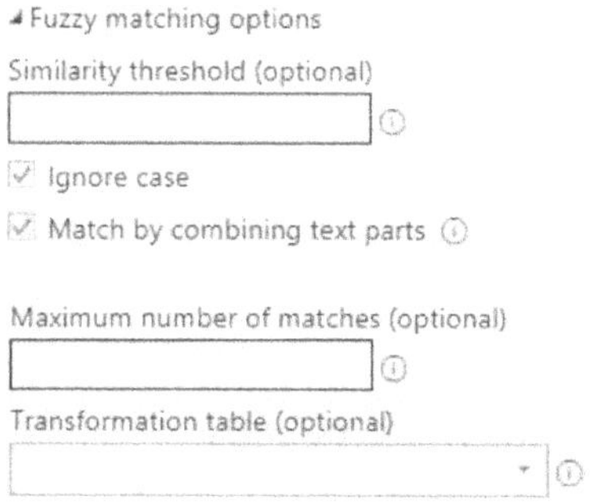

Figure 3.51: Expanded fuzzy matching options

Understanding the **Similarity threshold** field as follows:

- By default, this field is empty, which means Power Query uses the default 0.8 similarity threshold.

- The value can range from 0 to 1:
  - **Lower values (closer to 0):** More flexible matches (less strict).
  - **Higher values (closer to 1):** More precise matches (more strict).

For example:

- **0.95 similarity threshold**: Only 7 out of 15 rows would match.

- **0.2 similarity threshold**: 14 out of 15 rows would match.

Other default fuzzy matching options are as follows:

- **Ignore case (checked by default)**: Power Query ignores uppercase/lowercase differences.

- **Match by combining text parts (checked by default)**: Helps match text by ignoring spaces or combining partial text.

These options are best left enabled in most cases.

Choosing the best similarity threshold

The default (0.8) threshold works well in most cases, but it can be adjusted depending on the dataset. In this example, city names are quite different from each other, so we do not need to worry about incorrect matches. However, in some datasets, incorrect matches can occur, leading to cases where multiple rows match a single value instead of just one.

Setting the maximum number of matches

If we only want the closest match per row, we can set the maximum number of matches field to 1. If we set it to a higher value, Power Query will not force additional matches; it will only consider those that exceed the similarity threshold.

Using a transformation table

If we still have errors or missing matches, we can use a **Transformation Table** by selecting **tFromTo** in the **Transformation Table** field.

This table must have exactly two columns:

- **From:** Contains incorrect/misspelled values.
- **To:** Contains the correct values found in the related table.

Column names are case-sensitive; they must be named **From** and **To** exactly.

The final steps for this example are as follows:

1. In the fuzzy matching options, we add our **tFromTo** table.
2. We leave all other options at their default values.
3. We confirm the merge by clicking **OK**.
4. We expand the **tCities** column, extracting only the **City Name**.
5. We load the query into Excel.

If any corrections are still needed, we can update the tFromTo table. This involves adding new value replacements, where values in the **From** column are replaced with corresponding values from the **To** column.

Conclusion

This chapter covered the key techniques for combining data in Power Query through appending and merging. You learned how to append data from multiple sources while handling differences in structure and how to merge tables using different join types, including multi-condition merges. Additionally, we explored list comparisons, aggregations, and self-joins for hierarchical relationships.

Mastering these techniques will allow us to prepare only the relevant data for further analysis.

In the next chapter, we will learn how to group data by one or multiple columns and explore different aggregation methods during data grouping.

Multiple choice questions

1. **What is the primary difference between appending and merging data in Power Query?**
    a. Appending adds new columns, while merging adds new rows
    b. Appending adds new rows, while merging adds new columns
    c. Both appending and merging add new columns
    d. Both appending and merging add new rows

2. **Which Power Query join type includes only matching rows from both tables?**
    a. Left Outer join
    b. Right Outer join
    c. Inner join
    d. Full Outer join

3. When performing an append operation in Power Query, what must be consistent between the tables?

   a. The number of rows

   b. The column names and data types

   c. The presence of unique identifiers

   d. The sort order of data

4. Which of the following are valid use cases for merging queries in Power Query? (Select all that apply)

   a. Looking up product prices from a price list

   b. Adding sales records for a new year to an existing dataset

   c. Combining two datasets using multiple conditions

   d. Removing duplicates from a dataset

5. Which of the following statements about self-joins in Power Query are correct? (Select all that apply)

   a. A self-join is performed by merging a table with itself

   b. Self-joins are used to compare elements between two unrelated datasets

   c. They can be used to find hierarchical relationships, such as employees and their managers

   d. Self-joins require at least three tables to be performed

Answers

Question number	Answer option letter
1.	b.
2.	c.
3.	b.
4.	a., c.
5.	a., c.

CHAPTER 4

Grouping Data

Introduction

In the previous chapter, we explored how to combine data using Power Query, focusing on merging and appending queries from multiple sources. You learned how to integrate information from different tables, files, and connections to create unified datasets ready for analysis.

This chapter builds on those skills by introducing techniques for grouping and summarizing data. Effectively organizing and summarizing large datasets is crucial for meaningful analysis.

You will learn essential grouping operations, aggregation methods, ranking techniques, and how to handle duplicates or ties. By mastering these skills, you will simplify data analysis tasks, clarify your results, and enhance your decision-making.

Structure

This chapter covers the following topics:

- Basics of grouping
- Sales results summary using grouping
- Ranking with ties
- More functions with grouping

- Local grouping
- Data types

Objectives

By the end of this chapter, you will be able to group data in Power Query using both basic and advanced techniques. You will learn how to summarize data with built-in aggregation functions, extract unique values, and generate dynamic product lists. You will also understand how to create rankings, handle ties, and perform local grouping for sequential data analysis. Additionally, you will work with custom M code and Power Query functions to perform complex transformations and improve performance. This knowledge will help you organize, analyze, and present data more effectively in real-world reporting scenarios.

Basics of grouping

Grouping is most commonly seen in Excel within pivot tables. In these tables, it is possible to group or aggregate data based on a single column as well as multiple columns. This can be seen in *Figure 4.1*, where the first pivot table shows data grouped by the **Merchant** column, and the second one by both the **Merchant** and **City** columns:

	A	B	C	D	E	F	G	H	I	J	K	L
1	Date	City	Merchant	Product	Income		Merchant	Sum of Income		Merchant	City	Sum of Income
2	1/16/2025	Minas Tirith	Iago	Sapphire	$48,800		Abu	$510,400		Abu	Ankh-Morpork	$108,000
3	1/27/2025	Waterdeep	Abu	Sapphire	$65,600		Aladdin	$128,000		Abu	King's Landing	$60,000
4	2/2/2025	Rapture	Jasmine	Pearl	$20,000		Iago	$182,400		Abu	Minas Tirith	$189,600
5	3/2/2025	Waterdeep	Jasmine	Emerald	$38,400		Jasmine	$425,600		Abu	Waterdeep	$152,800
6	3/3/2025	Ankh-Morpork	Jasmine	Diamond	$36,800		Grand Total	$1,246,400		Aladdin	King's Landing	$51,200
7	3/14/2025	Rapture	Iago	Emerald	$71,200					Aladdin	Minas Tirith	$65,600
8	5/4/2025	Ankh-Morpork	Abu	Diamond	$108,000					Aladdin	Waterdeep	$11,200
9	5/15/2025	Rapture	Jasmine	Pearl	$119,200					Iago	Minas Tirith	$48,800
10	6/22/2025	King's Landing	Aladdin	Ruby	$51,200					Iago	Rapture	$133,600
11	6/22/2025	Waterdeep	Abu	Ruby	$87,200					Jasmine	Ankh-Morpork	$36,800
12	6/27/2025	Rapture	Iago	Sapphire	$62,400					Jasmine	Minas Tirith	$193,600
13	7/3/2025	Minas Tirith	Aladdin	Emerald	$65,600					Jasmine	Rapture	$139,200
14	8/25/2025	Waterdeep	Jasmine	Emerald	$17,600					Jasmine	Waterdeep	$56,000
15	10/14/2025	Minas Tirith	Abu	Ruby	$102,400					Grand Total		$1,246,400

Figure 4.1: Grouped data in pivot tables

Since we are working in Power Query, it may be important to note that in pivot tables, Excel stores a kind of smaller table or data range behind each summary cell. This smaller table represents the source data after applying the appropriate filter. For example, by double-clicking cell H2 in the PivotTable worksheet (*Figure 4.1*), we would receive a table showing only Abu's sales. This happens for every summary cell. A similar mechanism is also used in Power Query to ensure that calculations are performed on the smallest possible subset of data. For instance, when grouping by the **Merchant** column, Power Query would create four smaller tables behind the scenes, as shown in *Figure 4.2*, and only then, for example, sum the data in the **Income** column:

	A	B	C	D	E	F	G	H	I	J	K
1											
2							**Date**	**City**	**Merchant**	**Product**	**Income**
3							1/27/2025	Waterdeep	Abu	Sapphire	$65,600
4							5/4/2025	Ankh-Mor	Abu	Diamond	$108,000
	Date	**City**	**Merchant**	**Product**	**Income**		6/22/2025	Waterdeep	Abu	Ruby	$87,200
5	1/16/2025	Minas Tirith	Iago	Sapphire	$48,800		10/14/2025	Minas Tirit	Abu	Ruby	$102,400
6	1/27/2025	Waterdeep	Abu	Sapphire	$65,600		11/14/2025	Minas Tirit	Abu	Emerald	$87,200
7	2/2/2025	Rapture	Jasmine	Pearl	$20,000		11/29/2025	King's Lan	Abu	Sapphire	$60,000
8	3/2/2025	Waterdeep	Jasmine	Emerald	$38,400						
9	3/3/2025	Ankh-Morpork	Jasmine	Diamond	$36,800		**Date**	**City**	**Merchant**	**Product**	**Income**
10	3/14/2025	Rapture	Iago	Emerald	$71,200		6/22/2025	King's Lan	Aladdin	Ruby	$51,200
11	5/4/2025	Ankh-Morpork	Abu	Diamond	$108,000		7/3/2025	Minas Tirit	Aladdin	Emerald	$65,600
12	5/15/2025	Rapture	Jasmine	Pearl	$119,200		12/13/2025	Waterdeep	Aladdin	Pearl	$11,200
13	6/22/2025	King's Landing	Aladdin	Ruby	$51,200						
14	6/22/2025	Waterdeep	Abu	Ruby	$87,200		**Date**	**City**	**Merchant**	**Product**	**Income**
15	6/27/2025	Rapture	Iago	Sapphire	$62,400		1/16/2025	Minas Tirit	Iago	Sapphire	$48,800
16	7/3/2025	Minas Tirith	Aladdin	Emerald	$65,600		3/14/2025	Rapture	Iago	Emerald	$71,200
17	8/25/2025	Waterdeep	Jasmine	Emerald	$17,600		6/27/2025	Rapture	Iago	Sapphire	$62,400
18	10/14/2025	Minas Tirith	Abu	Ruby	$102,400						
19	11/1/2025	Minas Tirith	Jasmine	Diamond	$101,600		**Date**	**City**	**Merchant**	**Product**	**Income**
20	11/10/2025	Minas Tirith	Jasmine	Sapphire	$92,000		2/2/2025	Rapture	Jasmine	Pearl	$20,000
21	11/14/2025	Minas Tirith	Abu	Emerald	$87,200		3/2/2025	Waterdeep	Jasmine	Emerald	$38,400
22	11/29/2025	King's Landing	Abu	Sapphire	$60,000		3/3/2025	Ankh-Mor	Jasmine	Diamond	$36,800
23	12/13/2025	Waterdeep	Aladdin	Pearl	$11,200		5/15/2025	Rapture	Jasmine	Pearl	$119,200
24							8/25/2025	Waterdeep	Jasmine	Emerald	$17,600
25							11/1/2025	Minas Tirit	Jasmine	Diamond	$101,600
26							11/10/2025	Minas Tirit	Jasmine	Sapphire	$92,000

Figure 4.2: Sample layout of source data split into smaller tables

In the following examples, we will take a closer look at grouping in Power Query and the possibilities it offers.

Sales results summary using grouping

In this example, we will summarize sales data stored in the **tSales** table on the **Grouping** worksheet. We want to display sales results for individual merchants, which means we will group the data by the **Merchant** column. Our goal is to obtain two simple summaries (sum and average of the **Income** column) and a more complex calculation resulting in a list of products sold by each merchant. The source data and the results we want to achieve using Power Query are shown in *Figure 4.3*:

	A	B	C	D	E	F	G	H	I	J
1	**Date**	**City**	**Merchant**	**Product**	**Income**		**Merchant**	**Income**	**Average**	**Sold Products**
2	1/16/2025	Minas Tirith	Iago	Sapphire	$48,800		Abu	$510,400	$85,066.67	Sapphire, Diamond, Ruby, Emerald
3	1/27/2025	Waterdeep	Abu	Sapphire	$65,600		Aladdin	$128,000	$42,666.67	Ruby, Emerald, Pearl
4	2/2/2025	Rapture	Jasmine	Pearl	$20,000		Iago	$182,400	$60,800.00	Sapphire, Emerald
5	3/2/2025	Waterdeep	Jasmine	Emerald	$38,400		Jasmine	$425,600	$60,800.00	Pearl, Emerald, Diamond, Sapphire
6	3/3/2025	Ankh-Morpork	Jasmine	Diamond	$36,800					

Figure 4.3: Source data and results grouped using Excel functions

As usual, the data is imported into Power Query using the **From Table/Range** command from the **Data** tab (*Figure 1.1*). After the data is loaded into the editor, we can immediately proceed with grouping. All that needs to be done is to select the **Merchant** column and then click the **Group By** command on the **Home** tab, as shown in *Figure 4.4*:

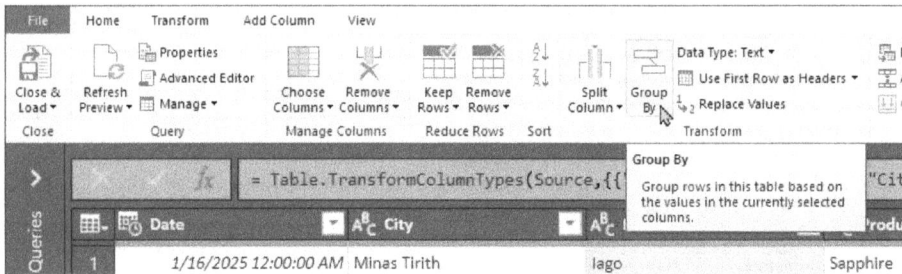

Figure 4.4: Group By command

This will open the **Group By** window, where the **Merchant** column will automatically be selected as the column to group by. By default, the **Basic** option will be selected using radio buttons, which allows grouping by only one column and performing only one aggregation operation, as shown in *Figure 4.5*:

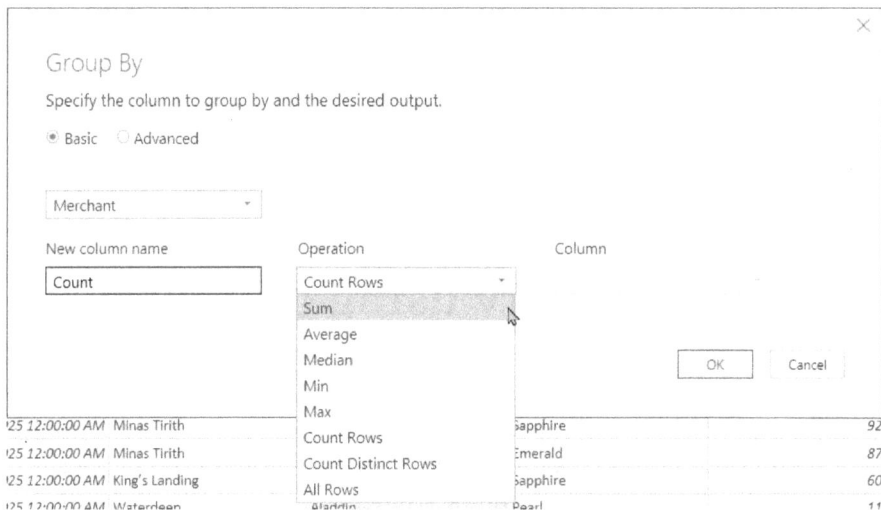

Figure 4.5: Basic Group By window

Tip: If several columns are selected before clicking the Group By command, the Group By window (Figure 4.5) will automatically open with the Advanced option selected and the chosen columns inserted as the grouping hierarchy. The order of the columns in the grouping hierarchy is based on their order in the current step, not on the order in which they were selected.

By default, the aggregation operation **Count Rows** will be selected, which simply counts the number of rows in the grouped table. This aggregation method does not require specifying a column for the calculation, so the **Column** field will remain empty. In the **New column name** field, the word **Count** will be entered.

Most of the remaining aggregation operations available from the drop-down list in *Figure 4.5* are basic mathematical calculations: **Sum**, **Average**, **Median**, **Min**, and **Max**. **The Count Distinct Rows** option works differently. It counts only those rows that are unique, meaning they differ from others by at least one column value.

The final operation, **All Rows**, allows all grouped rows to be preserved as a table embedded as a single cell in a new column. This option will be used in this example.

In this example, it is necessary to add more than one aggregation operation, so the option buttons must be switched to **Advanced**. It is not necessary to click the **Add grouping** button since grouping is only based on one column, but it is necessary to click the **Add aggregation** button twice, as three aggregation operations will be used. These will be **Sum**, **Average**, and **All Rows**, in that order. The first two will be performed on the **Income** column, and the third one does not require a column to be specified. The newly created columns will be named **Sum**, **Average**, and **All**, respectively. The fully completed **Group By** window is shown in *Figure 4.6*:

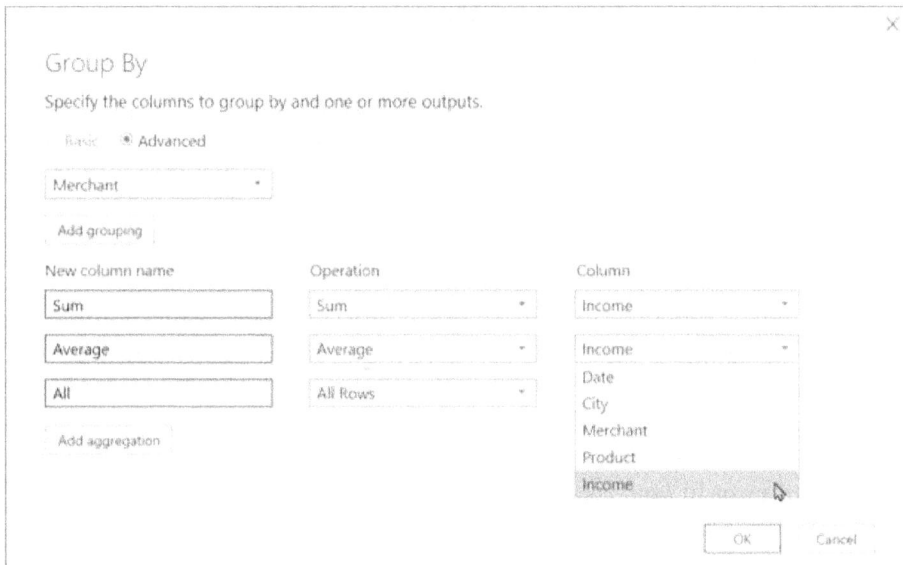

Figure 4.6: *Advanced Group By window*

Once the fields have been filled in correctly, it is enough to click the **OK** button, and Power Query will add a new step named **Grouped Rows**. In this step, just as in a PivotTable (*Figure 4.1*), the data will be grouped by the **Merchant** column, and calculations will be added to compute the **sum** and **average** of the **Income** column for each merchant, as shown in *Figure 4.7*:

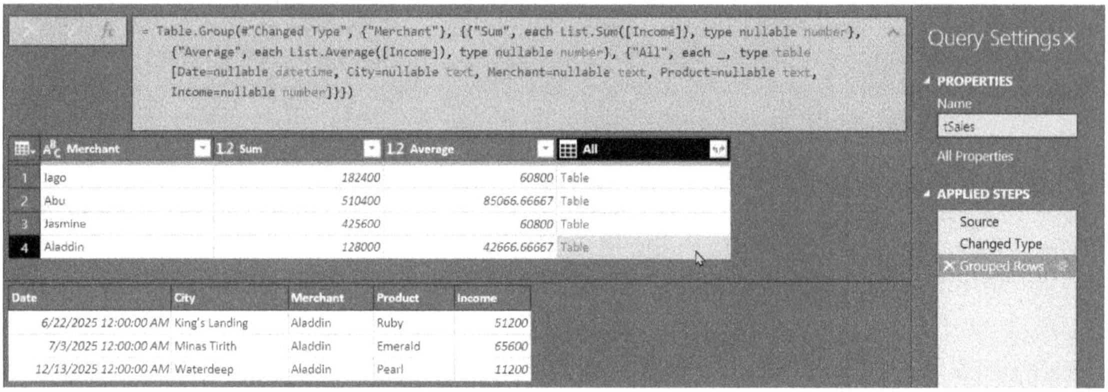

Figure 4.7: Grouped Rows step

The individual smaller tables (*Figure 4.2*) can be viewed as the **Table** data type in the individual cells of the **All** column.

If the result of this step is examined closely, it can be observed that the **Sum** and **Average** columns have been assigned the **Decimal Number** format. This does not match the **Whole Number** data type that was previously assigned to the column, as the data format is more closely related to the type of aggregation performed rather than the earlier data type. In this case, the desired data type is **Currency**. A new step could be added to change the data type of the relevant columns, but if the M code in the formula bar is examined:

```
= Table.Group(#"Changed Type", {"Merchant"}, {{"Sum", each List.Sum([Income]),
type nullable number}, {"Average", each List.Average([Income]), type nullable
number}, {"All", each _, type table [Date=nullable datetime, City=nullable
text, Merchant=nullable text, Product=nullable text, Income=nullable
number]}})
```

At the end of the blocks (opened and closed curly braces) related to individual columns, it is possible to see the assigned data type. To determine the exact M code for the **Currency** data type (or any other data type), a new step that changes the data type can be added and reviewed there. Alternatively, earlier examples can be examined, such as steps involving data type changes to **Currency** or operations that created a new column (for example, the multiplication of columns in *Figure 2.7*).

In this example, the word **number** should be replaced with **Currency.Type**. It is important to make this change in the block for the **Sum** and **Average** columns only, leaving the **All** column unchanged. The modified code should now appear as follows:

```
= Table.Group(#"Changed Type", {"Merchant"}, {{"Sum", each List.Sum([Income]),
type nullable Currency.Type}, {"Average", each List.Average([Income]),
type nullable Currency.Type}, {"All", each _, type table [Date=nullable
datetime, City=nullable text, Merchant=nullable text, Product=nullable text,
Income=nullable number]}})
```

If the data type has been correctly replaced, Power Query will change the data type icon for the relevant columns to a dollar sign.

Note: **Forcing the data type in the grouping step does not change how basic variable types are stored, nor does it affect number precision. Therefore, if there is a real need to change the data type, an additional Change Type step must be added, which will perform the actual transformation of data types or precision adjustment.**

Upon further analysis of the M code for this step, it can be observed that for aggregation (after the **each** keyword), the **List.Sum** function was used for the sum and **List.Average** for the average. Both perform calculations on the filtered **Income** column based on the grouping element. On the other hand, for the **All** column, only the underscore symbol appears after the **each** keyword. In M code, this symbol represents the entire row of a table, and in the context of grouping, it means retrieving all rows matching the grouping element in the current row. For this column, the data type expression is the most complex. In older versions of Power Query, only the phrase **type table** might appear, but now, the M code contains a list of all columns along with their data types enclosed in square brackets.

In the **All** column, it is not necessary to extract the entire data row. Only a single column, **Product**, is of interest. Therefore, in place of the underscore symbol, the column should be referenced using square brackets. Since the result is no longer a full table but a column, effectively a list, the data type **table** must be changed to a **list**. It is also important to remove the entire section within square brackets that specifies the data types of the individual table columns. After making all the changes, the M code should appear as follows:

```
= Table.Group(#"Changed Type", {"Merchant"}, {{"Sum", each List.Sum([Income]),
type nullable Currency.Type}, {"Average", each List.Average([Income]), type
nullable Currency.Type}, {"All", each [Product], type list}})
```

After confirming the changes in the formula bar by pressing *Enter*, Power Query will change the data type icon for the **All** column to a list. This change also results in different column expansion options compared to those for a table. Additionally, it can be observed that the individual cells in the **All** column now display product lists, as shown in *Figure 4.8*:

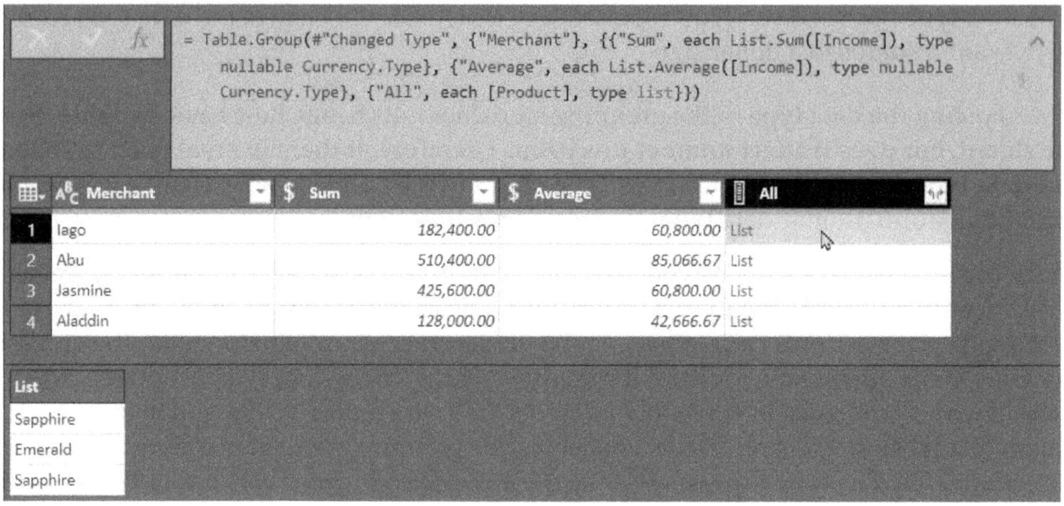

Figure 4.8: Grouped Rows step after changes

Introducing these changes will cause the gear icon for the **Grouped Rows** step to disappear. This is because the applied modifications deviate significantly from the standard structure available in the **Group By** window (*Figure 4.5* and *Figure 4.6*), which does not allow selecting a single data column instead of entire rows.

The code still requires the **List.Distinct** function to be added to remove duplicate products from the lists. Similar to the **List.Sum** and **List.Average** functions, the **Product** column from the **All** column needs to be inserted into it.

After this modification, the **All** column can now be expanded. To do this, click the expand icon in the header and from the context menu, select the **Extract Values** option, as shown in *Figure 4.9*:

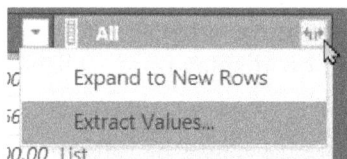

Figure 4.9: Expand options for a column containing lists

This will open the **Extract values from list** window, as shown in *Figure 4.10*, where **Custom** should be selected as the delimiter, and a comma followed by a space should be entered in the field that appears below:

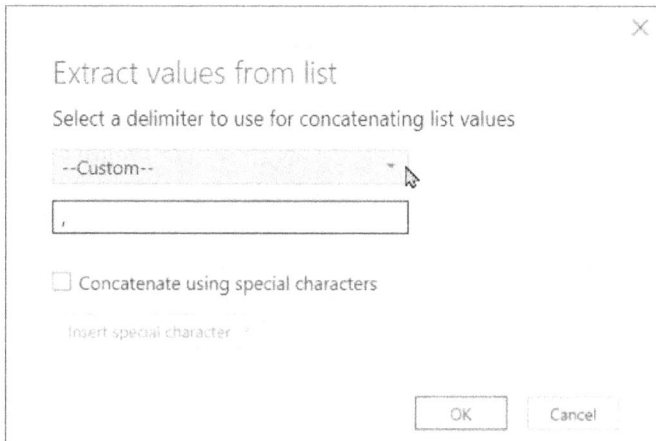

Figure 4.10: Extract values from the list window

It is worth mentioning here that, in addition to standard characters, it is possible to add special characters that have specific codes. These can be selected from the **Insert special character** list after checking the **Concatenate using special characters** checkbox. Instead of selecting from the list, they can also be entered manually, but the checkbox must still be selected. Without selecting the checkbox, Power Query will modify the special character codes, which will cause them to stop working. The list of special characters and their corresponding codes is presented in *Table 4.1*:

Special character name	Special character code
Tab	#(tab)
Carriage return	#(cr)
Line feed	#(lf)
Non-breaking space	#(00A0)

Table 4.1: Sample data and errors in ML models

After confirming the selected delimiter (it may consist of multiple characters) by clicking the **OK** button, Power Query will combine all items from the list into a single text string, as shown in *Figure 4.11*:

Figure 4.11: Result of the extracted values step

We have achieved almost the same result as with Excel formulas (*Figure 4.3*). At most, we can add a sorting step by clicking the **AZ** icon on the **Home** tab (*Figure 4.4*). Alternatively, this step can be added later in Excel. Refreshing the query will not affect the sorting applied from the Excel side. Let us assume that this is what we will do. Therefore, we now load the result of the query into Excel under the previous calculations, as shown in *Figure 4.12*:

	G	H	I	J
1	Merchant	Income	Average	Sold Products
2	Abu	$510,400	$85,066.67	Sapphire, Diamond, Ruby, Emerald
3	Aladdin	$128,000	$42,666.67	Ruby, Emerald, Pearl
4	Iago	$182,400	$60,800.00	Sapphire, Emerald
5	Jasmine	$425,600	$60,800.00	Pearl, Emerald, Diamond, Sapphire
6				
7	Merchant	Sum	Average	All
8	Abu	510400	85066.667	Sapphire, Diamond, Ruby, Emerald
9	Aladdin	128000	42666.667	Ruby, Emerald, Pearl
10	Iago	182400	60800	Sapphire, Emerald
11	Jasmine	425600	60800	Pearl, Emerald, Diamond, Sapphire

Figure 4.12: Sorted query result in Excel

The results are the same. It is important to remember that the **Currency** data type from Power Query does not convert to currency formatting in Excel. This formatting must be applied manually from within Excel. The number formatting we apply will remain even after the query is refreshed.

Ranking with ties

In this example, we want to determine the ranking of merchants, that is, to identify which one generated the highest **Income** and which one the lowest. It is important to note that the data in the **tRanking** table from the **Ranking** worksheet, which will be used in this task, has been specifically prepared to include ties resulting from identical cumulative sales totals across merchants. The data used for summing sales is presented in *Figure 4.13*:

	A	B	C	D	E
1	Date	City	Merchant	Product	Income
2	1/16/2025	Minas Tirith	Iago	Sapphire	$48,800
3	1/27/2025	Waterdeep	Genie	Sapphire	$59,200
4	2/2/2025	Rapture	Jafar	Pearl	$20,000
5	3/2/2025	Waterdeep	Abu	Emerald	$37,600
6	3/3/2025	Ankh-Morpork	Iago	Diamond	$61,600

Figure 4.13: Data in tRanking table

As usual, the data is imported into Power Query. Next, similar to the previous example (*Figure 4.4* and *Figure 4.5*), the data is grouped by the **Merchant** column. In this grouping, we want to include only one aggregation: a **Sum** of the **Income** column. This will generate a simple table, which can be seen in *Figure 4.14*:

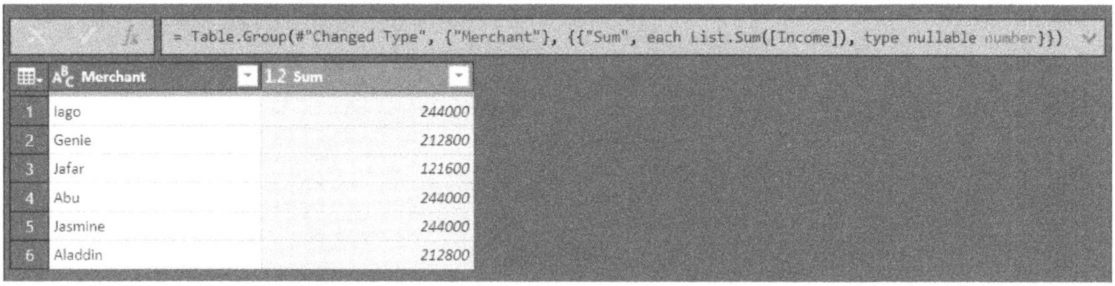

Figure 4.14: Grouped data

Now, the data needs to be sorted so that the top-performing sellers appear at the beginning of the table. To do this, simply select the **Sum** column and click the **ZA** command on the **Home** tab, which instructs Power Query to sort the data in descending order.

Next, a step can be added that will generate the initial ranking by assigning a position to each seller. This can be done using the **Index Column** command from the **Add Column** tab. It should be expanded to select the **Custom** option, as shown in *Figure 4.15*:

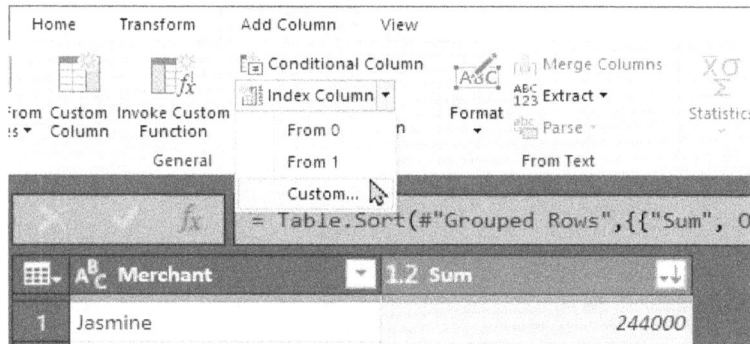

Figure 4.15: Index Column command

The **From 0** option will create a column with whole numbers starting from zero, while the **From 1** option will begin numbering from one. In this example, the **From 1** option would be sufficient, but the goal is to take a closer look at the capabilities of generating an index column, which is why the **Custom** option is selected. This will open the **Add Index Column** window, which contains two fields as follows:

- **Starting index**: The number from which row numbering in the index column begins.

- **Increment**: The value by which the number increases with each subsequent row.

In this case, the number **1** will be entered in both fields. This is equivalent to using the **From 1** option (*Figure 4.15*). However, before confirming the values by clicking **OK**, one of the whole numbers should be changed to a decimal, for example, to **1.2**. Power Query will display a warning icon next to the field with the decimal number along with an error message, as shown in *Figure 4.16*:

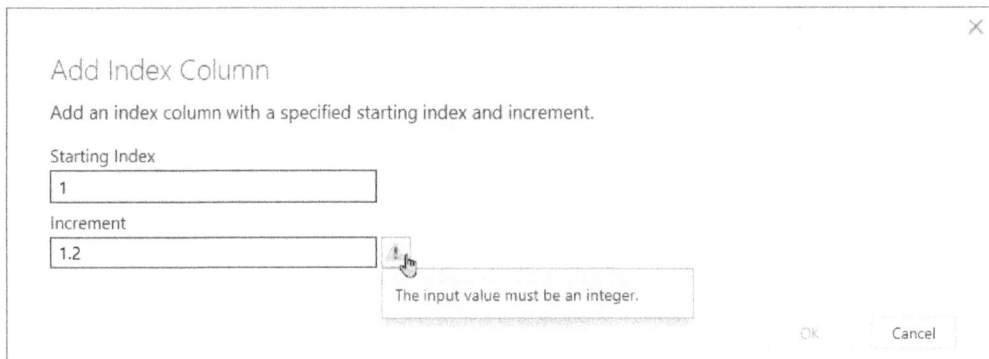

Figure 4.16: *Add Index Column window with an error*

Enter the correct numbers and confirm them by clicking the **OK** button.

Power Query will add a column with numbers that can be treated as the ranking of the sellers, as shown in *Figure 4.17*:

Figure 4.17: *First Index column*

Before starting to analyze the ranking in terms of ties, let us take a closer look at the M code in the formula bar:

```
= Table.AddIndexColumn(#"Sorted Rows", "Index", 1, 1, Int64.Type)
```

First of all, it shows the name of the column being created (**Index**). A more appropriate name for us would be **Ranking**, so we will want to change that in the code. Next, we see two whole numbers (**1**) and the data type **Int64.Type**. Because the **Index Column** command (*Figure 4.15*) by default returns whole numbers, it is not possible to enter a decimal number in the **Add Index Column** window (*Figure 4.16*).

However, we can enter a decimal number directly in the M code. We only need to remember to change the returned data type to **type number** to avoid errors in later steps or during data load into Excel. An example of the modified code may look as follows:

```
= Table.AddIndexColumn(#"Sorted Rows", "Ranking", -1, 1.2, type number)
```

Tip: **The `Table.AddIndexColumn` function allows the creation of index columns that differ by a decimal value. It only requires specifying the data type corresponding to a decimal number as its fifth argument. It is also possible to create descending indexes or indexes starting from a negative number. This only requires entering the appropriate values in the fourth and third arguments of the function, respectively.**

In our case, we only changed the name of the column being created in the `Table.AddIndexColumn` function.

Now, we can analyze the ties (*Figure 4.17*). At the beginning of the table, there are three values equal to 244,000 (a triple tie), followed by two values equal to 212,800 (a double tie), and finally, one value equal to 121,600 (no tie). These results do not exactly match the assigned ranks. Despite having the same value (in the **Sum** column), the three merchants have been assigned different ranks. We want each tied result to receive the same rank. We will consider three possible ranking schemes as follows:

- The **average** of all ranks is currently assigned to a tie. In this example, the first tie includes positions 1, 2, and 3. The average of these numbers is 2. Next, we have a double tie between positions 4 and 5, which results in an average of 4.5. The last value is not part of a tie, so the average is equal to its value, that is, rank 6.

- The **minimum** rank (in a sense, the best) among all ranks currently assigned to a tie. In this example, it would be rank 1 for the triple tie, then rank 4 for the double tie, and finally rank 6 for the last merchant.

- Each position in the tie receives **the same value**, and the next rank is incremented by 1. In this example, we would have three merchants with rank 1, two merchants with rank 2, and one merchant with rank 3.

For each of these ranking methods, grouping will be useful. This time, we need to group by the **Sum** column. We will need three aggregations: **Average** and **Sum** of the **Ranking** column, and **All Rows**. The properly filled **Group By** window is shown in *Figure 4.18*:

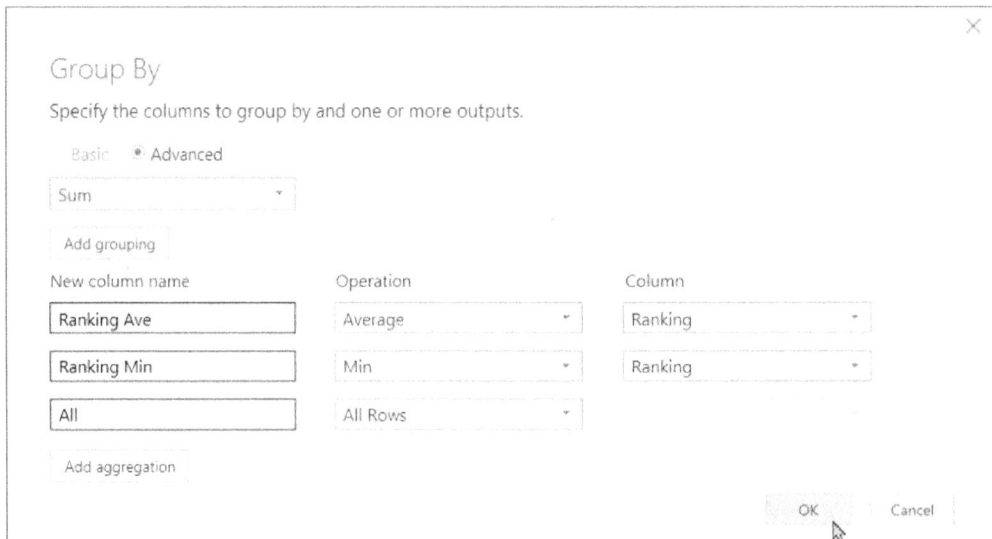

Figure 4.18: Grouping for different rankings

The grouping options selected (*Figure 4.18*) allow generating two out of the three discussed ranking methods. To obtain the third ranking, it is necessary to add another index column starting from 1 (*Figure 4.15*). As before, the name of the newly created index column should be changed. This time to **Ranking Same**.

Next, it is necessary to retrieve information about the merchants and their previous ranks. To do so, simply expand the **All** column, just as demonstrated in earlier examples (*Figure 2.19, Figure 3.14*). It is necessary to display the **Merchant** and **Ranking** columns again. The Prefixes and the **Sum** column should be excluded, as **Sum** already exists in the result table. It is the column used for grouping.

Finally, it would be helpful to change the column order, just as was done in *Chapter 1, Getting Started with Power Query*, in the example: *Retrieving data from a .txt file*. To do this, select the desired column or columns, then drag them using the left mouse button to the appropriate position.

Once the columns are arranged correctly, the final result should resemble what is shown in *Figure 4.19*:

Merchant	Sum	Ranking	Ranking Ave	Ranking Min	Ranking Same
Iago	244000	1	2	1	1
Abu	244000	2	2	1	1
Jasmine	244000	3	2	1	1
Genie	212800	4	4.5	4	2
Aladdin	212800	5	4.5	4	2
Jafar	121600	6	6	6	3

Figure 4.19: All rankings in a query

The only remaining task is to load the result of the query into Excel.

Tip: **If a query has the same name as an already existing Excel table, the result will be loaded into Excel as a table with a modified name. For example, tRanking would become tRanking_1.**

More functions with grouping

In this example, the goal is to group the data from the **tMostSales** table on the **MoreFunctions** sheet by the **Merchant** and **City** columns. For the grouped data, using selected and customized functions, the following values should be calculated:

- The total revenue.

- The number of sales transactions.

- A list of the most frequently sold products.

- A sorted list of all sold products (after removing duplicates).

The source data is shown in *Figure 4.20*:

	A	B	C	D	E
1	Date	Merchant	City	Product	Income
2	1/16/2025	Iago	Minas Tirith	Sapphire	$48,800
3	1/27/2025	Abu	Minas Tirith	Sapphire	$65,600
4	2/2/2025	Iago	Ankh-Morpork	Pearl	$20,000
5	3/2/2025	Abu	King's Landing	Ruby	$38,400
6	3/3/2025	Aladdin	Ankh-Morpork	Diamond	$36,800

Figure 4.20: Data in tMostSales table

We start the transformation by retrieving data from an Excel table using the From Table/ Range command from the **Data** tab (*Figure 1.1*).

The next step will be grouping the data. To do this, select the **Merchant** and **City** columns, then click the **Group By** command from the **Home** tab (*Figure 4.4*). Since two columns were selected, Power Query will automatically switch to the advanced grouping options.

Not all calculations that need to be performed can be done directly through the user interface. Therefore, the goal is to start by selecting aggregations that are either close to the final calculations or help better understand the grouping options. The following operations are selected in order: **Sum, Count Distinct Rows, Median,** and **All Rows.** For the **Sum,** an incorrect column (**Product**) is intentionally selected. All grouping options are shown in *Figure 4.21*:

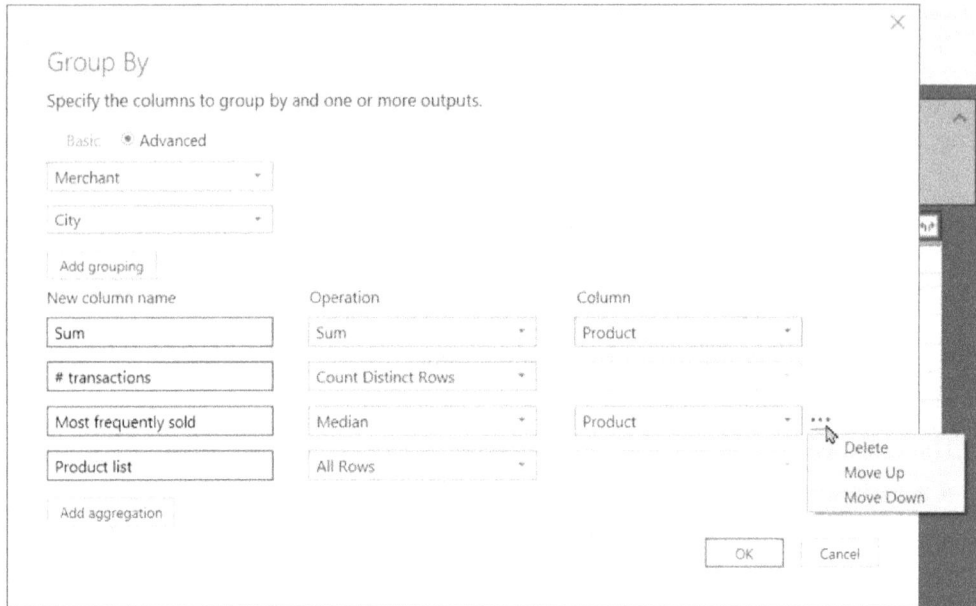

Figure 4.21: Filled Group By window

If too many aggregations were added or if their order needs to be changed, it is necessary to click on the ellipsis in the appropriate row. This will open a context menu where it is possible to select whether the given aggregation should be **Delete**, **Move Up**, or **Move Down**. This context menu is visible in the lower-right corner of *Figure 4.21*.

The first thing that should be noticed after clicking the **OK** button is the errors in the column with the sum, as shown in *Figure 4.22*:

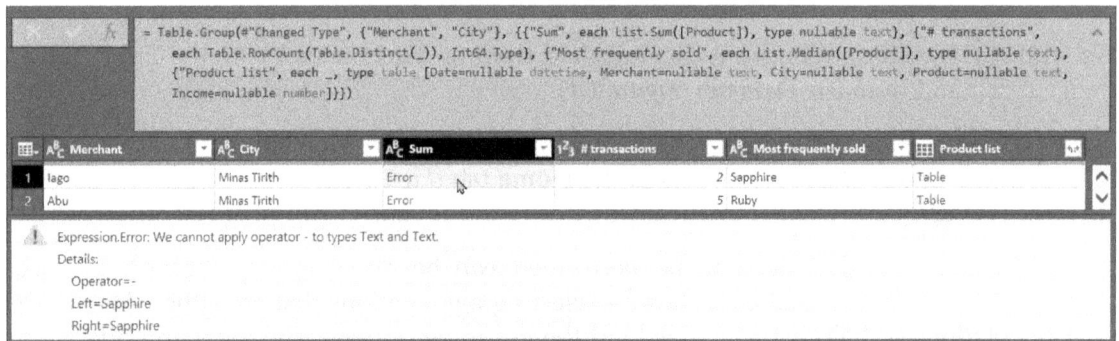

Figure 4.22: First grouped result

The reason for the error is clear from our perspective. A text column was selected for summation, and text values cannot be added together in the same way as numbers. Therefore, Power Query returns the value **Error** in each row. Additionally, in the most recent versions of Excel, a red line will appear, rather than a green one, indicating that errors have occurred in the column (more details are provided in *Chapter 7, Logical Operations and Conditional Columns*). When a cell with an error is selected, Power Query displays error details below the data (as shown at the bottom of *Figure 4.22*).

To correct this error, it is enough to click the gear icon next to the grouping step (**Grouped Rows**). This will reopen the **Group By** window, where the selected column for summation can be changed from **Product** to **Income**. After confirming the change by clicking **OK**, the **Sum** column will no longer display errors, as shown in *Figure 4.23*:

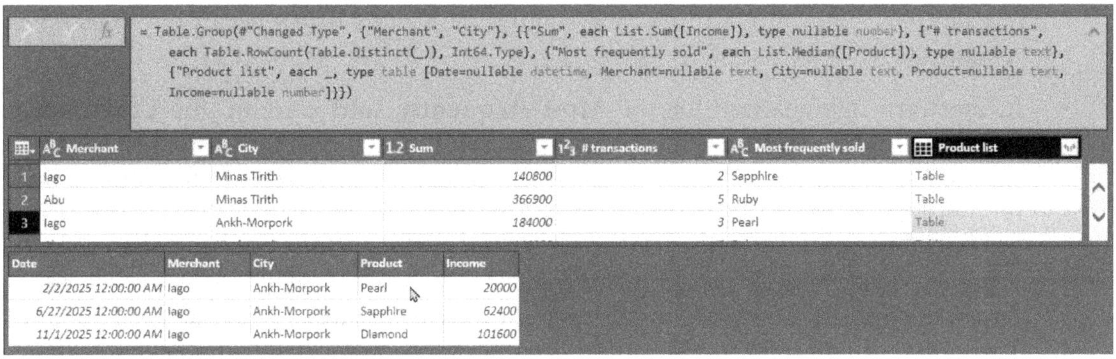

Figure 4.23: Tables in the corrected grouped result

Additionally, the data type for this column will change from text to a decimal number.

Fun fact: After correcting the error, a red line may still appear below the column header. This line should change after adding another step or switching to a previous step and back. Refreshing the query using the Refresh Preview command on the Home tab does not change the color of this line.

Let us now take a closer look at the functions used in the M code for each of the aggregations:

```
= Table.Group(#"Changed Type", {"Merchant", "City"}, {{"Sum", each List.
Sum([Income]), type nullable number}, {"# transactions", each Table.
RowCount(Table.Distinct(_)), Int64.Type}, {"Most frequently sold", each
List.Median([Product]), type nullable text}, {"Product list", each _, type
table [Date=nullable datetime, Merchant=nullable text, City=nullable text,
Product=nullable text, Income=nullable number]}})
```

To better understand how each aggregation works in this example, let us briefly examine the functions used in the M code:

- In the first aggregation, for the **Sum** column, the function **List.Sum** is used, which calculates the sum for a list of elements (it may also be a column of data). In previous examples, we could observe functions such as **List.Average**, **List.Min**, and **List. Max**, which respectively calculate the average, minimum, and maximum values.

- In the second aggregation, for the # **transactions** column, two functions are used. `Table.RowCount`, as the name suggests, calculates the number of rows in a table. Inside it, because the aggregation selected was **Count Distinct Rows**, the `Table.Distinct` function is also used, which removes duplicate rows from the table. For a row to be considered unique, it is sufficient for it to differ in at least one column. Therefore, in most cases, the **Count Distinct Rows** and **Count Rows** aggregations return the same result because, in multi-column tables, there is a low probability that all values in all columns will be identical across different rows. For performance optimization reasons, in examples similar to this one, we should use **Count Rows** because it uses fewer functions.

- In the third aggregation, for the **Most frequently sold** column, the `List.Median` function is used. This function returns the value in the middle of the list after it is sorted. For example, in the third row of the **Grouped Rows** step, in the filtered table for this row, we see three products: Pearl, Sapphire, and Diamond. This is not a sorted order. If the data were sorted, Pearl would be in the middle, and that is exactly the value the `List.Median` function returns for this row. However, we do not want to return the middle value in this column, but rather the most frequently sold product. Therefore, we will need to modify the calculation for this aggregation later.

- In the last aggregation, for the **Product list** column, there is no function. There is an underscore symbol (_), which represents the entire row, and a fully written data type **table** (with data types for individual columns).

We need to modify the functions used in the third and fourth aggregations. Therefore, we need to find out how to locate the appropriate functions and access their descriptions.

Searching for functions

Most functions used in aggregations begin with the word `List`. Therefore, we can begin typing this word in the formula bar, and in newer versions of Power Query, the editor will suggest all functions and other objects that start with or include this value. Additionally, by clicking the information icon or pressing the keyboard shortcut *Ctrl + Space*, we can display a brief description of the function. An example suggestion is shown in *Figure 4.24*:

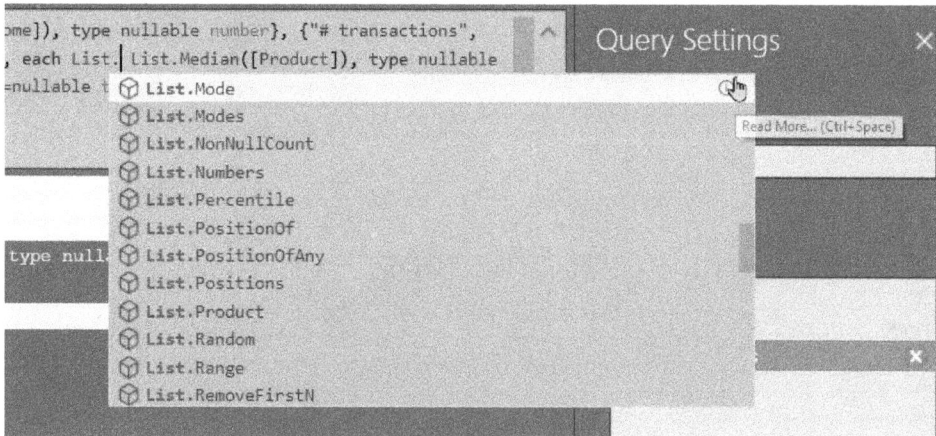

Figure 4.24: Editor suggestion for functions

If we were using an older version of Power Query, where no suggestions are provided while typing code, the most convenient solution would be to search for functions on the official Microsoft website, as shown in *Figure 4.25*:

https://learn.microsoft.com/en-us/powerquery-m/power-query-m-function-reference

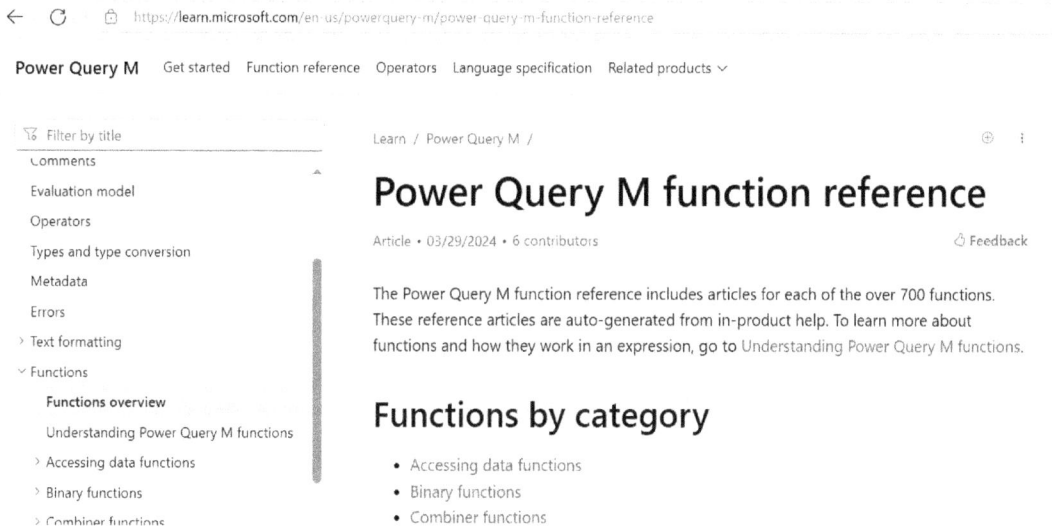

Figure 4.25: Official Microsoft website regarding Power Query functions

We can use the search box located in the top left corner of this website, or navigate through the list of topics shown in the following *Figure 4.26* to the page with **List** functions:

https://learn.microsoft.com/en-us/powerquery-m/list-functions

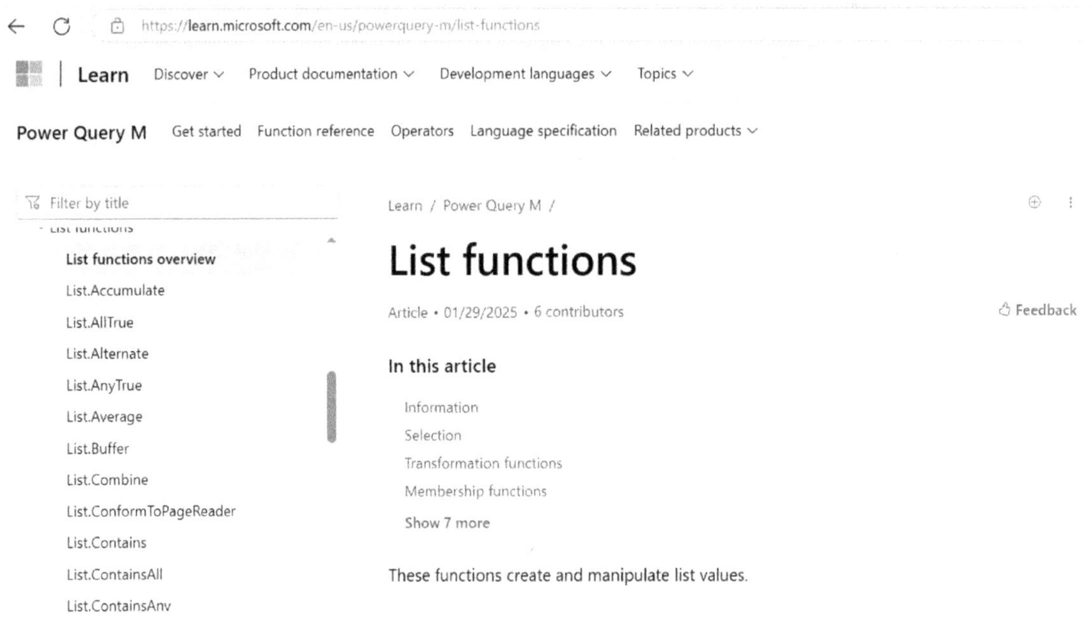
https://learn.microsoft.com/en-us/powerquery-m/list-functions
Learn
Discover
Product documentation
Development languages
Topics
Power Query M
Get started
Function reference
Operators
Language specification
Related products
Filter by title
List functions overview
List.Accumulate
List.AllTrue
List.Alternate
List.AnyTrue
List.Average
List.Buffer
List.Combine
List.ConformToPageReader
List.Contains
List.ContainsAll
List.ContainsAny
Learn / Power Query M /
List functions
Article • 01/29/2025 • 6 contributors
Feedback
In this article
Information
Selection
Transformation functions
Membership functions
Show 7 more
These functions create and manipulate list values.

***Figure 4.26**: Official Microsoft website regarding List functions*

If we add the information that, in mathematics, the most common number that appears in your set of data is called the mode, it should not be difficult for us to find the function we need here, namely, **`List.Mode`** and/or **`List.Modes`**, as shown in *Figure 4.27*:

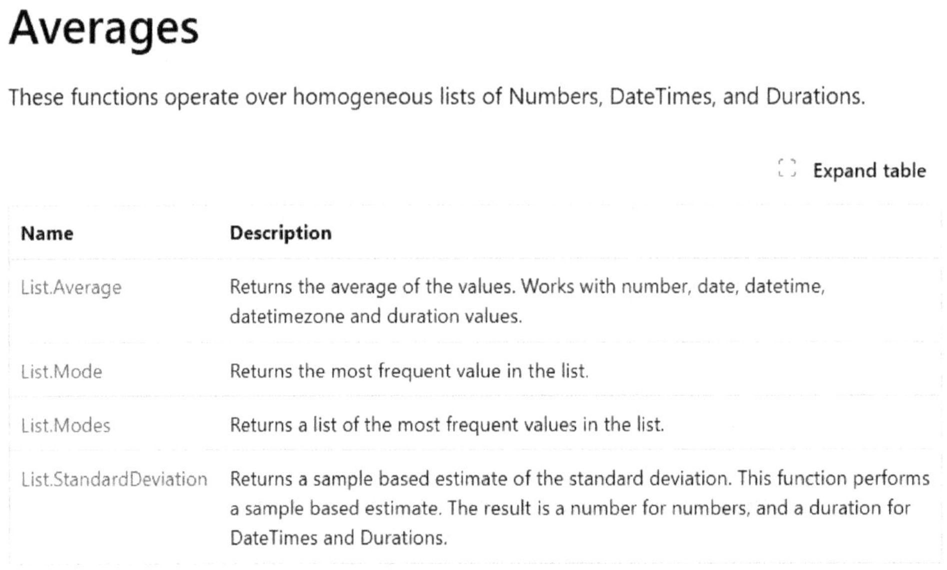
Averages
These functions operate over homogeneous lists of Numbers, DateTimes, and Durations.
Expand table
Name
Description
List.Average
Returns the average of the values. Works with number, date, datetime, datetimezone and duration values.
List.Mode
Returns the most frequent value in the list.
List.Modes
Returns a list of the most frequent values in the list.
List.StandardDeviation
Returns a sample based estimate of the standard deviation. This function performs a sample based estimate. The result is a number for numbers, and a duration for DateTimes and Durations.

***Figure 4.27**: List of List functions labeled as Averages*

Clicking on the appropriate links will redirect us to pages that describe the selected functions in more detail. From these pages, we learn that the **List.Modes** function returns a list of the most frequently occurring values in a list (or column), while the **List.Mode** function returns the single most frequently occurring value. If multiple values occur with the same frequency, the **List.Mode** function will return the last of these values. We can never be sure that there will be only one most common value, so in most situations, it is better to use the **List.Modes** function.

If we replace the **List.Median** function directly with **List.Modes**, we would also have to change the data type to **list**, similar to the first example in this chapter.

Tip: **Changing the function name in the Grouped Rows step to one not supported in the user interface of the Group By window will cause the gear icon to disappear from that step, because we have moved beyond the functionality supported by that window.**

In our case, we want to immediately receive concatenated values instead of expanding list data from a column later, which would create an additional step. Therefore, we need to find a function for combining the text. Among the many available options, we should be able to locate **List.Combine** and **Text.Combine** by searching the official Microsoft website. These functions combine lists of values (but not plain text) and combine text values with a specified delimiter. Therefore, in this example, we need the **Text.Combine** function. The M code for this step, after applying the necessary changes in the formula bar, should look as follows:

```
= Table.Group(#"Changed Type", {"Merchant", "City"}, {{"Sum", each List.
Sum([Income]), type nullable number}, {"# transactions", each Table.
RowCount(Table.Distinct(_)), Int64.Type}, {"Most frequently sold", each
Text.Combine(List.Modes([Product]), ", "), type nullable text}, {"Product
list", each _, type table [Date=nullable datetime, Merchant=nullable text,
City=nullable text, Product=nullable text, Income=nullable number]}})
```

Now, we can, similar to the first example, modify the fourth aggregation so that instead of referencing the entire row (underscore character), it extracts a single column (**Product**), and then apply the **List.Distinct** function to remove duplicate product names.

Following the same logic as in the third aggregation, we can also add the **Text.Combine** function to join the product names into one text string. We can optionally insert the **List.Sort** function beforehand to sort the list before combining it. We must also remember to change the data type from **table** to plain **text**, just like we did in the third aggregation.

After all modifications, the code in the formula bar should look as follows:

```
= Table.Group(#"Changed Type", {"Merchant", "City"}, {{"Sum", each List.
Sum([Income]), type nullable number}, {"# transactions", each Table.
RowCount(Table.Distinct(_)), Int64.Type}, {"Most frequently sold", each Text.
Combine(List.Modes([Product]), ", "), type nullable text}, {"Product list",
each Text.Combine(List.Sort(List.Distinct([Product])), ", "), type nullable
text}})
```

This will produce the updated result of the *Grouped Rows* step, as shown in *Figure 4.28*:

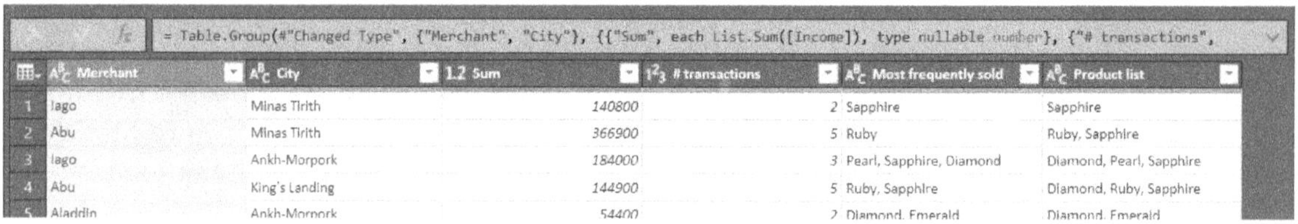

Figure 4.28: Changed result of the Grouped Rows step

Before we load the data into Excel, we want to sort it by the **Merchant** and **City** columns (using the **AZ** command from the **Home** tab). What is important here is the order in which the columns are sorted. When using the **AZ** or **ZA** command, Power Query applies sorting in the opposite order to Excel. In Power Query, the most important column must be sorted first, whereas in Excel, it must be sorted last.

After sorting multiple columns, the editor will add numbers to the sorted columns. These numbers may be difficult to see depending on your Excel color settings, but they are there, as shown in *Figure 4.29*:

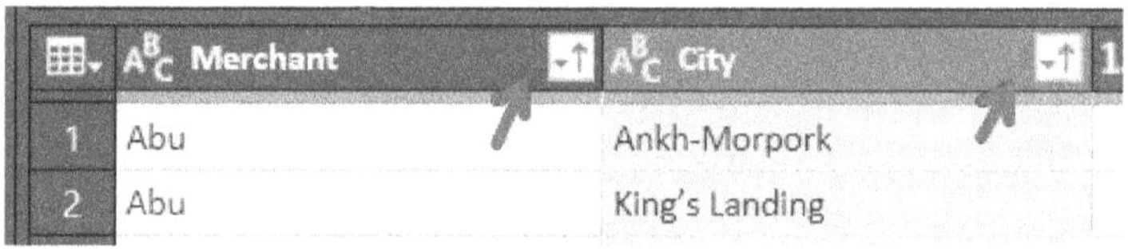

Figure 4.29: Columns sorting order

The sort order can also be determined from the order in which the columns are listed in the M code in the formula bar.

After this step, the query result can be loaded into Excel.

Local grouping

In this example, we want to group the data from the **tWeather** table from the *Local* worksheet in such a way that we combine sequences of repeating values, as shown in *Figure 4.30*:

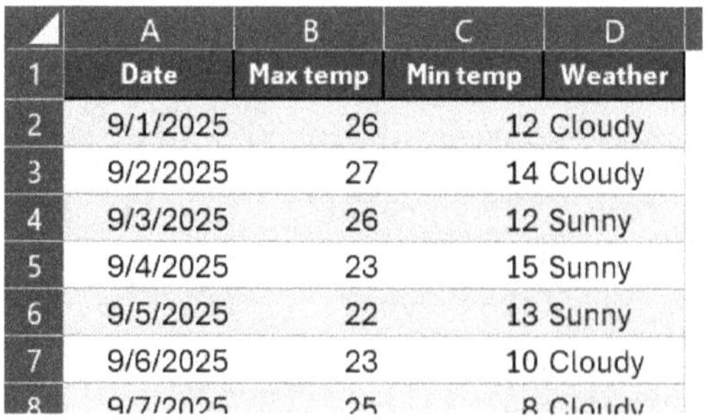

Figure 4.30: Data in tWeather table

So, we do not want to combine all days with *Cloudy* or *Sunny* weather together, but rather group only the rows with the same weather **that follow one another**. For example, as we can see in *Figure 4.30*, the first two days are marked as *Cloudy*, followed by three *Sunny* days, and then another stretch of *Cloudy* weather starting on September 6. We want to group the first two Cloudy days separately from the next Cloudy period beginning on September 6.

The first thing we need to do is import the data from the table into Power Query, as usual. The next step is to change the type from datetime to date for the **Date** column. After this, we can proceed to group the data, for now, in a standard way by the **Weather** column.

So, we select the **Weather** column and then click the **Group By** command from the **Home** tab (*Figure 4.4*). In the **Group By** window, we must switch to **Advanced** options and define three aggregations, which we will use in the next transformations. We want to count the number of days that a given weather period lasted (count rows) and determine the starting date (minimum date) and the ending date (maximum date) for each period. All the grouping settings in the **Group By** window are shown in *Figure 4.31*:

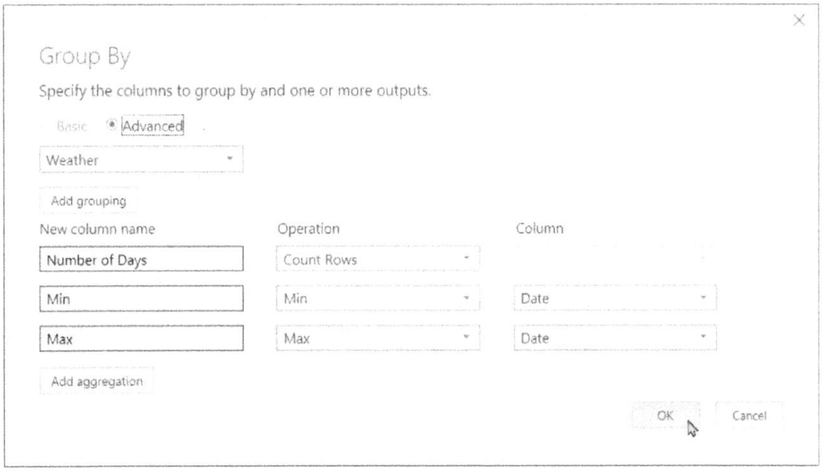

Figure 4.31: Grouping settings

After confirming the selected grouping parameters by clicking the **OK** button, Power Query will return the data grouped in the standard way, as shown in *Figure 4.32*:

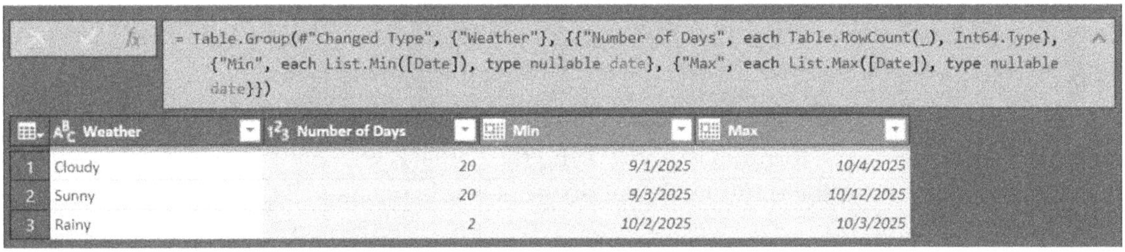

```
= Table.Group(#"Changed Type", {"Weather"}, {{"Number of Days", each Table.RowCount(_), Int64.Type},
  {"Min", each List.Min([Date]), type nullable date}, {"Max", each List.Max([Date]), type nullable
  date}})
```

	Aᴮ_C Weather	1²₃ Number of Days	Min	Max
1	Cloudy	20	9/1/2025	10/4/2025
2	Sunny	20	9/3/2025	10/12/2025
3	Rainy	2	10/2/2025	10/3/2025

Figure 4.32: Data grouped in the standard way

We need to change how the `Table.Group` function works. The current formula is visible in the formula bar as follows:

```
= Table.Group(#"Changed Type", {"Weather"}, {{"Number of Days", each Table.
RowCount(_), Int64.Type}, {"Min", each List.Min([Date]), type nullable date},
{"Max", each List.Max([Date]), type nullable date}})
```

To learn the full description of the function, we can either search for it on the website provided in the previous example or remove all of its arguments, leaving only the equal sign and the function name. The best approach is to cut the entire formula and paste it into a temporary text file or another clipboard. Once we confirm the changes by pressing *Enter*, Power Query will display a description of the function, its possible arguments, and even a few usage examples.

We will focus on the function's arguments. In particular, we are interested in the **groupKind** argument, for which we can see two possible options, as shown in *Figure 4.33*:

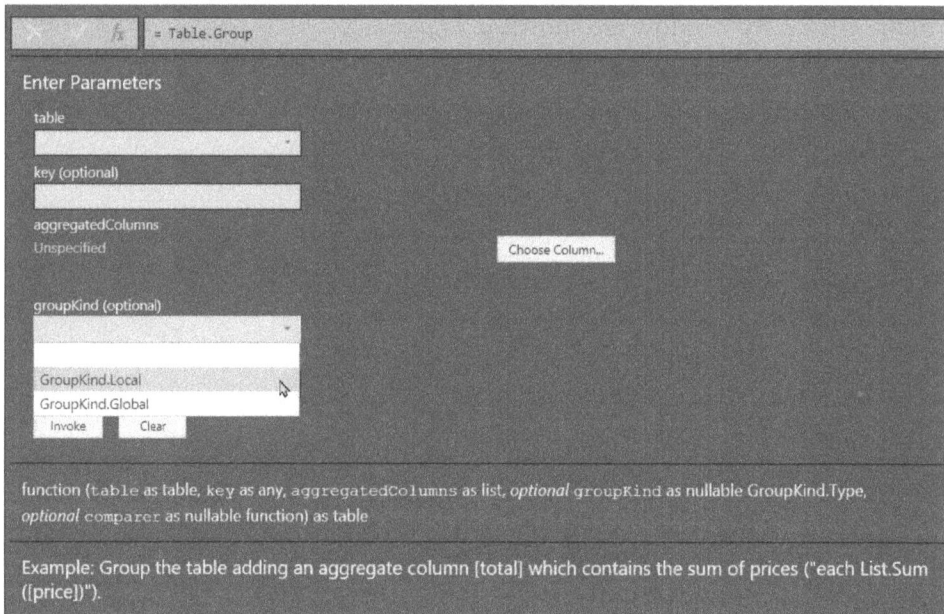

Figure 4.33: *Arguments for Table.Group function*

`GroupKind.Global` is the default option and provides the results we have seen so far. However, `GroupKind.Local` will allow us to achieve the effect we discussed earlier.

We can return to the previous version of the function. If we have not added any steps in the meantime, clicking on the formula bar and using the *Ctrl + Z* keyboard shortcut should undo the changes we made in the formula. If that does not work, we have kept the removed part in a temporary text file.

The argument we want to add is placed after the already written code, so just before the last parenthesis, we should add a comma and then enter its value. Once we add the comma, the latest versions of Power Query will start suggesting the syntax of the function, as shown in *Figure 4.34*:

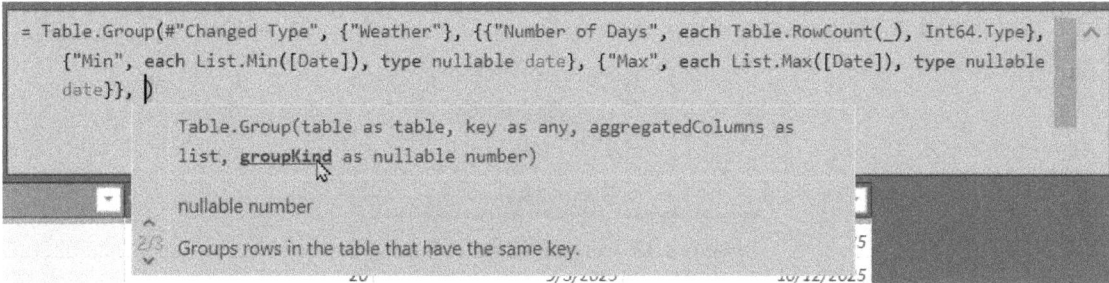

```
= Table.Group(#"Changed Type", {"Weather"}, {{"Number of Days", each Table.RowCount(_), Int64.Type},
    {"Min", each List.Min([Date]), type nullable date}, {"Max", each List.Max([Date]), type nullable
    date}}, )

            Table.Group(table as table, key as any, aggregatedColumns as
            list, groupKind as nullable number)

        nullable number

        Groups rows in the table that have the same key.
```

Figure 4.34: Power Query syntax suggestions

In this example, it is sufficient to add the grouping name: **GroupKind.Local**, which will also be suggested by the newer Power Query editor, as shown in *Figure 4.35*:

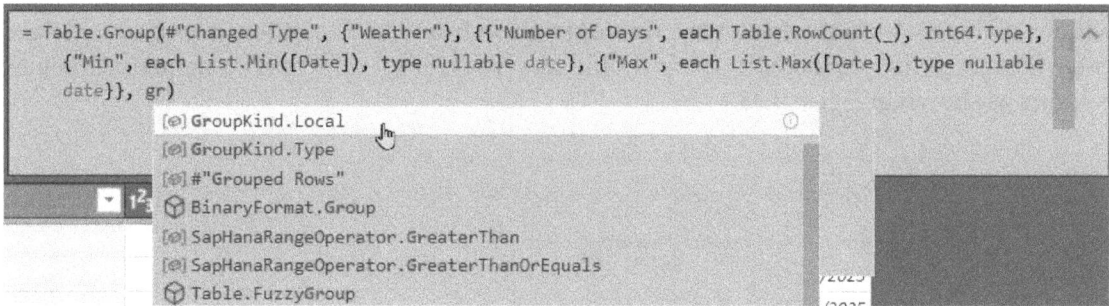

```
= Table.Group(#"Changed Type", {"Weather"}, {{"Number of Days", each Table.RowCount(_), Int64.Type},
    {"Min", each List.Min([Date]), type nullable date}, {"Max", each List.Max([Date]), type nullable
    date}}, gr)
        [@] GroupKind.Local
        [@] GroupKind.Type
        [@] #"Grouped Rows"
        BinaryFormat.Group
        [@] SapHanaRangeOperator.GreaterThan
        [@] SapHanaRangeOperator.GreaterThanOrEquals
        Table.FuzzyGroup
```

Figure 4.35: Power Query suggestions for constants, functions, etc.

After completing and confirming the formula, Power Query will return the data grouped locally, meaning according to sequences of repeating values, as shown in *Figure 4.36*:

	A\u1d2e\u1d04 Weather	1²₃ Number of Days	Min	Max
1	Cloudy	2	9/1/2025	9/2/2025
2	Sunny	3	9/3/2025	9/5/2025
3	Cloudy	4	9/6/2025	9/9/2025
4	Sunny	1	9/10/2025	9/10/2025
5	Cloudy	1	9/11/2025	9/11/2025
6	Sunny	2	9/12/2025	9/13/2025

Figure 4.36: Locally grouped data

Tip: **To confirm a formula written in the M language in the formula bar, you can either press the Enter key while positioned at the end of the code or click the checkmark located next to the formula bar. To cancel any changes made in the formula bar, simply press the Esc key or click the X icon next to the formula bar.**

Our next step will be to merge the columns containing the minimum and maximum dates. We need to select them in order, first, the **Min** column, then the **Max** column. Next, click the **Merge Columns** command on the **Transform** tab, as shown in *Figure 4.37*:

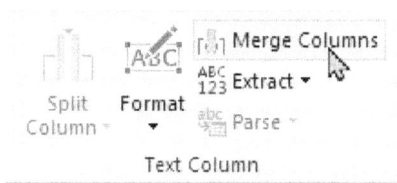

Figure 4.37: *Merge Columns command*

What matters for us is that we select this command from the **Transform** tab, not **Add Column**, because we want Power Query to remove the **Min** and **Max** columns and replace them with a new column rather than simply adding a new one to the existing columns.

After clicking the **Merge Columns** command, the editor will open the **Merge Columns** window, where we want to select the **Custom** option from the **Separator** drop-down list and enter the text *to* in the field below. We should also provide an appropriate name for the new column, as shown in *Figure 4.38*:

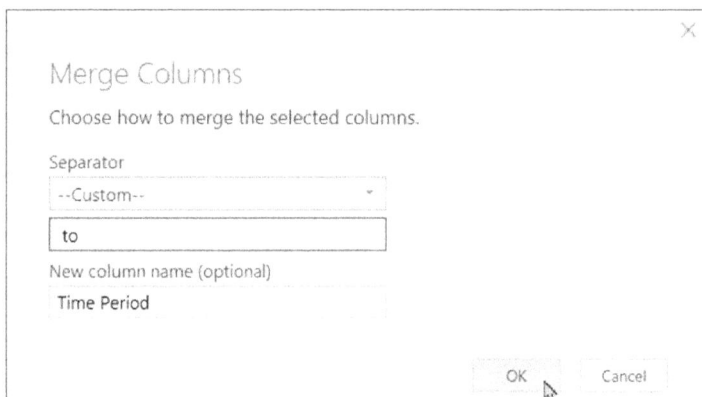

Figure 4.38: *Merge Columns window*

After confirming the settings by clicking the **OK** button, Power Query will generate the merged dates according to the regional settings, as shown in *Figure 4.39*:

Figure 4.39: *Merged Columns with date*

Tip: **For some functions, there may be an argument concerning culture or regional settings to be used for formatting, for example, a date. In our examples, we work with U.S. regional settings, which correspond to the text en-US in the function arguments (Figure 4.39). Power Query should recognize language codes listed in the Language Tag column of the table on the following page:**

https://learn.microsoft.com/en-us/openspecs/windows_protocols/ms-lcid/a9eac961-e77d-41a6-90a5-ce1a8b0cdb9c

To the **Time Period** column, we want to add a prefix. It is enough to select this column, then expand the **Format** command on the **Transform** tab (*Figure 1.12*) and choose the **Add Prefix** option. In the **Prefix** window that opens, simply enter the text from and confirm it by clicking the **OK** button, as shown in *Figure 4.40*:

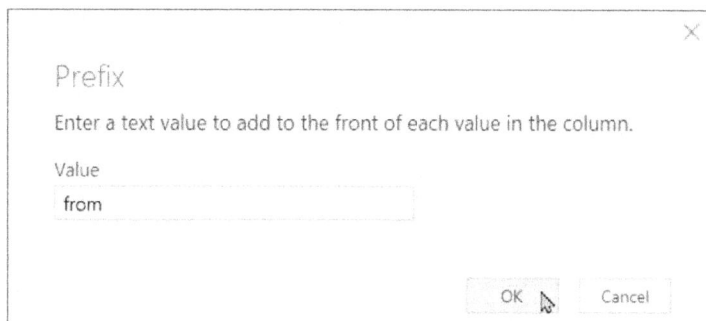

Prefix

Enter a text value to add to the front of each value in the column.

Value

from

OK   Cancel

Figure 4.40: Prefix window

After this transformation, we can load the data into Excel.

Data types

We have already discussed several examples. In each of them, the data types in individual columns were important. Now, we want to discuss them in more detail. Let us begin by presenting the basic data types. Their detailed description can be found in *Table 4.2*:

Data type	Description	Examples
Text	Stores text values (strings)	"Hello"; "Power Query"; "123"
Whole number	Integer value (Integer64)	10; -5; 1000
Decimal number	Decimal number with up to 15 decimal places	3.14159; -2.5; 100.0
Currency	Decimal number with up to 4 decimal places	100.1234; -50.99
Date	Date without time information	1/31/2025; #date(2013,02,26)
Time	Time without date information	12:30:45 AM; #time(09,15,00)

Date/Time	Date and time combined, stored as a floating-point number	1/31/2025 14:45; #datetime(2013,02,26,09,15,00)
Date/Time/Timezone	Date and time with a timezone	01/31/2025 2:45:00 PM +02:00; #datetimezone(2013,02,26, 09,15,00, 09,00)
Duration	Represents the difference between two points in time	2.00:30:00 (2 days, 30 min); #duration(0,1,30,0)
Boolean (True/False)	Logical value: True or false	true; false

Table 4.2: Basic data types

In addition to the basic data types, we can distinguish more complex data types, which we can refer to as structured types. They are described in *Table 4.3*:

Data type	Description	Examples
Binary	Stores binary data, such as files	.CSV file; JPG image
List	A collection of values, which can have different data types. They are written in the code within curly brackets	{1, 3, 9}; {"A", "Z", "X"}; {1.23, "a", false}
Record	A structured object [row] containing multiple fields of different types	[A = 1, B = 2]; [CustomerID = 1, price = 20]
Table	Stores data in a tabular structure (rows and columns)	#table({"X","Y"},{{0,1},{1,0}}); #table(type table [Digit = number, Name = text], {{1,"one"}, {2,"two"}, {3,"three"}})
Function	Represents a function that can be called in Power Query	(x) => x + 1
Type	Describes the data type used in Power Query	type { number } type table [A = any, B = text]

Table 4.3: Complex data types

In some categories of basic variables, we may encounter specially named values, but we will discuss them later in the chapter.

Conclusion

In this chapter, we covered key techniques for effectively grouping data in Power Query. You learned fundamental and advanced grouping operations, methods for summarizing and ranking data, handling duplicates, and local grouping techniques. Understanding and applying the correct Power Query data types were also emphasized. Mastering these methods will significantly enhance your data analysis capabilities.

In the next chapter, we will explore additional advanced data transformation techniques to further deepen your skills.

Multiple choice questions

1. **Which of the following aggregation methods can be used in Power Query in the Group By window?**

    a. Sum

    b. Average

    c. Maximum

    d. Concatenate text

2. **When grouping data, selecting All Rows will:**

    a. Count all rows in the dataset

    b. Aggregate numerical values

    c. Keep grouped rows as an embedded table

    d. Automatically delete duplicates

3. **Which Power Query function returns a list of the most frequently occurring items?**

    a. List.Median

    b. List.Max

    c. List.Modes

    d. List.Mode

4. **The GroupKind.Local option in Power Query groups data by:**

    a. Sequential repeating values

    b. Numeric order

    c. Alphabetical order

    d. Distinct values only

5. **What symbol represents an entire row of data in M code?**

    a. %

    b. @

    c. &

    d. _ (underscore)

6. **Which data types are essential to understand Power Query?**

    a. Text

    b. Decimal number (Currency)

    c. Boolean

    d. Font styles

Answers

Question number	Answer option letter
1.	a., b., c.
2.	c.
3.	c.
4.	a.
5.	d.
6.	a., b., c.

Join our Discord space

Join our Discord workspace for latest updates, offers, tech happenings around the world, new releases, and sessions with the authors:

https://discord.bpbonline.com

CHAPTER 5
Pivot and Unpivot

Introduction

In this book, we will discuss the **extract, transform, load (ETL)** tool known as Power Query.

Data used in reports is often formatted for readability, not analysis. Tables may include merged headers, repeated rows, or values spread across columns. This makes them difficult to process automatically.

This chapter introduces key Power Query techniques for pivoting and unpivoting data. Through practical examples, you will learn how to transform messy, report-style layouts into clean, structured tables ready for analysis. Common challenges like splitting headers, filling in missing values, and reshaping rows and columns will be addressed step by step.

Structure

This chapter covers the following topics:

- Pivoting and unpivoting basics
- First unpivoting of columns
- Splitting combined headers
- Splitting double headers

- Transforming repeated rows to columns
- Single row into multiple rows

Objectives

By the end of this chapter, you will be proficient in pivoting and unpivoting data using Power Query in Excel, enabling you to transform report-style data into structured datasets suitable for analysis. You will learn to effectively reorganize data into meaningful categories, manage complex header structures, and address irregularities, such as missing values. Mastering these skills will streamline your data preparation, enhance reporting efficiency, and enable insightful data analysis.

Pivoting and unpivoting basics

When creating reports in Excel, we most often use pivot tables. They perform a special transformation of the data along with its aggregation, which results in a clear summary. Example source data and the pivot table created from it are shown in *Figure 5.1*:

	A	B	C	D	E	F	G	H	I	J	K
1	Product	Country	Salesman	Month	Revenue		Country	Poland			
2	Pony	Poland	Richard	January	$3,544		Salesman	Richard			
3	Pony	Poland	Richard	February	$12,672						
4	Pony	Poland	Richard	March	$12,101		Sum of Revenue	Month			
5	Doll	Poland	Richard	January	$2,871		Product	January	February	March	Sum
6	Doll	Poland	Richard	February	$9,562		Car	$4,588	$3,914	$9,902	$18,404
7	Doll	Poland	Richard	March	$6,462		Doll	$2,871	$9,562	$6,462	$18,895
8	Lego	Poland	Richard	January	$8,206		Lego	$8,206	$2,463	$6,142	$16,811
9	Lego	Poland	Richard	February	$2,463		Pony	$3,544	$12,672	$12,101	$28,317
10	Lego	Poland	Richard	March	$6,142		Robot	$9,843	$11,735	$1,513	$23,091
11	Teddy	Poland	Richard	January	$3,103		Ship	$2,441	$9,998	$11,596	$24,035
12	Teddy	Poland	Richard	February	$4,636		Teddy	$3,103	$4,636	$5,931	$13,670
13	Teddy	Poland	Richard	March	$5,931		Train	$9,843	$11,735	$5,931	$27,509
14	Robot	Poland	Richard	January	$9,843		Sum	$44,439	$66,715	$59,578	$170,732
15	Robot	Poland	Richard	February	$11,735						

Figure 5.1: Source data and the pivot table created from it

In Power Query, there is a functionality very similar to pivot tables, which allows creating column headers from the values of a specified column and summarizing based on values from another column. This command is called **Pivot Column**. It does not offer the same capabilities as a pivot table, but it allows the creation of simple summaries.

However, because the main purpose of Power Query is to combine data from different sources and transform it for further processing, for example, by loading it directly into pivot tables (*Figure 1.14*), this command is used less frequently than its reverse counterpart, **Unpivot Columns**.

It often happens that users prepare data in a way that is convenient for manual data entry rather than structured for tools, such as Excel or databases, to process and analyze it easily. In other words, users do not create a proper data range (see *Chapter 1, Getting Started with Power Query*), and the task of tools like Power Query is to transform such data into the correct format. An example source might be a simple report resembling a pivot table, as shown in *Figure 5.1*.

To better understand how the unpivot columns command works, the file **Introduction to pivot and unpivot.xlsx** contains several sheets illustrating the transformation from a report-like structure into a proper dataset. The first rule of transformation that must be kept in mind is that one data type must be placed in a single data column. An example here would be the summary **Revenue** values across different months, excluding totals, which should be placed in a single **Revenue** column. A visual representation of this transformation is shown on the worksheet **Unpivot (2)** and illustrated in *Figure 5.2*:

	A	B	C	D	E	F	G	H	I	J	K
1	Country: Poland						Country	Salesman	Product	Month	Revenue
2	Salesman: Richard						Poland	Richard	Pony	January	$3,544
3							Poland	Richard	Pony	February	$12,672
4	Revenue		Month				Poland	Richard	Pony	March	$12,101
5	Product	January	February	March	Sum		Poland	Richard	Doll	January	$2,871
6	Pony	$3,544	$12,672	$12,101	$28,317		Poland	Richard	Doll	February	$9,562
7	Doll	$2,871	$9,562	$6,462	$18,895		Poland	Richard	Doll	March	$6,462
8	Lego	$8,206	$2,463	$6,142	$16,811		Poland	Richard	Lego	January	$8,206
9	Teddy	$3,103	$4,636	$5,931	$13,670		Poland	Richard	Lego	February	$2,463
10	Train	$9,843	$11,735	$5,931	$27,509		P			March	$6,142
11	Robot	$9,843	$11,735	$1,513	$23,091		P	All values of the same		January	$3,103
12	Car	$4,588	$3,914	$9,902	$18,404		P	type must go into 1		February	$4,636
13	Sum	$41,998	$56,717	$47,982	$146,697		P	column		March	$5,931
14							Poland	Richard	Robot	January	$9,843
15							Poland	Richard	Robot	February	$11,735

Figure 5.2: Moving summary values into a single column

The second condition is that each cell containing a summary value must be associated with row and column header cells, as well as with data that, for this book, will be referred to as **report metadata**. In a pivot table, this metadata is represented by selecting a single value in the report filter area.

All of these values must be included in a single row of a properly structured dataset. This condition is illustrated on the worksheet **Unpivot (3)** and shown in *Figure 5.3*:

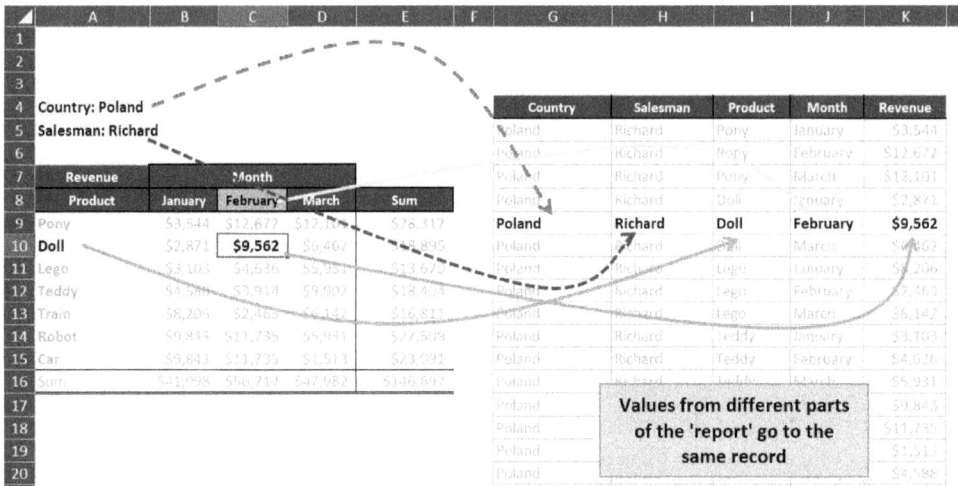

Figure 5.3: Moving descriptive values for each summary cell

Finally, it is necessary to ensure that the values from column headers, row headers, and report metadata are placed into their designated columns. At the same time, any redundant data, such as rows and columns with totals, should be removed.

This is demonstrated on the worksheet **Unpivot (4)**, as shown in *Figure 5.4*:

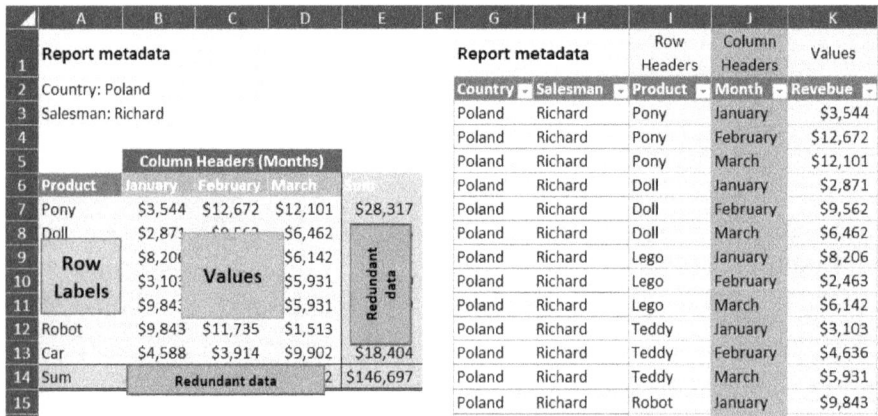

Figure 5.4: Fitting data into appropriate columns

The basic principles of the pivot and unpivot operations have already been covered, so it is now possible to proceed with practical examples of how to use them.

First unpivoting of columns

The data for this example is located on the **FirstReport** worksheet in the `Pivot and unpivot.xlsx` file. What is important here is that the data is not part of a table but rather loosely entered into the worksheet. This is illustrated in *Figure 5.5*:

	A	B	C	D	E	F
1	Coutry: Poland					
2						
3	Salesman	Product	January	February	March	Sum
4	Richard	Doll	$3,544	$12,672	$12,101	$28,317
5		Teddy	$2,871	$9,562	$6,462	$18,895
6		Train	$8,206	$2,463	$6,142	$16,811
7		Car	$3,103	$4,636	$5,931	$13,670
8	Mary	Doll	$9,843	$11,735	$1,513	$23,091
9		Teddy	$4,588	$3,914	$9,902	$18,404
10		Train	$2,441	$9,998	$11,596	$24,035
11		Car	$9,843	$11,735	$5,931	$27,509
12	Gabriel	Doll	$7,245	$3,472	$266	$10,983
13		Teddy	$4,647	$5,209	$5,399	$15,255
14		Train	$2,049	$6,946	$11,064	$20,059
15		Car	$9,451	$8,683	$6,729	$24,863

Figure 5.5: First report data

It can be observed that the reference to the country for which this report was prepared is located only in cell **A1**. There is also a lack of repeated data for the salespeople in the **Salesman** column. For a proper data source, this information is necessary. In contrast, the column with the total is unnecessary for the source data. Overall, the transformation must follow the Unpivot principle. Additionally, the result should be placed on the same worksheet as the source data.

The process of importing data from the current Excel file into Power Query involves the following steps:

1. Retrieve data from the Excel file, as shown in *Figure 2.8*.

2. Select the appropriate method for importing data into Power Query (also shown in *Figure 2.8*).

3. Locate and select the Excel file containing the data (*Figure 2.9*).

4. Import the data from the chosen Excel file.

5. Select a single worksheet containing the data needed for the current example.

6. Click the **Transform Data** button to load the selected data into Power Query, as shown in *Figure 5.6*:

Navigator

FirstReport

Coutry: Poland	Column2	Column3	Column4	Column5	Column6	Column7
	null	null	null	null	null	null
Salesman	Product	January	February	March	Sum	
Richard	Doll	3544	12672	12101	28317	null
null	Teddy	2871	9562	6462	18895	null
null	Train	8206	2463	6142	16811	null
null	Car	3103	4636	5931	13670	null
Mary	Doll	9843	11735	1513	23091	null
null	Teddy	4588	3914	9902	18404	null
null	Train	2441	9998	11596	24035	null
null	Car	9843	11735	5931	27509	null
Gabriel	Doll	7245	3472	266	10983	null
null	Teddy	4647	5209	5399	15255	null

Select multiple items

Display Options

▲ Pivot i unpivot.xlsx [8]
- tCombineHeaders
- tOneRow
- tRepeteadRows
- Combined Headers
- Double Headers
- FirstReport
- OneRow
- Repeated Rows

Load ▾   Transform Data   Cancel

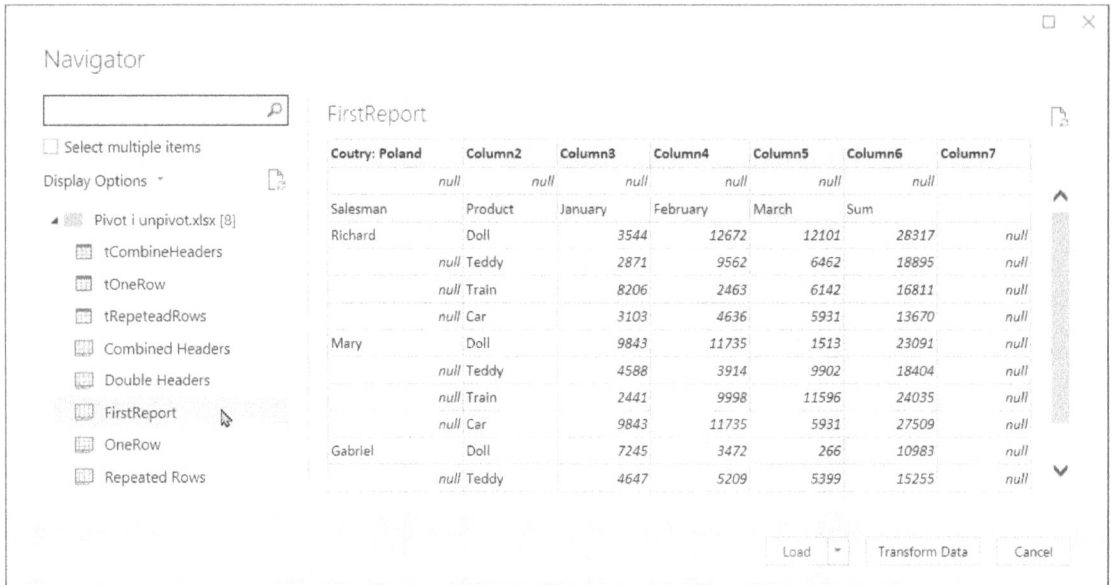

Figure 5.6: Worksheet selected for further transformations

When this worksheet is selected, it can be observed that Power Query automatically treats the first row as headers. However, this is not the case for every worksheet. In this example, it is an unfavorable situation, although in other cases, it could accelerate the transformations.

Empty text strings were intentionally placed in column **G** of the worksheet (cells **G2** and **G3**). This column appears as **Column7** in the data preview (*Figure 5.6*). These cells appear empty in the **Navigator** window, but in reality, the empty cells are represented by a special value, **null**, which means nothing.

To clean and prepare the data in Power Query, follow these steps:

1. After loading the data into Power Query, delete the default steps: **Changed Type** and **Promoted Headers**. This can be done by clicking the X icon next to each step name, starting from the bottom up.

2. Alternatively, right-click on the **Promoted Headers** step and select **Delete Until End** from the context menu, as shown in *Figure 5.7*:

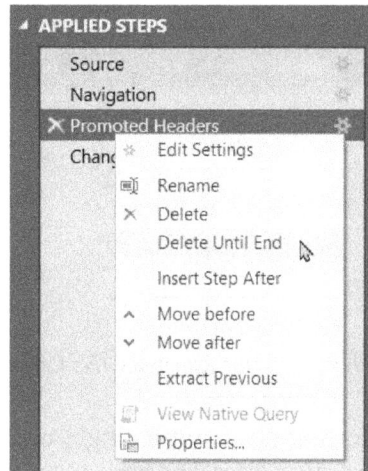

Figure 5.7: *Context menu for a query step*

3. Confirm the deletion by clicking the **Delete** button in the window that appears, as shown in *Figure 5.8*:

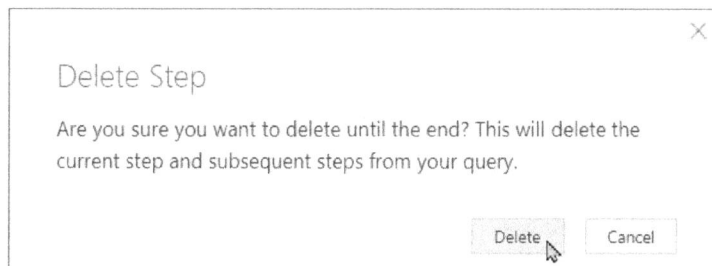

Figure 5.8: *The confirmation window for deleting steps to the end of the query*

4. Identify unnecessary columns in the data. In this case, Column6 and Column7. This means we want to keep other columns.

5. Select Column1 to Column5, right-click on any of the selected headers, and choose **Remove Other Columns** from the context menu (as shown in *Figure 2.18*).

Choosing this specific operation is especially important because we plan to load the query results onto the same worksheet (into a further column) from which we are retrieving the data. This step will ensure that any additional data beyond the first five columns will be excluded from the query's analysis.

When examining the current query result, we can notice that the first two rows of data are not needed, as shown in *Figure 5.9*:

```
= Table.SelectColumns(FirstReport_Sheet,{"Column1", "Column2", "Column3", "Column4", "Column5"})
```

Column1	Column2	Column3	Column4	Column5
1 Coutry: Poland		null	null	null	null
2	null	null	null	null	null
3 Salesman	Product	January	February	March
4 Richard	Doll	3544	12672	12101
5	null Teddy	2871	9562	6462
6	null Train	8206	2463	6142
7	null Car	3103	4636	5931
8 Mary	Doll	9843	11735	1513
9	null Teddy	4588	3914	9902

Figure 5.9: Result of the Removed Other Columns step

These rows contain only the information about a single country for which this report was generated. We will add this information later. For now, we need to remove the first two rows, so we expand the **Remove Rows** command on the **Home** tab and choose the **Remove Top Rows** option, just as we did in *Chapter 1* (*Figure 1.30*). Then, in the **Remove Top Rows** window (*Figure 1.31*), we confirm the removal of the first two rows.

The process of preparing the data for further transformations involves the following steps:

1. Use the **Use First Row as Headers** command from the table's context menu, as shown in *Figure 1.8*.

2. After applying this step, verify that the headers have been correctly promoted, as illustrated in *Figure 5.10*:

```
= Table.TransformColumnTypes(#"Promoted Headers",{{"Salesman", type text}, {"Product", type text},
    {"January", Int64.Type}, {"February", Int64.Type}, {"March", Int64.Type}})
```

Salesman	Product	January	February	March
1 Richard	Doll	3544	12672	12101
2	null Teddy	2871	9562	6462
3	null Train	8206	2463	6142
4	null Car	3103	4636	5931
5 Mary	Doll	9843	11735	1513
6	null Teddy	4588	3914	9902
7	null Train	2441	8008	11595

Figure 5.10: Query result after promoting headers

3. Proceed to fill in the data in the **Salesman** column. This column contains a salesperson's name only in the first row of each section, with **null** values in the following rows.

4. Copy the values in the **Salesman** column downward until a new value is encountered, and continue this process throughout the column. In Power Query, it is enough to select the column, expand the **Fill** command on the **Transform** tab, and choose the **Down** option, as shown in *Figure 5.11*:

Figure 5.11: *Fill Down command*

Tip: **The Fill command copies data either downward or upward, but only into cells containing the null value. If a cell contains an empty text value, it will not be replaced by another value. Only null values are replaced.**

To convert the monthly data into a more analysis-friendly format, follow these steps:

1. Select the **January**, **February**, and **March** columns in the Power Query editor.

2. Navigate to the **Transform** tab.

3. Expand the **Unpivot Columns** command.

4. Apply the command, as shown in *Figure 5.12,* to transform the selected columns into attribute-value pairs:

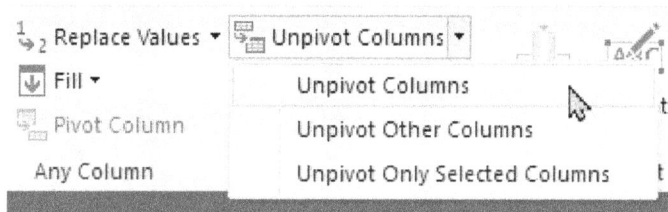

Figure 5.12: *Unpivot Columns command*

It is important to note which option is selected in this case. If the **Unpivot Columns** command is clicked directly, or that option is selected from the expanded list, Power Query will decide, behind the scenes, which of the following functions to apply, based on whether there are more selected or unselected columns. In this example, more columns are selected, so Power Query will generate the following code:

```
= Table.UnpivotOtherColumns(#"Filled Down", {"Salesman", "Product"},
"Attribute", "Value")
```

In this code, it is clear that the second option was used, listing only the two initial column names. This guarantees that only those two columns remain unchanged, and all remaining columns will be involved in the unpivot operation. In theory, if additional columns with subsequent months were to appear, they would be included in this transformation. However, due to the previous step that removed other columns, this operation would not work correctly if new valid month columns were added.

If, in this example, the unpivoting is forced on selected columns only (by clicking the **Unpivot Only Selected Columns** option), then a different code will be generated:

```
= Table.Unpivot(#"Filled Down", {"January", "February", "March"}, "Attribute", "Value")
```

In this version, more columns are explicitly listed in the unpivot operation. The selection of an unpivoting method does not need to be based on the number of columns. More importantly, it should be guided by which part of the report (which columns) must remain unchanged. If there is a chance that additional month columns may appear in the future, then it is better to use the version with the **Table.UnpivotOtherColumns** function. However, if it is certain that the number of columns to be unpivoted will remain the same, but the other columns may vary, then it is better to use the version with the **Table.Unpivot** function.

For this example, the **Table.Unpivot** function will be used. Thus, the columns with month names in their headers are selected, and the **Unpivot Only Selected Columns** option is chosen from the **Unpivot Columns** command menu (*Figure 5.12*).

After this operation, the original column headers will appear in the **Attribute** column, and the values from those columns will be placed in the **Value** column. This is shown in *Figure 5.13*:

	A_C Salesman	A_C Product	A_C Attribute	1²₃ Value
1	Richard	Doll	January	3544
2	Richard	Doll	February	12672
3	Richard	Doll	March	12101
4	Richard	Teddy	January	2871
5	Richard	Teddy	February	9562
6	Richard	Teddy	March	6462

Figure 5.13: *Result after the unpivot operation*

This is the result that was expected, except for the column names. Fortunately, those names can be changed directly in the formula bar to **Month** and **Revenue**, respectively. After applying those changes, the code in the formula bar should appear as follows:

```
= Table.Unpivot(#"Filled Down", {"January", "February", "March"}, "Month", "Revenue")
```

To complete the transformation, follow these final steps to add the country name:

1. Go to the **Add Column** tab in Power Query.

2. Click the **Custom Column** command, as shown in *Figure 5.14*:

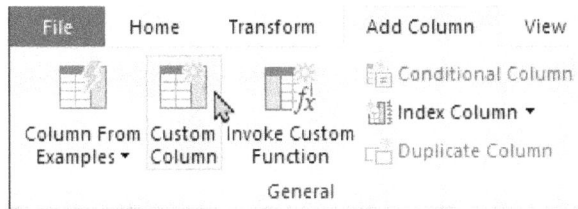

Figure 5.14: Custom Column command

3. In the **Custom Column** window that appears, enter **Country** as the column name.

4. In the formula field, type **"Poland"** (including the quotation marks) after the equals sign to insert a fixed text value.

5. The formula in the **Custom Column** window should match what is shown in *Figure 5.15*:

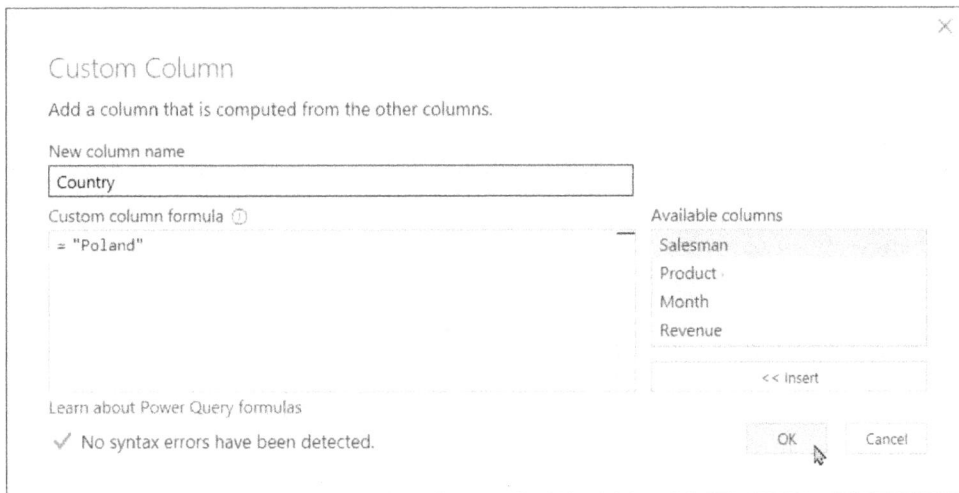

Figure 5.15: Correctly filled Custom Column window

6. Confirm the operation with the **OK** button.

More information on inserting columns and the **Custom Column** window will be provided in *Chapter 6, Adding Columns*.

To finalize the process and load the transformed data into Excel, follow these steps:

1. Locate the newly created column, which is placed at the end of the dataset by default.

2. Click and drag the column to the left to move it to the beginning of the table.

3. Go to the **Home** tab in Power Query and expand the **Close & Load** command.

4. Choose **Close & Load To** (as shown in *Figure 1.13*) to open the loading options.

5. Specify where the data should be inserted. In this example, select cell **H1** on the **FirstReport** worksheet as the destination.

6. Load the query and save the file.

7. Refresh the query to ensure it runs correctly, especially after new data is added to the worksheet.

Note: **In general, although it is possible, it is not recommended to load the query result into the same worksheet from which the data is being retrieved. This can easily lead to errors or force additional steps to be added for the query to function correctly.**

Splitting combined headers

The work is performed on data from the **Combined Headers** worksheet in the `Pivot i unpivot.xlsx` file. In the table from which the data is being retrieved, the last four columns contain combined headers. Specifically, each header describes both the month and whether the data in the column refers to worked hours or costs. This is illustrated in *Figure 5.16*:

	A	B	C	D	E	F	G	H
1	Project ID	Project Name	Task	Responsible	Sep Hours	Oct Hours	Sep Costs	Oct Costs
2	1001	Master of Power Query	Promotional Materials (photos)	Stephan	14	8	2000	1730
3	1001	Master of Power Query	Promotional Materials (videos)	Stephan	12	16	3030	4810
4	1001	Master of Power Query	Advertisement	Mary	0	14	0	1650
5	1001	Master of Power Query	Videos	Olive		8		2590
6	1001	Master of Power Query	Partners	Olive	12	16	1570	1030

Figure 5.16: Table with combined headers

Additionally, the dataset contains two empty cells and two cells filled with zero values, allowing comparison of Power Query's behavior with these different values. In total, there are 20 data cells that should be split into different columns.

Since the data is located in an Excel table, it can be imported into the editor using the **From Table/Range** command from the **Data** tab (*Figure 1.1*).

After the data is loaded, Power Query replaces the empty cells with **null** values. It is important to note that these values appear in the row where the responsible person is Olive and the task is video editing.

To ensure the structure meets the requirements of a proper dataset format, follow these steps:

1. Select the first four columns of the table.

2. Right-click on any of the selected column headers to open the context menu.

3. Choose the **Unpivot Other Columns** option from the menu, as illustrated in *Figure 5.17*:

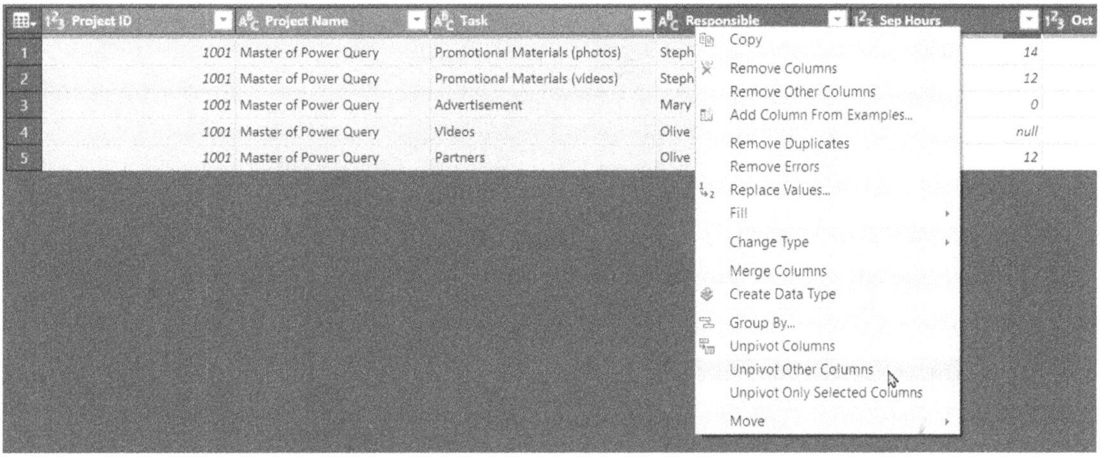

Figure 5.17: Data and context menu for selected columns

After this transformation, Power Query will display only 18 rows of data. As in the previous example, column headers will be moved into the **Attribute** column, and the values from cells will appear in the **Value** column. An exception applies to cells containing **null** values. For these, Power Query does not generate rows. This is illustrated in *Figure 5.18*:

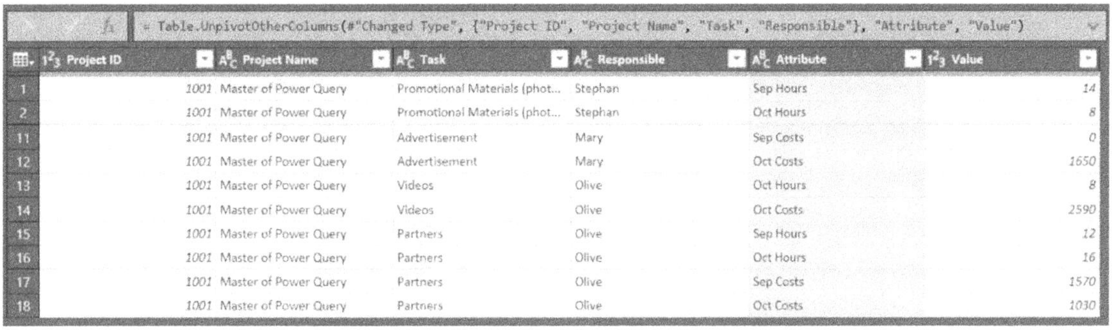

Figure 5.18: Data after using the Unpivot command

To ensure that rows containing null values are also included after unpivoting, the following steps are to be followed. In this approach, the previously created unpivot step is not removed, but instead the replacement step is inserted earlier in the query:

1. Select the step that appears before the **Unpivoted Other Columns** step. Typically, this will be the **Changed Type** step.

2. Highlight the last four columns that are to be unpivoted.

3. On the **Home** tab, click the **Replace Values** command, as shown in *Figure 5.19*:

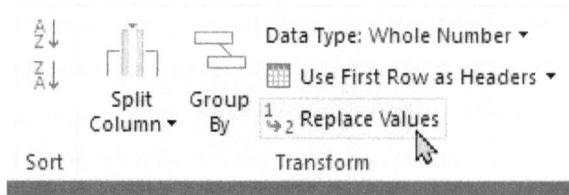

Figure 5.19: *The Replace Values command on the Home tab*

4. Power Query will display the **Insert Step** window. Confirm the action by clicking the **Insert** button, as shown in *Figure 5.20*:

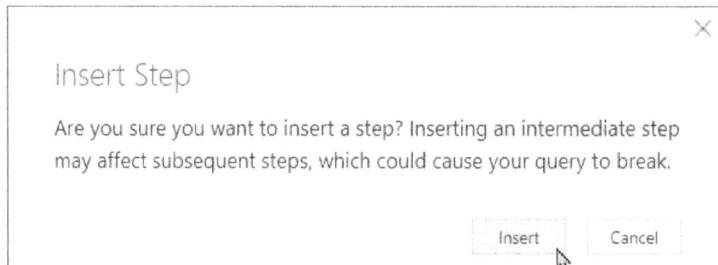

Figure 5.20: *Insert Step window*

5. Once the **Replace Values** window opens, verify that the data types are correctly detected by Power Query based on the icons shown next to the **Value To Find** and **Replace With** fields, as illustrated in *Figure 5.21*:

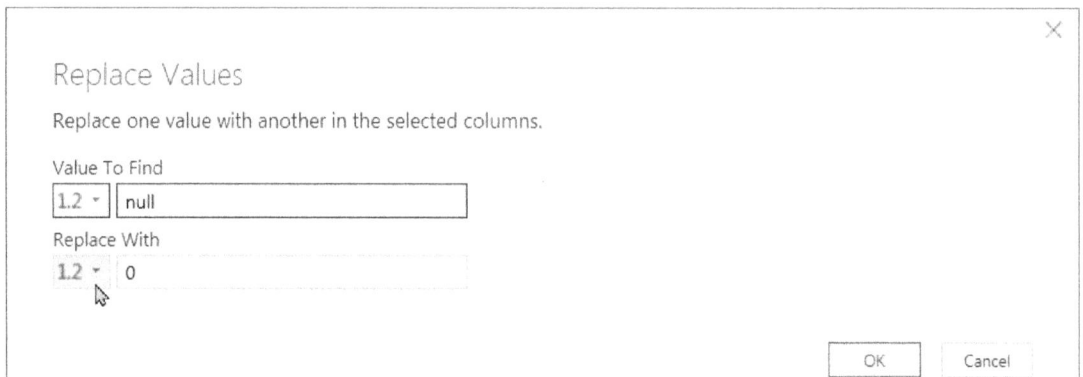

Figure 5.21: *Replace Values window*

6. Enter **null** as the value to find, and zero as the replacement value.

7. After applying the replacement, return to the **Unpivoted Other Columns** step to ensure the rows previously containing nulls are now retained with zeros.

Power Query generates the following M code for this step:

```
= Table.ReplaceValue(#"Changed Type",null,0,Replacer.ReplaceValue,{"Sep
Hours", "Oct Hours", "Sep Costs", "Oct Costs"})
```

Sometimes, we want to distinguish cells that originally contained zeros from those that were empty. In this example, it is enough to replace the zero in the code with an empty text string, that is, two double quotation marks. The code after the modification will look as follows:

```
= Table.ReplaceValue(#"Changed Type",null,"",Replacer.ReplaceValue,{"Sep
Hours", "Oct Hours", "Sep Costs", "Oct Costs"})
```

It is important to note that this change will result in a shift in the data type from **Whole Number** to the general type (**ABC123: any**). This change will apply to all columns for which the **Replace Value** operation was performed, even those where no **null** value was replaced.

After such a code modification, it is advisable to test whether the shift to a more general data type will negatively affect the query's performance. This is more likely to occur with large datasets.

After applying all changes, we can return to the **Unpivoted Other Columns** step and observe that the resulting table now has 20 rows, meaning there are four rows for **Olive** and the **Videos** task, as shown in *Figure 5.22*:

1²₃ Project ID	Aᵇ꜀ Project Name	Aᵇ꜀ Task	Aᵇ꜀ Responsible	Aᵇ꜀ Attribute	123 Value
1	1001 Master of Power Query	Promotional Materials (phot...	Stephan	Sep Hours	14
2	1001 Master of Power Query	Promotional Materials (phot...	Stephan	Oct Hours	8
11	1001 Master of Power Query	Advertisement	Mary	Sep Costs	0
12	1001 Master of Power Query	Advertisement	Mary	Oct Costs	1650
13	1001 Master of Power Query	Videos	Olive	Sep Hours	
14	1001 Master of Power Query	Videos	Olive	Oct Hours	8
15	1001 Master of Power Query	Videos	Olive	Sep Costs	
16	1001 Master of Power Query	Videos	Olive	Oct Costs	2590
17	1001 Master of Power Query	Partners	Olive	Sep Hours	12
18	1001 Master of Power Query	Partners	Olive	Oct Hours	16
19	1001 Master of Power Query	Partners	Olive	Sep Costs	1570
20	1001 Master of Power Query	Partners	Olive	Oct Costs	1030

Figure 5.22: Data after using the Unpivot command and replacing null values with an empty text string

In this example, it is not necessary to change the names of the **Attribute** and **Value** columns, as further transformations will alter them regardless. However, it is important to note that the **Value** column now stores data of a general type and is not specified as whole numbers. To facilitate subsequent transformations involving this column, we convert its data type to **Whole Number**. This action will add another step (**Changed Type1**) and convert the empty cells back to **null** values.

The process of splitting the **Attribute** column into two separate columns can be completed by following these steps:

1. Select the **Attribute** column in the Power Query editor.

2. On the **Home** tab, expand the **Split Column** command and choose **By Delimiter**, as shown in *Figure 1.22*.

3. In the **Split Column by Delimiter** window that appears, confirm that Power Query has automatically detected a space character as the delimiter (similar to *Figure 1.23*).

4. Since the column contains only one space per value, no additional adjustments are needed. Click **OK** to confirm.

5. A new step named **Split Column by Delimiter** will be added to the **Applied Steps** list, and the **Attribute** column will be divided into two columns.

6. Power Query may also add a **Changed Type2** step automatically. This step is not required in this case and can be safely removed.

7. Verify that the correct M code appears in the formula bar for the splitting operation:

```
= Table.SplitColumn(#"Unpivoted Other Columns", "Attribute",
Splitter.SplitTextByDelimiter(" ", QuoteStyle.Csv), {"Attribute.1",
"Attribute.2"})
```

The name of the second newly created column is not relevant in this context, so it can be left unchanged. However, the first column should be renamed to **Month**, so the code after modification should look as follows:

```
= Table.SplitColumn(#"Unpivoted Other Columns", "Attribute", Splitter.
SplitTextByDelimiter(" ", QuoteStyle.Csv), {"Month", "Attribute.2"})
```

Tip: **When splitting a column by a delimiter, the specified delimiter is removed from the row value (replaced by the column split) and will not appear in any of the newly created columns.**

Now, we can use the headers from the **Attribute.2** column to create proper data column headers corresponding to the values in the **Value** column. To do this, simply select the **Attribute.2** column and then click the **Pivot Column** command located on the **Transform** tab, as shown in *Figure 5.23*:

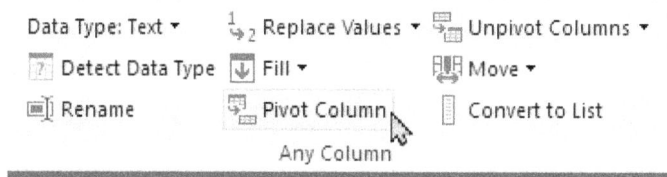

Figure 5.23: The Pivot Column command on the Transform tab

This will open the **Pivot Column** window, where unique values from the **Attribute.2** column will be used to create new columns. We only need to ensure that the values used to populate the cells in those new columns are taken from the **Value** column. Since we previously changed the data type for this column to **Whole Number**, we do not need to expand the **Advanced options**. The correctly configured **Pivot Column** window is shown in *Figure 5.24*:

Figure 5.24: Pivot Column window

After completing this step, the data will take the form of a proper data range or table. It only remains to rename the query, for example, to **Proper Headers**, and then load the query result into Excel. One additional observation: since Excel does not have an equivalent for the special **null** value, such values are loaded into Excel as empty cells, as shown in *Figure 5.25*:

	A	B	C	D	E	F	G
8	Project ID	Project Name	Task	Responsible	Month	Hours	Costs
17	1001	Master of Power Query	Videos	Olive	Oct	8	2590
18	1001	Master of Power Query	Videos	Olive	Sep		

Figure 5.25: Cells with the null value imported into Excel as empty cells

Splitting double headers

The data used in this example is located in the **Double Headers** sheet of the **Pivot and unpivot.xlsx** file. It is important to note that the data is not stored in an Excel table but placed directly into worksheet cells, as shown in *Figure 5.26*:

	A	B	C	D	E	F	G	H
1						Sep		Oct
2	Project ID	Project Name	Task	Responsible	Hours	Costs	Hours	Costs
3	1001	Master of Power Qu	Promotional Materials (p	Stephan	14	2000	8	1730
4	1001	Master of Power Qu	Promotional Materials (vi	Stephan	12	3030	16	4810
5	1001	Master of Power Qu	Advertisement	Mary	0	0	14	1650
6	1001	Master of Power Qu	Videos	Olive			8	2590
7	1001	Master of Power Qu	Partners	Olive	12	1570	16	1030

Figure 5.26: Data with double headers

These are the same data as in the previous example, but the division into months and the number of hours worked and costs in the last four columns are presented differently. The month names appear in an additional row above the rest of the data and are visually centered above the columns they relate to. This layout may be convenient for data entry, but it is unsuitable for data analysis. Therefore, as in the previous example, we will need to transform it into a proper data table.

Tip: Visually centering data in Excel does not mean that the value is present in all cells above which it appears. In practice, it means that the value is located in the first cell of the aligned area, and the remaining cells are empty, which means that after importing into Power Query, they will appear as null values.

The process of converting the range into an Excel table involves the following steps:

1. Select any cell within the data range you want to convert.
2. Press *Ctrl + T* to open the **Create Table** window.
3. In the window that appears, uncheck the **My table has headers** checkbox, as shown in *Figure 5.27*:

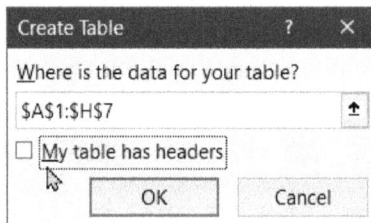

Figure 5.27: Create Table window

4. Confirm the creation of the table by clicking the **OK** button.

If a table is created in Excel without specifying headers, Excel will automatically add a header row using default column names, as shown in *Figure 5.28*:

	A	B	C	D	E	F	G	H
1	Column1	Column2	Column3	Column4	Column5	Column6	Column7	Column8
2					Sep		Oct	
3	Project ID	Project Name	Task	Responsible	Hours	Costs	Hours	Costs
4	1001	Master of Power Qu	Promotional Materials (p	Stephan	14	2000	8	1730
5	1001	Master of Power Qu	Promotional Materials (vi	Stephan	12	3030	16	4810
6	1001	Master of Power Qu	Advertisement	Mary	0	0	14	1650
7	1001	Master of Power Qu	Videos	Olive			8	2590
8	1001	Master of Power Qu	Partners	Olive	12	1570	16	1030

Figure 5.28: Table with default headers added

To prepare the data for further transformations, follow these steps:

1. Load the data into Power Query by selecting the table and clicking the **From Table/ Range** command on the **Data** tab (*Figure 1.1*).

2. Leave the default table name unchanged during the import.

3. After loading, observe that the table contains 8 columns and 7 rows.

4. If the **Changed Type** step was automatically added, remove it to reduce unnecessary steps.

5. Note that many columns contain a mix of numeric and text values, which causes Power Query to assign a general data type (**ABC123: any**). Data types will be adjusted after initial transformations.

   Tip: **The special value null can appear for any data type and does not affect the detected data type of a column.**

6. Click the **Transpose** command on the **Transform** tab to switch rows and columns, as shown in *Figure 5.29*:

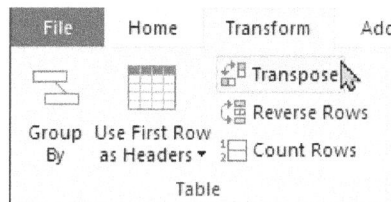

Figure 5.29: *Transpose command on Transform tab*

After this transformation, the resulting table will contain 7 columns and 8 rows. This is shown in *Figure 5.30*:

	Column1	Column2	Column3	Column4	Column5	Column6	
1		null Project ID	1001	1001	1001	1001	
2		null Project Name	Master of Power Query	Master of Power Query	Master of Power Query	Master of Power Query	
3		null Task	Promotional Materials (photos)	Promotional Materials (videos)	Advertisement	Videos	
4		null Responsible	Stephan	Stephan	Mary	Olive	
5	Sep	Hours	14	12	0	null	
6		null Costs	2000	3030	0	null	
7	Oct	Hours	8	16	14	8	

Figure 5.30: *Table after transposition*

Important: **The Transpose command (Figure 5.29) does not preserve original header names. The transposition occurs within the data area, and new columns are assigned default column names.**

This transformation is necessary because, unlike in the previous example, information about the months is located in a single column, and it needs to be associated with both the **Hours** and **Costs** values. Thanks to the transposition, the first column will now display the names of the months along with several **null** values. This is an ideal scenario because the column can be selected and the **Fill** command from the **Transform** tab expanded, then the **Down** option is selected (*Figure 5.11*). **Null** values at the beginning of the column will not be changed, as there is no fixed value above them.

To proceed with the transformation, follow these steps:

1. Select the first two columns in the transposed table.

2. Click the **Merge Columns** command on the **Transform** tab (*Figure 4.37*).

3. In the **Merge Columns** window, ensure that the **None** option is selected as the separator.

4. Leave the default name for the new merged column, as it will be removed in the next step.

5. Confirm the settings by clicking **OK**. These steps are illustrated in *Figure 5.31*:

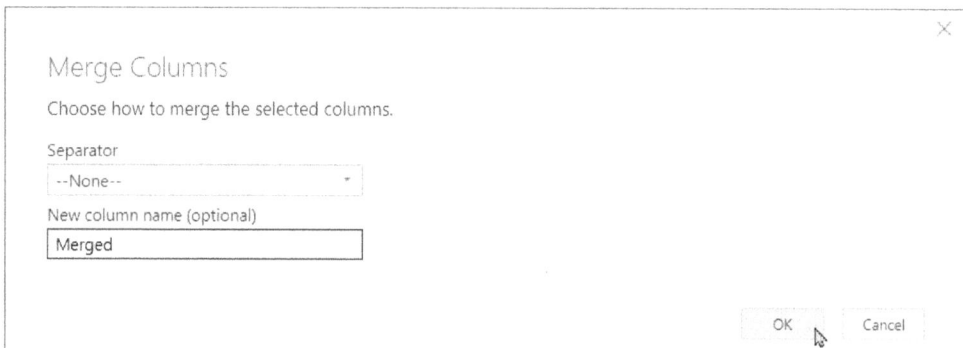

Figure 5.31: Merge Columns window

The data after merging the first two columns is shown in *Figure 5.32*:

	Merged	Column3	Column4	Col
1	Project ID	1001	1001	
2	Project Name	Master of Power Query	Master of Power Query	Master
3	Task	Promotional Materials (photos)	Promotional Materials (videos)	Adverti
4	Responsible	Stephan	Stephan	Mary
5	SepHours	14	12	
6	SepCosts	2000	3030	
7	OctHours	8	16	
8	OctCosts	1730	4810	

Figure 5.32: Data after merging

Important: **When a `null` value is concatenated with another text value, the result will be only the appended text. A separator, if used, may also appear before or after the appended text, depending on which side the null value was on during the concatenation process.**

Now, the **Transpose** command can be used again (*Figure 5.29*), followed by the **Use First Row as Headers** command, which can be accessed from the table's context menu (*Figure 1.8*). After this operation, Power Query should also automatically detect data types for each column. This step should now be retained because there is a clear and appropriate data type in each column.

At this point, the data looks nearly identical to the starting state of the previous example, so the same steps will be applied, as follows:

1. Select the last four columns in the table, which contain numeric values and potential **`nulls`**.
2. Click the **Replace Values** command from the **Home** tab (*Figure 5.19*).
3. In the **Replace Values** window (*Figure 5.21*), set the value to find as **`null`** and replace it with 0.
4. Confirm the changes by clicking **OK**.
5. Select the first four columns of the dataset.
6. Right-click on one of the selected headers and choose the **Unpivot Other Columns** option from the context menu (*Figure 5.17*).
7. Observe that, unlike in the previous example, the values in the **Attribute** column are now joined together without delimiters, as shown in *Figure 5.33*:

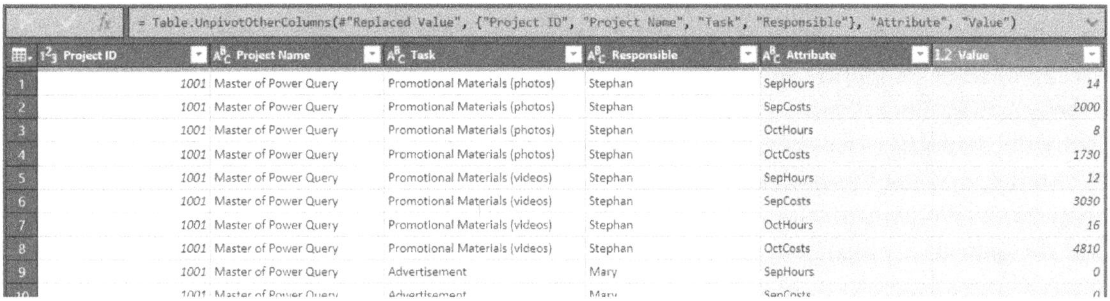

= Table.UnpivotOtherColumns(#"Replaced Value", {"Project ID", "Project Name", "Task", "Responsible"}, "Attribute", "Value")

	Project ID	Project Name	Task	Responsible	Attribute	Value
1	1001	Master of Power Query	Promotional Materials (photos)	Stephan	SepHours	14
2	1001	Master of Power Query	Promotional Materials (photos)	Stephan	SepCosts	2000
3	1001	Master of Power Query	Promotional Materials (photos)	Stephan	OctHours	8
4	1001	Master of Power Query	Promotional Materials (photos)	Stephan	OctCosts	1730
5	1001	Master of Power Query	Promotional Materials (videos)	Stephan	SepHours	12
6	1001	Master of Power Query	Promotional Materials (videos)	Stephan	SepCosts	3030
7	1001	Master of Power Query	Promotional Materials (videos)	Stephan	OctHours	16
8	1001	Master of Power Query	Promotional Materials (videos)	Stephan	OctCosts	4810
9	1001	Master of Power Query	Advertisement	Mary	SepHours	0
10	1001	Master of Power Query	Advertisement	Mary	SepCosts	0

Figure 5.33: Column Attribute with data without separator

Therefore, it is not possible to split these values based on a specific delimiter. Fortunately, in this example, abbreviated month names are used, consisting of three letters.

To correctly split the values in the **Attribute** column, follow these steps:

1. Select the **Attribute** column in the query.
2. On the **Home** tab, expand the **Split Column** command and choose **By Number of Characters** (*Figure 1.22*).

Fun fact: The Split Column command can only be used on one column at a time. If multiple columns are selected, this command will become inactive.

3. In the **Split Column by Number of Characters** window, enter the value **3** in the **Number of characters** field.

4. In the **Split** section, select the **Once, as far left as possible** radio button to ensure the value is only split after the first three characters.

5. Confirm the settings by clicking the **OK** button. A correctly completed window is shown in *Figure 5.34*:

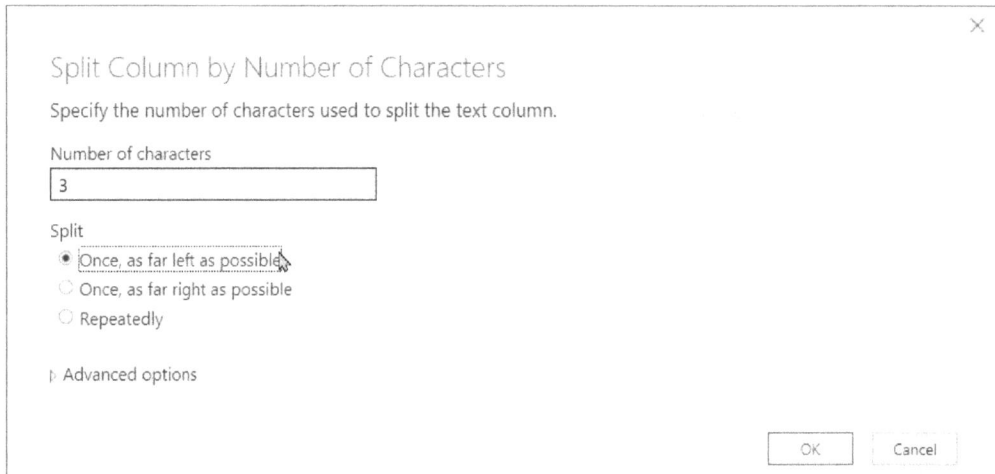

Figure 5.34: Split Column by Number of Characters window

TIP: Instead of using the Split Column command, you can achieve the same result by using functions like `Text.Start`, `Text.End`, or `Text.Middle` in a custom column. These functions allow you to extract a specific number of characters from the beginning, end, or middle of a text string, making them ideal for dynamic scenarios where a fixed split position might not be enough. This approach is also useful when you want to keep both the original column and the one containing the extracted text.

Power Query will create a column-splitting step, for which the M code should look as follows:

```
= Table.SplitColumn(#"Unpivoted Other Columns", "Attribute", Splitter.
SplitTextByPositions({0, 3}, false), {"Attribute.1", "Attribute.2"})
```

The editor will also add a step that changes the data type. However, in this example, that step does not provide any value, so it should be removed. The assigned column name in the M code should also be changed: the first column should be renamed from **Attribute.1** to **Month**. After this change, the M code should look as follows:

```
= Table.SplitColumn(#"Unpivoted Other Columns", "Attribute", Splitter.
SplitTextByPositions({0, 3}, false), {"Month", "Attribute.2"})
```

In newer versions of Power Query, the **By Lowercase to Uppercase** option can also be used. Selecting this option will not open a new window but instead will immediately generate a step using the following M code:

```
= Table.SplitColumn(#"Unpivoted Other Columns", "Attribute", Splitter.
SplitTextByCharacterTransition({"a".."z"}, {"A".."Z"}), {"Attribute.1",
"Attribute.2"})
```

The key element here is the function **Splitter.SplitTextByCharacterTransition**. Even if this option does not appear under the **Split Column** command (*Figure 1.22*), the column can still be split this way if the Power Query editor supports this function. The splitting will occur at each transition between the specified character lists.

Important: **The expression {"a".."z"} generates a list of lowercase English letters from a to z. More precisely, it generates a list of characters from letter a to letter z based on their Unicode values. The two dots represent the list-generation operator, and the curly braces indicate a list. It is also possible to concatenate lists in this way. For example: {"a".."z", "A".."Z", 0..9} will generate a list of lowercase letters, then uppercase letters, and finally numbers from 0 to 9. These character sequences will be combined into one larger list.**

The following steps outline how to complete the transformation and load the data:

1. Select the **Attribute.2** column in the query.
2. On the **Transform** tab, click the **Pivot Column** command (*Figure 5.23*).
3. In the **Pivot Column** window, choose the **Value** column as the values column to populate the new headers (*Figure 5.24*).
4. Rename the query to a meaningful name, such as **Proper Headers 2**.
5. Load the transformed data into Excel.

The result should closely resemble the outcome of the previous example, with the only difference being the presence of zeroes instead of empty text strings in previously **null** cells.

Transforming repeated rows to columns

We are working with data from the **Repeated Rows** worksheet in the **Pivot and unpivot. xlsx** file. The table in *Figure 5.35* contains only two columns; however, this data should be split into five separate columns to form a proper data range or table. Some rows should also be filtered out.

	A	B
1	Parametr/Column name	Value
2	Name	Stephan
3	Date of employment	18/05/2013
4	Hourly rate	$30
5	Number of hours worked	85
6	Total cost	$2,550
7		
8	Sum:	$2,550
9		
10	Name	Richard
11	Date of employment	07/06/2014
12	Hourly rate	$25
13	Number of hours worked	40
14	Total cost	$1,000
15		
16	Sum:	$1,000

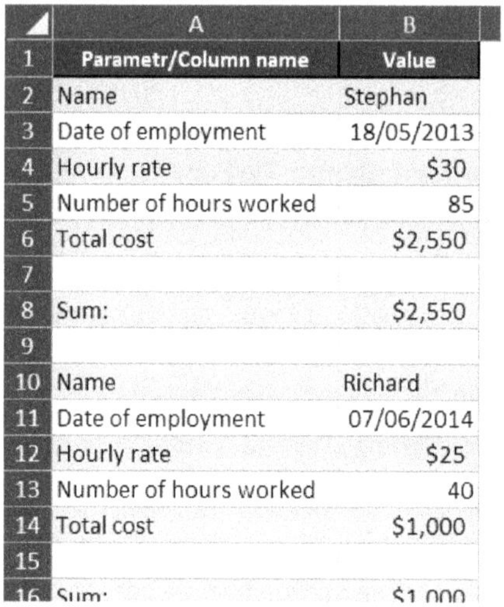

Figure 5.35: Data to be split into appropriate columns

The process of cleaning and filtering the data in Power Query includes the following steps:

1. Import the data using the **From Table/Range** command from the **Data** tab (*Figure 1.1*).
2. Locate the column named **Parametr/Column name**, which contains rows with either `null` values or `blank` entries represented by empty text strings from Excel.
3. Expand the filter for that column, as shown in *Figure 5.36*:

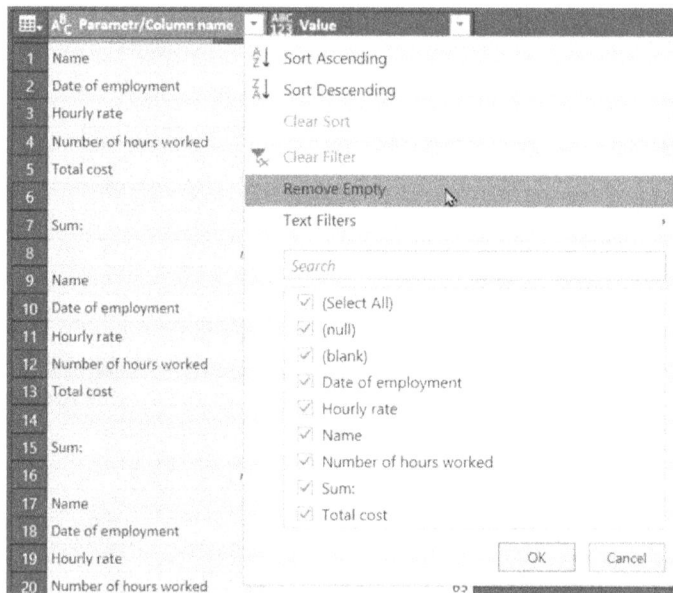

Figure 5.36: Filter for the Parametr/Column name column

4. In the filter window, click the **Remove Empty** option to exclude both **null** and **blank** values.

5. Confirm the filter step, which adds the following M code:

```
= Table.SelectRows(#"Changed Type", each [#"Parametr/Column name"] <>
null and [#"Parametr/Column name"] <> "")
```

6. This expression ensures that only rows with meaningful values in the **Parametr/Column name** column are retained for further transformations.

We can see that Power Query, for each row (keyword **each**), checks whether the value is different (**not equal** operator as in Excel: **<>**) from **null**, and also (keyword **and**) different from the empty text string represented in the code as two double quotation marks (in the filter in *Figure 5.36* labeled as **blank**).

These are not the only values we want to filter out. We also want to exclude cells with the text **Sum:**. We can add this condition by reopening the filter and deselecting this value from the list, or we can add the appropriate code fragment, similar to the one previously discussed. After this modification, the M code for the step should be as follows:

```
= Table.SelectRows(#"Changed Type", each ([#"Parametr/Column name"] <> null
and [#"Parametr/Column name"] <> "" and [#"Parametr/Column name"] <> "Sum:"))
```

Power Query is case-sensitive when evaluating such conditions.

Tip: **If a column name contains a special character (e.g., space, slash, etc.), Power Query might enclose the name in double quotation marks and precede it with a hash sign. For example: [#"Parametr/Column name"]. In the case of step names, this is required. However, when referring to column names, it should be sufficient to enclose the column name in square brackets.**

The following steps describe how to pivot the cleaned data in Power Query:

1. After removing unnecessary rows, verify that only the relevant data remains in the table.

2. Select the **Parametr/Column name** column.

3. On the **Transform** tab, click the **Pivot Column** command (*Figure 5.23*).

4. In the **Pivot Column** window that appears, expand **Advanced options**.

5. From the **Aggregate Value Function** drop-down list, select the **Don't Aggregate** option, as shown in *Figure 5.37*:

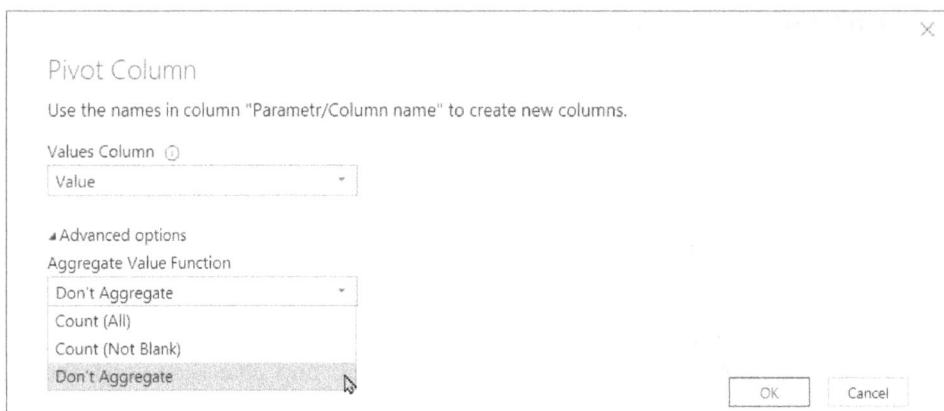

Figure 5.37: Pivot Column window with the expanded Aggregate Value Function list

6. Confirm the transformation to pivot the data without applying any aggregation to the values.

The list of available aggregation methods depends on the data type in the column selected in the **Values Column** list.

After performing the **Pivot Column** operation without aggregation, the next step will return errors for all columns. When one of the columns is selected, the following error message appears:

Expression.Error: There were too many elements in the enumeration to complete the operation.

This occurs because Power Query groups values for each column (it creates a list of values) and is unable to place them correctly in a single column. It lacks row-level uniqueness. The simplest way to introduce uniqueness is to add an index column by clicking the **Index Column** command on the **Add Column** tab (*Figure 4.15*).

To correctly organize the pivoted data with a unique index, follow these steps:

1. Delete the **Pivoted Column** step from the **Applied Steps** pane.

2. Add a new step by creating an index column. This can be done either by using the **Add Column** tab and choosing the **Index Column** command, or by right-clicking the **Filtered Rows** step and inserting the step there, which will require confirmation.

3. Once the index column is added, return to the **Pivot Column** window (*Figure 5.36*) and reapply the pivoting operation.

4. After pivoting, observe the results. Each pivoted value will be in a separate row, which breaks the relationship between corresponding data values, as shown in *Figure 5.38*:

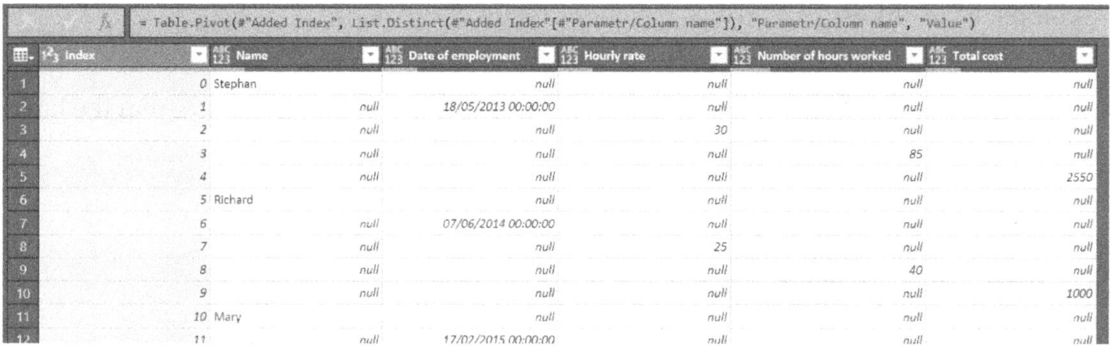

```
= Table.Pivot(#"Added Index", List.Distinct(#"Added Index"[#"Parametr/Column name"]), "Parametr/Column name", "Value")
```

	Index	Name	Date of employment	Hourly rate	Number of hours worked	Total cost
1	0	Stephan	null	null	null	null
2	1	null	18/05/2013 00:00:00	null	null	null
3	2	null	null	30	null	null
4	3	null	null	null	85	null
5	4	null	null	null	null	2550
6	5	Richard	null	null	null	null
7	6	null	07/06/2014 00:00:00	null	null	null
8	7	null	null	25	null	null
9	8	null	null	null	40	null
10	9	null	null	null	null	1000
11	10	Mary	null	null	null	null
12	11	null	17/02/2015 00:00:00	null	null	null

***Figure 5.38**: Data after pivoting columns with a unique index column*

5. To correct this issue, assign appropriate data types to the columns. Use either the **Detect Data Type** command on the **Transform** tab (*Figure 2.21*) or manually adjust them, ensuring that **Date of employment** is set to **Date**.

6. Select the last four columns and apply the **Fill Up** command from the **Transform** tab (*Figure 5.11*).

7. Confirm that the top row of each group now contains all correctly filled-in values, as shown in *Figure 5.39*:

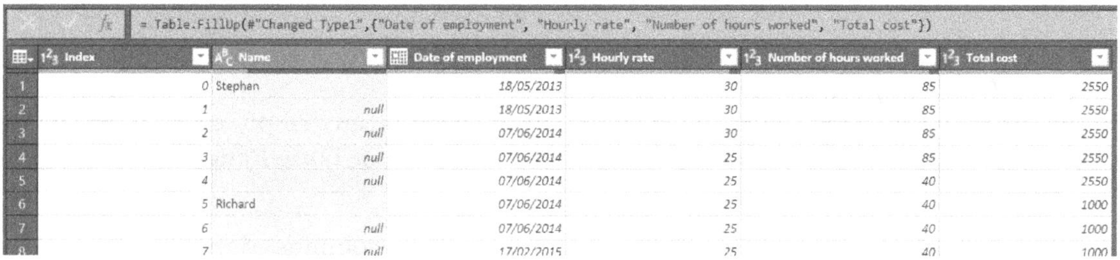

```
= Table.FillUp(#"Changed Type1",{"Date of employment", "Hourly rate", "Number of hours worked", "Total cost"})
```

	Index	Name	Date of employment	Hourly rate	Number of hours worked	Total cost
1	0	Stephan	18/05/2013	30	85	2550
2	1	null	18/05/2013	30	85	2550
3	2	null	07/06/2014	30	85	2550
4	3	null	07/06/2014	25	85	2550
5	4	null	07/06/2014	25	40	2550
6	5	Richard	07/06/2014	25	40	1000
7	6	null	07/06/2014	25	40	1000
8	7	null	17/02/2015	25	40	1000

***Figure 5.39**: Data after the Fill Up operation*

The **Name** column was intentionally excluded from the **Fill Up** operation so that it would retain its **`null`** values, which now need to be filtered out, just as was done previously (*Figure 5.36*). After this step, the result will include only valid rows with complete data, as shown in *Figure 5.40*:

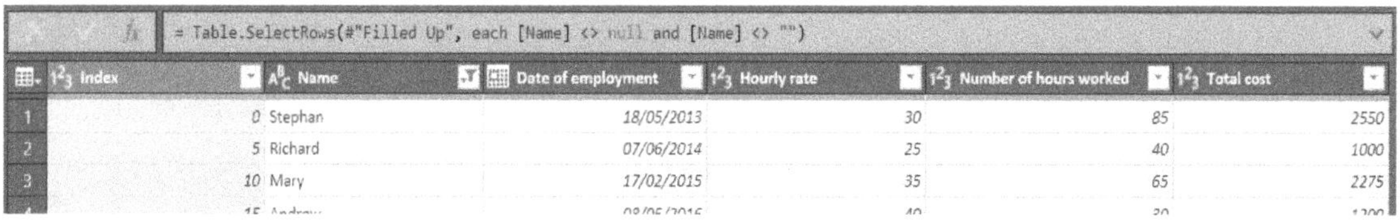

```
= Table.SelectRows(#"Filled Up", each [Name] <> null and [Name] <> "")
```

	Index	Name	Date of employment	Hourly rate	Number of hours worked	Total cost
1	0	Stephan	18/05/2013	30	85	2550
2	5	Richard	07/06/2014	25	40	1000
3	10	Mary	17/02/2015	35	65	2275

***Figure 5.40**: Data with correct data rows*

To complete the process and finalize the query, follow these steps:

1. Select the **Index** column that was used earlier for pivoting.
2. Press the **Delete** key on your keyboard to remove the selected column from the table.
3. Rename the query to **Repeated Rows** to reflect the transformation performed.
4. Load the cleaned and structured data into Excel.

Single row into multiple rows

We are working with the data from the **OneRow** worksheet in the `Pivot and unpivot.xlsx` file. The source table contains basic information about stores in selected cities. What is important here is that not every city has the same number of stores, so some rows are filled to the maximum length, while others describe only a single store. This structure is presented in *Figure 5.41*:

	A	B	C	D	E	F	G	H	I	J
1	Country	City	Shop1	Street1	Shop2	Street2	Shop3	Street3	Shop4	Street4
2	Poland	Warsaw	Zeta	Marszałkowska	Mino	Piłsudskiego	Lira	Puławska	Riko	Dolna
3	Italy	Rome	Tivo	Via del Corso						
4	Poland	Kielce	Luno	Sienkiewicza	Tiva	Warszawska				
5	Spain	Madrid	Nova	Gran Vía	Lumo	Calle de Alcalá	Zuno	Paseo del Prado		
6	France	Paris	Elix	Rue de Rivoli	Lumo	Rue de Rivoli				

Figure 5.41: Basic store data by city

We need to transform this data into a valid table and remove any empty cells. As usual, the first step is to import the data into Power Query using the **From Table/Range** command from the **Data** tab (*Figure 1.1*).

Once the data has been loaded, we can select the first two columns, right-click any of the selected column headers, and from the context menu, choose **Unpivot Other Columns**, just as we did in the earlier example (*Figure 5.17*).

In this example, it works to our advantage that the **Unpivot** operation ignores empty cells. As a result, the city names are repeated the appropriate number of times in the output. This is shown in *Figure 5.42*:

⊞▾	A^Bc Country	▾	A^Bc City	▾	A^Bc Attribute	▾	A^Bc Value	▾
1	Poland		Warsaw		Shop1		Zeta	
2	Poland		Warsaw		Street1		Marszałkowska	
3	Poland		Warsaw		Shop2		Mino	
4	Poland		Warsaw		Street2		Piłsudskiego	
5	Poland		Warsaw		Shop3		Lira	
6	Poland		Warsaw		Street3		Puławska	
7	Poland		Warsaw		Shop4		Riko	
8	Poland		Warsaw		Street4		Dolna	
9	Italy		Rome		Shop1		Tivo	
10	Italy		Rome		Street1		Via del Corso	
11	Poland		Kielce		Shop1		Luno	
12	Poland		Kielce		Street1		Sienkiewicza	

Figure 5.42: Data after the Unpivot operation

At this stage, the dataset resembles the previous example before applying the **Pivot** operation. However, the column names are still unique for each store (**Shop1, Shop2, …**), while we need them to be identical for the same type of data. In this example, newer versions of Power Query allow splitting values in the **Attribute** column at the transition from a letter to a digit by using the **Split Column** command on the **Home** tab and selecting the **By Non-Digit to Digit** option (*Figure 1.22*).

After choosing this option, Power Query will immediately generate a step with the following code:

```
= Table.SplitColumn(#"Unpivoted Other Columns", "Attribute", Splitter.
SplitTextByCharacterTransition((c) => not List.Contains({"0".."9"}, c),
{"0".."9"}), {"Attribute.1", "Attribute.2"})
```

This code even contains a generated inline function (**(c) => ...**), which will be explained in detail in *Chapter 9, Creating Custom Functions*.

At this point, the code can be modified so that the second column (with digits) is not created, as it seems unnecessary. Simply remove the name of the second column and the preceding comma. The modified code should look like the following:

```
= Table.SplitColumn(#"Unpivoted Other Columns", "Attribute", Splitter.
SplitTextByCharacterTransition((c) => not List.Contains({"0".."9"}, c),
{"0".."9"}), {"Attribute.1"})
```

If it were not possible to split the data into clearly defined components, we would need to manually generate an appropriate column. The easiest approach would start with adding an index column beginning from zero by selecting the **Index Column** command from the **Add Column** tab (*Figure 4.15*). Next, we would select this column and from the **Transform** tab, expand the **Standard** command and choose the **Modulo** option, as shown in *Figure 5.43*:

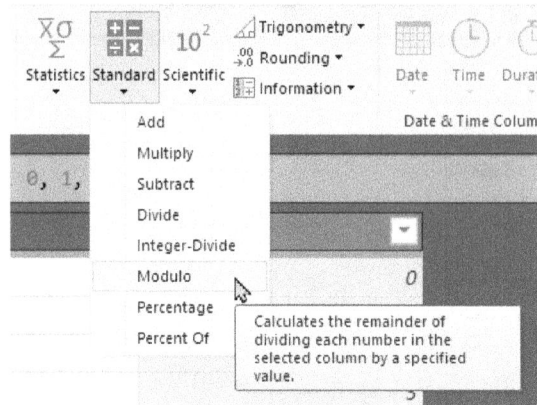

Figure 5.43: Standard Modulo operation

The following steps explain how to apply the modulo operation to divide data evenly between two columns that describe the store in a given city:

1. In the Power Query editor, open the **Modulo** window by selecting the appropriate column and navigating to the **Standard** operations under the **Transform** tab.

2. In the **Value** field of the **Modulo** window, enter **2**, as shown in *Figure 5.44*:

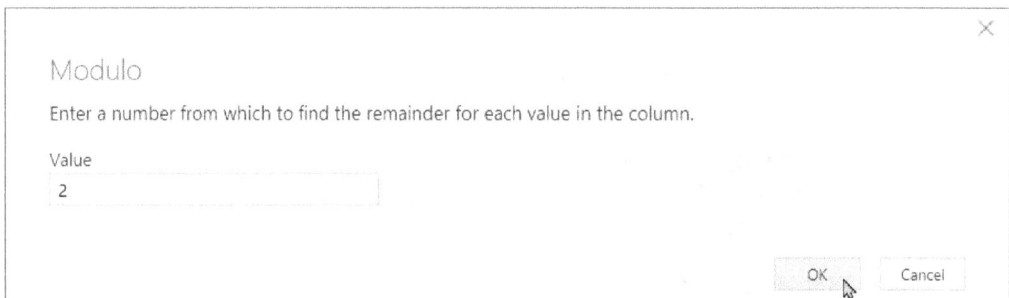

Figure 5.44: Modulo window

3. Confirm the operation by clicking **OK** to create a new column that assigns alternating values (0 or 1), which can be used to split the data into two distinct categories.

This will allow us to calculate the remainder after dividing the value in the **Index** column by the number we entered. This creates an association between a value from the **Value** column and a specific label. It works analogously to the situation with the **Attribute.1** column, where we already have the correct column names assigned.

In such a case, we would need to convert the numeric values in the column into valid column names using the **Replace Values** command on the **Home** tab (*Figure 5.19*) or, after performing the **Pivot**, rename the numeric columns to proper descriptive labels.

To ensure the proper grouping of column headers before pivoting, follow these steps:

1. Confirm that the data has been structured correctly and that all column headers are located in the **Attribute.1** column.

2. Add an index column by selecting the **Index Column** command from the **Add Column** tab (*Figure 4.15*). This will help group repeating values.

3. With the new index column selected, go to the **Transform** tab, expand the **Standard** command group, and choose **Integer-Divide**, as shown in *Figure 5.45*:

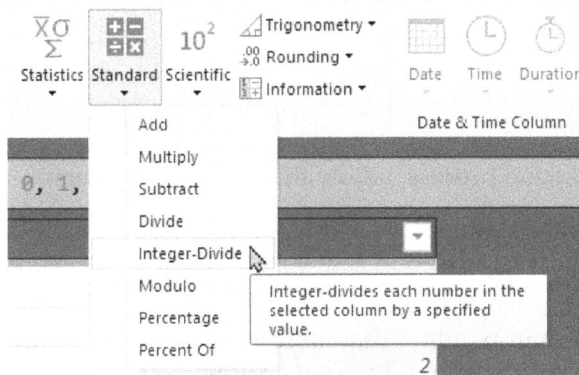

Figure 5.45: Standard Integer-Divide operation

4. In the **Integer-Divide** window that appears, enter the value **2** into the **Value** field (*Figure 5.46*), since each group of data is described by two columns.

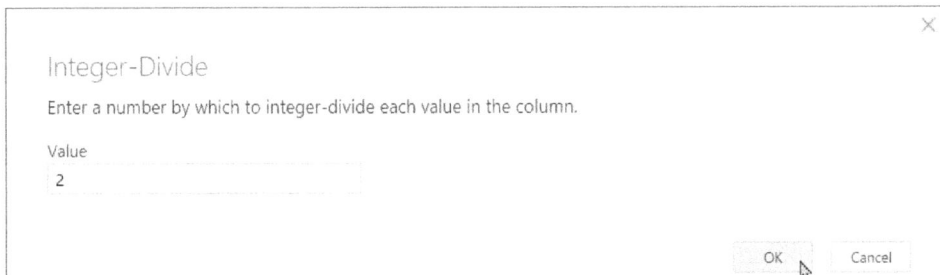

Figure 5.46: Integer-Divide window

5. Click **OK** to apply the transformation. This prepares the data for a correct pivot by creating a repeating group identifier.

This operation returns only the integer part of the division result of values from the **Index** column by the number provided. As a result, we create group identifiers for Power Query to recognize individual sets of data. This is illustrated in *Figure 5.47*:

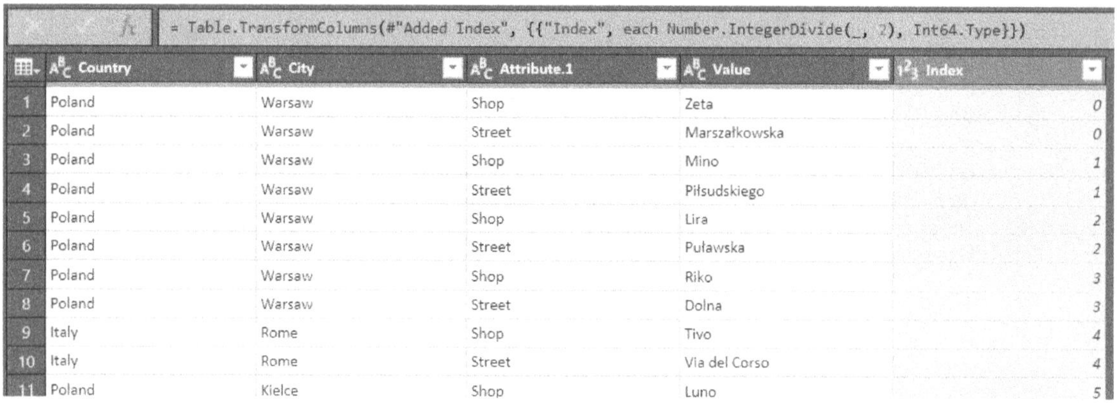

```
fx    = Table.TransformColumns(#"Added Index", {{"Index", each Number.IntegerDivide(_, 2), Int64.Type}})
```

▦▾	A^B_C Country	A^B_C City	A^B_C Attribute.1	A^B_C Value	1$^2_3$ Index
1	Poland	Warsaw	Shop	Zeta	0
2	Poland	Warsaw	Street	Marszałkowska	0
3	Poland	Warsaw	Shop	Mino	1
4	Poland	Warsaw	Street	Piłsudskiego	1
5	Poland	Warsaw	Shop	Lira	2
6	Poland	Warsaw	Street	Puławska	2
7	Poland	Warsaw	Shop	Riko	3
8	Poland	Warsaw	Street	Dolna	3
9	Italy	Rome	Shop	Tivo	4
10	Italy	Rome	Street	Via del Corso	4
11	Poland	Kielce	Shop	Luno	5

Figure 5.47: Groups of store information for cities

To finalize the transformation process, follow these remaining steps:

1. Select the **Attribute.1** column.

2. From the **Transform** tab, click the **Pivot Column** command (*Figure 5.23*).

3. In the **Pivot Column** window that appears, choose the **Value** column as the values to be distributed and, under **Advanced options**, select **Don't Aggregate** (*Figure 5.37*).

4. Confirm the transformation to pivot the data correctly.

5. Remove the **Index** column, as it is no longer needed.

6. Rename the query to **One Row**.

7. Load the final result into Excel.

Conclusion

This chapter introduced core techniques for pivoting and unpivoting data in Power Query, showing how to convert messy, report-style layouts into clean, structured tables. We addressed challenges like combined headers, repeated rows, and scattered values.

These transformations are key to preparing data for analysis and automation. In the next chapter, we will expand on this by creating custom columns and exploring Power Query's formula language.

Multiple choice questions

1. **Which Power Query command is used to reverse the effect of pivoting data?**

   a. Combine columns

   b. Merge queries

   c. Unpivot columns

   d. Expand table column

2. **What are the key steps in preparing a report for unpivoting?**

   a. Remove totals

   b. Promote headers

   c. Protect worksheet

   d. Fill down missing values

3. **What is the primary purpose of using the Fill Down command in Power Query?**

   a. To propagate values into null cells below

   b. To fill empty text values

   c. To delete unnecessary rows

   d. To group similar records

4. **In Power Query, null values:**

   a. Are treated the same as empty text strings

   b. Are automatically removed during unpivoting

   c. Represent missing data and can be filled or replaced

   d. Cannot be detected by filters

5. **What is a key reason to avoid loading a query result to the same worksheet as the source?**

   a. It may lead to errors or circular references

   b. Power Query does not allow it

   c. Excel will not save the file

   d. The workbook will close unexpectedly

6. **What are some benefits of using the Unpivot Other Columns command instead of selecting columns manually?**

   a. It automatically includes new columns added later

   b. It prevents the need for filtering

   c. It reduces the chance of missing relevant columns

   d. It simplifies M code maintenance

Answers

Question number	Answer option letter
1.	c.
2.	a., b., d.
3.	a.
4.	c.
5.	a.
6.	a., c., d.

CHAPTER 6
Adding Columns

Introduction

In the previous chapter, we explored how to reshape data using Power Query's pivot and unpivot transformations. Those tools allow reorganizing tables to better support analysis. We learned how to convert repeated values into columns and how to normalize wide datasets into structured formats.

This chapter explores key column transformation techniques in Power Query, essential for preparing data for analysis. We will learn how to calculate and round values, split text using custom delimiters. We will also learn how to extract and combine values using the **Column From Examples** feature, as well as how to handle durations and apply time rounding.

Structure

This chapter covers the following topics:

- Calculating and rounding discount
- Splitting data into rows
- Splitting a column by various delimiters
- Column from examples

- Calculating work time
- Rounding time

Objectives

By the end of this chapter, we will be able to perform calculations involving null values, apply rounding techniques to both numbers and time values, and split data into rows or columns using various delimiters. We will learn how to transform messy text fields into structured formats, extract useful components using examples, and calculate working time with rounding adjustments. These techniques will help us clean, restructure, and enhance datasets for more accurate analysis and reporting in Excel.

Calculating and rounding discount

In this chapter, we are working with data from the **AddingColumns.xlsx** file. We begin with an analysis of simple sales data, for which we need to calculate the total amount after applying a discount. The information is located in the **Sales2025** table on the **Simple** worksheet. It is shown in *Figure 6.1*:

	A	B	C	D	E
1	Date	Product	Quantity	Price	Discount
2	1/1/2025	Diamond	5	$5.00	0%
3	1/2/2025	Pearl	5	$5.00	
4	1/2/2025	Emerald	16	$1.22	13%
5	1/2/2025	Diamond	93	$5.00	8%
6	1/3/2025	Pearl	107	$25.00	8%
7	1/4/2025	Ruby	4	$2.00	8%
8	1/4/2025	Pearl	7	$25.00	0%
9	1/5/2025	Emerald	12	$1.00	15%
10	1/7/2025	Sapphire	7	$5.00	8%

Figure 6.1: Sales data with discount information

The first two rows in the table have been intentionally prepared so that the **Discount** column contains, respectively, a value of zero and an empty cell, which will appear in Power Query as a **null** value.

Since the data is located in an Excel table, it is sufficient to load it into the editor using the **From Table/Range** command from the **Data** tab (*Figure 1.1*). As is standard, the date column from Excel will be recognized as a **Date/Time** format. It is advisable to convert it to the **Date** format only.

Now, we can begin calculating the total amount after the discount.

The process for initiating the calculation of the total amount with discount involves the following steps:

1. Multiply the three columns: **Quantity**, **Price**, and **Discount**. This step does not produce the correct final value, but it enables a more efficient progression toward the intended result.

2. Select the columns, ensuring the order of selection matches the column order in the table.

3. Navigate to the **Add Column** tab.

4. Expand the **Standard** command.

5. Choose the **Multiply** option, as shown in *Figure 6.2*:

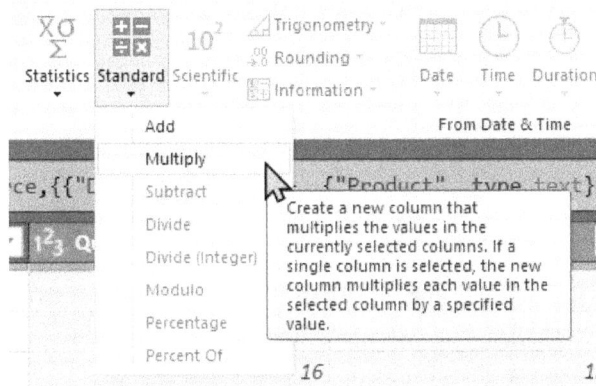

Figure 6.2: Standard command, Multiply option

Tip: **When more than two columns are selected, most options within the Standard command will become inactive (Figure 6.2).**

Power Query will add a column named **Multiplication**, where the values from the three selected columns are multiplied together. This is shown in *Figure 6.3*:

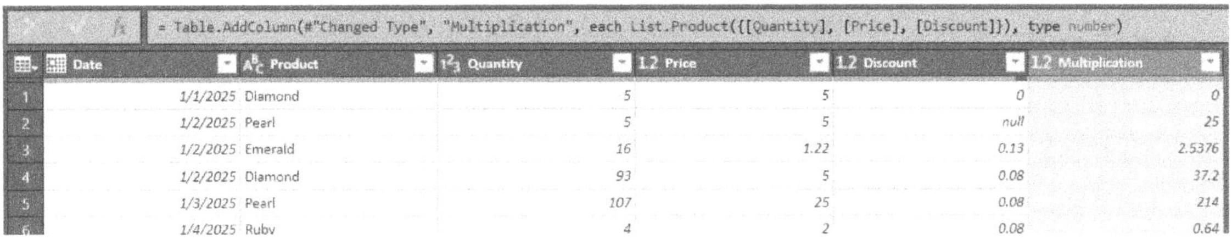

Figure 6.3: Multiplication results from three columns

Tip: **For the multiplication result (Figure 6.3), it does not matter that the values in the Discount column are not treated as percentages, as they were in Excel (Figure 6.1).**

Now, it is important to analyze the results, especially for the first two rows. We can see that the result in the first row is **0**, but in the second row, it is **25**, even though the values in the **Quantity** and **Price** columns are the same. The difference lies in the **Discount** column, but it is not the only factor. What also matters is the operation or function Power Query used to calculate the product. It can be seen in the formula bar. The full code is as follows:

```
= Table.AddColumn(#"Changed Type", "Multiplication", each List.
Product({[Quantity], [Price], [Discount]}), type number)
```

We can observe that the function `List.Product` was used. It multiplies the given list of elements. This is not stated in its official documentation, but it ignores **null** values. This means that for the first row, Power Query performed the multiplication **5 * 5 * 0**, while for the second row, it only calculated **5 * 5**. This results in a difference in the output.

Note: **If regular multiplication had been used instead of the `List.Product` function, the result for the second row (Figure 6.3) would have been null because the value from the Discount column would not have been ignored.**

Upon further analysis of the results, it becomes evident that they are incorrect. The **Discount** value should not be directly multiplied but instead subtracted from one (100%) and only then multiplied by the remaining values. At the same time, the default name of the new column can be changed to a more appropriate one, such as **Total Price**. After the modification, the code in the formula bar should look as follows:

```
= Table.AddColumn(#"Changed Type", "Total Price", each List.
Product({[Quantity], [Price], 1-[Discount]}), type number)
```

After confirming this formula, we will obtain correct results, as shown in *Figure 6.4*:

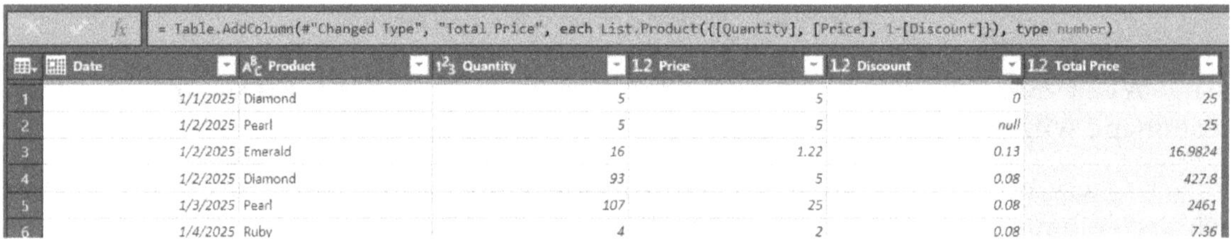

	Date	Product	Quantity	Price	Discount	Total Price	
1	1/1/2025	Diamond	5	5	0	25	
2	1/2/2025	Pearl	5	5	null	25	
3	1/2/2025	Emerald	16	1.22	0.13	16.9824	
4	1/2/2025	Diamond	93	5	0.08	427.8	
5	1/3/2025	Pearl	107	25	0.08	2461	
6	1/4/2025	Ruby	4	2	0.08	7.36	

Formula bar: `= Table.AddColumn(#"Changed Type", "Total Price", each List.Product({[Quantity], [Price], 1-[Discount]}), type number)`

Figure 6.4: Correct total price after discount

For the first row, Power Query now calculates **5 * 5 * (1 - 0)**, and for the second row, it still evaluates only **5 * 5** because in the subtraction **1 - null**, the result is **null**, which is ignored by the `List.Product` function.

The next transformation we will perform is related to the result in the third row (*Figure 6.3* and *Figure 6.4*). We can observe a number with four decimal places. Since we are dealing with prices, this value should be rounded to two decimal places (to the nearest cent).

To round the values in the Total Price column, the following steps are to be followed:

1. Select the **Total Price** column.

2. On the **Transform** tab, expand the **Rounding** command.

3. Select the **Round** option, as shown in *Figure 6.5*:

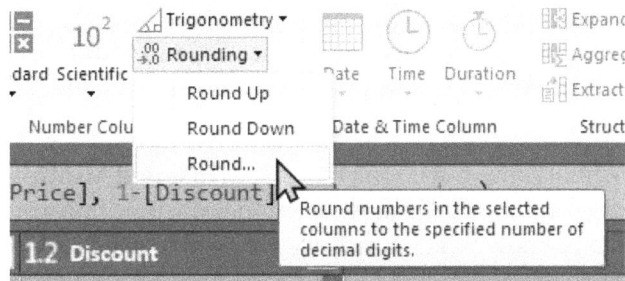

Figure 6.5: Rounding command from the Transform tab

Tip: **The Round Up and Round Down options (Figure 6.5) do not open a dialog window with options but immediately apply rounding up or down to whole numbers, respectively. They use Number.RoundUp and Number.RoundDown functions.**

The following steps explain how to apply rounding to the existing column without creating a new one:

1. Avoid using the **Rounding** command from the **Add Column** tab, since the objective is to transform the existing column rather than retain the original unrounded column alongside a new one.

2. Select the column containing the result to be rounded.

3. On the **Transform** tab, expand the **Rounding** command.

4. Choose the **Round** option.

5. The **Round** window will then appear, as shown in *Figure 6.6*:

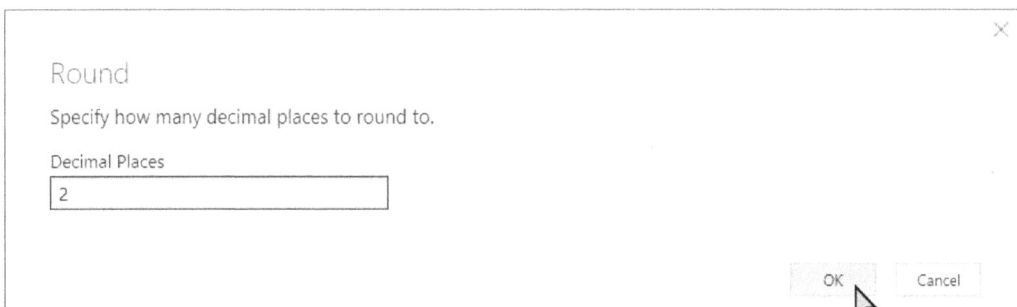

Figure 6.6: Round window

It is enough to enter **2** in the **Decimal Places** field and confirm the transformation by clicking the **OK** button in order to round the numbers to two decimal places. Power Query will add the appropriate step using the following rounding function:

```
= Table.TransformColumns(#"Inserted Multiplication",{{"Total Price", each
Number.Round(_, 2), type number}})
```

Tip: **We can enter the value 0 in the Decimal Places field to round to whole numbers, and by entering negative numbers, rounding is performed to tens, hundreds, thousands, and so on.**

We have calculated the final price, but it took two steps (**Inserted Multiplication** and **Rounded Off**) and additional transformations. Now, we want to write the appropriate formula ourselves in a single step. We already know which functions we need to use (`List.Product`, and `Number.Round`) from earlier transformations.

The following steps outline how to create a new column using a custom formula:

1. Click the **Custom Column** command on the **Add Column** tab (*Figure 3.6*).

2. The **Custom Column** window will open, as shown in *Figure 6.7*:

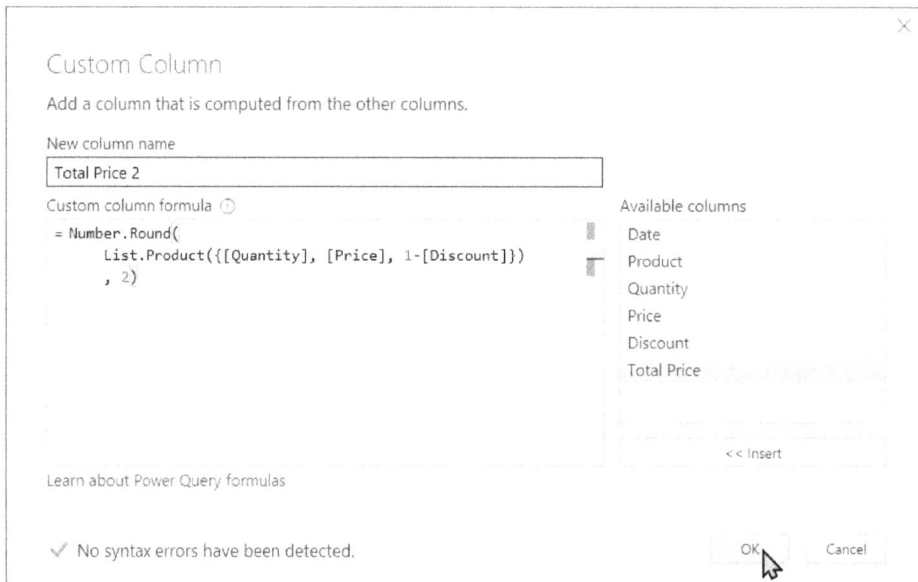

Figure 6.7: Custom Column window with whole formula

First, change the default column name (the value in the **New Column Name** field) to **Total Price 2**. Then, in the **Custom column formula** field below, we need to enter a formula that combines multiplication to calculate the discount using `List.Product({[Quantity], [Price], 1-[Discount]})` with `Number.Round` function.

The list of all column names (**Available columns**) on the right side of the window makes it easier to create the appropriate formula. Simply double-click any name to insert the correct column reference (the column name in square brackets). The full formula should be written as follows:

```
Number.Round(List.Product({[Quantity], [Price], 1-[Discount]}), 2)
```

If no syntax error has been made, a confirmation message will be displayed at the bottom of the window.

After confirming the formula by clicking the **OK** button, Power Query will insert a new column where the results will be the same as in the previously created column. This is shown in *Figure 6.8*:

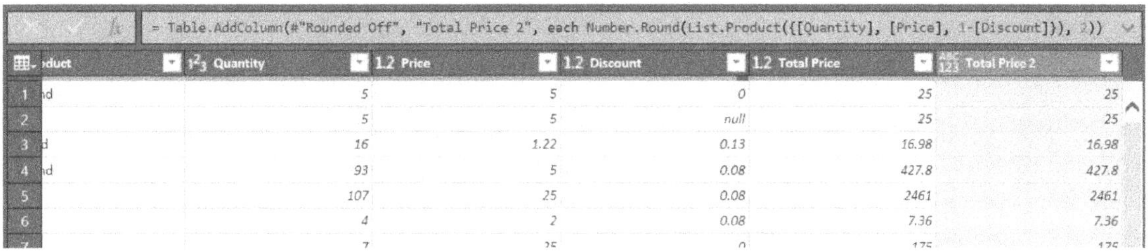

iduct	Quantity	Price	Discount	Total Price	Total Price 2	
1 nd	5	5	0	25	25	
2	5	5	null	25	25	
3 d	16	1.22	0.13	16.98	16.98	
4 nd	93	5	0.08	427.8	427.8	
5	107	25	0.08	2461	2461	
6	4	2	0.08	7.36	7.36	
7	7	25	0	175	175	

Formula bar: `= Table.AddColumn(#"Rounded Off", "Total Price 2", each Number.Round(List.Product({[Quantity], [Price], 1-[Discount]}), 2))`

Figure 6.8: Correct results in two columns

There is only a minor error related to the data type. The **Custom Column** command does not automatically assign a specific data type. This means that the newly created column stores data using the general data type (**ABC123/any**). For code optimization purposes, we should append a data type argument (**type number**) at the end of the **Table.AddColumn** function used in this step. After making this change, the code for this step should look as follows:

```
= Table.AddColumn(#"Rounded Off", "Total Price 2", each Number.Round(List.
Product({[Quantity], [Price], 1-[Discount]}), 2), type number)
```

When we do not yet have experience with Power Query functions, we can confidently use the user interface to obtain the desired result. However, for optimization purposes (including the number of steps), it is necessary to learn how to modify the M code displayed in the formula bar and how to nest functions.

At this point, all that remains is to rename the query and optionally remove the **Price**, **Quantity**, and **Discount** columns, as they are no longer relevant (no further transformations will be applied to them, and they do not need to be displayed).

After this, the data can be loaded into Excel.

Splitting data into rows

This example uses data from the **tClasses** table on the **Row** worksheet. The table contains information about classes and individuals attending them. It is shown in *Figure 6.9*:

	A	B	C	D
1	Class ID	Class Name	Category	List of people registered
2	1102	Eggcellent Omelettes 101	Cooking	Grace, Sophia, Emma,
3	1203	Serial Grillers	Cooking	James, Elizabeth, Lily,
4	1305	Potheads	Pottery	James, Alexander, Isabella, Emma,
5	1407	Knit Happens	Knitting	Olivia, James, Thomas, Emma, Charlotte, William, Edward
6	1511	Hammer Time	Woodworking	Grace, Henry, Olivia, Isabella, Thomas
7	1613	Crochet All Day	Crocheting	Isabella, Charlotte, Elizabeth
8	1717	Board to be Wild	Woodworking	Lily, Elizabeth, Charlotte
9	1819	Birdhouse Builders Anonymous	Woodworking	Elizabeth, James, Olivia, William, Samuel, Edward, Sophia, Emma
10	1923	Drama Llamas	Theater	Henry, Sophia, Isabella, Samuel, Lily
11	2029	Plant Parenthood	Gardening	Sophia, Lily, Charlotte, William, Isabella

Figure 6.9: Data on classes with minor errors

The task is to extract information from this data, showing how many and which classes each person is registered for. Additionally, the **List of people registered** column contains minor errors that will need to be corrected during the data transformation process.

Since the data is stored in an Excel table, it can be imported into the editor using the **From Table/Range** command from the **Data** tab (*Figure 1.1*).

After loading the data, it is noticeable that the last column is wider than the others. This is shown in *Figure 6.10*:

	Class ID	Class Name	Category	List of people registered
1	1102	Eggcellent Omelettes 101	Cooking	Grace, Sophia, Emma,
2	1203	Serial Grillers	Cooking	James, Elizabeth, Lily,
3	1305	Potheads	Pottery	James, Alexander, Isabella, Emma,
4	1407	Knit Happens	Knitting	Olivia, James, Thomas, Emma, Charlotte, William, Edward

Figure 6.10: Data loaded into Power Query

Tip: **The width of a column can be adjusted by clicking and dragging its edge with the left mouse button. In newer versions of Power Query, each column has a minimum width, which is determined by the properties of the data it contains. These properties will be discussed in more detail in Chapter 7, Logical Operations and Conditional Columns.**

The focus now needs to be on the **List of people registered** column. Specifically, this column should be selected, then the **Split Column** command from the **Home** tab should be expanded, and the **By Delimiter** option selected (*Figure 1.22*).

In the **Split Column by Delimiter** window that appears, the advanced options will need to be expanded. There, radio buttons will be visible that allow choosing whether to split the data into columns or into rows. By default, the data is split into columns, and in this example, the result would be 8 columns. This is shown in *Figure 6.11*:

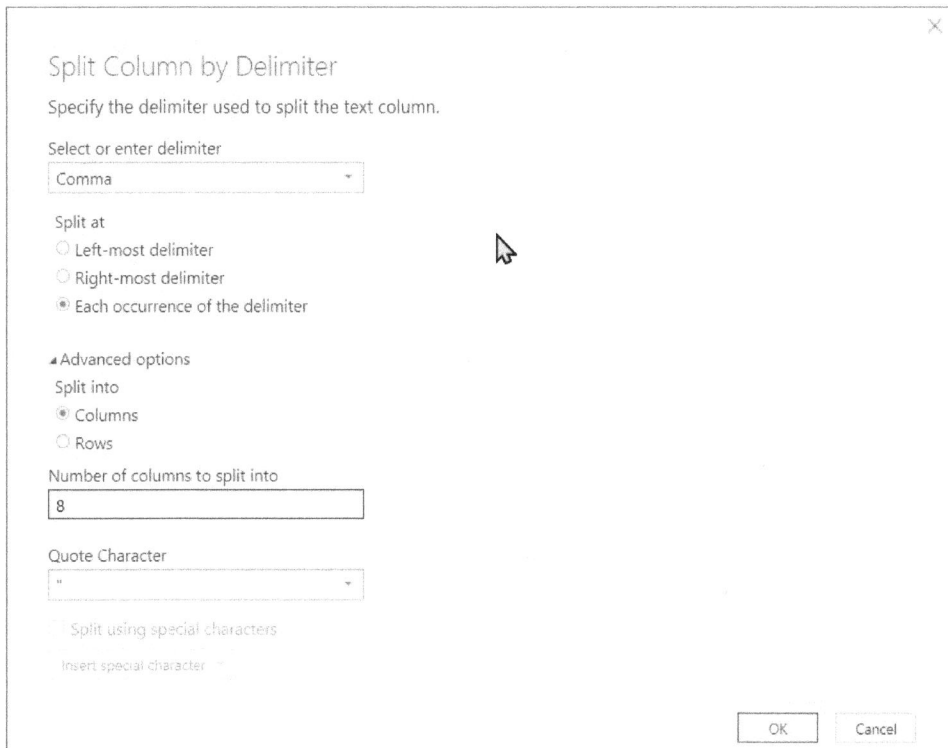

Figure 6.11: Advanced column splitting options

We can also observe that Power Query has selected **Comma** as the default delimiter. Unfortunately, this is not the correct delimiter because the values in the **List of people registered** column are separated by two characters: a comma and a space. Therefore, the **Custom** option must be selected, and the correct delimiter should be entered in the field below.

It is also important to avoid splitting the data into columns. The main reason is that when splitting into columns, Power Query imposes a limit on the number of columns created. In this case, eight. If more people were registered for a class, some of the entries would be lost during the column split. Therefore, a much safer solution in this case is to choose the option to split into **rows**, which does not have such limitations. This approach also simplifies further transformations.

At the bottom of the window, there is a **Quote Character** field. This option is useful when the data contains text that includes the chosen delimiter, but the delimiter should not be considered for splitting. If the text is enclosed in double quotation marks, all characters within will be ignored during the split. In most examples, there is no need to change this setting.

Following that is an option to split by special characters. These were previously discussed (*Table 4.1*). In this example, this option is not needed. The correctly filled **Split Column by Delimiter** window is shown in *Figure 6.12*:

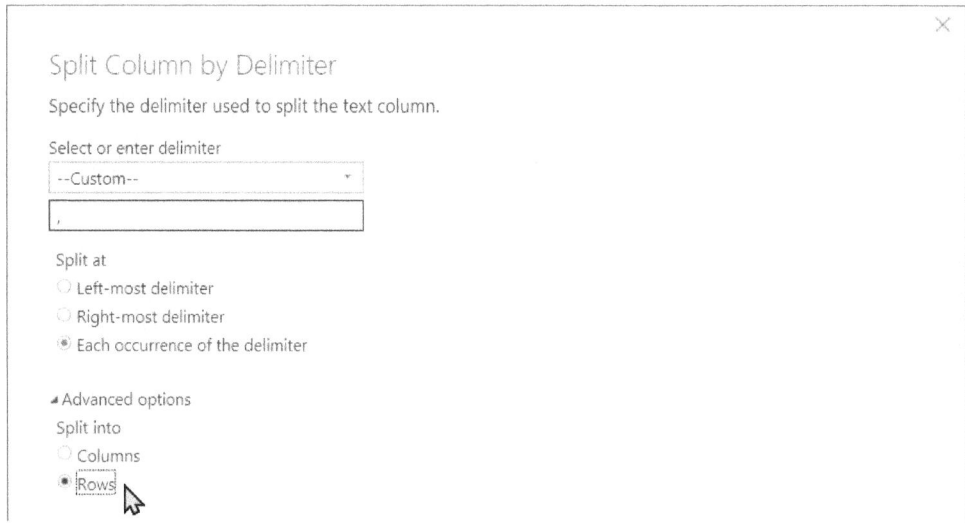

Figure 6.12: *Properly filled Split Column by Delimiter window*

After confirming the selected options by clicking the **OK** button, we obtain a table shown in *Figure 6.13*:

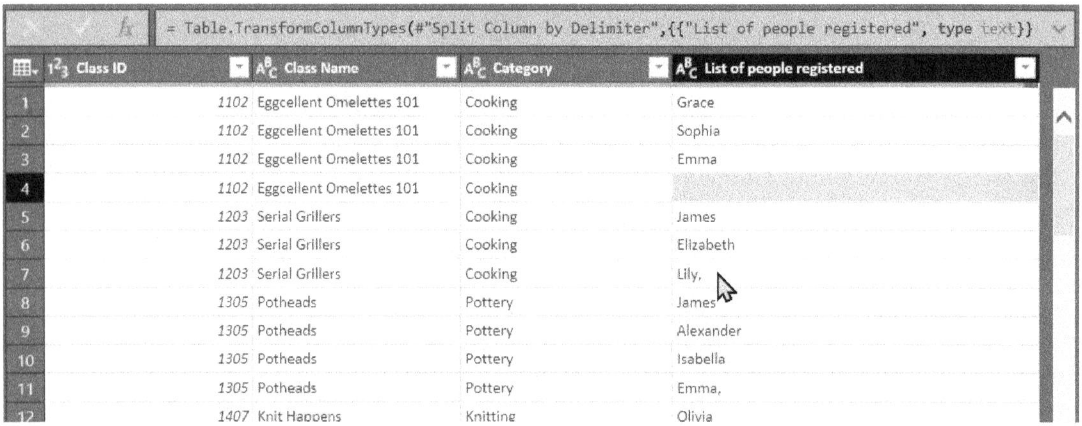

Figure 6.13: *Table after splitting a column by delimiter into rows*

If a step appears that changes the data types for the columns, it can be removed because the transformed column has already been assigned the text data type. We follow the same approach in similar situations.

Next, we can observe several issues in the data. First, in the fourth row, there is an empty cell. In the seventh and eleventh rows, we can see a comma after the name of the registered person. This is an unacceptable situation because the additional character will prevent these names from being grouped correctly with their other occurrences.

Both of these issues stem from errors in the source data (*Figure 6.9*). In the first row, at the end of the data in the **List of people registered** column, a comma followed by a space is included, which is our entire delimiter. This causes a split into a new row. Since there are no characters after the delimiter, Power Query inserts a blank value.

In the second and third rows, only a comma is present at the end, so no new row is created, but the trailing character is considered part of the name/value returned to the row.

If possible, we should correct the source data by removing the unnecessary characters, but for this example, we assume that we do not have that option. Therefore, we need to add transformations that will correct the erroneously added characters.

The steps to remove the commas from the column are as follows:

1. Select the column that contains the values to be cleaned.
2. On the **Home** tab, click the **Replace Values** command (*Figure 5.19*).
3. In the **Replace Values** window that appears, type a comma in the **Value To Find** field.
4. Leave the **Replace With** field empty.
5. Confirm the changes to apply the transformation.

This is shown in *Figure 6.14*:

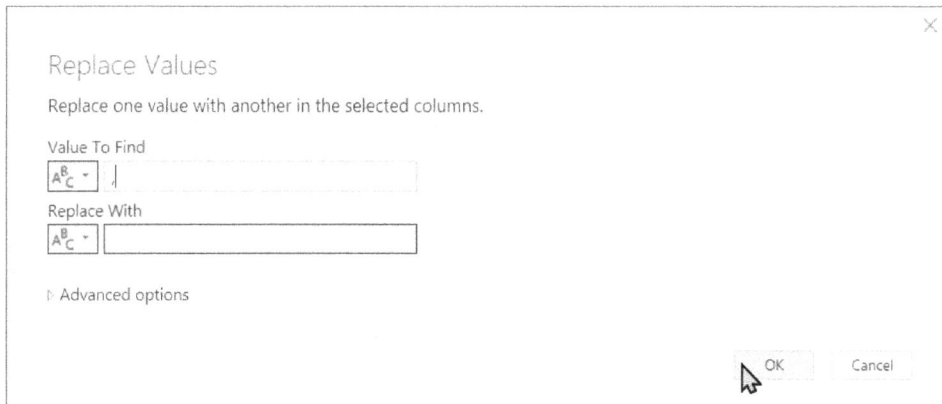

Figure 6.14: Removing a comma using the Replace Values window

After confirming the option by clicking the **OK** button, the editor will remove the commas. More precisely, it will replace them with blank values, but the result will be the same.

The next correction will involve filtering out empty rows. It is enough to expand the filter window for the **List of people registered** column and choose the **Remove Empty** option, just as we did in previous examples (*Figure 5.36*).

The steps to group the data based on the **List of people registered** column are as follows:

1. Select the List of people registered column.

2. Go to the **Home** tab.

3. Click the **Group By** command (*Figure 4.4*).

Next, as we learned in *Chapter 4, Grouping Data*, we need to properly fill in the **Group By** window. First of all, we need to switch to **Advanced** options because we want to perform two aggregations. The first is a simple row count, which we will name **Number of classes**. In the second, we need to retrieve **All Rows**, which we will name **Classes**. This aggregation will need to be modified in the formula bar (we will change its M code). The properly filled-in **Group By** window is shown in *Figure 6.15*:

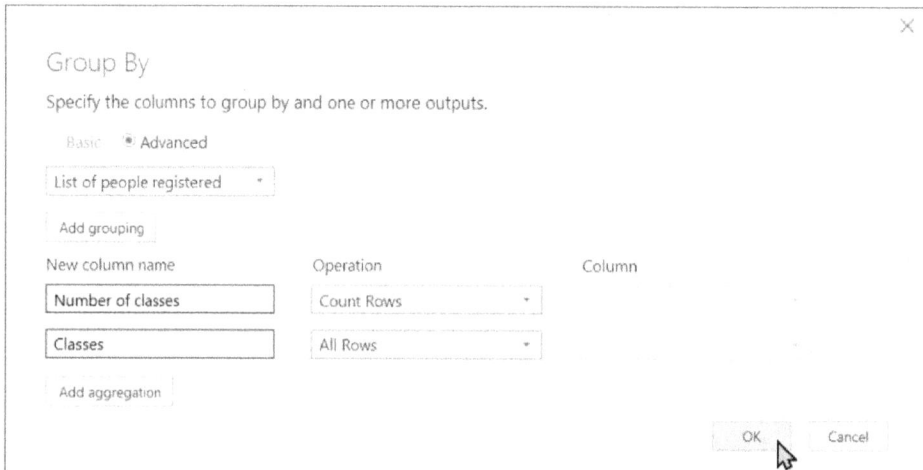

Figure 6.15: *Filled-in Group By window*

After grouping, we obtain a table consisting of three columns. The first contains the name of the person registered for classes. The second contains the calculated number of classes the person is attending. The third column includes the rows from the table that are related to the given person. This is shown in *Figure 6.16*:

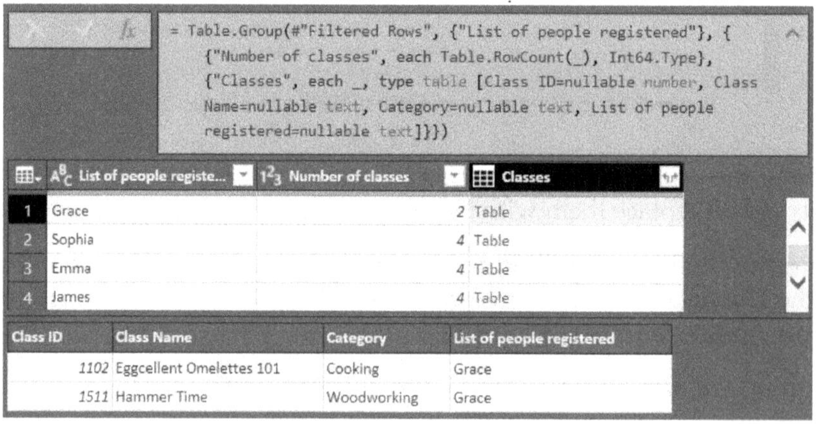

Figure 6.16: *Grouped data*

We do not need an entire table in the third column, but rather just a column with the class names. Therefore, we need to modify the code in the formula bar. Specifically, we must replace the underscore with the column name (written in square brackets) and change the data type from a table with a detailed schema to a list. So, instead of the following code:

```
= Table.Group(#"Filtered Rows", {"List of people registered"}, {{"Number of
classes", each Table.RowCount(_), Int64.Type}, {"Classes", each _, type table
[Class ID=nullable number, Class Name=nullable text, Category=nullable text,
List of people registered=nullable text]}})
```

We should have the following:

```
= Table.Group(#"Filtered Rows", {"List of people registered"}, {{"Number of
classes", each Table.RowCount(_), Int64.Type}, {"Classes", each [Class Name],
type list}})
```

This will result in a list of classes for each person. This is shown in *Figure 6.17*:

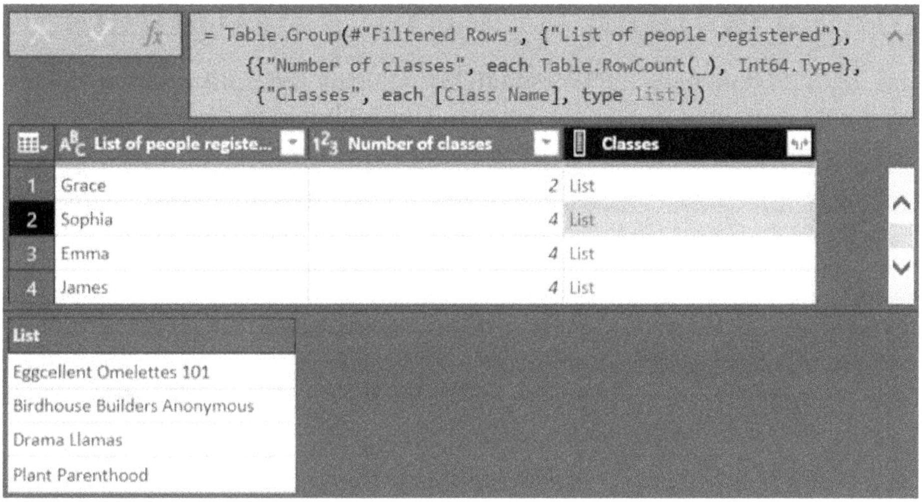

Figure 6.17: Class list for a sample participant

Now, it is sufficient to expand the column by clicking the arrow icon in the header and selecting the **Extract Values** option (*Figure 4.9*). In the **Extract values from list** window that appears, enter a comma and a space as the delimiter for concatenating data (*Figure 4.10*).

After confirming the expansion of the list, we can manually shorten or rename the first column to **Attendee** (simply double-click the column header and enter the new name). This could not have been done in the previous step in the formula bar because the original column name was required for the grouping to function correctly. This will produce the desired result, as shown in *Figure 6.18*:

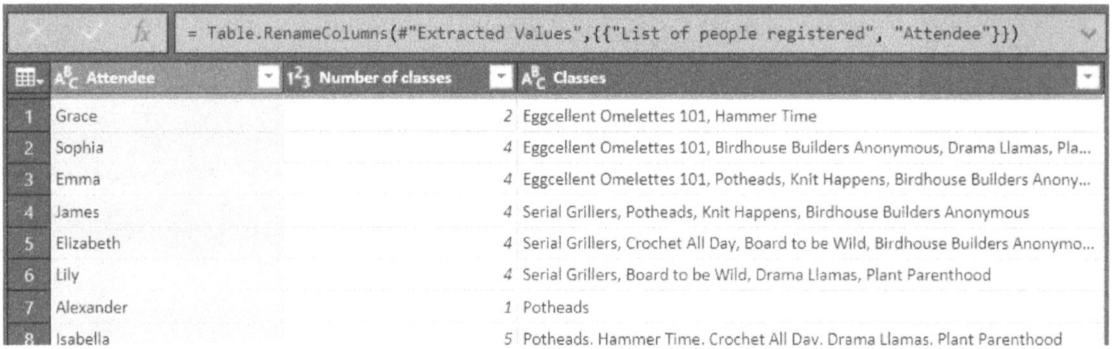

Figure 6.18: Table after the final transformation

All that remains is to rename the query to **AttendeeClasses** and load the result into Excel.

Splitting a column by various delimiters

We are working with data from the **tPersonalData** table on the **Split** worksheet. Here, we see concatenated data contained in a single column. This is shown in *Figure 6.19*:

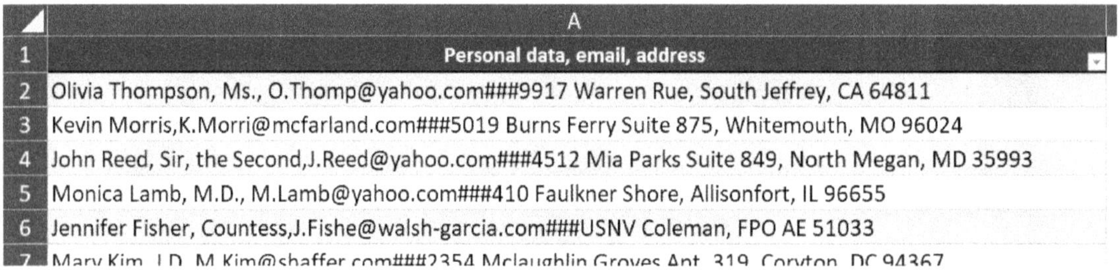

Figure 6.19: Concatenated data in a single column

Our task is to split this data so that each piece of information ends up in the appropriate column. Ultimately, we want to have four columns containing what we will identify as **Personal data**, **email**, **address**, and **honorifics**.

The process of splitting the data into columns using the proper delimiter consists of the following steps:

1. Import the data from the Excel table using the **From Table/Range** command on the **Data** tab (*Figure 1.1*).

2. Observe that the data contains many commas, but they are not used consistently as delimiters.

3. The data is not enclosed in double quotation marks, so the **Quote Character** option in the **Split Column by Delimiter** window (*Figure 6.11*) cannot be applied effectively.

4. Identify a unique and consistent delimiter: a sequence of three hash symbols (**###**).

5. Click the **Split Column** command from the **Home** tab.

6. Select the **By Delimiter** option (*Figure 1.22*).

7. In the **Split Column by Delimiter** window, observe that Power Query may automatically select the hash symbol (**#**) as the custom delimiter.

8. Modify the delimiter input to the full sequence **###** to ensure correct splitting.

9. Avoid accepting the default single-character delimiter, which would result in four columns, two of which would be empty due to the adjacent delimiter characters.

Tip: Information about the number of columns that will be created is available after expanding the Advanced Options section in the Split Column by Delimiter window, as shown in Figure 6.11.

Therefore, in this example, it is necessary to enter the sequence of three hash symbols (**###**) as a single delimiter. For this type of delimiter, the **Split at** setting does not matter since the delimiter appears only once in the data. After the split, we will obtain two columns of data, as shown in *Figure 6.20*:

```
= Table.SplitColumn(#"Changed Type", "Personal data, email, address",
    Splitter.SplitTextByDelimiter("###", QuoteStyle.Csv), {"Personal data, email,
    address.1", "Personal data, email, address.2"})
```

Aᴮ꜀ Personal data, email, address.1	Aᴮ꜀ Personal data, email, address.2
Olivia Thompson, Ms., O.Thomp@yahoo.com	9917 Warren Rue, South Jeffrey, CA 64811
Kevin Morris,K.Morri@mcfarland.com	5019 Burns Ferry Suite 875, Whitemouth, MO 96024
John Reed, Sir, the Second,J.Reed@yahoo.com	4512 Mia Parks Suite 849, North Megan, MD 35993
Monica Lamb, M.D., M.Lamb@yahoo.com	410 Faulkner Shore, Allisonfort, IL 96655
Jennifer Fisher, Countess, J.Fishe@walsh-garcia.com	USNV Coleman, FPO AE 51033

Figure 6.20: Data split by the hash sequence

We can observe that the second column contains the full address, which corresponds exactly to one of the target columns we intended to extract. Therefore, it is recommended to immediately rename this column in the formula bar to a shorter name, **Address**, instead of keeping the default full column name with a numeric suffix (**Personal data, email, address.2**).

The process of splitting the column **Personal data, email, address.1** into two separate columns consists of the following steps:

1. Replace the text between the double quotation marks to assign a clear name to the second column, such as **Address**.

2. Prepare to split the **Personal data, email, address.1** column into two new columns: one for personal data and one for the email address.

3. Open the **Split Column** command from the **Home** tab.

4. Select the **By Delimiter** option.

5. In the **Split Column by Delimiter** window (*Figure 6.11*), choose the last comma as the delimiter by setting the split option to split at the right-most delimiter.

6. Confirm that the earlier split (shown in *Figure 6.20*) was necessary to isolate this part of the data for accurate processing.

7. Execute the split to produce two new columns.

8. Review the result of this operation, as shown in *Figure 6.21*:

f_x	= Table.SplitColumn(#"Split Column by Delimiter", "Personal data, email, address.1", Splitter.SplitTextByEachDelimiter({","}, QuoteStyle.Csv, true), {"Personal data, email, address.1.1", "Personal data, email, address.1.2"})	
A^Bc Personal data, email, address.1.1	**A^Bc Personal data, email, address.1.2**	**A^Bc Address**
1 Olivia Thompson, Ms.	O.Thomp@yahoo.com	9917 Warren Rue, South Jeffrey, CA 64811
2 Kevin Morris	K.Morri@mcfarland.com	5019 Burns Ferry Suite 875, Whitemouth, MO 96024
3 John Reed, Sir, the Second	J.Reed@yahoo.com	4512 Mia Parks Suite 849, North Megan, MD 35993
4 Monica Lamb, M.D.	M.Lamb@yahoo.com	410 Faulkner Shore, Allisonfort, IL 96655
5 Jennifer Fisher, Countess	J.Fishe@walsh-garcia.com	USNV Coleman, FPO AE 51033

Figure 6.21: Result of splitting at the last comma

9. In the added step, within the formula bar, rename the newly created columns to **Personal data** and **email**, respectively.

It is important to note that in some rows containing email addresses, a leading space appears at the beginning (for example, the first and fourth rows, as seen in *Figure 6.21*). We have already learned how to remove unnecessary spaces from the beginning and end of text values. This can be done using the **Trim** option, available after expanding the **Format** command on the **Transform** tab (*Figure 1.40*).

All that remains is to create a column containing **honorifics**. However, we want to retain the existing first column (*Figure 6.21*) that stores the combined information. Therefore, we **cannot** use the **Split Column** command.

To extract the honorifics from the combined column, the following steps are to be followed:

1. Go to the **Add Column** tab in the Power Query editor.

2. Click the **Extract** command.

3. From the dropdown, select **Text After Delimiter** (*Figure 2.32*).

4. In the **Text After Delimiter** window that opens, enter a comma as the delimiter.

5. Optionally, enter a comma followed by a space if, after reviewing the source data

(*Figure 6.19*), it is confirmed that honorifics always follow this exact pattern after the full name.

6. Ensure that the delimiter setting reflects the correct structure of the data to extract the desired portion accurately.

Such an assumption can only be made because we are working with a small dataset, and we assume the structure of the data will remain unchanged. A safer approach would be to split on a comma only and then use the **Trim** option to remove any leading spaces.

The following steps outline how to configure the delimiter settings correctly when using the **Text After Delimiter** command:

1. Before adding the new column, expand the **Advanced options** in the **Text After Delimiter** window.

2. In the advanced settings, select whether to search for the delimiter from the start of the input or the end of the input.

3. In this case, choose the option to search from the start of the input, as the delimiter is expected to appear before the honorifics.

4. Confirm that the editor is set to extract the text following the selected delimiter.

5. Proceed to extract the desired portion of the text accordingly.

The correctly filled **Text After Delimiter** window is shown in *Figure 6.22*:

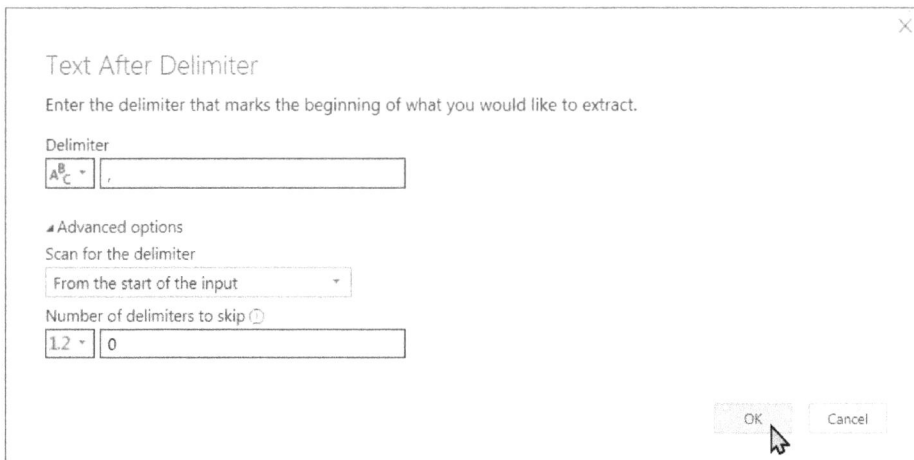

Figure 6.22: Text After Delimiter window

The results of the split are visible in *Figure 6.23*:

Figure 6.23: *Result of adding a column with data after the delimiter*

As in previous steps, it is a good idea to immediately change the default name of the column (**Text After Delimiter**) to **Honorifics** directly in the formula bar. Then, we must remember to remove excess spaces using the **Trim** option (*Figure 1.40*).

After this step, all that remains is to rename the query to **SplitData** and load it into Excel.

Column from examples

We are working with data from the **tFromExample** table on the **FromExample** worksheet. The source data consists of five columns, as shown in *Figure 6.24*. We will transform this data using the **Column From Examples** command, providing the output manually as examples for the new column.

Figure 6.24: *Source data for further transformation*

The process of preparing and using the **Column From Examples** command proceeds as follows:

1. As usual, load data from the Excel table using the **From Table/Range** command from the **Data** tab (*Figure 1.1*).

2. Change the data type of the **Date of Birth** column from **Date/Time** to **Date** only.

3. Go to the **Add Column** tab and expand the **Column From Examples** command.

4. Two options will appear: **From All Columns** and **From Selection**, as shown in *Figure 6.25*:

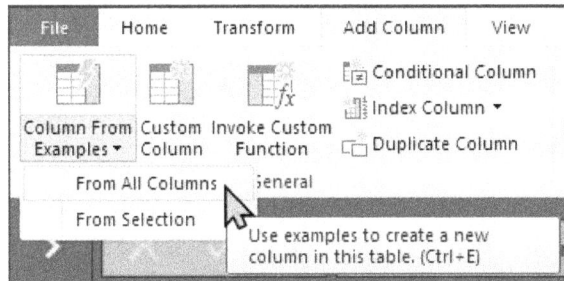

Figure 6.25: Expanded Column From Examples command

Fun fact: **The Column From Examples command is the only command discussed in this book from the Power Query editor tabs that has an assigned keyboard shortcut: Ctrl + E for all columns and Ctrl + Shift + E for selected columns.**

In reality, it does not make much difference which option is selected because during the process of creating a new column from examples, it is possible at any point to check or uncheck the columns to be considered in the formula creation. In the column headers, there will be checkboxes whose state determines whether the column is included in the generation of the new column formula. These checkboxes, along with the view for creating the new column after clicking the **Column From Examples** command, are shown in *Figure 6.26*:

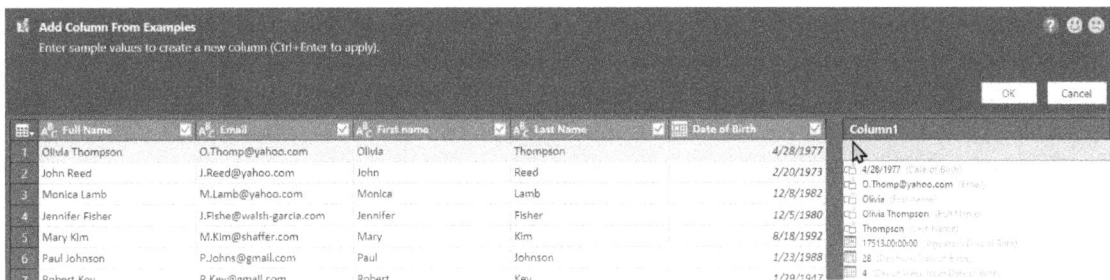

Figure 6.26: View of creating a new column from examples

Columns with the most basic transformations can be selected by double-clicking on any cell in the new column. A portion of the list of available transformations can be seen on the right side of *Figure 6.26*. In addition to the value that will be inserted for the selected row, the editor also describes what is being extracted and from which column.

The number of these basic options in the list depends on how many columns are selected and on the data types they contain. All columns have been selected here, so a wide range of suggestions is available, especially for the column with dates.

A more complex transformation is desired than what Power Query proposes, so in the first cell of the new column, the name **OLIVIA** is entered in uppercase, and the easiest way to confirm the entry is by pressing the *Enter* key. The editor will have no trouble suggesting the correct transformation function. The full formula will appear above the columns. The new column will be assigned a default name associated with the applied function, and all cells in the column will be populated according to the suggested formula.

Tip: **The name of the newly created column can also be changed manually by double-clicking the header and entering the desired text.**

Only the manually entered value (**OLIVIA**) will appear in black. The remaining values will be grayed out (indicating that they are inferred, not manually entered). This is shown in *Figure 6.27*:

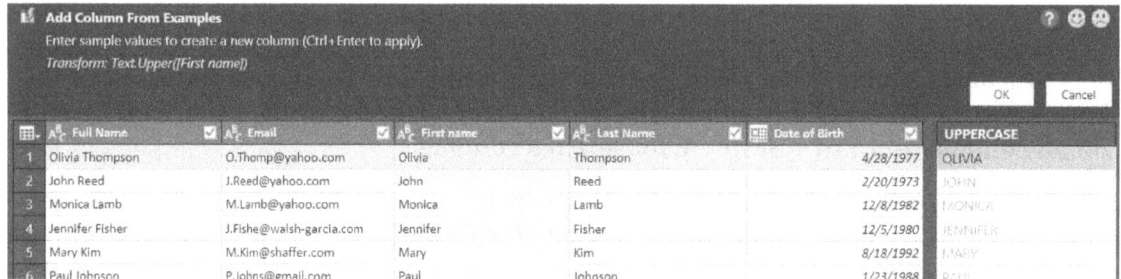

Figure 6.27: Formula proposed for uppercase first name

For the currently entered value, Power Query immediately suggested the correct formula (**Text.Upper([First name])**), as the result in each visible row matched expectations. It is also possible to identify the function used for the transformation instantly. There is no need to search for it elsewhere, and a practical example of its application is visible. If this were the only transformation required, it would be enough to confirm the creation of the new column by clicking the **OK** button.

The process of adding further values to the column using the **Column From Examples** command continues as follows:

1. To cancel the operation, the **Cancel** button must be clicked (both buttons are located above the new column, as shown in *Figure 6.27*).

2. However, since the goal is to explore the **Column From Examples** command more thoroughly, additional values will be added to the new column.

3. In the next step, the last name is added after the uppercase first name.

4. The first row is edited, and the full text entered should be: **OLIVIA Thompson**.

5. Power Query correctly suggests the appropriate formula despite its increased complexity and the requirement for nested functions:

```
Text.Combine({Text.Upper([First name]), " ", [Last Name]})
```

This is shown in *Figure 6.28*:

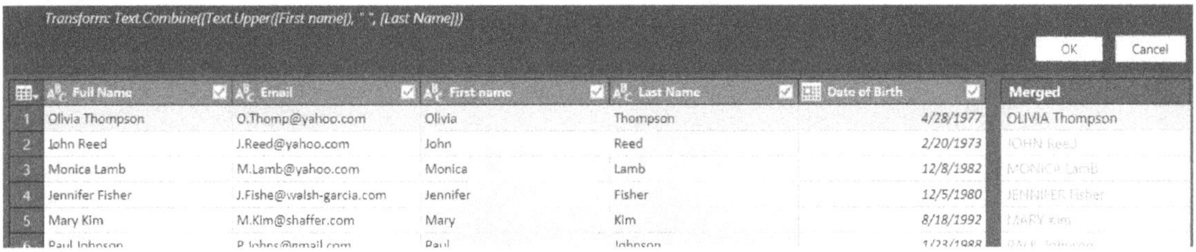

Figure 6.28: *Formula proposed for first and last name*

In addition to the proposed formula, the name of the new column was also changed.

Once again, the complexity of Power Query is increased. This time, a semicolon and information about the year of birth are to be added. The exact text to be entered should be: **OLIVIA Thompson; year of birth 1977**. In this case, the editor did not correctly detect the pattern and instead treated the entire text as a static value, resulting in the following formula:

```
Text.Combine({Text.Upper([First name]), " ", [Last Name], "; year of birth
1977"})
```

This is shown in *Figure 6.29*:

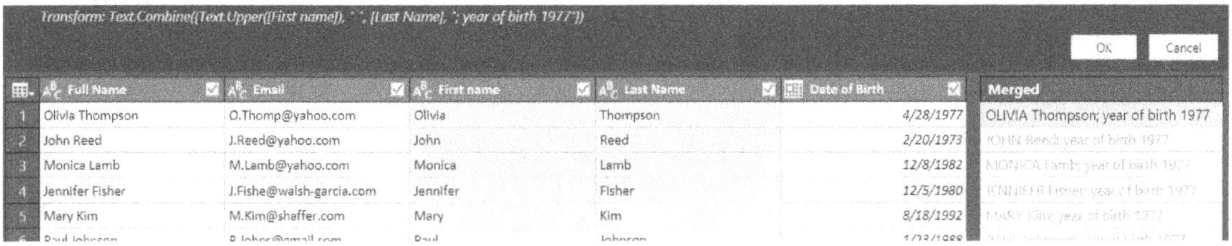

Figure 6.29: *Incorrect formula after adding year of birth*

If Power Query does not generate the correct formula based on a single example row, the formula created so far can be accepted and manually adjusted later, or another gray row can be modified to provide Power Query with more accurate data to work with. For example, in the second row, the year of birth should be entered as *1973*. It is sufficient to double-click the second cell and enter the correct year of birth.

After this modification, Power Query should return correct results, but it will do so using a very complex formula, as shown in *Figure 6.30*:

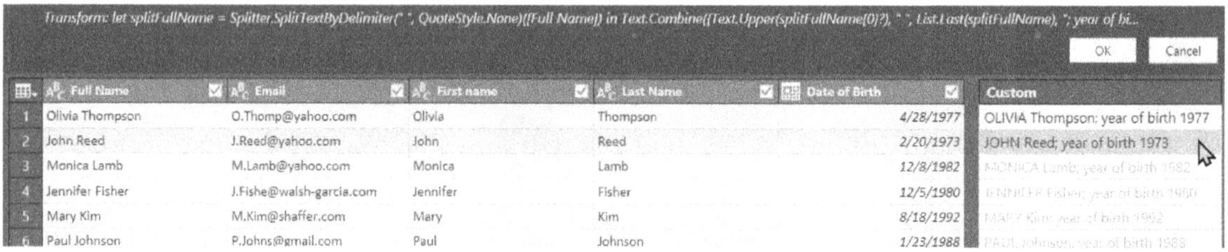

Figure 6.30: Correct result including year of birth

We can now observe that in the first two rows, the examples are displayed in black font. This indicates that these values were entered manually by the user, not suggested by Excel.

Tip: **Examples for the Column From Examples command do not need to be entered in row order. We can start entering values from any visible row, and further examples can be entered in any non-filled row.**

The automatically generated formula is overly complex, so it is useful to confirm one more example manually, for example, in the fourth row. After doing so, Power Query should generate a much simpler formula. It may also happen that, depending on the version of the editor, a shorter formula will be generated after two examples. The desired formula is as follows:

```
Text.Combine({Text.Upper([First name]), " ", [Last Name], "; year of birth "
Date.ToText([Date of Birth], "yyyy")})
```

The result is shown in *Figure 6.31*:

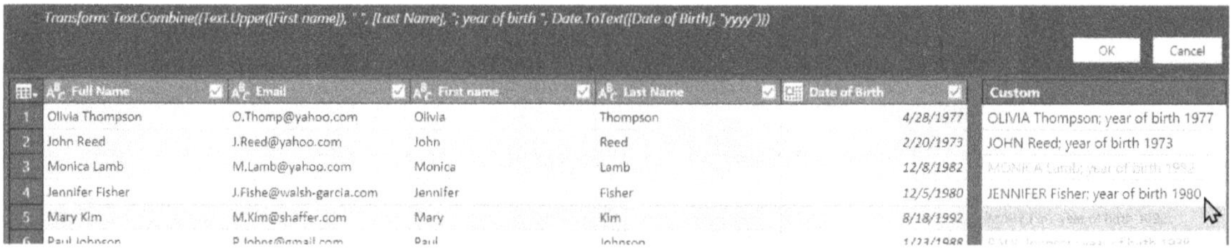

Figure 6.31: Shorter formula with year of birth

We want to add one more piece of information to the column we are creating: the name of the day of the week on which the person was born. For the first row, this value will be **Thursday**.

If we input this additional information manually, Power Query will not be able to infer the formula and will instead generate a very long expression. Even more critically, it will populate only the values that were entered manually and will return **null** for all other rows. This situation is shown in *Figure 6.32*:

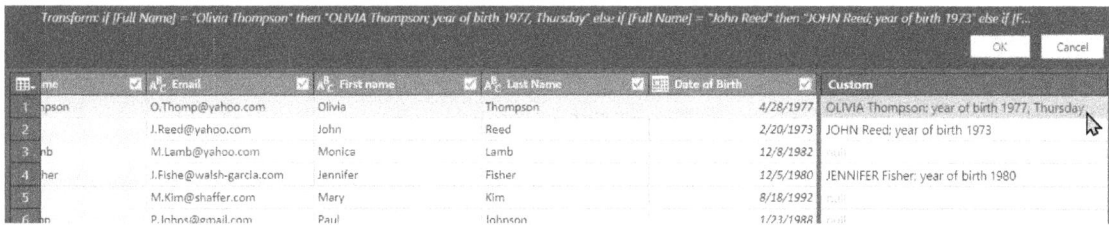

Figure 6.32: *Null values when the pattern was not recognized*

Fortunately, it is enough to include the day of the week in the other examples we provide (e.g., based on the source data in *Figure 6.24*) for Power Query to suggest the correct formula:

```
Text.Combine({Text.Upper([First name]), " ", [Last Name], "; year of birth
", Date.ToText([Date of Birth], "yyyy"), ", ", Date.ToText([Date of Birth],
"dddd")})
```

This formula is shown in *Figure 6.33*:

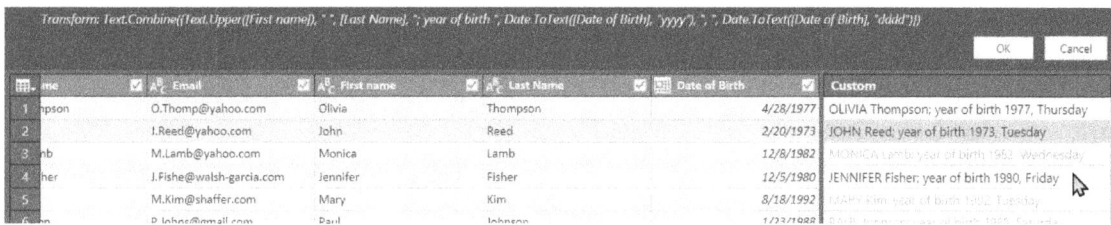

Figure 6.33: *Final correct formula*

Before confirming the creation of the new column by clicking the **OK** button, it is possible to rename the new column to **Date of birth** information. This change can also be made later in the formula bar, as has been done multiple times before. It makes no difference to Power Query. Either method will yield the same result, so the choice depends on convenience.

It is important to note that after confirming the new column created using the **Column From Examples** command, even though a gear icon appears next to the step name, it is not possible to return to editing the column through the same interface. Instead of reopening the **Column From Examples** view, Power Query will open the **Custom Column** window, where the formula must be written manually without the assistance of the editor interpreting example values.

The **Custom Column** window for the newly added step is shown in *Figure 6.34*:

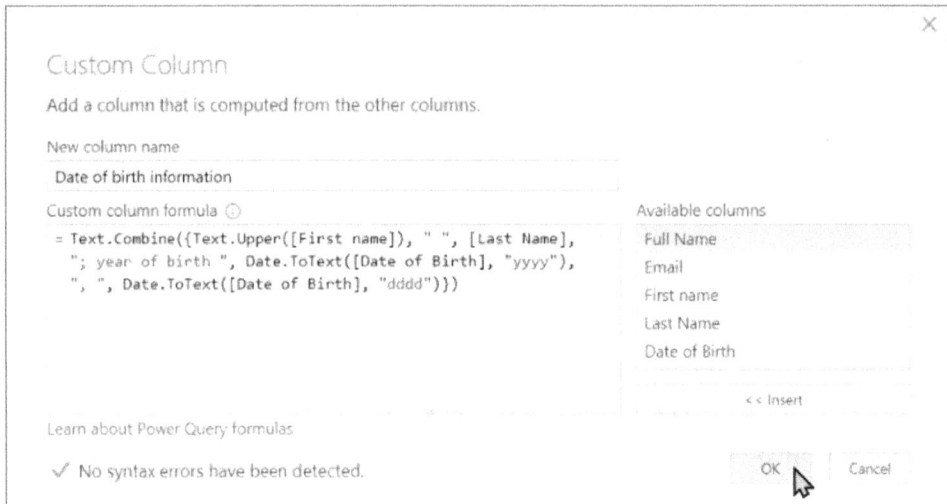

Figure 6.34: Custom Column window for the column created from examples

It is possible to simplify the formula proposed by Power Query because the year and day of the week from the date of birth can be extracted using a single function. The shortened formula should be as follows:

```
=Text.Combine({Text.Upper([First name]), " ", [Last Name], "; year of birth ", Date.ToText([Date of Birth], "yyyy, dddd")})
```

Such edits can only be made effectively once there is a solid understanding of Power Query functions. At the early stages of learning, it is perfectly acceptable to use the formulas proposed by the editor, provided they return the correct result.

The final improvement that should be made to the newly created column is to assign it the appropriate data type rather than the general type (**ABC123/any**). This can be done by either changing it via the icon in the column header or by modifying the M code by adding type text before the final parenthesis.

In this example, the intention is to create one more column from an example, so the shortcut *Ctrl + E* is used to quickly enter the **Column From Examples** interface again. This time, the goal is to have the last name written in uppercase, followed by the first letter of the first name. The correct value for the first row should be: **THOMPSON, O**.

However, as shown in *Figure 6.35*, Power Query did not correctly identify the appropriate formula:

Figure 6.35: Example-based formula for the last name in uppercase

Therefore, two additional examples are provided, for instance, for the third and fourth rows. This is shown in *Figure 6.36*:

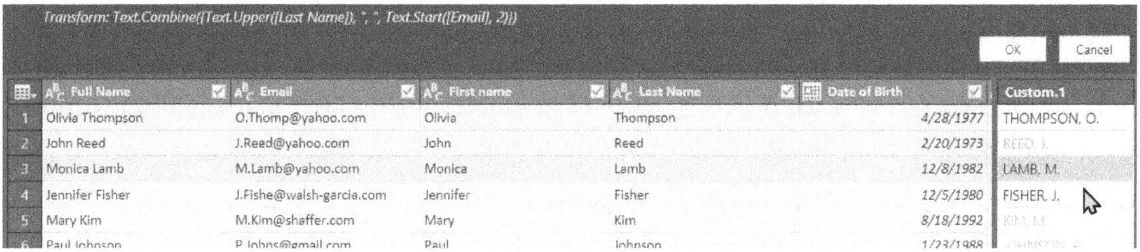

Figure 6.36: Correct result after providing more examples

The formula proposed by the editor is as follows:

```
Text.Combine({Text.Upper([Last Name]), ", ", Text.Start([Email], 2)})
```

It returns correct results, but using the **Email** column instead of the **First name** column does not seem to be the proper approach. Therefore, only the columns **First name** and **Last Name** should be selected for analysis. The result of such an operation is shown in *Figure 6.37*:

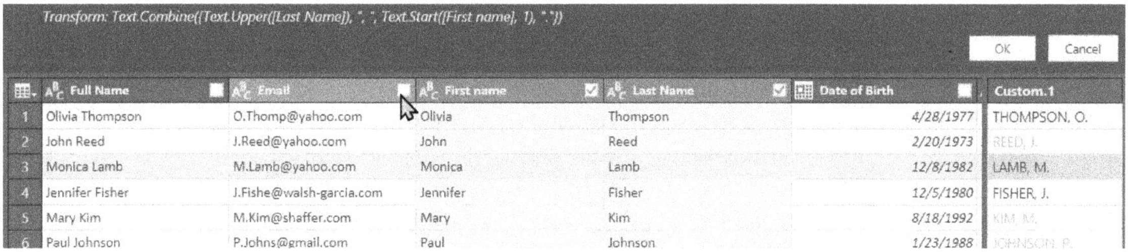

Figure 6.37: Correct result based on two columns

The formula now uses the **First name** column instead of **Email**, but the functions used have not changed:

```
Text.Combine({Text.Upper([Last Name]), ", ", Text.Start([First name], 1),
"."})
```

More values are now being concatenated in the formula. If the goal is code optimization, it would be better to revert to the earlier result. However, in this example and with such a small dataset, this has no impact. What matters most is that the result is correct. Therefore, rename the column to **Name UPPER** and confirm its addition by clicking **OK**.

For this column, in contrast to the previously added column using examples, Power Query should automatically assign the text data type. This is because only columns containing text are referenced. The earlier column extracted values from both text and date columns, which is why the editor did not assign a specific data type, and it had to be set manually.

Tip: **Based on user experience, if Power Query is unable to return correct results after providing three examples, it is recommended to limit or change the columns used by the editor to generate the formula. If this operation is ineffective, the next step is to try entering examples for different rows. In general, providing more than three examples rarely helps Power Query recognize the correct formula. Therefore, if, after entering examples and narrowing down the analyzed columns, the Column From Examples command still does not produce correct results, it is advisable to manually write the transformation formula or break the creation of the new column into intermediate steps.**

The final steps to complete this example are as follows:

1. Rename the query to **New Columns**.

2. Load the result into Excel.

Calculating work time

We are working with data from the **tWorkHours** table on the **WorkTime** sheet (the source data is shown in *Figure 6.38*). Based on this table, we want to calculate the working time for each employee on a daily basis.

	A	B	C	D
1	Employee	Date	Entry Time	Exit Time
2	Monica Lamb	10/1/2025	8:00	16:00
3	Monica Lamb	10/2/2025	8:05	16:10
4	Monica Lamb	10/3/2025	8:00	16:20
5	Monica Lamb	10/4/2025	8:30	17:30
6	Monica Lamb	10/5/2025	8:00	15:30
7	Monica Lamb	10/8/2025	8:00	16:00

Figure 6.38: Source data on working hours

As usual, the data is imported from the Excel table using the **From Table/Range** command from the **Data** tab (*Figure 1.1*).

The first thing we notice after importing the data into Power Query is that the automatic detection of data types did not work correctly for the columns containing time values. This is illustrated in *Figure 6.39*:

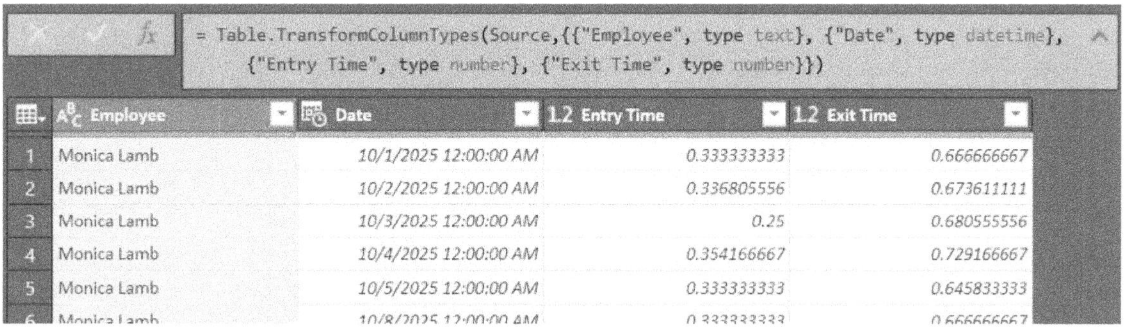

```
= Table.TransformColumnTypes(Source,{{"Employee", type text}, {"Date", type datetime},
  {"Entry Time", type number}, {"Exit Time", type number}})
```

▦	A⁸_C Employee	🗂 Date	1.2 Entry Time	1.2 Exit Time
1	Monica Lamb	10/1/2025 12:00:00 AM	0.333333333	0.666666667
2	Monica Lamb	10/2/2025 12:00:00 AM	0.336805556	0.673611111
3	Monica Lamb	10/3/2025 12:00:00 AM	0.25	0.680555556
4	Monica Lamb	10/4/2025 12:00:00 AM	0.354166667	0.729166667
5	Monica Lamb	10/5/2025 12:00:00 AM	0.333333333	0.645833333
6	Monica Lamb	10/8/2025 12:00:00 AM	0.333333333	0.666666667

Figure 6.39: Incorrectly detected data types for time columns

Instead of time values, we see decimal numbers. This is consistent with how time is stored in Excel (and Power Query), where a decimal number represents the fraction of the day that has passed. For example, 8:00 is $8/24 = ⅓ = 0.3333333$, and 6:00 is $6/24 = ¼ = 0.25$.

However, we want to display actual time values. Therefore, we change the data type for the **Entry Time** and **Exit Time** columns to **Time** and for the **Date** column to **Date** only. After making these transformations, we will obtain the desired time representation. This is shown in *Figure 6.40*:

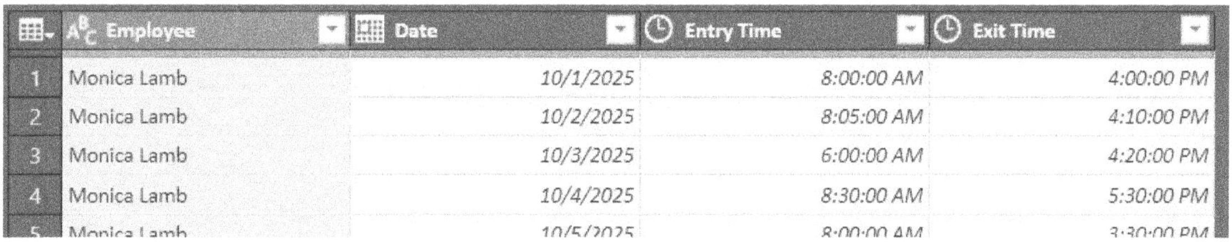

▦	A⁸_C Employee	▦ Date	🕐 Entry Time	🕐 Exit Time
1	Monica Lamb	10/1/2025	8:00:00 AM	4:00:00 PM
2	Monica Lamb	10/2/2025	8:05:00 AM	4:10:00 PM
3	Monica Lamb	10/3/2025	6:00:00 AM	4:20:00 PM
4	Monica Lamb	10/4/2025	8:30:00 AM	5:30:00 PM
5	Monica Lamb	10/5/2025	8:00:00 AM	3:30:00 PM

Figure 6.40: Correctly formatted time and date

The steps to calculate the working time based on the **Entry Time** and **Exit Time** columns are as follows:

1. Select the **Entry Time** and **Exit Time** columns in the correct order.

2. Go to the **Add Column** tab.

3. Expand the **Time** command.

4. Select the **Subtract** option, as shown in *Figure 6.41*:

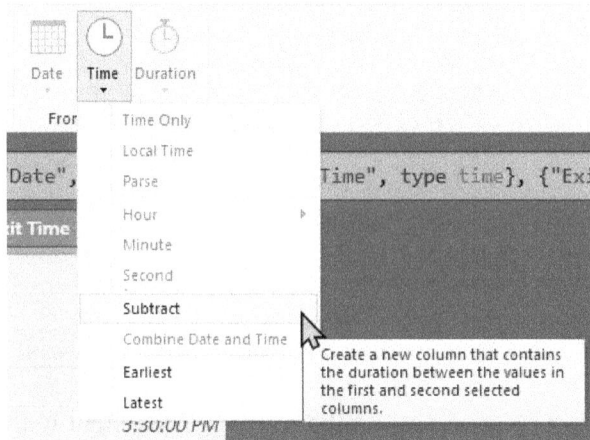

Figure 6.41: Expanded Time command

Tip: **Depending on the data type stored in a column, only certain transformations are available for it.**

After performing the subtraction, the editor will insert a new column with the calculated working time. The result is shown in *Figure 6.42*:

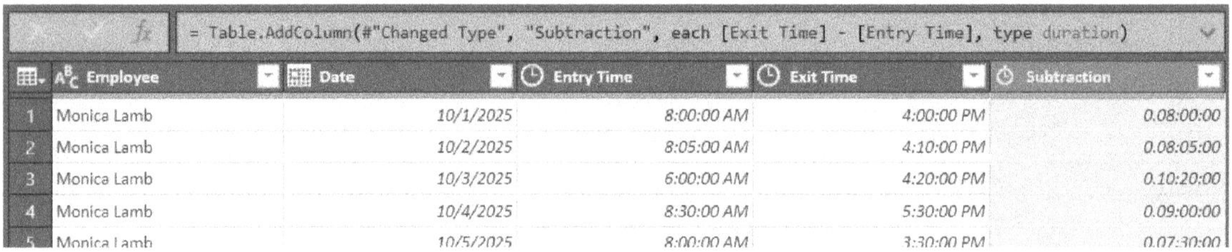

Figure 6.42: Time subtraction result

For our purposes, it is important to note that the new column has automatically been assigned the duration data type, which represents the number of days, hours, minutes, and seconds that passed between the specified times. The result of the subtraction is correct. It is only necessary to rename the new column in the formula bar to Work Time. We have to remember that renaming the new column directly in the M code, when possible, helps optimize the query, mainly by reducing the number of steps in the query.

Fun fact: **Power Query, unlike Excel, does not have any issues displaying negative time values. Such a situation could occur, for example, if the value from the Entry Time column were subtracted from the value in the Exit Time column.**

The process of extracting the exact number of hours worked from a duration column involves the following steps:

1. Create a new column using one of the options from the **Time** command group.

2. Note that this step could be completed using the **Custom Column** command (see *Figure 3.6*), though this would require manually entering a formula.

3. Understand that using the **Time** command is a more optimal solution because it assigns the data type automatically.

4. Recognize that working with whole-number hour values may be more intuitive than dealing with fractions of a day, which is how durations are stored internally.

5. Select the column that contains the **duration** data type.

6. Go to the **Add Column** or **Transform** tab.

7. Expand the **Duration** command.

8. Choose the **Total Hours** option, as shown in *Figure 6.43*:

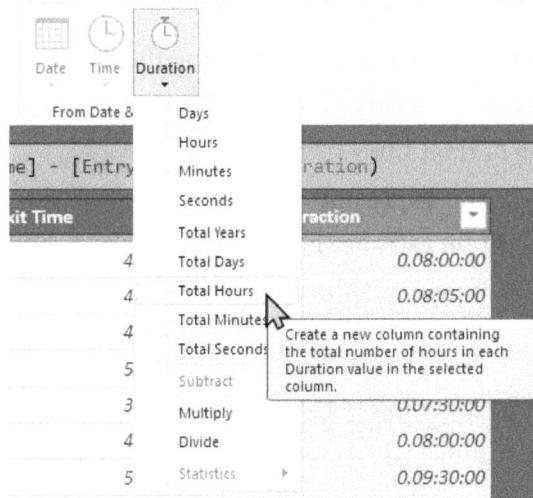

Figure 6.43: Duration command options

A key distinction between the **Total** options and the ones above them is that the **Total** options return the cumulative value of a given unit of time. For example, for a duration of **8:20**, the **Minutes** option would return the value **20**, while **Total Minutes** would return **500**, which represents the total number of minutes in the specified duration.

By choosing the **Total Hours** option, the exact number of hours is calculated. Minutes are also included in this result. For instance, **20** minutes will be converted to $20 \div 60 = 1/3 = 0.333333$. The result of this transformation is shown in *Figure 6.44*:

▦	A^B_C Employee	▼	▦ Date	▼	🕑 Entry Time	▼	🕑 Exit Time	▼	🕑 Work Time	1.2 Total Hours	▼
1	Monica Lamb		10/1/2025		8:00:00 AM		4:00:00 PM		0.08:00:00	8	
2	Monica Lamb		10/2/2025		8:05:00 AM		4:10:00 PM		0.08:05:00	8.083333333	
3	Monica Lamb		10/3/2025		6:00:00 AM		4:20:00 PM		0.10:20:00	10.33333333	
4	Monica Lamb		10/4/2025		8:30:00 AM		5:30:00 PM		0.09:00:00	9	
5	Monica Lamb		10/5/2025		8:00:00 AM		3:30:00 PM		0.07:30:00	7.5	
6	Monica Lamb		10/8/2025		8:00:00 AM		4:00:00 PM		0.08:00:00	8	

The formula bar reads: `= Table.AddColumn(#"Inserted Time Subtraction", "Total Hours", each Duration.TotalHours([Work Time]), type number)`

Figure 6.44: Exact number of hours in the duration

The desired results have been obtained, so the query can be renamed to **Work Hours** and loaded into Excel.

Now, it is possible to review the number formatting for the **Work Time** column.

To check or adjust the formatting of duration values in Excel, the following steps are to be followed:

1. Select a sample cell from the column containing the duration values.
2. Press the keyboard shortcut *Ctrl + 1*.
3. Excel will open the **Format Cells** window.
4. Ensure the window is on the **Number** tab.
5. Confirm that the **Custom** category is selected.
6. The window should appear as shown in *Figure 6.45*:

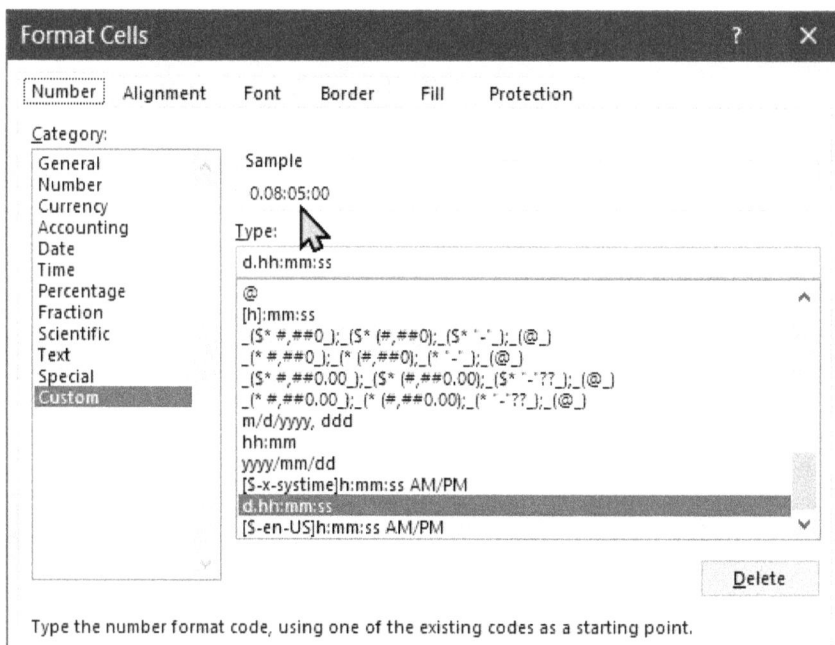

Figure 6.45: Custom number format in Excel for duration data type

The format code for this is **d.hh:mm:ss**, meaning Excel will first display the number of days, followed by the exact remaining time for the partial day. However, if we take a closer look at Excel's custom number formatting, we will see that a single letter **d** represents the day number within the month. Therefore, this formatting will correctly display up to 31 days, as this is the number of days in the first month (January) from which Excel starts counting dates. If the number of days exceeds this limit, Excel will move into the next month and will start showing incorrect day counts. Power Query does not have such limitations, but since data is most commonly presented in Excel, in similar situations we should consider splitting the duration into separate columns for days and time.

Rounding time

In this example, we will want to return to the previous query and round the work time to 15 minutes. To return to editing an already created query, we can select the **Edit** option from the query's context menu (*Figure 1.26*) or by clicking the **Edit** command on the **Query** tab (*Figure 1.15*).

In Power Query, there are far fewer rounding options than in Excel. There is only one **Rounding** command (*Figure 6.5*) and three functions related to it. All of them are associated with rounding numbers, not time. Therefore, to round the value from the **Work Time** column, we will need to use additional functions and calculations.

Although the Date, Time, and Duration data types are backed by numerical values, Power Query does not always automatically convert these types to numbers. This leads to situations where some calculations or functions used with these types return an error. That is why we will need functions that convert data types. The first function we will use is **Number.From**, which can convert any meaningful value into a number.

Now, create a new column using the **Custom Column** command from the **Add Column** tab (*Figure 3.6*). Name the new column **Work time rounded to 15 minutes**, and then enter the following formula:

```
Number.From([Work Time])
```

To better understand why we are adding individual functions, let us confirm this formula right away by clicking the **OK** button. Power Query will convert the duration into a number, as shown in *Figure 6.46*:

fx	= Table.AddColumn(#"Inserted Total Hours", "Work time rounded to 15 minutes", each Number.From([Work Time]))			
try Time	**Exit Time**	**Work Time**	**1.2 Total Hours**	**Work time rounded to 15 minutes**
1	8:00:00 AM	4:00:00 PM	0.08:00:00	8	0.333333333
2	8:05:00 AM	4:10:00 PM	0.08:05:00	8.083333333	0.336805556
3	6:00:00 AM	4:20:00 PM	0.10:20:00	10.33333333	0.430555556
4	8:30:00 AM	5:30:00 PM	0.09:00:00	9	0.375
5	8:00:00 AM	3:30:00 PM	0.07:30:00	7.5	0.3125

Figure 6.46: Duration converted to a number

The results resemble the time values we saw earlier (*Figure 6.39*). Now, we need to appropriately convert these values to reflect how many 15-minute intervals (quarters of an hour) these numbers represent. This means we need to multiply each value by the number of quarters in a day. There are 24 hours in a day, and each hour contains 4 quarters, so we need to multiply the formula by 24 and then again by 4. From an optimization perspective, we should multiply directly by 96 (24 * 4), but in this example, we want to emphasize the individual reasoning behind each step in the calculation.

The steps involved in modifying the formula to calculate the number of 15-minute intervals are as follows:

1. Add the multiplication directly in the formula bar or click the gear icon next to the step to reopen the **Custom Column** window.

2. Enter the multiplication: `24 * 4 * Number.From([Work Time])`

3. Power Query will return the result shown in *Figure 6.47*:

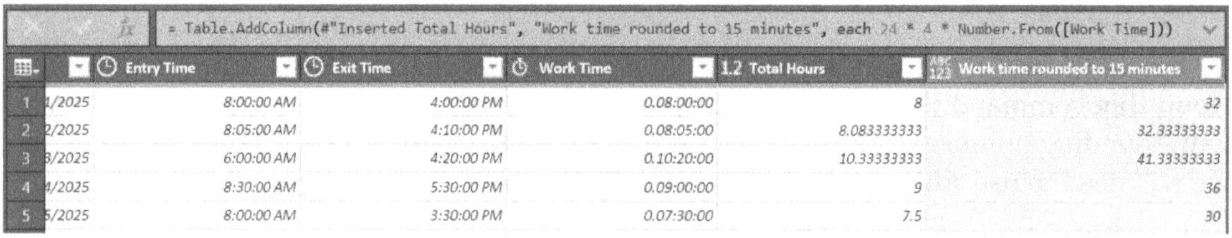

	Entry Time	Exit Time	Work Time	1.2 Total Hours	Work time rounded to 15 minutes
1	1/2025	8:00:00 AM	4:00:00 PM	0.08:00:00	8	32
2	2/2025	8:05:00 AM	4:10:00 PM	0.08:05:00	8.083333333	32.33333333
3	3/2025	6:00:00 AM	4:20:00 PM	0.10:20:00	10.33333333	41.33333333
4	4/2025	8:30:00 AM	5:30:00 PM	0.09:00:00	9	36
5	5/2025	8:00:00 AM	3:30:00 PM	0.07:30:00	7.5	30

Formula bar: `= Table.AddColumn(#"Inserted Total Hours", "Work time rounded to 15 minutes", each 24 * 4 * Number.From([Work Time]))`

Figure 6.47: Number of quarters

For work times that correspond to whole quarters, we see whole numbers, but where additional minutes are present, we see decimal values.

Now, we can round these values using one of the available rounding functions that we discussed in the first example of this chapter. We assume that we always want to round down to whole numbers, so we need to use the **Number.RoundDown** function with only one argument. Based on this assumption, the new formula should look as follows:

```
Number.RoundDown(24 * 4 * Number.From([Work Time]))
```

Once we have only the full number of quarters, we must return to the time format. First, we need to divide the obtained number by the number of quarters in a day, which is *96 (24 * 4)*. Now, we need the following formula:

```
Number.RoundDown(24 * 4 * Number.From([Work Time]))/96
```

The result of this formula is shown in *Figure 6.48*:

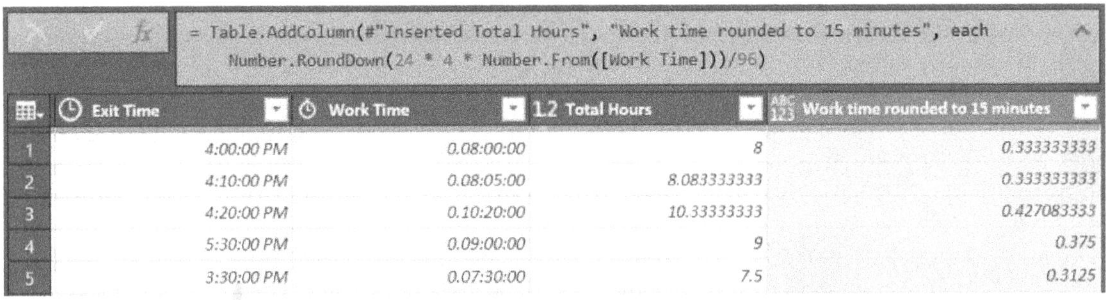

```
= Table.AddColumn(#"Inserted Total Hours", "Work time rounded to 15 minutes", each
    Number.RoundDown(24 * 4 * Number.From([Work Time]))/96)
```

	Exit Time	Work Time	1.2 Total Hours	Work time rounded to 15 minutes
1	4:00:00 PM	0.08:00:00	8	0.333333333
2	4:10:00 PM	0.08:05:00	8.083333333	0.333333333
3	4:20:00 PM	0.10:20:00	10.33333333	0.427083333
4	5:30:00 PM	0.09:00:00	9	0.375
5	3:30:00 PM	0.07:30:00	7.5	0.3125

Figure 6.48: Number of quarters converted to time as a number

At this point, we could finish writing the formula and add a new step to change the general data type of the **Work time rounded to 15 minutes** column to the **Time** type. However, we want to include this transformation directly in the formula, because sometimes it may be necessary to perform the conversion directly within the formula. We only need to add the `Time.From` function, so the complete formula becomes:

```
Time.From(Number.RoundDown(24 * 4 * Number.From([Work Time]))/96)
```

The formula contains several nested functions. Sometimes, such a formula can be more readable in the **Custom Column** window if we add a few line breaks and indentations in strategic places, as shown in *Figure 6.49*:

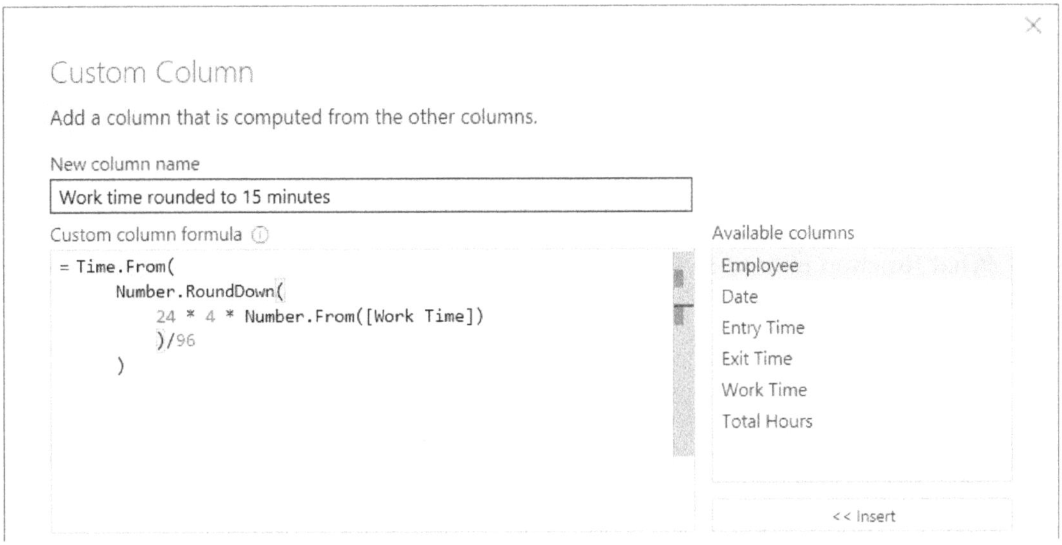

Figure 6.49: Formula with additional line breaks

Such formatting of the formula does not affect the result but allows the user to better understand where each function starts and ends. After confirming the formula, it appears that the result is a valid time, as shown in *Figure 6.50*:

	⊙ Exit Time		⊙ Work Time		1.2 Total Hours		Work time rounded to 15 minutes	
1	4:00:00 PM		0.08:00:00		8		8:00:00 AM	
2	4:10:00 PM		0.08:05:00		8.083333333		8:00:00 AM	
3	4:20:00 PM		0.10:20:00		10.33333333		10:15:00 AM	
4	5:30:00 PM		0.09:00:00		9		9:00:00 AM	
5	3:30:00 PM		0.07:30:00		7.5		7:30:00 AM	

Figure 6.50: Result that appears to be the correct time

However, it is important to remember the data type. Although the values in the column are displayed as time, the column still has the general data type. This will result in the time being displayed in Excel as a decimal number. Therefore, it is necessary to add the following to the end of the M code in the formula bar: `, type time`, just before the final closing parenthesis. After making this correction, the data can safely be loaded back into Excel.

Conclusion

In this chapter, we focused on practical transformation techniques essential for real-world data preparation in Power Query. We learned how to calculate values with nulls, apply rounding to numbers and durations, split data into rows or by custom delimiters, and use the Column From Examples command to automate column creation. We also covered work time calculations and how to round time values to fixed intervals. These skills strengthen our ability to clean and restructure data efficiently.

In the next chapter, we will explore logical operations and conditional columns. Those tools will allow us to build more dynamic, rule-based transformations for more flexible data shaping.

Multiple choice questions

1. **What function is used in Power Query to multiply several values at once, ignoring null values?**

    a. Number.Multiply

    b. List.Multiply

    c. List.Product

    d. Table.Multiply

2. **In Power Query, what is the result of the expression 1 - null?**

    a. 1

    b. 0

    c. null error

    d. null

3. **When using Column From Examples, which actions can help Power Query correctly detect the pattern?**
   a. Providing multiple example rows
   b. Limiting selected input columns
   c. Rewriting M code manually
   d. Adjusting the sequence of input values

4. **What data type is automatically assigned when subtracting two-time columns?**
   a. Time
   b. Decimal
   c. Duration
   d. Whole Number

5. **Which operations are available in the Duration menu in Power Query?**
   a. Total Hours
   b. Total Minutes
   c. Median
   d. Count Rows

6. **When using Column From Examples, what should we do if Power Query does not detect a pattern correctly? (Multiple choice)**
   a. Provide more example values
   b. Restart the editor
   c. Limit the selected columns
   d. Manually adjust the formula later

Answers

Question number	Answer option letter
1.	c.
2.	d.
3.	a., b., d.
4.	c.
5.	a., b.
6.	a., c., d.

Join our Discord space

Join our Discord workspace for latest updates, offers, tech happenings around the world, new releases, and sessions with the authors:

CHAPTER 7
Logical Operations and Conditional Columns

Introduction

In the previous chapter, we focused on techniques for adding columns in Power Query, a fundamental step in data transformation. This included creating new columns using examples, custom formulas, and built-in operations.

This chapter explores how to apply logic to transform and analyze that data using conditional expressions and logical operators.

You will learn how to calculate overtime, assign bonuses, and grade results by evaluating values against defined rules. The chapter introduces key tools, such as if, and, or, and try, along with methods for comparing rows, handling errors, and working with thresholds.

These techniques are essential for automating decisions, handling exceptions, and preparing data for reporting or further analysis.

Structure

This chapter covers the following topics:

- Overtime hours
- Logical operators combining multiple tests
- Grading with nested if

- Grading with appending
- Counting days of absence
- Numbers and errors
- Compare with the previous row using merge
- Compare with the previous row using index

Objectives

By the end of this chapter, you will be able to create conditional logic using both the user interface and M code in Power Query. You will learn how to calculate overtime hours, apply grading logic with multiple thresholds, and assign bonuses based on combined conditions. You will also gain skills in handling errors, comparing values across rows, and analyzing time-based data such as absence periods. These techniques are essential for dynamic reporting, quality control, and data validation in real-world business scenarios.

Overtime hours

This example uses data from the **OverTime** worksheet. Specifically, the analysis will focus on the query named **OverTime**, which was created based on transformations of data from the **tWork** table. Both tables are shown in *Figure 7.1*:

	A	B	C	D	E	F	G	H	I	J	K
1	Employee	Date	Entry Time	Exit Time		Employee	Date	Entry Time	Exit Time	Work Time	Total Hours
2	Monica Lamb	10/1/2025	8:00	16:00		Monica Lamb	10/1/2025	8:00:00 AM	4:00:00 PM	0.08:00:00	8
3	Monica Lamb	10/2/2025	8:10	16:25		Monica Lamb	10/2/2025	8:10:00 AM	4:25:00 PM	0.08:15:00	8.25
4	Monica Lamb	10/3/2025	6:00	16:20		Monica Lamb	10/3/2025	6:00:00 AM	4:20:00 PM	0.10:20:00	10.33333333
5	Monica Lamb	10/4/2025	8:30	17:30		Monica Lamb	10/4/2025	8:30:00 AM	5:30:00 PM	0.09:00:00	9
6	Monica Lamb	10/5/2025	8:00	15:30		Monica Lamb	10/5/2025	8:00:00 AM	3:30:00 PM	0.07:30:00	7.5
7	Monica Lamb	10/8/2025	8:00	16:00		Monica Lamb	10/8/2025	8:00:00 AM	4:00:00 PM	0.08:00:00	8
8	Monica Lamb	10/9/2025	8:00	17:30		Monica Lamb	10/9/2025	8:00:00 AM	5:30:00 PM	0.09:30:00	9.5

Figure 7.1: Source data on working time

The goal is to add columns to the query that calculate the number of overtime hours. Calculations will be performed using both the **Work Time** and **Total Hours** columns in order to illustrate the differences between working with time stored as the **duration** data type and as numeric values.

To return to editing an already created query, one can select the **Edit** option from the query's context menu (*Figure 1.26*) or click the **Edit** command on the **Query** tab (*Figure 1.15*). It is also possible to double-click the name of the query in the **Queries & Connections** pane.

Overtime occurs when an employee works more than eight hours. All time beyond the eight-hour threshold is considered overtime. The analysis will begin with the **Work Time** column. To do this, the following steps are to be followed:

1. Select the **Work Time** column.

2. On the **Add Column** tab, click the **Conditional Column** command, as shown in *Figure 7.2*:

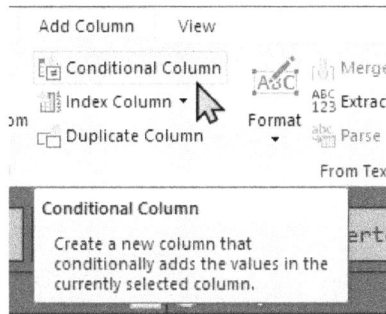

Figure 7.2: *Conditional Column command*

This command opens the **Add Conditional Column** window, where the conditions for calculating the new column must be defined. The steps are as follows:

1. In the **New column name** field, enter the name of the new column: **OverTime**.

2. From the **Column Name** drop-down list, select the **Work Time** column, as this is the column to be evaluated.

3. In the **Operator** field, choose **is greater than**, since the goal is to identify work durations exceeding eight hours.

4. In the **Value** field, decide whether to use a fixed value, a value from another column, or a parameter (parameters will be discussed in more detail in *Chapter 8, Parameters and Query Parameterization*). In this example, manually enter the value **8:00**.

5. Next, define the **Output**, which is the result to be returned when the condition is met. In this case, the number of overtime hours should be calculated by subtracting eight hours from the **Work Time** value. Since the interface does not support entering formulas in this field, Power Query will be tricked by manually typing the formula: `[Work Time] - 8:00`

6. Lastly, complete the **Else** field with the value to return when the condition is not met. In this example, it will be zero, meaning no overtime.

A correctly completed **Add Conditional Column** window is shown in *Figure 7.3*:

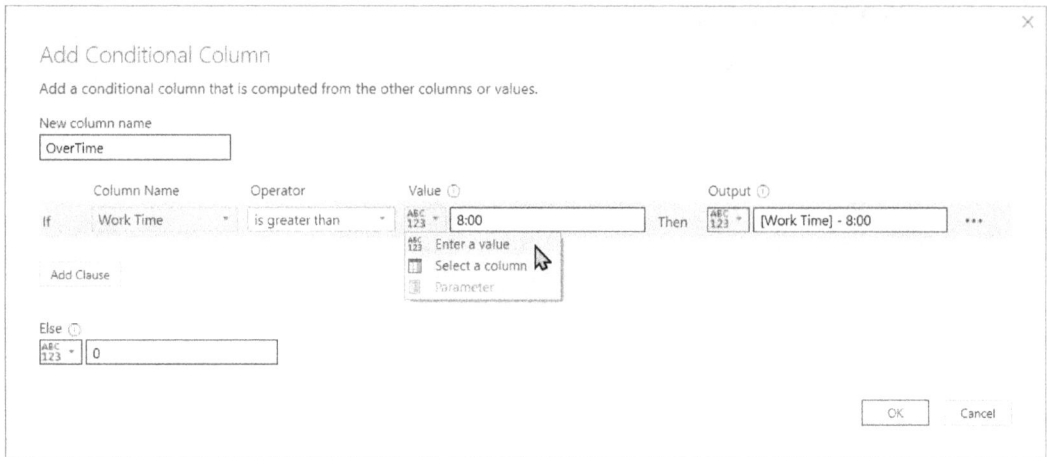

Figure 7.3: Filled Add Conditional Column window

7. After confirming the setup by clicking the **OK** button, Power Query returns an incorrect result, as shown in *Figure 7.4*:

= Table.AddColumn(#"Inserted Total Hours", "OverTime", each if [Work Time] > #duration(0, 8, 0, 0) then "[Work Time] - 8:00" else 0)

	Date	Entry Time	Exit Time	Work Time	Total Hours	OverTime
1	10/1/2025	8:00:00 AM	4:00:00 PM	0.08:00:00	8	0
2	10/2/2025	8:10:00 AM	4:25:00 PM	0.08:15:00	8.25	[Work Time] - 8:00
3	10/3/2025	6:00:00 AM	4:20:00 PM	0.10:20:00	10.33333333	[Work Time] - 8:00
4	10/4/2025	8:30:00 AM	5:30:00 PM	0.09:00:00	9	[Work Time] - 8:00
5	10/5/2025	8:00:00 AM	3:30:00 PM	0.07:30:00	7.5	0

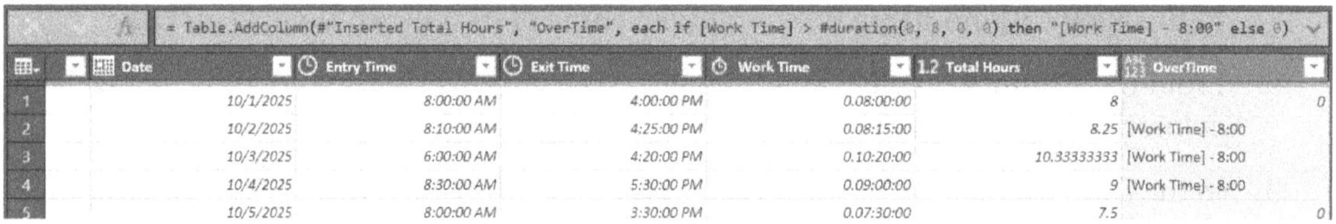

Figure 7.4: Incorrect conditional column result

If the formula bar is examined, the exact logic used to create the new column becomes visible. It resembles **Visual Basic for Applications** (**VBA**) code utilizing an if conditional statement. The code to be analyzed is as follows:

```
if [Work Time] > #duration(0, 8, 0, 0) then "[Work Time] - 8:00" else 0
```

Begin by reviewing the general syntax of the **if** statement in Power Query:

```
if <test> then <result> else <alternative result>
```

This expression follows a specific logic, which can be broken down into three parts as follows:

1. First, the keyword `if` is used, followed by a logical test.
2. Then, the keyword `then` introduces the result to be returned when the test is true.
3. Finally, the `else` keyword is used to define the alternative result, which is returned when the logical test is false.

In the current example, after the `if` keyword, the test checks whether the value from the `Work`

Time column (column reference is enclosed in square brackets) is greater than eight hours. Power Query automatically converts the entered time **8:00** into **#duration(0, 8, 0, 0)**. This is a valid use of the **#duration** function, where the arguments represent days, hours, minutes, and seconds, respectively.

Following the **then** keyword, a result is defined. However, this expression was not interpreted correctly by Power Query and has been enclosed in double quotation marks, meaning it is treated as a text string. This occurred because the **Add Conditional Column** interface does not allow entering a formula directly. It only accepts manually entered values, column values, or parameters. Therefore, the first necessary correction is to remove the double quotation marks.

The alternative result, placed after the **else** keyword, is the valid numeric value zero, so no modifications are required there.

After correcting the formula, the code in the formula bar should look as follows:

```
= Table.AddColumn(#"Inserted Total Hours", "OverTime", each if [Work Time] >
#duration(0, 8, 0, 0) then [Work Time] - 8:00 else 0)
```

Unfortunately, Power Query will not understand this code and will return an error, as illustrated in *Figure 7.5*:

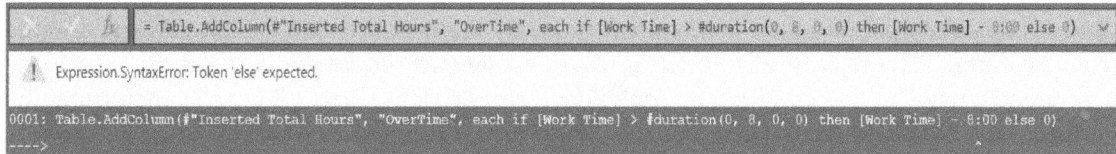

Figure 7.5: Error caused by incorrect time subtraction

The error analysis indicates that the editor identified a syntax error and expected the **else** keyword at the position of the colon (pointed to by the arrow shown in *Figure 7.5*). However, this error message does not specify the actual cause. The underlying reason for the issue is that Power Query, in M code, does not recognize the **8:00** notation.

An attempt can be made to correct the formula using the Excel style by entering the time as text. That is, by enclosing **8:00** in double quotation marks as follows:

```
= Table.AddColumn(#"Inserted Total Hours", "OverTime", each if [Work Time] >
#duration(0, 8, 0, 0) then [Work Time] – "8:00" else 0)
```

Unfortunately, Power Query is much more sensitive to operations involving mismatched data types than Excel (as demonstrated in the previous chapter), and once again returns an error, this time with a different message, as shown in *Figure 7.6*:

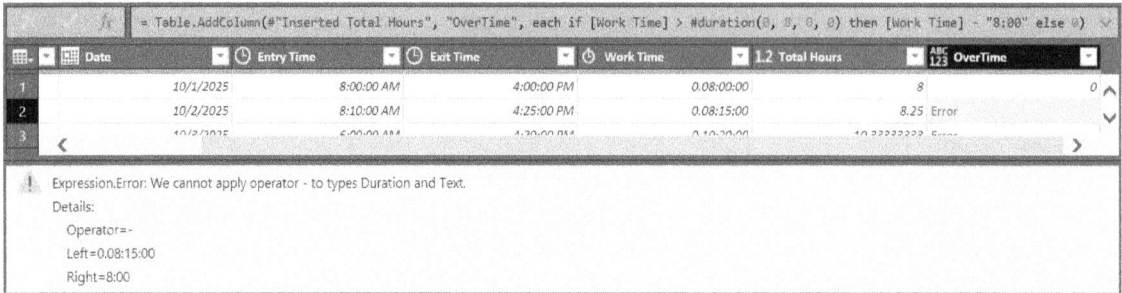

Figure 7.6: Error caused by an invalid operation between different data types

In short, the editor displays a message stating that it cannot perform a subtraction operation between data types **Duration** and **Text**.

Tip: **Power Query does not perform automatic data type conversions, which users might be accustomed to from working in Excel, because in Power Query, data types play a much more important role in calculations than in Excel, particularly due to performance optimization.**

Therefore, manual conversion is required. Although the **Duration.From** function could be used, in this example, the goal is to subtract exactly eight hours rather than convert a value from a column. A more natural solution is to use the **#duration** function, which Power Query has already used in the previously analyzed formula. The correct M code, including the addition of a data type for the new column, should be written as follows:

```
= Table.AddColumn(#"Inserted Total Hours", "OverTime", each if [Work Time] >
#duration(0, 8, 0, 0) then [Work Time] - #duration(0, 8, 0, 0) else 0, type
duration)
```

Tip: **From the first correction to the M code (shown in Figure 7.4), the gear icon next to the step name will begin to open the Custom Column window instead of the Add Conditional Column window, because the formula now exceeds the structure supported by the user interface of the Conditional Column command.**

After this transformation, the formula returns the correct result, as shown in *Figure 7.7*:

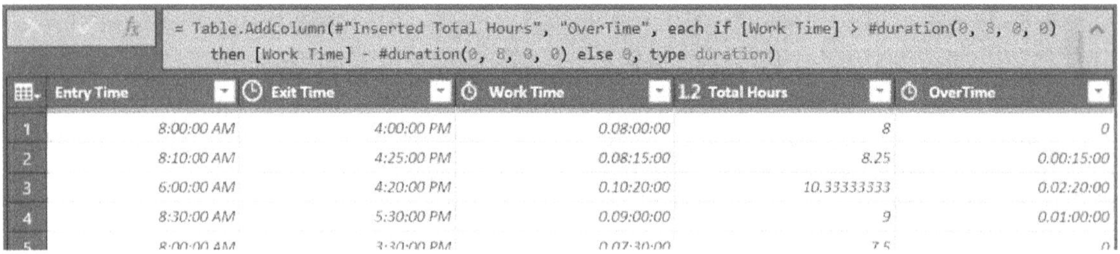

Figure 7.7: Correct calculation of overtime

The data in the **OverTime** column appears to be correct. However, if it were loaded into Excel, empty cells would appear in place of the zero values. This is because the editor would fail to correctly convert a numeric zero into a zero of the **duration** type. Therefore, it is necessary to modify the formula by replacing **0** with **#duration(0, 0, 0, 0)**:

```
= Table.AddColumn(#"Inserted Total Hours", "OverTime", each if [Work Time]
> #duration(0, 8, 0, 0) then [Work Time] - #duration(0, 8, 0, 0) else
#duration(0, 0, 0, 0), type duration)
```

It is now possible to proceed with calculating overtime based on the **Total Hours** column, where the number of hours is recorded as a numeric value. This significantly simplifies the creation of the formula. The formula will be entered directly in the **Custom Column** window, as the **Add Conditional Column** window does not support inserting formulas as arguments within individual fields. Therefore, the **Custom Column** command should be selected from the **Add Column** tab (*Figure 5.14*).

The new column will be named **OverTime 2**. The formula, similar to that used for the **Work Time** column, checks whether the number of hours is greater than eight and, if so, returns the value exceeding eight, which is calculated by subtraction. The formula subtracts eight from the value in the **Total Hours** column. If the number of hours is not greater than eight, zero is returned. The formula in the **Custom Column** window should be written as follows:

```
if [Total Hours] > 8 then [Total Hours] - 8 else 0
```

This formula is simpler than the one used when working with the **duration** data type. Its readability can be further improved by adding line breaks and indentation in strategic places, as shown in *Figure 7.8*:

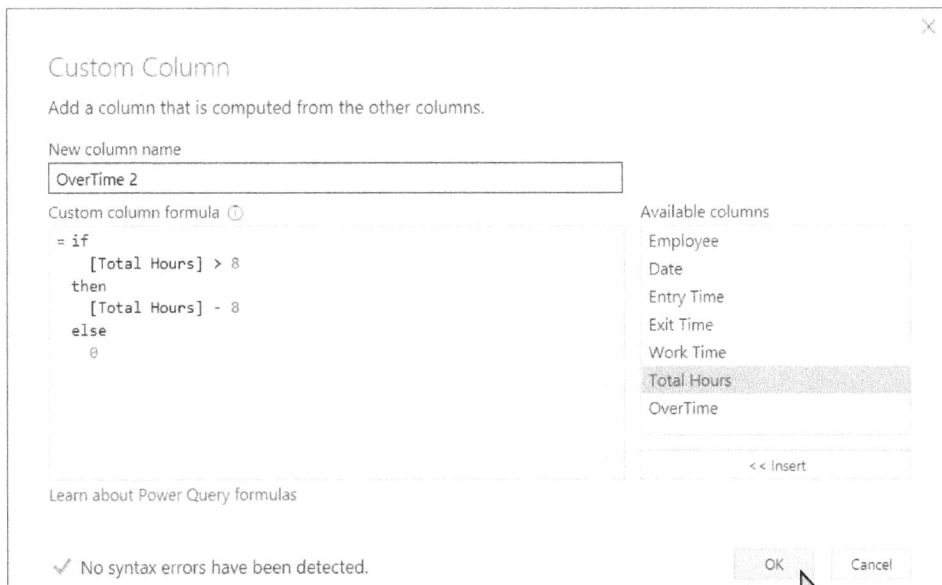

***Figure 7.8**: Formatted formula in the Custom Column window*

After confirming the formula, the appropriate data type (type number) should be appended at the end of the formula in the current step to ensure the result is returned as a numeric value. This is shown in *Figure 7.9*:

⊞.	Exit Time	○ Work Time	1.2 Total Hours	○ OverTime	1.2 OverTime 2
1	4:00:00 PM	0.08:00:00	8	0	0
2	4:25:00 PM	0.08:15:00	8.25	0.00:15:00	0.25
3	4:20:00 PM	0.10:20:00	10.33333333	0.02:20:00	2.333333333
4	5:30:00 PM	0.09:00:00	9	0.01:00:00	1
5	3:30:00 PM	0.07:30:00	7.5	0	0

Figure 7.9: Formatted formula in the formula bar and correct result

Now, all that remains is to reload the query into Excel.

Logical operators combining multiple tests

The data is located on the **AND|OR** worksheet in the **tLogical** table. The goal is to determine whether individual employees qualify for a bonus based on values in the **Sales Quantity** and **Sales Value** columns. Two types of logical combinations will be created using the logical **and** and **or** operators. The source data, combination conditions, and the result of logical tests written in Excel are shown in *Figure 7.10*:

	A	B	C	D	E	F	G H I
1	Employee	Sales Quantity	Sales Value		Bonus OR	Bonus AND	**Conditions OR**
2	Olivia	20	$5,605		FALSE	FALSE	Sales Quantity > 60
3	John	62	$9,490		TRUE	TRUE	OR
4	Monica	43	$9,610		TRUE	FALSE	Sales Value > 8000
5	Jennifer	54	$5,420		FALSE	FALSE	
6	Mary	61	$4,790		TRUE	FALSE	**Conditions AND**
7	Paul	43	$6,095		FALSE	FALSE	Sales Quantity > 50
8	Robert	39	$8,340		TRUE	FALSE	AND
9	Emily	65	$8,585		TRUE	TRUE	Sales Value > 7000
10	Nicholas	37	$6,730		FALSE	FALSE	

Figure 7.10: Source data and conditions for logical tests

As usual, the data should be loaded from the table into Power Query using the **From Table/ Range** command on the **Data** tab (*Figure 1.1*).

In this example, two logical tests will be combined at once. Therefore, the **Conditional Column** command (*Figure 7.2*) cannot be used because this command processes logical tests sequentially. That is, if the first logical test is not satisfied, only then does Power Query proceed to evaluate the next test. For this reason, the appropriate formula must be written manually using the **Custom Column** command (*Figure 3.6*), which will be used to add two new columns: **BonusOR** and **BonusAND**.

The first scenario involves awarding a bonus to an employee when they have sold more than 60 units (value in the **Sales Quantity** column) or when the total sales value (value in the **Sales Value** column) is greater than 8000. In such a case, the two logical tests must be connected using the **or** keyword. The general syntax of the **if** expression is as follows:

```
if <test1 or test2> then <result> else <alternative result>
```

In this example, it is sufficient to return the text *Bonus* when the conditions are met. This means placing the word *Bonus* after the **then** keyword. If neither of the two conditions is met, the result should be **null**, which is specified after the **else** keyword.

Tip: **Logical tests combined with the or operator will return a logical value of false only when both combined tests return false. If at least one of them returns true, the or operation will return true.**

The full formula should be written as follows:

```
if [Sales Quantity] > 60 or [Sales Value] > 8000 then "Bonus" else null
```

This formula, divided into individual components, is shown in *Figure 7.11*:

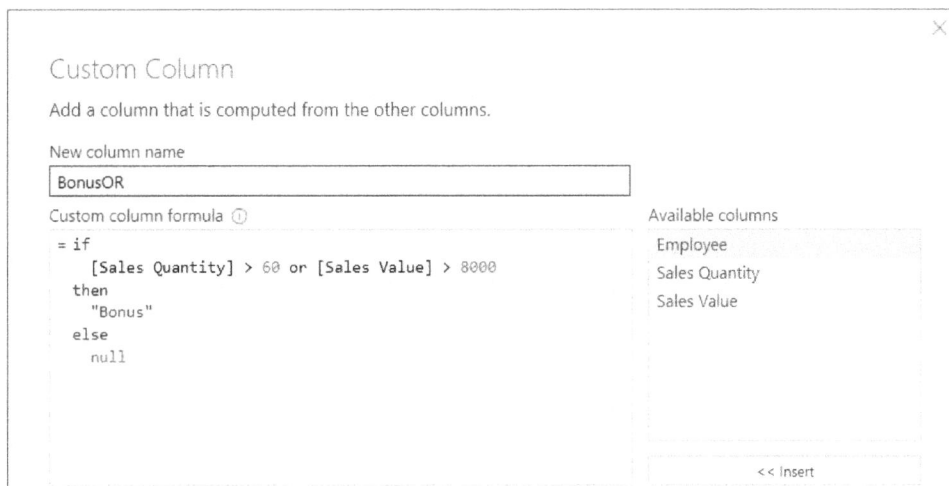

Figure 7.11: Formula using the logical or operator in the Custom Column window

Now, a new column can be created to assign a bonus based on two logical tests connected by the **and** operator. This time, the focus is on identifying rows where the value in the **Sales Quantity** column is greater than 50 **and** the value in the **Sales Value** column is greater than 7000.

Tip: **Logical tests combined using the and operator will return a logical value of true only if both tests return true. If at least one of them returns false, the result of the and operation will also be false.**

The general syntax of the `if` function is almost identical to the one used with the **or** operator. The only difference lies in the logical operator, as follows:

`if <test1 and test2> then <result> else <alternative result>`

In this use of the `if` function, the intention is to return the text **Bonus** when the defined conditions are met. When the combined logical tests return **false**, the desired output is an empty text string, written as two double quotation marks. The complete formula should be written as follows:

`if [Sales Quantity] > 50 and [Sales Value] > 7000 then "Bonus" else ""`

This formula, broken into separate sections, is shown in *Figure 7.12*:

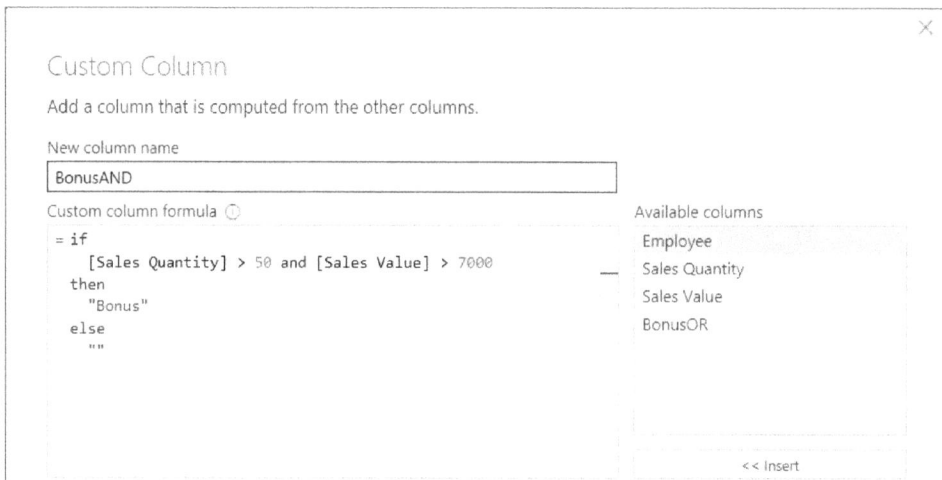

Figure 7.12: Formula with the logical and operator in the Custom Column window

After confirming the addition of both columns and changing their data types to text (ideally by appending **, type text** in the formula bar before the final parenthesis), the results will appear as shown in *Figure 7.13*:

	A♭C Employee	1²₃ Sales Quantity	1²₃ Sales Value	A♭C BonusOR	ABC₁₂₃ BonusAND
1	Olivia	20	5605	*null*	
2	John	62	9490 Bonus		Bonus
3	Monica	43	9610 Bonus		
4	Jennifer	54	5420	*null*	
5	Mary	61	4790 Bonus		
6	Paul	43	6095	*null*	
7	Robert	39	8340 Bonus		
8	Emily	65	8585 Bonus		Bonus
9	Nicholas	37	6730	*null*	

Figure 7.13: Results of combining logical tests with different operators in the if function

It can be observed that the word **Bonus** appears in the same rows where the logical tests in Excel returned **TRUE** (*Figure 7.10*).

Finally, the query should be renamed, for example, to **Logical OR I AND**, and the data should be loaded into Excel.

Tip: **Both null values and empty text strings (represented by two double quotation marks) will be loaded into Excel as blank cells.**

Grading with nested if

We are working with two tables (**tPoints** and **tGrades**) located on the **ApproximateIF** worksheet. These are shown in *Figure 7.14*:

	A	B	C	D	E
1	Student	No. of points		No. of points	Exam grade
2	Olivia	48		0	Bad
3	John	64		50	OK
4	Monica	82		80	Good
5	Jennifer	13			
6	Mary	96			
7	Paul	81			
8	Robert	34			
9	Emily	73			
10	Nicholas	77			
11					

Figure 7.14: Exam results and grading thresholds table

Based on the exam results and the grading threshold table, the goal is to assign an appropriate descriptive grade to each student. In this example, only the exam results table is imported into Power Query. The table containing grade thresholds serves as a reference for the values to be used in the logic. It is assumed that a student must achieve **at least** the number of points specified as the minimum in the grading table to be awarded a particular grade. In other words, the logical condition should be formulated as **greater than or equal to**.

It is important to understand that in such situations, where a value must be tested against multiple thresholds, systematic evaluation of the entire list is required. This can be done by starting from either the lower or higher thresholds. The direction depends solely on the user's preference in expressing the conditions. For Power Query, the order of operations is irrelevant. However, the logic must be continuous, since in the **Add Conditional Column** window, subsequent tests are only executed after the previous one evaluates to `false` (i.e., the condition is not met).

In this example, the thresholds will be evaluated from the **highest to the lowest**. Thus, the first condition checks whether the exam score is **greater than or equal to 80**. If this condition is not met, the next condition checks whether the score is **greater than or equal to 50**. When progressing to the next condition, the outcome of the previous check should be considered. For instance, if the score is **not greater than or equal to 80**, it must be **less than 80**. Therefore, the second condition essentially evaluates whether the score is in the range between 50 (inclusive) and 80 (exclusive). Due to this cumulative logic, there is no need to explicitly define a condition for the lowest grade. It can be assigned using the `else` clause, which instructs Power Query to return a predefined value when none of the previous conditions are met.

This approach is equivalent to creating an approximate match lookup function in Excel, based on threshold values.

After thoroughly analyzing the data, thresholds, and importing the table into Power Query, the **Conditional Column** command is selected (as shown in *Figure 7.2*). The **Add Conditional Column** window is then filled out as illustrated in *Figure 7.15*:

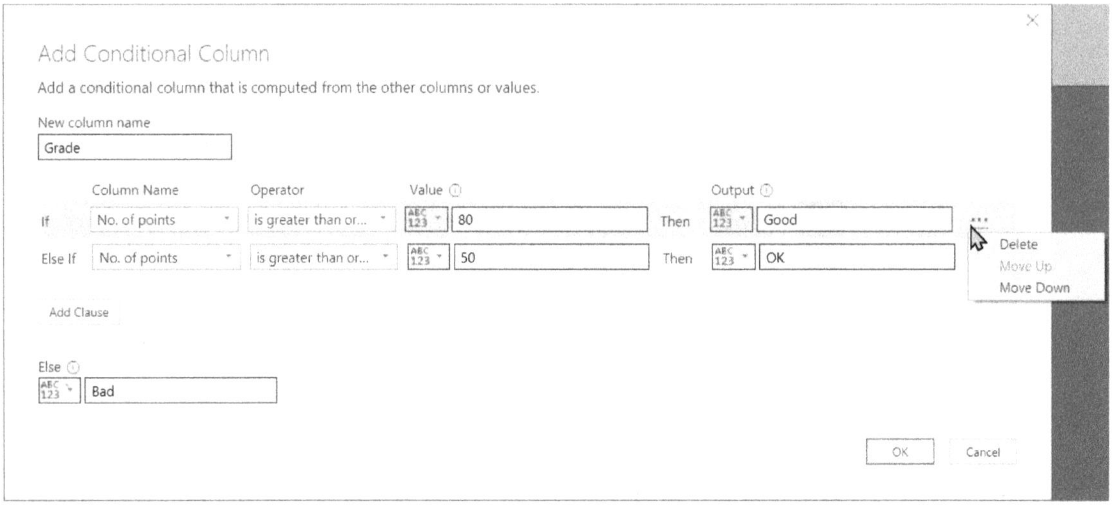

Figure 7.15: Filled conditional logic for assigning descriptive grades

To add a new condition in the **Add Conditional Column** window, the **Add Clause** button must be clicked. To change the position of a condition or delete it, the ellipsis icon located to the right of the condition must be selected, and the appropriate option chosen from the context menu (such a list is shown in *Figure 7.15*).

Tip: **The operators available in the Add Conditional Column window depend on the data type present in the analyzed column.**

After confirming the conditions by clicking the **OK** button, Power Query will insert a step containing the following M code:

```
= Table.AddColumn(#"Changed Type", "Grade", each if [No. of points] >= 80 then
"Good" else if [No. of points] >= 50 then "OK" else "Bad")
```

Fun fact: **If the data type of the column selected in the Add Conditional Column window is Date, a calendar icon will appear next to the Value field, which can also be used to insert a date.**

If the gear icon next to the step name *(Added Conditional Column)* is clicked, the **Add Conditional Column** window will reopen. Based on the analysis of the first example discussed in this chapter, it is known that any modification of the condition formula in this step (for example, changing **80** to **80 + 0**) will cause Power Query to switch to the **Custom Column** window. This behavior can be useful when basic logic is created with the help of the user interface and later refined manually.

Switching to the **Custom Column** window also allows for clearer formatting of the formula. After inserting line breaks and indentations, as shown in *Figure 7.16*, it becomes evident that this example uses nested **if** functions:

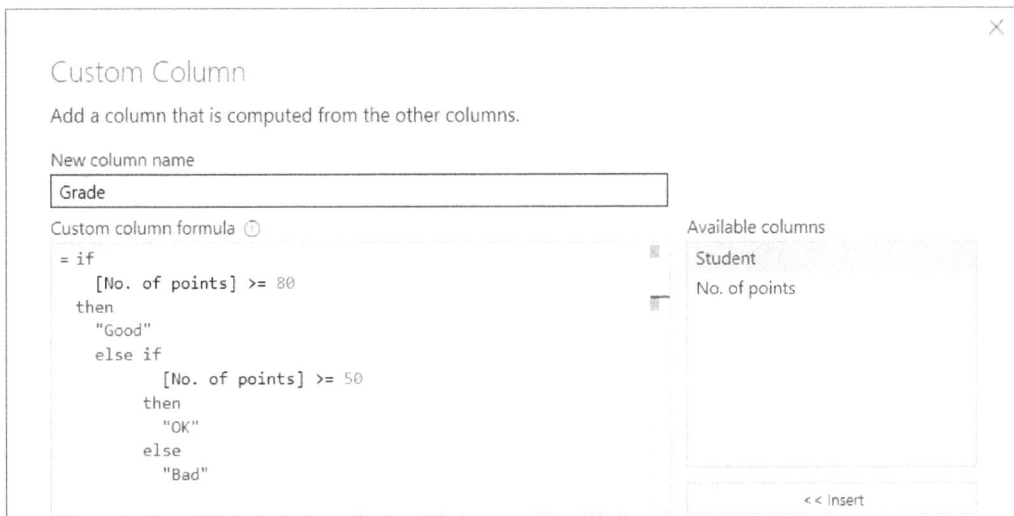

Figure 7.16: Formatted nested if function formula

Properly formatting the formula highlights that the alternative result of the first **if** function is another **if** function in which the next logical test is executed. In this example, it is not necessary to change the inner formula, so if the **Custom Column** window was opened, it can be closed by clicking the **X** in the top-right corner of the window and reverting any code modifications that were made.

Since the data type was not assigned in the M code when the conditional column was created, it must be added manually by appending the **type text** before the final parenthesis in the formula bar. It is also necessary to add a comma before the data type to separate the arguments of the **Table.AddColumn** function. Therefore, the full code for this step is as follows:

```
= Table.AddColumn(#"Changed Type", "Grade", each if [No. of points] >= 80 then
"Good" else if [No. of points] >= 50 then "OK" else "Bad", type text)
```

This modification in the code will not affect the functionality of the **Conditional Column** created through the user interface.

At this point, all that remains is to rename the query, for example, to **Marks**, and load it into Excel.

> Tip: **In this example, the threshold values were entered manually in the Add Conditional Column window; therefore, any changes made to the tGrades table will not affect the query results. Such changes must be made directly in the query either using the user interface or by editing the M code. The next example will present a solution that uses the values from the table as thresholds.**

Grading with appending

In this example, work is performed with two tables (**tPoints2** and **tGrades2**) located on the **ApproximateJoin** worksheet. These tables are presented in *Figure 7.17*:

	A	B	C	D	E
1	Student	No. of points		No. of points	Exam grade
2	Olivia	40		0	F
3	John	64		40	E
4	Monica	82		50	D
5	Jennifer	13		65	C
6	Mary	90		75	B
7	Paul	81		90	A
8	Robert	34			
9	Emily	73			
10	Nicholas	77			

Figure 7.17: Exam results and grade threshold table

Grades are assigned again, but this time there are significantly more thresholds, and using the **Conditional Column** command would be impractical. It would require considerable effort and would not allow for easy adjustment when thresholds or grade labels change. Therefore, in this scenario, the **Append** command will be used (see *Figure 3.2*), which was discussed in *Chapter 3, Combining Data Queries*.

Before loading the tables into the editor, it is important to note that the point-related columns in both tables have identical names, including case. This is crucial because Power Query is case-sensitive, and if the column names were identical except for letter case, Power Query would treat them as different columns, preventing proper data merging.

To correctly perform the Append operation for the **tPoints2** and **tGrades2** tables, these steps are to be followed:

1. Load the table with the grade thresholds into Power Query using the **From Table/ Range** command from the **Data** tab (*Figure 1.1*).

2. Without renaming the query, close the editor using the **Close & Load To** command (*Figure 1.13*).

3. In the **Import Data** window that opens (*Figure 1.14*), select the **Only Create Connection** option, since there is no need to load the table into Excel again.

4. Ensure the query is now available in the editor for further use.

5. Load the **tPoints2** table into Power Query.

6. Once loaded, select the **Append Queries** command on the **Home** tab (*Figure 3.2*).

7. In the **Append** window that appears, choose the **tGrades2** table to be merged with **tPoints2**, as shown in *Figure 7.18*:

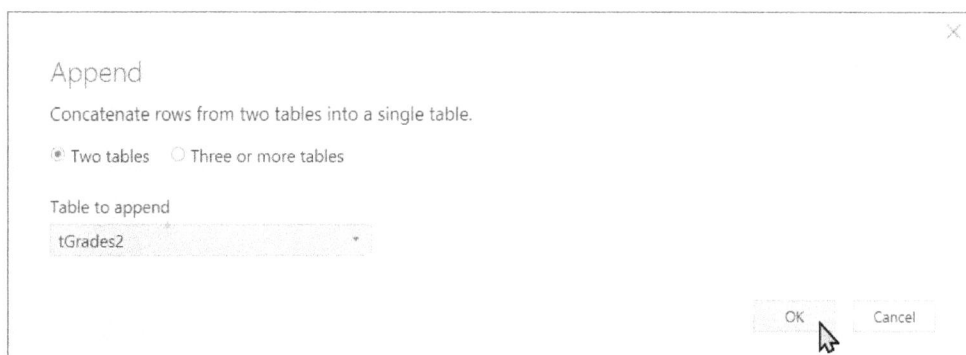

Figure 7.18: Append window combining two tables

8. After confirming the merge by clicking the **OK** button, Power Query will generate a combined query, as shown in *Figure 7.19*:

= Table.Combine({#"Changed Type", tGrades2})

	Student	No. of points	Exam grade	
1	Olivia	40	null	
2	John	64	null	
3	Monica	82	null	
4	Jennifer	13	null	
5	Mary	90	null	
6	Paul	81	null	
7	Robert	34	null	
8	Emily	73	null	
9	Nicholas	77	null	
10		null	0 F	
11		null	40 E	
12		null	50 D	
13		null	65 C	
14		null	75 B	
15		null	90 A	

Figure 7.19: Merged tPoints2 and tGrades2 tables

9. It is clear that the **No. of points** columns have merged correctly. However, in the two remaining columns, the editor has inserted **null** values wherever data was missing.

To correctly assign grades based on this dataset, the data must be sorted in ascending order by the **No. of points** column. To do this, the column should be selected, and then the **AZ** command from the **Home** tab should be clicked. The result of this sorting step is shown in *Figure 7.20*:

= Table.Sort(#"Appended Query",{{"No. of points", Order.Ascending}})

	Student	No. of points	Exam grade	
1		null	0 F	
2	Jennifer	13	null	
3	Robert	34	null	
4		null	40 E	
5	Olivia	40	null	
6		null	50 D	
7	John	64	null	
8		null	65 C	
9	Emily	73	null	
10		null	75 B	
11	Nicholas	77	null	
12	Paul	81	null	
13	Monica	82	null	
14		null	90 A	
15	Mary	90	null	

Figure 7.20: Sorted query

Tip: **During sorting, the null value is considered smaller than any number, text, or other value.**

It is important to note that in the case of duplicate values in the **No. of points** column, the row from the **tGrades2** table will appear above the row from the **tPoints2** table. As a result, it is sufficient to select the **Exam grade** column and use the **Fill Down** option from the **Transform** tab (*Figure 5.11*). This will propagate each grade downward (replacing **null** values) until the next non-null value is encountered.

10. Once the grades have been assigned to individual students, it is necessary to filter out the empty rows in the **Student** column (as demonstrated in *Figure 5.36*). The grades will be assigned correctly, as shown in *Figure 7.21*:

	Student	No. of points	Exam grade
1	Jennifer	13	F
2	Robert	34	F
3	Olivia	40	E
4	John	64	D
5	Emily	73	C
6	Nicholas	77	B
7	Paul	81	B
8	Monica	82	B
9	Mary	90	A

`= Table.SelectRows(#"Filled Down", each [Student] <> null and [Student] <> "")`

Figure 7.21: Grades assigned to students

11. The final steps are to rename the query (for example, to **Marks**) and load the result into Excel.

Since the grade thresholds were used intelligently in this example, it is sufficient to update the thresholds or grade labels in the source table and refresh the query to reflect the changes. Unlike in the previous example, there is no need to modify the query manually.

Counting days of absence

In this example, the data comes from the **TimeOff** worksheet, specifically from the **tOffWork** table. The source data contains information about periods during which individual employees were not at work. Based on this information, the goal is to generate a report that shows the number of days off in each month for all salespeople. The source data is shown in *Figure 7.22*:

◢	A	B
1	Id	Absence from work
2	1002	1/2/2025 - 1/7/2025; 7/19/2025; 10/11/2025 - 10/18/2025
3	1003	11/12/2025; 2/5/2025 - 2/15/2025; 6/30/2025 - 7/4/2025
4	1005	6/5/2025
5	1007	3/4/2025 - 3/18/2025; 5/6/2025 - 5/13/2025; 7/7/2025; 8/7/2025; 8/9/2025 - 8/10/2025
6	1011	5/13/2025 5/20/2025; 9/1/2025 9/4/2025

Figure 7.22: Source data with periods of work absence

A key detail for these transformations is that the third row in the table contains only a single date. Since it is right-aligned, Excel has recognized it as a date rather than a text value, which is how the other rows are treated. This inconsistency in data types within a single column will cause issues during the transformation process. This becomes even more evident after loading the data into Power Query using the **From Table/Range** command from the **Data** tab (*Figure 1.1*), because Excel imports dates with both date and time components by default, as shown in *Figure 7.23*:

⊞▾	1²₃ Id	▾	ᴬᴮᶜ₁₂₃ Absence from work	▾
1	1002		1/2/2025 - 1/7/2025; 7/19/2025; 10/11/2025 - 10/18/2025	
2	1003		11/12/2025; 2/5/2025 - 2/15/2025; 6/30/2025 - 7/4/2025	
3	1005		6/5/2025 12:00:00 AM	
4	1007		3/4/2025 - 3/18/2025; 5/6/2025 - 5/13/2025; 7/7/2025; 8/7/2025; 8/...	
5	1011		5/13/2025 - 5/20/2025: 9/1/2025 - 9/4/2025	

Figure 7.23: Source data loaded into Power Query

This occurs because the **Absence from work** column has **any** data type (indicated by the **ABC123** icon), which allows it to store any kind of data. However, attempts to remove the portion `12:00:00 AM` at this stage would be unsuccessful. This is because the time component is not stored as a separate time value but instead results from the formatting of the cell as **Date/Time**. This issue will need to be addressed later in the transformation.

The first transformation that must be performed is splitting the absence periods for each employee. To do this, the following steps are to be followed:

1. Select the **Absence from work** column.

2. Expand the **Split Column** command from the **Home** tab.

3. Select the **By Delimiter** option (*Figure 1.22*).

4. In the **Split Column by Delimiter** window, choose a semicolon as the delimiter.

5. Expand the advanced options and select to split into rows rather than columns, as done previously (*Figure 6.12*).

The result will be that each separate period (including single dates) is placed into a separate row for each employee, with each value represented as text. This is shown in *Figure 7.24*:

▦▾ 1²₃ Id		A^B_C Absence from work	
1	1002	1/2/2025 - 1/7/2025	
2	1002	7/19/2025	
3	1002	10/11/2025 - 10/18/2025	
4	1003	11/12/2025	
5	1003	2/5/2025 - 2/15/2025	
6	1003	6/30/2025 - 7/4/2025	
7	1005	6/5/2025 12:00:00 AM	
8	1007	3/4/2025 - 3/18/2025	
9	1007	5/6/2025 - 5/13/2025	

Figure 7.24: Absence periods split into separate rows

After splitting, it becomes clear that the actual delimiter is a semicolon followed by a space. However, for safety, it is better to perform the split using only the semicolon and then apply the **Trim** option available after expanding the **Format** command on the **Transform** tab (*Figure 1.40*), in case a space is missing and the split does not occur as expected.

The precise steps for cleaning the **Absence from work** column at this stage are as follows:

1. Change the data type to **text** (this step should be added automatically after splitting the column into rows).

2. Use the **Trim** option to remove any leading spaces. Depending on later transformations, this step may turn out to be unnecessary.

3. Remove the text **12:00:00 AM** using the **Replace Values** command from the **Home** tab by entering the value in the **Value To Find** field and leaving the **Replace With** field blank, as done previously (*Figure 6.14*).

Once the **Absence from work** column has been cleaned of unnecessary elements, it should be split into two columns using the hyphen as a delimiter. This is done by using the **Split Column by Delimiter** command again. Since the data was cleaned beforehand, Power Query should automatically change the data type for both columns to **Date**, as shown in *Figure 7.25*:

Figure 7.25: Absence periods in two separate columns

In cases where there was only one day of absence, the second column is filled with a **null** value. For further transformations, this value should be replaced with the corresponding value from the first column. This transformation is performed using a conditional column, created with the **Conditional Column** command from the **Add Column** tab (*Figure 7.2*). In this step, the condition checks whether the value in the second column is **null**. If it is, the value from the first column is returned; otherwise, the value from the second column is used. The correctly filled **Add Conditional Column** window is shown in *Figure 7.26*:

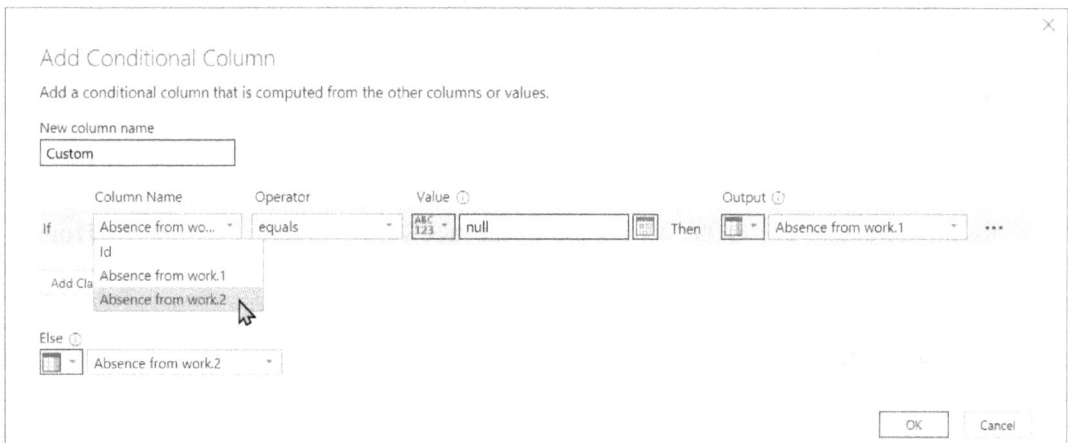

Figure 7.26: Filled Add Conditional Column window

The name of the new column, just like the previously created columns after splitting by hyphen, is not relevant, as they will be removed shortly. Therefore, their default names are retained.

Once the end date has been determined for each absence period, a sequence of days (numbers) from the first to the last day of the absence period can be generated. The topic of creating sequences was previously mentioned in *Chapter 5*, in the *Pivot and unpivot* section, specifically in the *Splitting double headers* subsection, when discussing the **By Lowercase to Uppercase** column split. The sequence operator, consisting of two dots, was used for that purpose.

Unfortunately, this operator cannot be applied directly to date values, so the `Number.From` function will be used to convert dates into numbers.

To generate the required list of values, the following steps should be performed:

1. Click the **Custom Column** command on the **Add Column** tab (*Figure 3.6*).

2. Name the new column **Month** (for use in later transformations).

3. Enter the formula that creates a list of days (as numbers) from the start date of the absence period (**Absence from work.1** column) to the end date of that period (**Custom** column). The complete formula is as follows:

```
{Number.From([Absence from work.1])..Number.From([Custom])}
```

The **Custom Column** window with the formula and renamed column is shown in *Figure 7.27*:

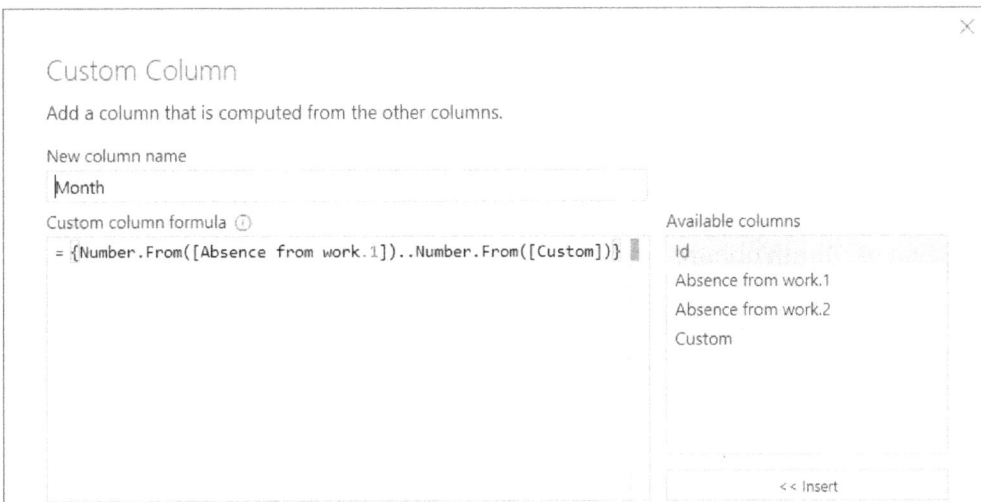

Figure 7.27: Custom Column window with a formula generating a list of days (numbers)

4. Confirm the addition of the new column by clicking the **OK** button.

5. Remove the columns **Absence from work.1**, **Absence from work.2**, and **Custom** by selecting them and pressing the *Delete* key.

6. Expand the **Month** column using the icon in the header and select the **Expand to New Rows** option (*Figure 4.9*).

7. Change the data type of the **Month** column to **Date**.

After completing these transformations, a table will be produced showing employee IDs alongside a list of dates on which each employee was absent. This result is shown in *Figure 7.28*:

Figure 7.28: Table with employee absence days

The objective was to generate a report indicating the number of absence days per month for each employee. To accomplish this, it is necessary to extract month names from the dates in the Month column and then group the data to count the days of absence. The steps should be executed in the following order:

1. Select the **Month** column.

2. On the **Transform** tab, expand the **Date** command, then expand **Month**, and select the **Name of Month** option, as shown in *Figure 7.29*:

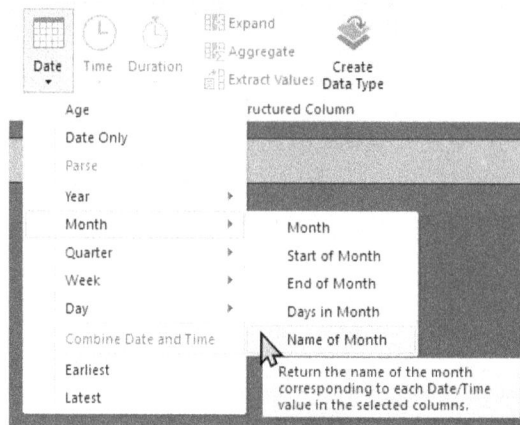

Figure 7.29: Name of Month option from the Date command

3. Select the **Id** and **Month** columns in that order.

4. Click the **Group By** command on the **Home** tab (*Figure 4.4*).

5. Leave the default aggregation method (**Count Rows**) and the default name for the aggregation column (**Count**).

6. Confirm the grouping by clicking the **OK** button.

This produces the required information, as shown in *Figure 7.30*:

Id	Month	Count
1002	January	6
1002	July	1
1002	October	8
1003	November	1
1003	February	11
1003	June	1
1003	July	4
1005	June	1
1007	March	15

Figure 7.30: Result showing the number of absence days by month

Finally, the query should be renamed, for example, to **Absences**, and the result loaded into Excel.

Numbers and errors

We are working with data from the **tNumbers** table located on the **Numbers** sheet. This table contains several different values, including special numeric values, as shown in *Figure 7.31*:

	A	B
1	**Client**	**Deposit**
2	John	1000
3	Monica	500
4	Jennifer	Gold
5	Mary	NA
6	Paul	Not a Number
7	Carlos	NaN
8	Positive	∞
9	Negative	-∞
10	Nothing	null

Figure 7.31: Table with special numeric values

This example will be used to demonstrate how to handle errors that may occur in Power Query results. The goal is to manage errors using the user interface, by writing a formula, and by extracting the error description. Three separate queries will be required to accomplish this.

To prepare the dataset for demonstrating multiple error-handling methods, these steps are to be followed:

1. Import the table into the Power Query editor using the **From Table/Range** command from the Data tab (*Figure 1.1*).

2. Rename the current query to `ErrorHandling` to reflect its purpose.

3. Expand the **Queries** list on the left side of the editor.

4. Right-click the `ErrorHandling` query and select the **Duplicate** option from the context menu, as shown in *Figure 7.32*:

Figure 7.32: Query duplication option

The new query will be given the default name `ErrorHandling (2)`, which will be addressed later. For now, the original query will be modified.

Since the **Deposit** column contains both numbers and text, Power Query has assigned it **any** data type (indicated by the **ABC123** icon), which supports all types of values. The first transformation involves changing the data type to **Whole Number**. Most cells contain values of incompatible types, and therefore, Power Query will return errors in those cells. Only one exceptional value (`null`) will be interpreted correctly and will not result in an error, as shown in *Figure 7.33*:

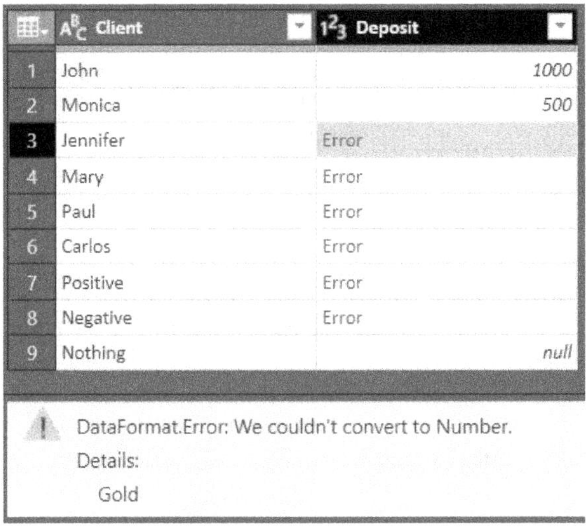

Figure 7.33: Errors after changing the data type to Whole Number

For the remaining values that are not numeric, errors will appear. Selecting a cell that contains an error will cause the editor to display a detailed description of the error beneath the data. As shown in *Figure 7.33*, this description includes information, such as the type of error, a short explanation, and **Details**, which typically contain a copy of the value in the selected cell.

Before handling the errors in this query, the data type for the **Deposit** column should be changed again. This time, the data type should be set to **Decimal Number**. If Power Query prompts whether the current step should be modified, the **Replace Current** button should be clicked (*Figure 2.6*). After changing the data type, the editor will recognize additional special values, as shown in *Figure 7.34*:

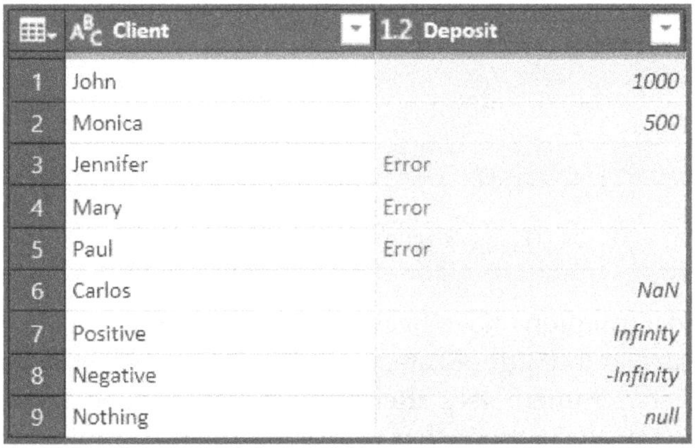

Figure 7.34: Errors after changing the data type to Decimal Number

The **Decimal Number** data type includes special values such as positive and negative **Infinity**, the **NaN** value (Not a Number), and **null**.

Tip: **Every data type supports the special value null. Special values are written in italics.**

In this query, the goal is to handle the errors in the **Deposit** column by replacing them with the number zero. In this case, the **Replace Values** command from the **Home** tab (*Figure 5.19*) cannot be used because, unlike **null**, the editor and the **Replace Values** window (*Figure 5.21*) do not recognize the word **Error** as a special value. To replace errors, the following steps are to be followed:

1. The **Replace Values** command from the **Transform** tab must be expanded.

2. The **Replace Errors** option is selected, as shown in *Figure 7.35*:

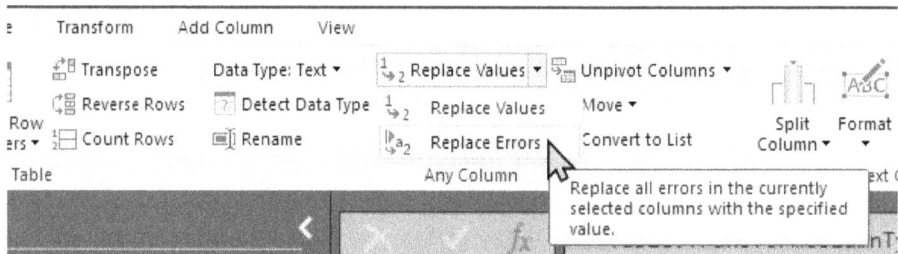

Figure 7.35: Replace Errors command

3. This will open the **Replace Errors** window, where the value zero should be entered into the **Value** field and the changes confirmed by clicking the **OK** button, as shown in *Figure 7.36*:

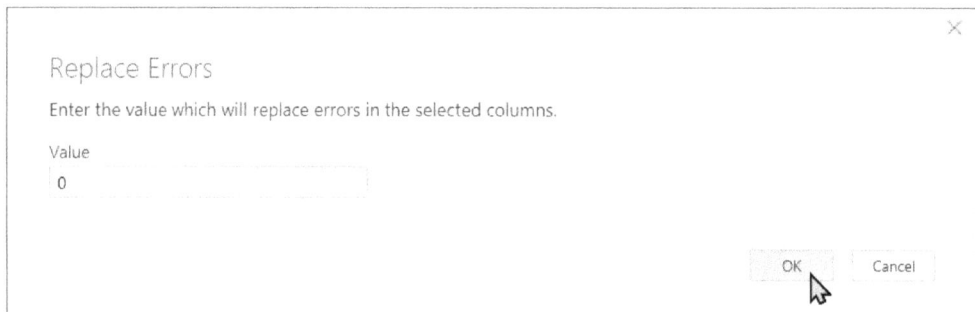

Figure 7.36: Replace Errors window

All the necessary transformations have been completed for the **ErrorHandling** query. Now, attention should be turned to its duplicate, **ErrorHandling (2)**. It is important to note that the query was duplicated immediately after the initial import, so **ErrorHandling (2)** does not contain any of the transformations that were subsequently applied to the **ErrorHandling** query.

The first operation to be added to the duplicated query is the creation of a new column using the **Custom Column** command from the **Add Column** tab (*Figure 3.6*). To complete this operation, these steps are to be followed:

1. The new column should be named **Try**.

2. The following formula should be entered: **Number.From([Deposit])**

3. The new column should be confirmed by clicking the **OK** button.

4. The data type for the new column should be explicitly defined by adding the code, type number before the final closing parenthesis in the formula bar.

After adding the new column, both the original column with data from Excel and the results of converting those values to decimal numbers will be visible in the query, as shown in *Figure 7.37*:

	A^B_C Client	ABC 123 Deposit	1.2 Try
1	John		1000	1000
2	Monica		500	500
3	Jennifer	Gold	Error	
4	Mary	NA	Error	
5	Paul	Not a Number	Error	
6	Carlos	NaN		NaN
7	Positive	∞		Infinity
8	Negative	-∞		-Infinity
9	Nothing	null		null

Figure 7.37: Data before conversion and after conversion to a number

At this stage, the **ErrorHandling (2)** query should be duplicated. The new query will automatically receive the name **ErrorHandling (3)**. This duplicate will include the step for adding a new column, but further transformations will be applied independently in each query.

Return to the **ErrorHandling (2)** query. The formula in the newly added column will be modified so that errors are replaced with zero values, similar to what was done in the **ErrorHandling** query. In Excel, this could be achieved using the **IFERROR** function. In Power Query, a more complex expression must be used. First, the keyword **try** is added before the current formula to test its result. Then, the **otherwise** keyword is appended, followed by the value to return in case of an error. In this case, zero. The formula update process is as follows:

1. Click the gear icon next to the last step (**Added Custom**).

2. In the **Custom Column** window, update the formula to:

   `try Number.From([Deposit]) otherwise 0`

3. Confirm the formula update by clicking **OK**.

Now, the **Try** column will return the same results as the **Deposit** column in the `ErrorHandling` query.

Proceed to the `ErrorHandling` **(3)** query. Here, the formula in the newly added column should also be modified, but only the **try** keyword is to be added before the `Number.From` function. The entire formula should be: `try Number.From([Deposit])`

This change may be made in the **Custom Column** window as before, or directly in the formula bar by inserting the word **try** in the appropriate place.

As a result of using only the **try** keyword (without **otherwise**), the outcome will be records that contain detailed information about the evaluated expressions. If the evaluated formula does not return an error, the record will include a **HasError** field with the value **false**, and a **Value** field with the result of the formula. If the formula does return an error, the record will include **HasError** set to **true** and an **Error** field, which itself contains a record with a detailed description of the error. These cases are shown in *Figure 7.38*:

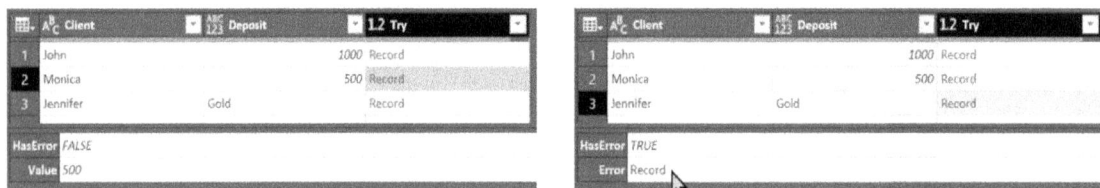

Figure 7.38: Results of evaluating a formula using the try keyword

The goal now is to expand the records stored in the **Try** column. However, this is currently not possible because one of the previous transformations set the column's data type to **number**. The data type must be changed to **any** or removed entirely from the formula bar to restore the ability to expand the internal contents.

Once the column can be expanded, click the expand icon in the column header. It is important to select the **Load more** option, as shown in *Figure 7.39*, to ensure Power Query retrieves the complete list of fields. By default, it may only scan a sample of rows and present an incomplete list of columns.

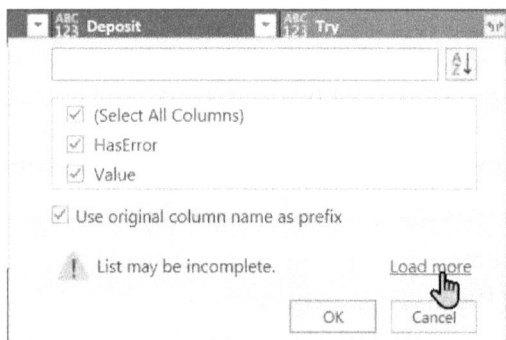

Figure 7.39: Load more option when expanding the Try column

The exact process of expanding the **Try** column consists of the following steps:

1. Click the arrow icon in the header of the **Try** column.

2. Click the **Load more** option to ensure additional data columns (including **Error**) are loaded.

3. Leave all checkboxes selected, including the **Use original column name as prefix** option.

4. Click **OK** to confirm the expansion.

After expanding the **Try** column, three new columns will appear as follows:

- **Try.HasError**: Contains a logical value indicating whether an error occurred.

- **Try.Value**: Returns the value from the **Deposit** column when no error occurred, or null if an error occurred.

- **Try.Error**: Contains a record describing the error if one occurred, or null if no error occurred.

The results of the column expansion are shown in *Figure 7.40*:

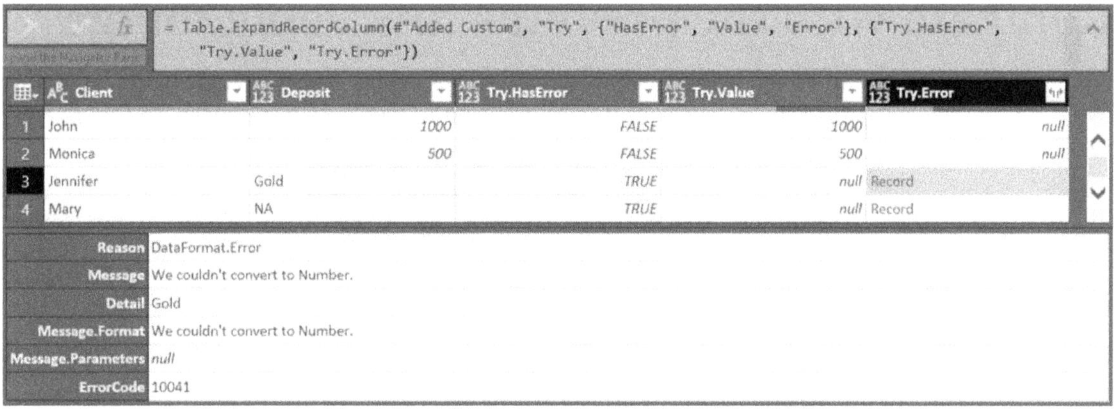

Figure 7.40: Result after expanding the Try column

To retrieve additional error information, the **Try.Error** column should be expanded. When doing so, exclude the **Message.Format** and **Message.Parameters** fields and uncheck the prefix option. Once this column is expanded, the data can be loaded into Excel.

Since multiple queries were created simultaneously, they cannot be inserted into a specific worksheet directly. Instead, choose the option to place them on a new worksheet (*Figure 1.14*). After loading the tables into Excel, they can be moved by cutting (*Ctrl + X*) and pasting (*Ctrl + V*) them into another worksheet.

When importing special values into Excel, they may not always be displayed correctly. This is illustrated by the result of the **ErrorHandling (2)** query, shown in *Figure 7.41*:

Figure 7.41: ErrorHandling (2) query loaded into Excel

Tip: **Some values and data types recognized by Power Query are not recognized by Excel. Therefore, the null value is imported as an empty cell. Special values such as Not a Number and Infinity are returned as the #NUM! error. Complex values such as Record and Table are imported as the text [Record] or [Table].**

Compare with the previous row using merge

We are working with data from the **tInvoices** table located on the **Merge** worksheet. This table contains information about invoices issued to clients. The source data is shown in *Figure 7.42*:

Figure 7.42: Source data about invoices

The objective is to determine when a client previously made a purchase and, based on this, assess whether the client is a returning customer. A client is considered returning if no more than 14 days have passed since their last purchase.

The process of preparing the table in Power Query for row-by-row comparison involves the following steps:

1. Load the table into the Power Query editor using the **From Table/Range** command from the **Data** tab (*Figure 1.1*).

2. Change the data type of the **Date** column to **Date** (not Date/Time).

3. Sort the data by the **Client** or **Client ID** column.

4. Then, sort by the **Date** column in ascending order using, for example, the **AZ** button on the **Home** tab.

5. Review the sorted data, where each client's rows are arranged chronologically so that the previous invoice or purchase appears directly above the current row, as shown in *Figure 7.43*:

⊞▾ 1²₃ Client ID	A^BC Client	A^BC Invoice	▦ Date
1	1 Colorful Butterfly	FV2025/02	10/4/2025
2	1 Colorful Butterfly	FV2025/13	11/10/2025
3	1 Colorful Butterfly	FV2025/17	11/12/2025
4	2 Digging Mole Ltd.	FV2025/03	10/6/2025
5	2 Digging Mole Ltd.	FV2025/11	10/29/2025
6	3 Jumping Frog	FV2025/05	10/8/2025
7	3 Jumping Frog	FV2025/07	10/12/2025
8	3 Jumping Frog	FV2025/19	11/22/2025
9	3 Jumping Frog	FV2025/23	11/29/2025

Figure 7.43: Sorted data

Unfortunately, in Power Query, referring to a row other than the current one is significantly more complex than in Excel. This example will demonstrate how this can be achieved by merging a query with itself. A technique discussed in detail in *Chapter 3, Combining Data Queries*, in the subsection *Merging query with itself*.

Before merging the query, two index columns must be added using the **Index Column** command from the **Add Column** tab (*Figure 4.15*). The first index column should be numbered starting from one, and the second from zero.

After adding the index columns, the query can be merged using the **Merge Queries** command from the **Home** tab (*Figure 3.9*). The **Merge** window will open, in which the same query (**tInvoices**) is selected as both the top and bottom table. It is also necessary to select the index starting from zero at the top and the index starting from one at the bottom, as shown in *Figure 7.44*:

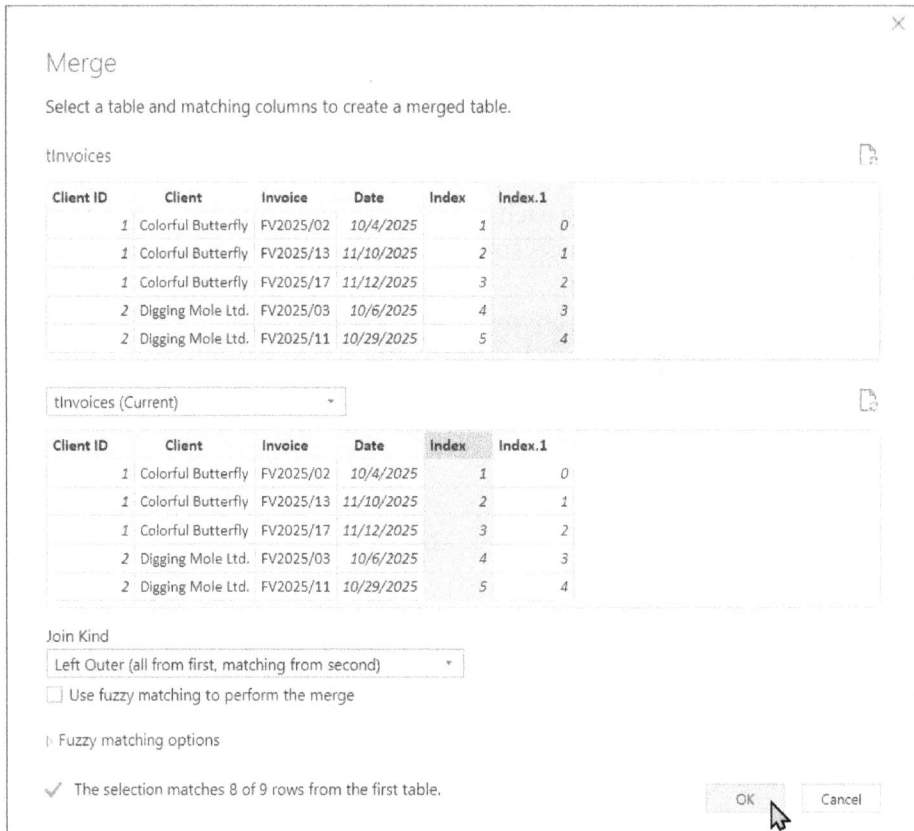

Figure 7.44: Merging with the previous row

The offset between the index columns ensures that each row is merged with the preceding row. From the previous row, the required information is found in the **Client** and **Date** columns. Therefore, the newly created column is expanded to include only those two columns, without prefixes. The index columns can be deleted, as they are no longer needed. The data after these transformations is shown in *Figure 7.45*:

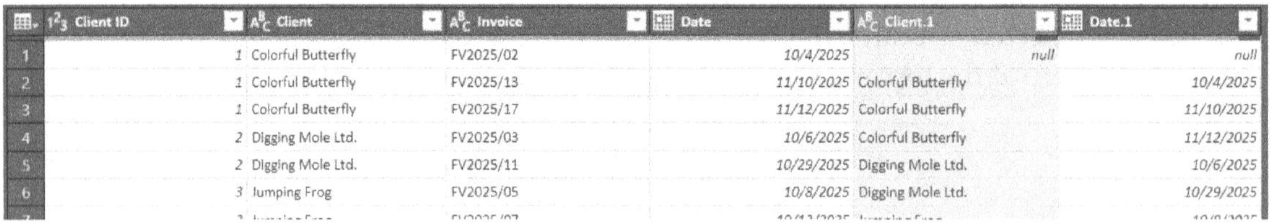

Figure 7.45: Data from the previous and current row

At this point, it is possible to determine whether the client is a returning customer. This will be done by writing an appropriate logical formula. Two conditions must be satisfied simultaneously, which means they will be joined using the **and** operator. The first condition is that the client in the previous row (**Client.1** column) must be the same as the client in the current row (**Client** column). The second condition is that the difference between the dates must be less than 14 days. Since date calculations cannot be directly compared to numeric values, the first example will use the **#duration** function. The complete formula is as follows:

```
if [Client] = [Client.1] and [Date] - [Date.1] < #duration(14, 0, 0, 0) then
"YES" else null
```

A new column containing this formula is added using the **Custom Column** command from the **Add Column** tab (*Figure 3.6*). The complete formula and the name of the new column (**Returning Customer?**) are shown in *Figure 7.46*:

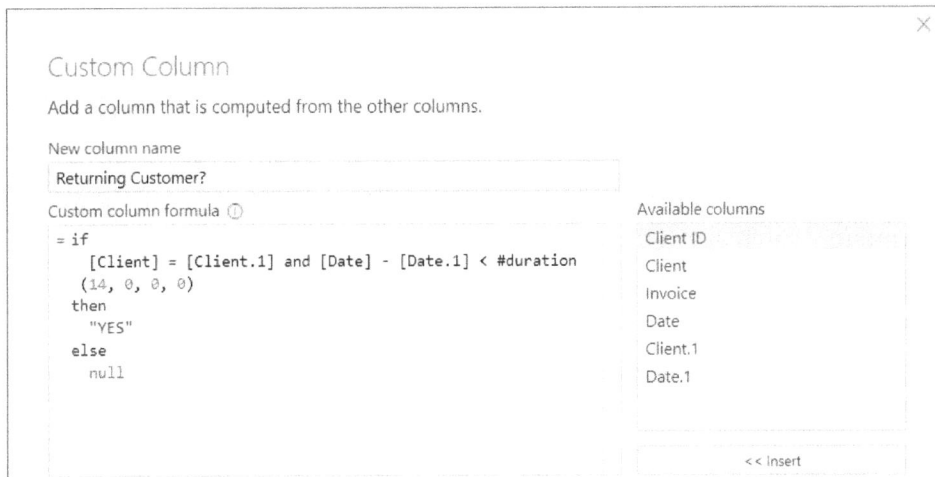

Figure 7.46: Formula checking whether the client is a returning customer

An alternative version of the formula could use the **Duration.Days** function as follows:

```
if [Client] = [Client.1] and Duration.Days([Date] - [Date.1]) < 14 then "YES"
else null
```

This formula answers the question posed at the beginning of the example. The final steps are as follows:

1. Rename the query, for example, to **Returning Customers**.
2. Remove the **Client.1** and **Date.1** columns.
3. Load the data into Excel.

Compare with the previous row using index

We are working with data from the **tIncome** table located on the **Index** worksheet. This table contains information about the company's income in individual months. The task is to calculate the difference in income between consecutive months. In Excel, this is a straightforward formula, as illustrated in *Figure 7.47*:

	A	B	C	D	E	F
1	**Month**	**Income**				
2	January	$17,306		0.0%		
3	February	$17,936		=1-B2/tIncome[@Income]		
4	March	$15,206		▼ -18.0%		
5	April	$17,703		▲ 14.1%		
6	May	$17,770		▲ 0.4%		
7	June	$17.934		▲ 0.9%		

Figure 7.47: Source data and formula calculating the income difference

In Power Query, as shown in the previous example, this task is not as simple. In this case, a method based on the row index will be used.

Begin by loading the data from the table into the editor. Then, right-click on the cell in the *Income* column for March. From the context menu that opens, select the **Drill Down** option, as shown in *Figure 7.48*:

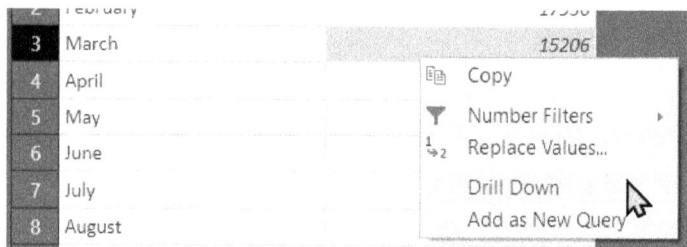

Figure 7.48: Context menu for the cell

The previous operation added a new step that returns the value from the specified cell. However, the main point of interest here is the M code visible in the formula bar, which is as follows:

```
= #"Changed Type"{2}[Income]
```

This line includes the following components:

1. A reference to the previous step: #"Changed Type"
2. A row index in curly brackets: {2}
3. A reference to the column: [Income]

It is particularly important to note that although the third row was selected (as shown in *Figure 7.48*), Power Query used the number two as the index. This is because Power Query indexes values such as list elements or row numbers starting from zero (a convention similar to many programming languages). Therefore, the first row is assigned the index zero, the second row is indexed as one, and so on.

The step just added served as an illustration of how to reference a specific cell within a Power Query table and can now be removed.

Next, an index column should be added using the **Index Column** command from the **Add Column** tab (*Figure 4.15*), starting with the value minus one. Based on the values in this column, it will be possible to reference previous rows by constructing a formula based on the M code used after applying the **Drill Down** option.

All formulas seen so far in the formula bar have referred to the immediately preceding step. However, Power Query allows referencing any earlier step in the query.

Tip: **In Power Query, references can be made only to previous steps. It is not possible to reference subsequent steps, as this would result in a circular dependency.**

To create a formula that retrieves the income value from the previous month, it is necessary to reference a specific earlier step that contains the income column sorted in chronological order. In this example, the desired reference point is the step named **Changed Type**, where data types have already been assigned, and which is not the step immediately preceding the one being added.

The next part of the reference is the row number from which the value should be extracted. This number is stored in the newly created **Index** column. Therefore, instead of manually entering a static index such as **2** (as seen earlier), a dynamic reference to the **Index** column should be used. The reference to the **Income** column remains unchanged.

This means the formula to be used is as follows:

```
= #"Changed Type"{[Index]}[Income]
```

The column is added using the **Custom Column** command from the **Add Column** tab (*Figure 3.6*), and it is named **Change**. The resulting table is shown in *Figure 7.49*:

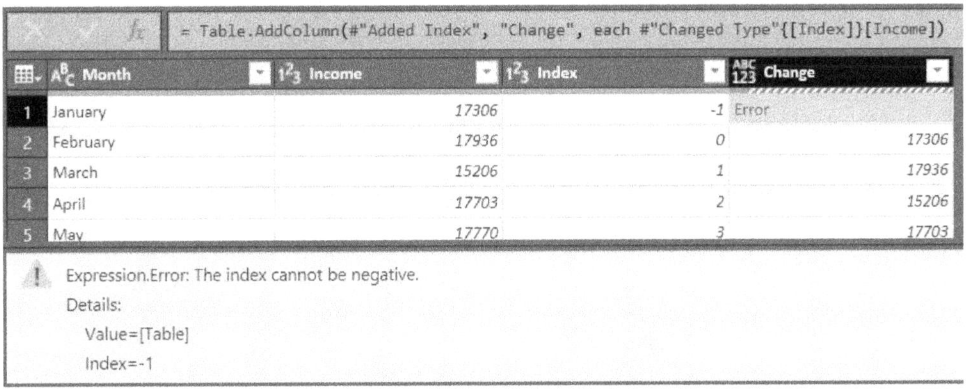

Figure 7.49: Reference to the previous cell from the Income column

In the first row, an error is visible. This results from the fact that the index or row number cannot be negative. However, before addressing it, the formula should be modified to calculate the change in income between months. Based on the Excel formula (*Figure 7.47*), the Power Query formula should be written as follows:

```
1 - #"Changed Type"{[Index]}[Income] / [Income]
```

After modifying the formula, it is recommended to change the data type to percentage. To do so, append the data type **Percentage.Type** before the final closing parenthesis in the formula bar. The complete M code for the final step should be as follows:

```
= Table.AddColumn(#"Added Index", "Change", each 1 - #"Changed Type"{[Index]}
[Income] / [Income], Percentage.Type)
```

This produces the result shown in *Figure 7.50*:

	A^B_C Month	1²₃ Income	1²₃ Index	% Change
1	January	17306	-1	Error
2	February	17936	0	3.51%
3	March	15206	1	-17.95%
4	April	17703	2	14.10%
5	May	17770	3	0.38%

Figure 7.50: Calculated percentage change between incomes for consecutive months

The error is still present in the first row of the table. However, if the query were loaded into Excel, a blank cell would appear in place of the error, which would be an acceptable result. Nevertheless, the goal is to display a zero instead of an empty cell, which requires modifying the formula once more by adding error handling using the try and otherwise keywords. The updated formula should be as follows:

```
try 1 - #"Changed Type"{[Index]}[Income] / [Income] otherwise 0
```

The formatted version of the formula is shown in *Figure 7.51*:

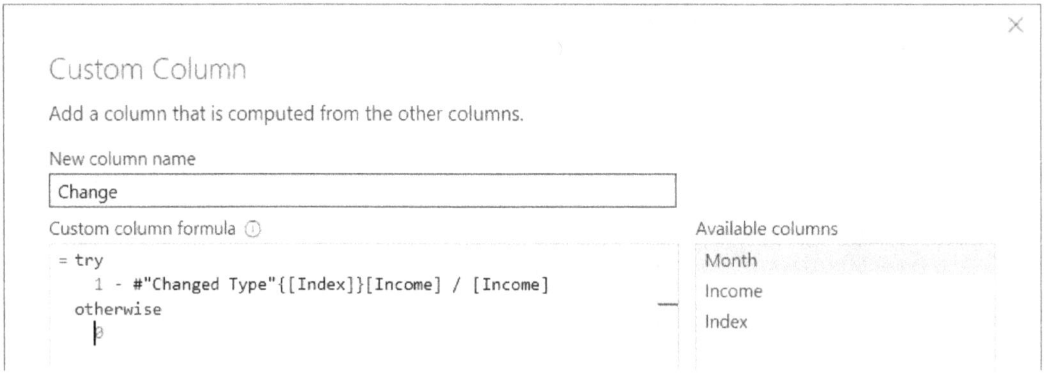

Figure 7.51: Formatted formula with error handling

Before loading the query result into Excel, several final transformations should be performed as follows:

1. Rename the **Changed Type** step. Right-click the step and choose **Rename** from the context menu (*Figure 5.7*) or select the step and press **F2**. The new step name should be a single word: **Types**.

    After renaming, all references to the original step name are updated automatically. The formula calculating the change in income will now appear as follows:

    ```
    try 1 - Types{[Index]}[Income] / [Income] otherwise 0
    ```

2. Delete the **Index** column by selecting it and pressing the **Delete** key.

3. Rename the query to % **change in Income**.

4. If the **Percentage** data type for the **Change** column has been lost, reapply it.

5. Load the final query result into Excel.

6. Apply percentage formatting to the **Change** column in Excel.

Fun fact: **Since the query was named with a special character at the beginning (the percent sign), Excel omits it when naming the resulting table. Therefore, the table in Excel will be named change_in_Income.**

Conclusion

In this chapter, we focused on logical operations and conditional column creation in Power Query. You learned how to build both simple and complex conditions using the graphical interface and custom M formulas. Key techniques included calculating overtime, assigning grades based on thresholds, handling errors, and comparing values across rows.

In the next chapter, you will learn how to make your queries dynamic by incorporating user-defined inputs and reusable settings.

Multiple choice questions

1. **In which window can you manually define conditions using drop-downs and input fields?**

    a. Custom Column

    b. Add Conditional Column

    c. Replace Values

    d. Group By

2. **Which function is used to return the number of days from a duration?**

   a. DateTime.Diff

   b. Time.Days

   c. Duration.Days

   d. Date.Difference

3. **What keywords are used to safely evaluate a formula that might return an error?**

   a. IFERROR

   b. otherwise

   c. try

   d. catch

4. **How can logical tests be combined in Power Query formulas?**

   a. Using + and – operators

   b. Using IF THEN ELSE blocks only

   c. Using parentheses only

   d. Using and and or keywords

5. **In a nested if structure, what should appear after the else keyword?**

   a. Only null

   b. Another if or a final result

   c. A try statement

   d. A Date value

6. **Which of the following are correct uses of the #duration function in Power Query?**

   a. #duration(0, 8, 0, 0)

   b. #duration(8, 0)

   c. #duration(0, 0, 0, 0)

   d. #duration("08:00")

7. **Which of the following are valid logical operators in Power Query?**

   a. and

   b. not

   c. &

   d. or

Answers

Question number	Answer option letter
1.	b.
2.	c.
3.	b., c.
4.	d.
5.	b.
6.	a., c.
7.	a., b., d.

Join our Discord space

Join our Discord workspace for latest updates, offers, tech happenings around the world, new releases, and sessions with the authors:

https://discord.bpbonline.com

CHAPTER 8
Parameters and Query Parameterization

Introduction

In the previous chapter, we explored logical operations and conditional columns, enabling dynamic data transformations based on rules and conditions.

This chapter introduces parameters and query parameterization, essential tools for making queries flexible, reusable, and interactive. We will learn how to extract specific values using Drill Down, filter data based on parameter values, and dynamically reference file paths.

Key topics include creating parameters from lists, queries, or worksheet cells, and writing M code to build fully parameterized queries. Along the way, challenges such as non-unique keys, privacy settings, and dynamic file locations will be addressed.

Structure

This chapter covers the following topics:

- Drill down information
- Parameterized query using filter
- Parameterized query using file path

- Extracting parameters from a cell
- Parameterized directly in M code

Objectives

By the end of this chapter, you will be able to create and apply parameters in Power Query to build flexible, reusable queries that adapt to changing inputs or file locations. You will understand how to extract specific cells, rows, and columns using both positional and key-based referencing, and how to handle common issues, such as non-unique or missing keys. The chapter also equips you with the skills to use parameters in filters, replace hardcoded file paths, and reference dynamic values from worksheet cells. Additionally, you will gain a foundational understanding of parameter-related M code, enabling you to modify and integrate parameters directly within queries for more advanced data transformations.

Drill down information

In this example, the mechanics of drill down and associated methods for detailing information, for example, from a specific column or row, are examined closely.

The example uses data from the **DrillDown** worksheet in the file **DrillDown.xlsx**, as shown in *Figure 8.1*:

	A	B	C	D	E	F	G	H	I	J	K	L
1	No. Excel	No. PQ	ID	Seller	Product	Jan	Feb	Mar				
2	1	0	1002	Alex	Pony	$35,800	$44,400	$34,100		ID	1017	
3	2	1	1003	Alex	Doll	$64,850	$55,500	$52,350		Month	Feb	
4	3	2	1005	Alex	Teddy	$51,000	$35,500	$39,000		Row	7	=MATCH(K2,tSales[ID],0)
5	4	3	1007	Alex	Car	$37,250	$18,700	$24,150		Column	2	=MATCH(K3,tSales[[#Headers],[Jan]:[Mar]],0)
6	5	4	1011	Richard	Pony	$44,150	$45,700	$42,600		Lookup Cell	$38,650	=INDEX(tSales[[Jan]:[Mar]],K4,K5)
7	6	5	1013	Richard	Doll	$57,650	$17,700	$52,550		Lookup Row	$84,750	=SUM(INDEX(tSales[[Jan]:[Mar]],K4,0))
8	7	6	1017	Richard	Teddy	$19,650	$38,650	$26,450		Lookup Column	$513,700	=SUM(INDEX(tSales[[Jan]:[Mar]],0,K5))
9	8	7	1019	Richard	Car	$41,550	$57,900	$23,900				
10	9	8	1023	Marlene	Pony	$47,900	$23,950	$53,850				
11	10	9	1029	Marlene	Doll	$48,950	$36,750	$23,450				
12	11	10	1031	Marlene	Teddy	$27,100	$29,050	$54,900				
13	12	11	1037	Marlene	Car	$59,600	$66,150	$69,400				
14	13	12	1041	Marlene	Train	$23,250	$43,750	$24,900				

Figure 8.1: Source data connected to the drill down option

The first important point to mention about detailing data in Power Query is the row and list numbering method. Power Query, similar to some programming languages, begins numbering from zero. This might be confusing for users who have not previously worked with such tools and are accustomed to Excel, which numbers rows and columns starting from one. Therefore, the first two columns in *Figure 8.1* illustrate the difference between standard Excel numbering and Power Query row numbering.

Another important aspect involves the calculations shown on the right side of *Figure 8.1*. From the top, these include the following:

- The selected ID number from the ID column (linked to the row number).
- The selected month from column headers (linked to the column number).
- Row number calculated based on the provided ID.
- Column number calculated based on the given month name.
- Value retrieved from a cell based on row and column numbers (range F2:H14).
- Sum of values from the selected row (based on its position).
- Sum of values from the selected column (based on its position).

Where necessary, the Excel formulas used to determine these values are indicated. It should be noted that the results are not strictly based on row or column numbers, but rather on their positions found using Excel functions. Translated into Power Query terms, this corresponds to searching by key. This means that even if the data were sorted or column positions were altered in the analyzed table (range C1:H14), the results of the last three formulas would remain unchanged, as they search for the position of a single ID in the ID column and the position of the selected month in the headers.

Next, the analysis will move into Power Query to demonstrate how specific details, such as data from a cell, row, or column, can be extracted.

Drill down cells

The process of drilling down into a specific cell in Power Query can be performed as follows:

1. Select any cell within the range **C1:H14** and use the **From Table/Range** command from the **Data** tab (*Figure 1.1*) to import the data into Power Query.

2. Right-click, for example, the **fifth cell in the Feb column**, and choose the **Drill Down** option from the context menu, as demonstrated in the previous chapter (*Figure 7.48*).

3. Observe that the editor now displays only the value from the selected cell, and examine the generated M code in the formula bar:

```
= Source{4}[Feb]
```

4. Understand the structure of the M code:
   - Source refers to the table/query step.
   - {4} specifies the fifth row (Power Query indexing starts at 0).
   - [Feb] refers to the column by name (not position).

This corresponds to the standard drill down syntax used in Power Query:

```
TableName {row index number}[ColumnName]
```

5. Note that since the row index is hardcoded, any changes to the row order (e.g., sorting) may return a different value. Column order, however, does not affect the result because the column is referenced by name.

6. Delete the last step created by the **Drill Down** command (typically named **Navigation**) to explore the underlying source.

7. Review the original **Source** step, which should resemble:

```
= Excel.CurrentWorkbook(){[Name="tSales"]}[Content]
```

8. Test the behavior of **Excel.CurrentWorkbook()** by removing the code after it. This displays a list of tables and named ranges from the current workbook (*Figure 8.2*):

	Content	Name
1	Table	tSales
2	Table	Table1
3	Table	Month
4	Table	Sheet1!Print_Area

Figure 8.2: Result of the Excel.CurrentWorkbook() function

Tip: **The Excel.CurrentWorkbook() function presents a list of tables and named ranges from the current Excel workbook as tables. Unlike Excel.Workbook function (Figure 2.11), it does not return worksheets.**

9. Recognize that in the Source step, the row is selected by key comparison using the Name column to the **tSales** value. The syntax for such key-based access is:

```
TableName {[ColumnName1 = "search key"]}[ColumnName2]
```

Using this syntax removes concerns about the order of data within the column.

The default difference in detailing data depends on the existence of keys in the table. For the currently modified Source step, columns with keys assigned by Power Query can be checked using the **Table.Keys** function.

To check which columns have keys assigned and then add your own, follow these steps:

1. Add a new step in the query by clicking the **fx** icon located next to the formula bar. This inserts a new step that, by default, contains only a reference to the previous step.

2. In the formula bar of the new step, enter the following code:

```
= Table.Keys(Source)
```

This will return a record that lists the column names to which keys have been assigned. The result is shown in *Figure 8.3*:

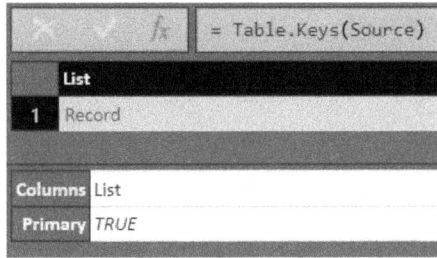

Figure 8.3: Record with a list of columns that have assigned keys

3. Understand that in the context of the **Source** step, specifically the one using `Excel.CurrentWorkbook()`, Power Query treats the **Name** column as a primary key. Therefore, when retrieving data from this table, the editor can use key-based comparison to identify a row.

4. However, in the default **Source** step that includes the line:

```
= Excel.CurrentWorkbook(){[Name="tSales"]}[Content])
```

Power Query does not automatically assign any keys to the resulting table. As a result, in the previously generated **Navigation** step, the **Drill Down** operation selected a row based on its position, not a key.

5. Delete the step that was used to check for key assignments, so that the query returns to the original **Source** step.

6. Add another step by clicking the **fx** icon again, and in the formula bar, enter the following code to assign a key manually:

```
= Table.AddKey(Source, {"ID"}, true)
```

This will not change the appearance of the table but will designate the **ID** column as the primary key. In this case, the **ID** column is suitable because it uniquely identifies each row in the dataset.

7. After assigning the key, repeat the **Drill Down** operation on the fifth row of the **Feb** column. This time, the M code will appear as:

```
= Custom1{[ID=1011]}[Feb]
```

This confirms that Power Query now selects the row based on the **ID** value rather than the row number.

Tip: **An example of an operation that automatically adds primary keys to a table is the removal of duplicate rows. This operation is available from the options list for the Remove Rows command on the Home tab (Figure 1.30).**

Having discussed extracting information from individual cells, the next section will focus on extracting information from entire columns.

Drill down columns

To extract information from a specific column using the Drill Down feature in Power Query, follow these steps:

1. In the Power Query editor, right-click the **header of the column** you want to extract. For example, the **Feb** column. Then select the **Drill Down** option from the context menu, as shown in *Figure 8.4*:

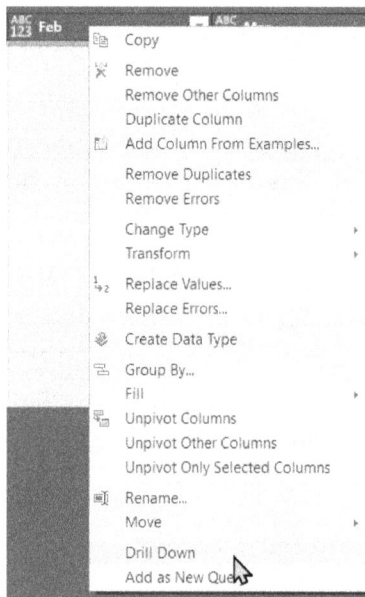

Figure 8.4: Drill Down information from a column

Power Query will return the contents of the selected column as a **list of values**, not as a table. This change in data structure is reflected in the interface, which now shows the **Transform** tab labeled as **List Tools**, as shown in *Figure 8.5*:

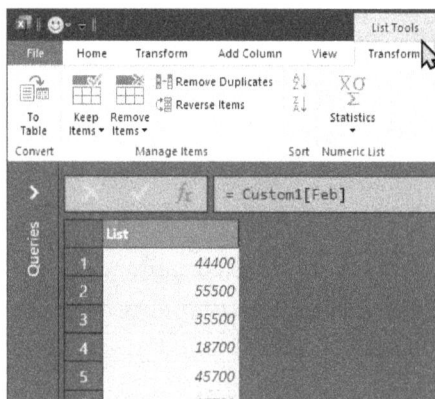

Figure 8.5: Column Feb extracted as a list of values

2. If you want to convert this list back into a proper table, use the **To Table** command available on the **Transform, List Tools** tab.

3. Alternatively, you can quickly convert the list to a table by modifying the M code directly in the formula bar. To do this, replace the existing formula with:

```
= Custom1[[Feb]]
```

This will return the **Feb** column as a single-column table.

4. If you wish to include additional columns, you can extend the list of column names inside the double square brackets. For example:

```
= Custom1[[Mar],[Feb],[Jan]]
```

This modification will extract the specified columns and return them as a multi-column table.

5. Note that the **order in which columns are listed** in the formula determines the order in which they appear in the resulting table. In the example above, the table will contain the **Mar**, **Feb**, and **Jan** columns in that specific sequence, as illustrated in *Figure 8.6*:

Mar	Feb	Jan
34100	44400	35800
52350	55500	64850
39000	35500	51000
24150	18700	37250
42600	45700	44150

Figure 8.6: Three extracted month columns in reversed order as a table

This completes the process of extracting selected columns. The next section will explain how to extract specific rows.

Drill down rows

First, the last step should be deleted in order to extract an entire row from the source table. Right-clicking the row number does not open any context menu from which the **Drill Down** option can be selected. Therefore, the appropriate code must be written manually, as follows:

1. Click the **fx** icon next to the formula bar.

2. Add curly brackets to the name of the previous step with the row number that should be extracted.

Considering that Power Query indexes from zero, the code to extract the fifth row should appear as follows:

```
= Custom1{4}
```

The result of this code is shown in *Figure 8.7*:

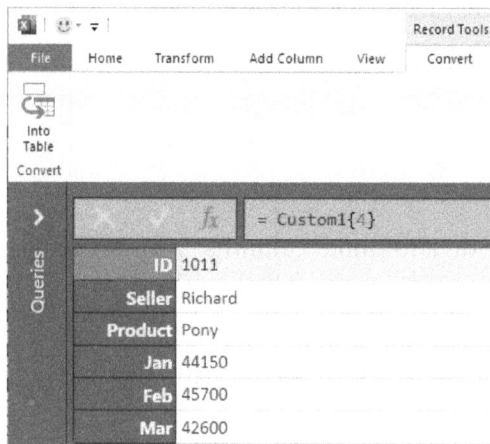

Figure 8.7: Extracted fifth row as a record

A row extracted in this manner is presented as a data record. This is also indicated by the appearance of the **Convert** tab, additionally labeled as **Record Tools**. Only one conversion option is available here: converting the record to a data table. This table will consist of two columns. The first contains the record field names, and the second contains the corresponding values.

Note: **The method of extracting a row shown in Figure 8.7 allows only a single row to be extracted. To extract multiple non-adjacent rows by their index, filtering based on an added index column may be used.**

The record shown in *Figure 8.7* can be limited to specific fields by appending syntax similar to the one used for extracting entire columns. The complete code in the formula bar might appear as follows:

```
= Custom1{4}[[Mar],[Feb],[Jan]]
```

This returns a record with three fields, as shown in *Figure 8.8*:

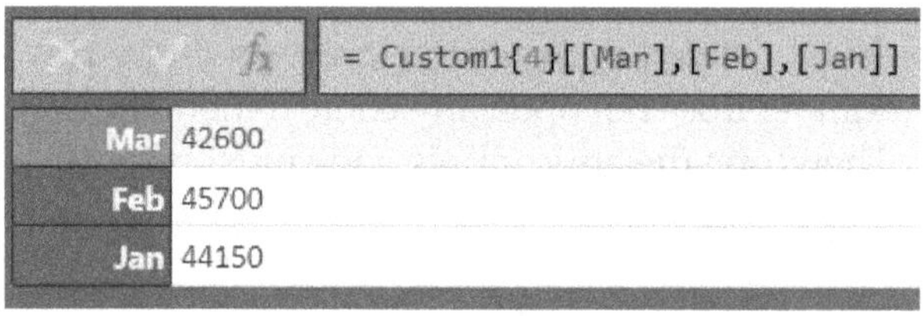

Figure 8.8: Record from a row limited to three fields

Information has been extracted from various sections of the table in Power Query. The final part of this example addresses errors that may occur when attempting to extract information using a non-unique key.

Errors with non-unique keys

First, remove all unnecessary steps that were added. Only the **Source** step and the step adding keys to the table should remain.

Next, a key match will be forced on a column containing duplicate values (**Product**), to which no key has been assigned. Since no key has been assigned to this column, the code must be written manually.

Begin with code for a value that appears only once in the **Product** column, such as **"Train"**. For this example, only the value from the **ID** column will be extracted, not the entire row. To extract a specific cell value based on a key column (in this case, Product), follow these steps:

1. Click the **fx** icon to create a new step.

2. Enter the following code:
   ```
   = Custom1{[Product="Train"]}[ID]
   ```

   This returns the correct cell value, as shown in *Figure 8.9*:

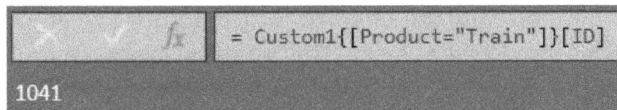

Figure 8.9: Correctly extracted value based on a unique key in the Product column

3. Next, change the key value to **"Pony"**, as follows:
   ```
   = Custom1{[Product="Pony"]}[ID]
   ```

   This code generates an error stating that more than one row matches the key condition, as shown in *Figure 8.10*:

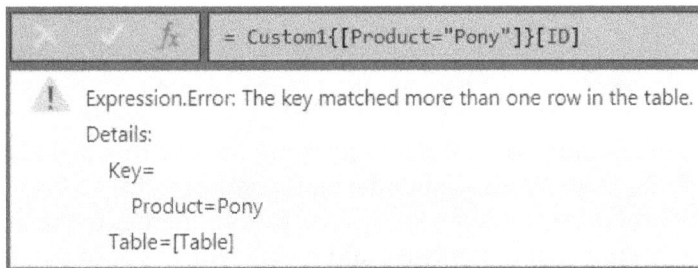

Figure 8.10: Error for a key value that appears multiple times

4. Next, change the key value to one that does not exist in the Product column, for example, **"car"**. The lowercase form is used deliberately to emphasize that Power Query is case-sensitive. For the new code:
   ```
   = Custom1{[Product="car"]}[ID]
   ```

The editor will not find the specified key value and will return an error, as shown in *Figure 8.11*:

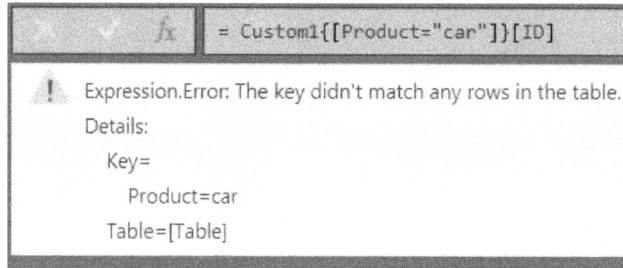

Figure 8.11: Error for a key value that does not exist in the specified column

These are all the operations and transformations intended for this query. In this example, the **Drill Down** command and its related operations have been thoroughly discussed, although no result offering additional value has been generated.

Therefore, click the **x** in the upper-right corner of the editor window to close it. Then, in the **Power Query Editor** window, click the **Discard** button to remove all changes, including the loading of data or queries into Power Query. This window is shown in *Figure 8.12*:

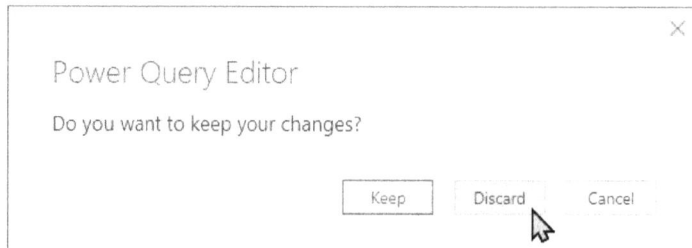

Figure 8.12: The discard changes window in Power Query

Parameterized query using filter

This example uses already transformed data regarding the one thousand largest cities in the world from the website **https://public.opendatasoft.com/**, which has been inserted into the file **LargestCitiesWorld.xlsx**. On the Queries worksheet, there is a query (**LargestCities**) containing basic information about the cities and a table with a list of continents loaded into Power Query (**Continents**), as shown in *Figure 8.13*:

	A	B	C	D	E	F	G	H
1	No.	Name	Country name EN	Population	Continent	Modification date		Continent
2	1	Shanghai	China	22,315,474	Asia	10/15/2023		Asia
3	2	Beijing	China	18,960,744	Asia	3/7/2022		Africa
4	3	Shenzhen	China	17,494,398	Asia	10/25/2023		Europe
5	4	Guangzhou	China	16,096,724	Asia	10/25/2023		Australia
6	5	Kinshasa	Congo, Democratic R	16,000,000	Africa	11/29/2023		South America
7	6	Lagos	Nigeria	15,388,000	Africa	10/25/2023		North America
8	7	Istanbul	Turkey	14,804,116	Europe	10/25/2023		
9	8	Chengdu	China	13,568,357	Asia	10/25/2023		
10	9	Mumbai	India	12,691,836	Asia	1/29/2024		

Figure 8.13: Source queries about the largest cities and a list of continents

The task is to add a parameterized filter to the **LargestCities** query to display the largest cities for a selected continent. To begin creating a parameterized filter in Power Query, perform the following steps:

1. Open the query editor. This can be done, for example, by selecting the **Edit** option from the query's context menu (*Figure 1.26*) or by clicking the **Edit** command on the **Query** tab (*Figure 1.15*).

2. Ensure that the **Always allow** checkbox is selected in the **Parameters** command group on the **View** tab (*Figure 1.6*).

3. Expand the filter menu for the column (*Figure 2.15*), select **Text filters**, then choose **Equals**.

Since parameter support has been enabled, it is possible not only to type a text value as the filter condition or select it from a drop-down list, but also to use or create a new parameter to be applied as the filter condition. As no parameter has been created yet, only the creation of a new parameter is available at this point, as shown in *Figure 8.14*:

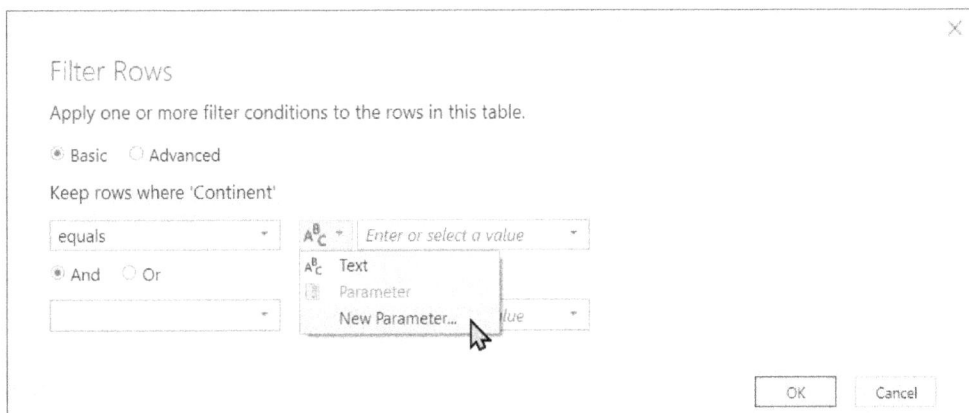

Figure 8.14: The Filter Rows window with the add parameter option expanded

Selecting the new parameter option opens the **Manage Parameters** window, in which two settings should be changed immediately, as follows:

1. Enter **Continent** as the name of the new parameter in the **Name** field.

2. Change the data type using the **Type** drop-down list to **Text**.

The window after these modifications is shown in *Figure 8.15*:

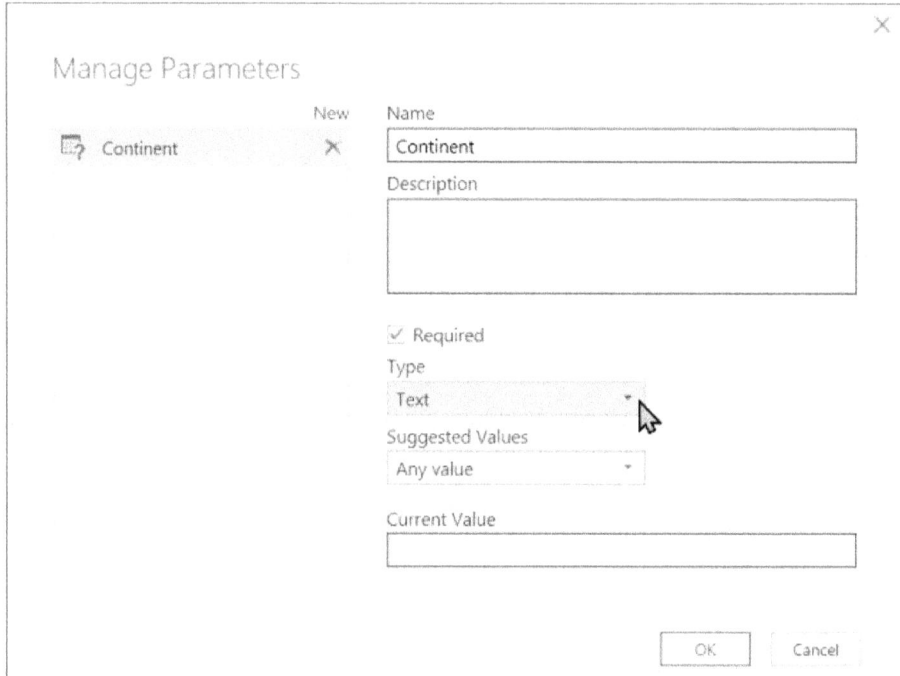

Figure 8.15: The Manage Parameters window with the new text parameter Continent

Individual elements of the **Manage Parameters** window include the following:

*   A list of parameters on the left side, with a **New** button above it to add a new parameter. When hovering over a parameter name, an **x** icon appears on the right, which allows the associated parameter to be deleted. A parameter can also be removed by clicking its name and pressing the **Delete** key.

*   The **Name** field for entering the parameter name.

*   The **Description** field for optional additional notes about the parameter.

*   The **Required** checkbox, indicating that the parameter is mandatory if it is used in a query, meaning the **Current Value** field cannot be empty.

*   The **Type** drop-down list containing data types that can be assigned to the argument.

- The **Suggested Values** drop-down list, which contains three options:

  o **Any value**, indicating the parameter can accept any value matching the selected data type.

  o **List of values**, allowing a predefined list of acceptable values to be entered. When selected, a **Default Value** field appears where the default parameter value can be entered or selected.

  o **Query**, assigning the parameter's values from the result of a query. When selected, a **Query** field appears to select the query returning the list of values.

- The **Current Value** field containing the current value assigned to the parameter.

To restrict the possible values that can be assigned to the parameter, change the **Suggested Values** option to **List of values**.

List of values

After selecting the **List of values** option, manually fill in the list of continents according to the list available on the **Queries** worksheet (*Figure 8.13*), as follows:

- Click the empty cell in the first row.

- Type the name of a continent.

- Press *Enter* to confirm the entry.

This action adds the value to the list and inserts another empty row. Additional empty rows can also be added by clicking the plus icon at the bottom of the list.

After entering all values, select **Europe** from the **Default Value** list and **Asia** from the **Current Value** list, as shown in *Figure 8.16*:

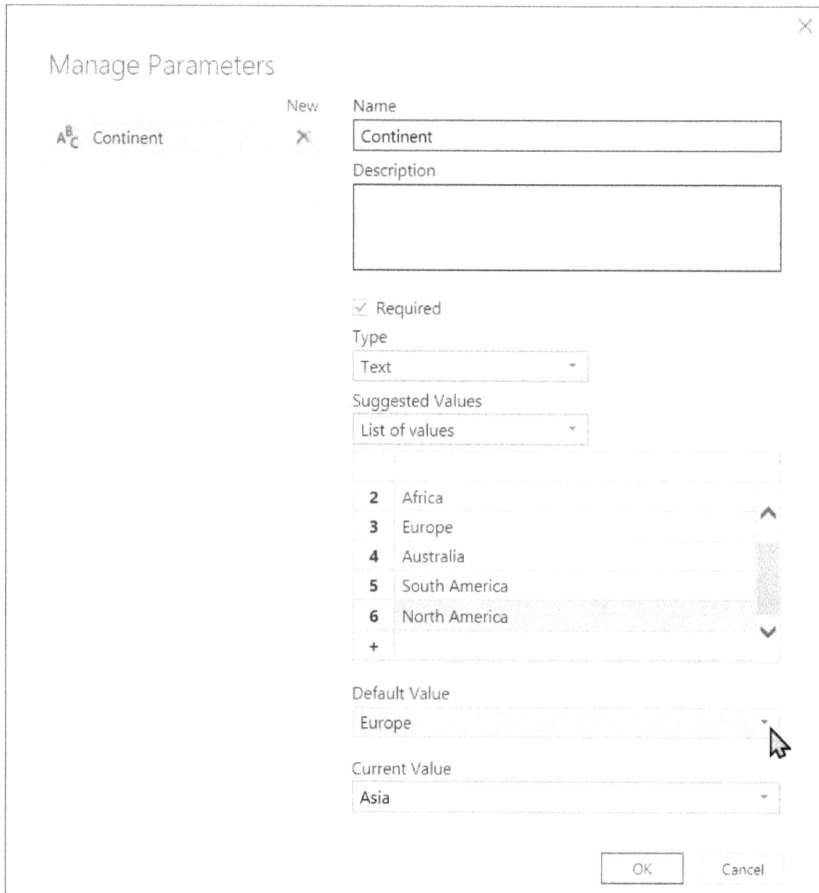

Figure 8.16: The Manage Parameters window with a list of values

Confirm the **Manage Parameters** window by clicking **OK**. This returns to the **Filter Rows** window, where the icon next to the value selection field changes from **ABC** to the icon assigned to the parameter. From this point on, instead of a list of column values, parameters can be selected. Currently, only one parameter is available, as shown in *Figure 8.17*:

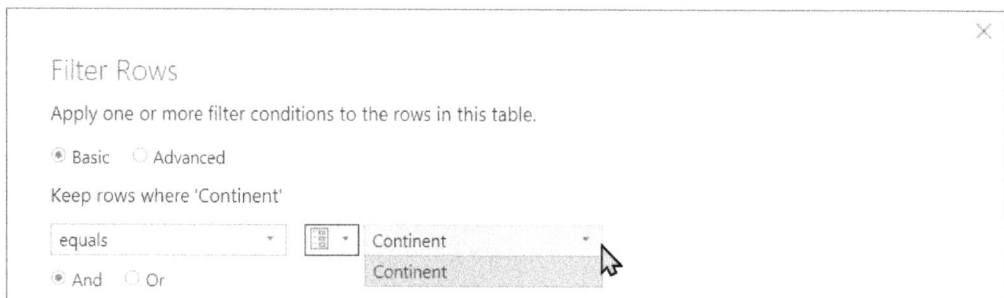

Figure 8.17: The Filter Rows window with the selected parameter

Confirming the filter by clicking **OK** adds a new step with the following M code visible in the formula bar:

```
= Table.SelectRows(#"Removed Columns", each [Continent] = Continent)
```

The code assigns a filter indicating that values in the **Continent** column (identified by square brackets) must equal the value stored in the **Continent** parameter. As the current value of the **Continent** parameter was set to **Asia** (*Figure 8.16*), the `LargestCities` query will return only cities from **Asia**.

To change the current parameter value, the following steps are to be followed:

1. Expand the query pane on the left side of the editor.

2. Click the name of the desired parameter (the current value is displayed in parentheses next to the name).

The query results area will display the **Current Value** field, where the parameter's assigned value can be changed, as shown in *Figure 8.18*:

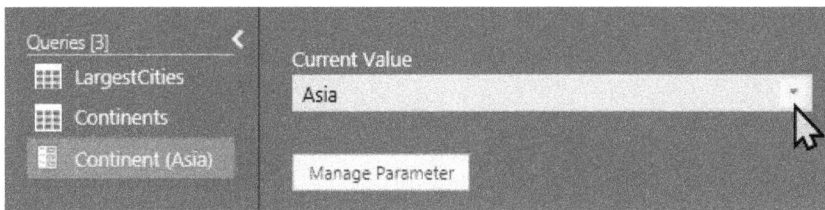

Figure 8.18: The query list including the added parameter

Tip: **Although the Continent parameter has a defined list of values (Figure 8.18), it is still possible to assign a different value. Instead of selecting from the list, type the value manually.**

Below the **Current Value** field (*Figure 8.18*) is the **Manage Parameter** button, which opens the **Manage Parameters** window (*Figure 8.15*, *Figure 8.16*). This window can also be opened by clicking or expanding the **Manage Parameters** command on the **Home** tab.

An additional option available when expanding the **Manage Parameters** command, besides creating a new parameter, is the option to edit all parameters from the current file, as shown in *Figure 8.19*:

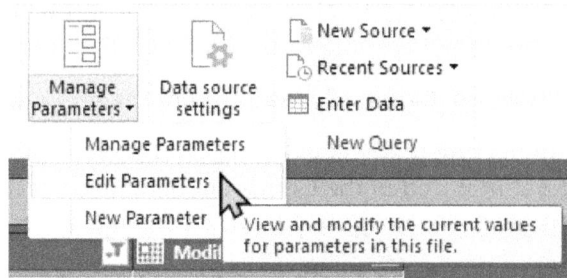

Figure 8.19: The Manage Parameters command

Selecting this option opens the **Edit Parameters** window, which lists all parameters and their assigned values, allowing them to be edited. As only one parameter has been created in this example, only that parameter is shown in the window. Change its value to **Africa**, as shown in *Figure 8.20*, to observe the change in the filtering results:

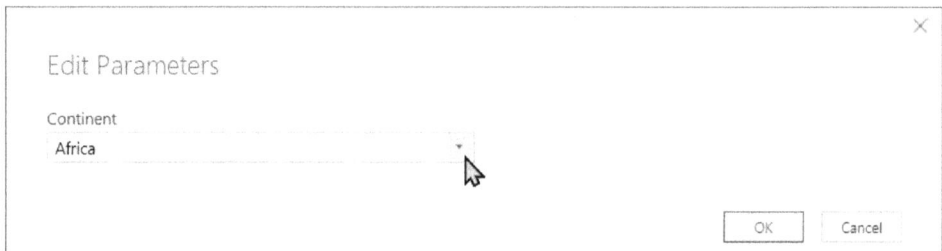

Figure 8.20: Edit Parameters window

Next, the value in the **Suggested Values** field in the **Manage Parameters** window will be changed to **Query**.

Query

Simply changing the value in the **Suggested Values** field to **Query** does not allow selecting from any of the currently existing queries to assign to the parameter, because parameters require queries that return lists.

Although the **Continents** query has already been imported into the editor and might be considered a list by a user, Power Query recognizes it as a table (as indicated by the icon next to the query name in *Figure 8.18*). Therefore, it is necessary to proceed to that query and then, on the **Transform** tab, click the **Convert to List** command, as shown in *Figure 8.21*:

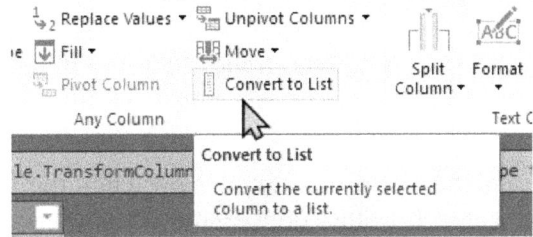

Figure 8.21: Convert to List command

This converts the selected column of data into a list, like how a column of data was extracted from a table earlier in this chapter (*Figure 8.5*). An important detail not previously emphasized is that this operation changes the data type of the query and the associated icon, as shown in *Figure 8.22*:

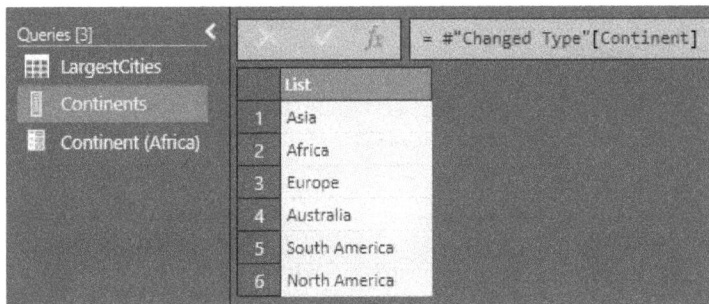

Figure 8.22: A query returning a list of elements

Now, this query can be selected as the input data for the **Continent** parameter, as shown in *Figure 8.23*:

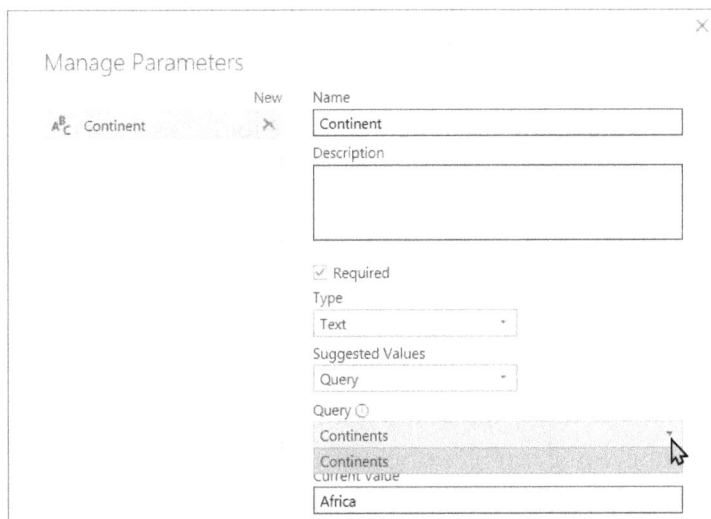

Figure 8.23: The Manage Parameters window with a parameter linked to a query

Confirm this change by clicking **OK**.

Unlike the **List of values** option, the **Query** option removes the ability to select parameter values from a list in the query pane (*Figure 8.18*). However, the list remains available in the **Edit Parameters** window (*Figure 8.20*).

These are all the changes intended for the editor. Now, click the **Close & Load** command located on the **Home** tab (*Figure 1.13*). Since only existing queries were edited and a parameter was added, Power Query does not load new data into Excel but simply updates the result table for the `LargestCities` query.

> Tip: **If the results of associated queries do not refresh after changing the parameter value, their refresh can be forced by clicking or expanding the Refresh Preview command on the Home tab.**

The **Refresh Preview** command is shown in *Figure 8.24*:

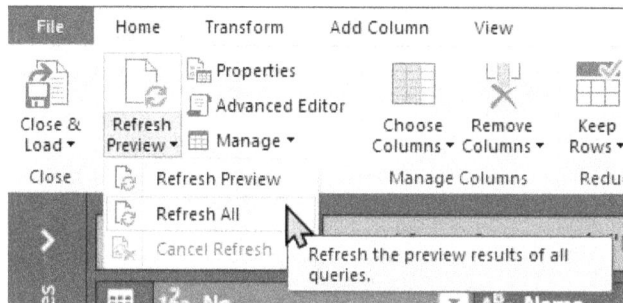

Figure 8.24: Refresh Preview command

Parameterized query using file path

In this example, data is imported into the file **FilePath.xlsx** from two other Excel files (**PriceList.xlsx** and **Sales.xlsx**) located in the same folder, as shown in *Figure 8.25*:

Figure 8.25: Files used in this example

These files contain a simple sales table and a price list table, respectively, as illustrated in *Figure 8.26*:

	A	B	C
1	Date	Product	Quantity
2	10/1/2025	Jadeite	8
3	10/1/2025	Diamonds	5
4	10/1/2025	Topazes	136
5	10/2/2025	Emeralds	6
6	10/3/2025	Pearls	17
7	10/3/2025	Pearls	14
8	10/3/2025	Emeralds	28
9	10/3/2025	Sapphires	50
10	10/3/2025	Jadeite	10
11	10/4/2025	Pearls	5
12	10/4/2025	Rubies	5
13	10/5/2025	Gold coins	4
14	10/5/2025	Jadeite	9
15	10/5/2025	Gold coins	20

	A	B
1	Product	Price
2	Emeralds	$14.80
3	Pearls	$8.40
4	Diamonds	$19.90
5	Sapphires	$14.00
6	Rubies	$16.00
7	Topazes	$15.00
8	Jadeite	$12.00
9	Gold coins	$10.00

Figure 8.26: The tSales table from Sales.xlsx and the tPrices table from PriceList.xlsx

Both imported tables are joined together, and the result of that merge is stored in the **FilePath.xlsx** file. This example focuses on handling the situation when the source files are moved to another folder. The location of the main file does not matter from Power Query's perspective, because the path to it is not referenced in any query.

Note: **When transferring files from another computer and importing data from other transferred files, the target path in the Source step may not match the one stored in the query (even a single character or letter case difference is enough). In that case, the path must be corrected for the queries to function properly.**

Therefore, the first step is to move the **PriceList.xlsx** and **Sales.xlsx** files to a parent folder, and then refresh the **Sales** query in the **FilePath.xlsx** file. Since the data is no longer in the previously specified location, the editor displays a warning message, as shown in *Figure 8.27*:

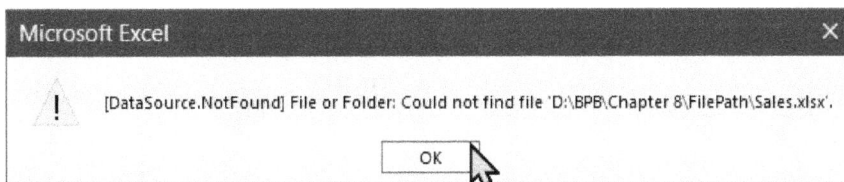

Microsoft Excel ✕

⚠ [DataSource.NotFound] File or Folder: Could not find file 'D:\BPB\Chapter 8\FilePath\Sales.xlsx'.

OK

Figure 8.27: Message indicating that the source file could not be found

After attempting to refresh, the **Queries & Connections** pane under the **Sales** query should display the message **Download did not complete**. To restore proper functionality of the queries, the file path must be updated in the **Source** step of both queries. To reduce the number of necessary adjustments in similar situations, the file path will be parameterized so that changes only need to be made in one place, even when working with multiple files from the same folder.

The following steps should be completed:

1. Move the **PriceList.xlsx** and **Sales.xlsx** files to the same folder as the **FilePath.xlsx** file.

2. Refresh the **Sales** query.

3. Open the query editor for the **Sales** query by selecting the **Edit** option from the query's context menu (*Figure 1.26*) or by clicking the **Edit** command on the **Query** tab (*Figure 1.15*).

4. If necessary, refresh the queries in the editor. To do so, expand the **Refresh Preview** command and choose **Refresh All** (*Figure 8.24*).

5. Go to the **Source** step.

    In the **Source** step's formula bar, the M code should resemble the following:

    ```
    = Excel.Workbook(File.Contents("D:\BPB\Chapter 8\FilePath\Sales.xlsx"),
    null, true)
    ```

    This path points to the exact location of the Excel file, including its name and extension.

To parameterize this file path, the following steps are to be followed:

1. Click the gear icon next to the **Source** step name.

2. In the **Excel Workbook** window that appears, click the **Advanced** button.

3. Cut the file name and extension and paste it into the second field in the **File path parts** section, as shown in *Figure 8.28*:

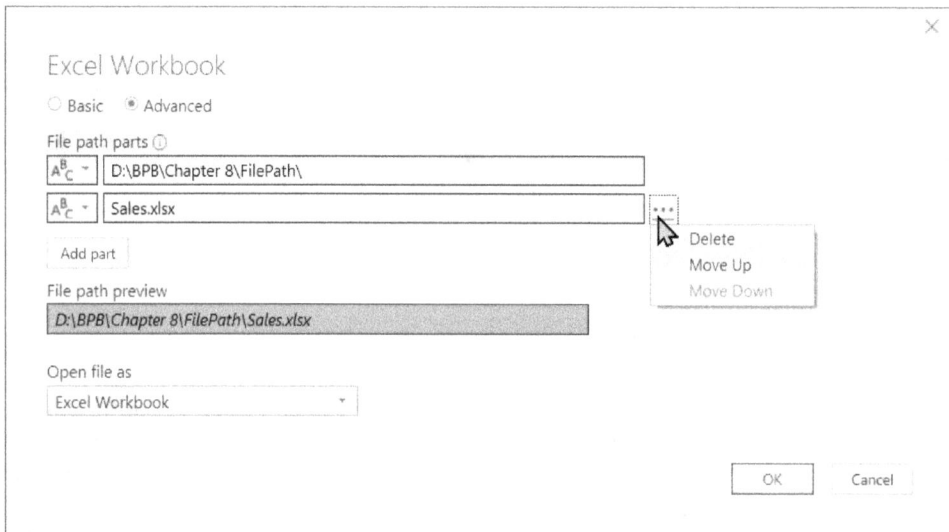

Figure 8.28: The Excel Workbook window with the file path split into two parts

4. Copy the first part of the file path.

5. Click the ABC icon next to the first part of the file path and select **New parameter** from the context menu. For this option to be available, the **Always allow** checkbox in the **Parameters** group on the **View** tab must be selected (*Figure 1.6*).

These steps open the **Manage Parameters** window, where the following settings must be changed:

1. Change the parameter name in the **Name** field to **FilePath**.

2. Change the parameter type in the **Type** field to Text.

3. Paste the previously copied file path into the **Current Value** field.

All of these settings are reflected in *Figure 8.29*:

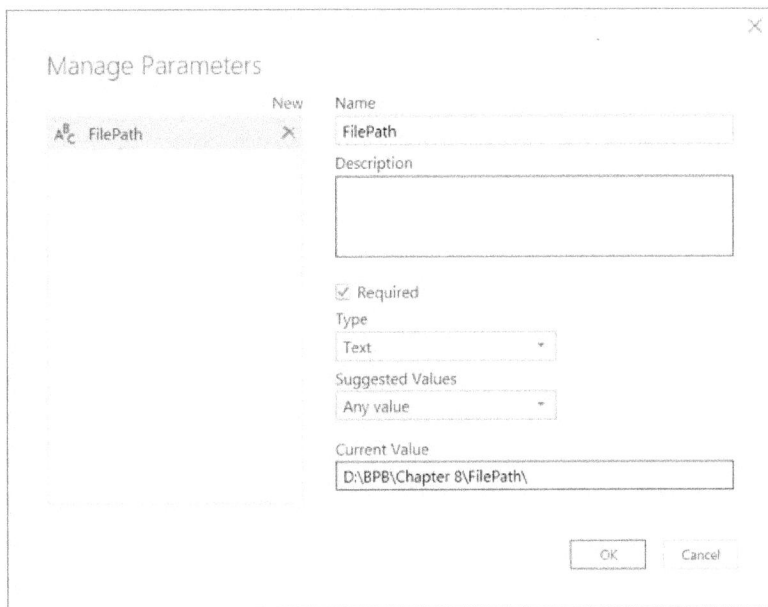

Figure 8.29: The new FilePath parameter

After confirming the creation of the new parameter by clicking **OK**, the editor returns to the **Excel Workbook** window. This time, instead of a literal text path, the first field contains a reference to the parameter, as shown in *Figure 8.30*:

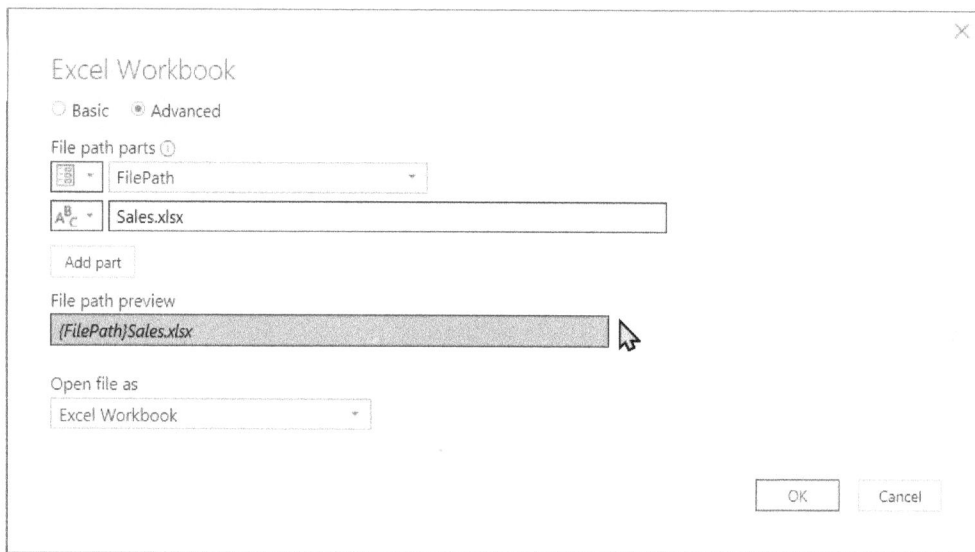

Figure 8.30: The Excel Workbook window with a parameterized path

Due to the changes in the **File path parts** section, the **File path preview** field also changes. Instead of the previously visible full path **D:\BPB\Chapter 8\FilePath\Sales.xlsx** (*Figure 8.28*), the field now displays **{FilePath}Sales.xlsx**. This is a combination of the parameter name in curly brackets and the remaining text.

Tip: **If the file path is more complex or contains multiple variable parts, additional segments can be added in the Excel Workbook window using the Add part button (Figure 8.28, Figure 8.30).**

Confirm the modified **Source** step by clicking **OK**. This updates the M code in the formula bar to the following:

```
= Excel.Workbook(File.Contents(FilePath & "Sales.xlsx"), null, true)
```

In this instance, the parameter name is not enclosed in curly brackets but is concatenated with the file name using the text concatenation operator, the ampersand (&).

The same change can now be made for the **Prices** query either using the user interface or by editing the formula directly in the formula bar. The updated code should be as follows:

```
= Excel.Workbook(File.Contents(FilePath & "PriceList.xlsx"), null, true)
```

Now that both queries use the parameter to reference the file path, whenever the **Sales.xlsx** and **PriceList.xlsx** files are moved simultaneously, only the parameter value must be updated. This can be done either directly from the query pane (*Figure 8.18*) or the **Edit Parameters** window (*Figure 8.20*).

The next step is to examine the M code for the parameter in detail.

Parameter M code

To do this, first select the parameter in the query pane, then on the **Home** tab, click the **Advanced Editor** command, as shown in *Figure 8.31*:

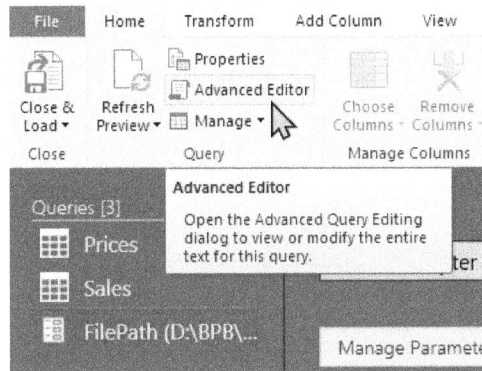

Figure 8.31: Advanced Editor command

This opens the **Advanced Editor** window, which displays the code used to create the parameter, as shown in *Figure 8.32*:

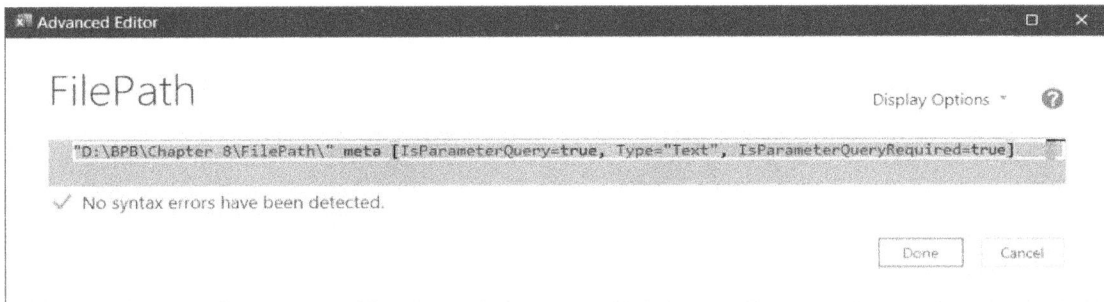

Figure 8.32: Advanced Editor window

The displayed M code:

```
"D:\BPB\Chapter  8\FilePath\"  meta  [IsParameterQuery=true,  Type="Text",
IsParameterQueryRequired=true]
```

Shows the following elements:

- The current value of the parameter: **"D:\BPB\Chapter 8\FilePath\"**

- The **meta** keyword.

- Parameter options, enclosed in square brackets. Depending on the parameter type, different sets of options may appear here.

Clicking the **Done** button confirms any changes made. Clicking **Cancel** or the **x** in the top-right corner cancels the changes. Since no changes have been made to the M code in this case, the method of closing the window does not matter.

In general, it is simpler to modify parameter settings using the **Manage Parameters** window. This code has been presented here for reference and to support a transition to more advanced examples involving the M language.

One more step can now be taken to begin examining M code more closely.

Blank query

On the **Home** tab, expand the **New Source** command, navigate to **Other Sources**, and then select **Blank Query**, as shown in *Figure 8.33*:

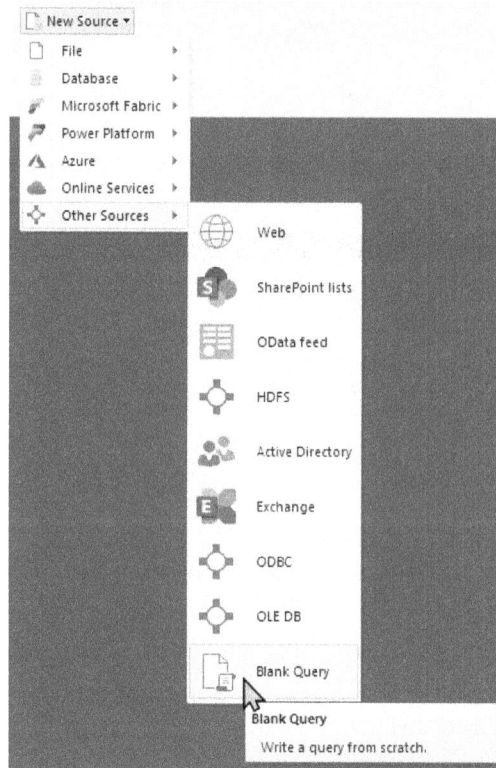

Figure 8.33: Creating a blank query

A blank query named **Query1** is created with a single step named **Source**. In the empty formula bar for this initial (and only) step, enter the following file path:

```
D:\BPB\Chapter 8\FilePath\
```

The next step is to check the resulting M code for this simple query by clicking the **Advanced Editor** command on the **Home** tab (*Figure 8.31*).

This opens the **Advanced Editor** window, where the M code for the simple query can be viewed, as shown in *Figure 8.34*:

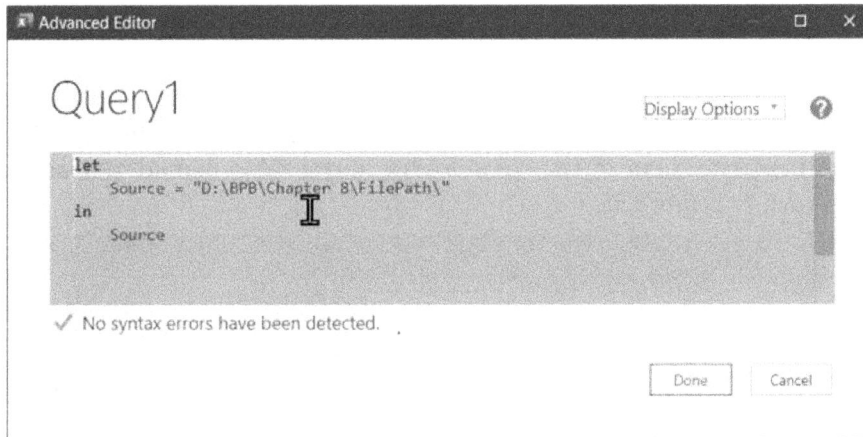

Figure 8.34: The Advanced Editor window with basic query code

The exact code is as follows:

```
let
    Source = "D:\BPB\Chapter 8\FilePath\"
in
    Source
```

The most important components are as follows:

- The **let** keyword, which begins the query.

- The **in** keyword, followed by the name of the step returned as the query result. It does not have to be the last step in the list, but if the step order (the basic structure of the M language) is disrupted, the editor may not display the full list of steps in the **Applied Steps** section (*Figure 1.6*).

In this simple example, there is only one step named **Source**, which is assigned a text value entered directly into the formula bar without quotation marks. Since the editor recognized the input as text, it automatically added double quotation marks in the full M code.

No additional modifications will be made to the M code in this example, so the **Advanced Editor** window can be closed by clicking **Done**. Then, click the **Close & Load** command (*Figure 1.13*) to exit Power Query. As only a parameter and a simple query returning text have been created in this example, the **Import Data** window (*Figure 1.14*) will not open. Instead, the result of **Query1** will be inserted into Excel on a new worksheet as a table with one column named after the query (**Query1**) and a single cell containing the file path/text entered in the formula bar.

Tip: **Parameters are always loaded as a connection only.**

Extracting parameters from a cell

In this example, the data and queries are located in the **FilePath2** folder. The file **FilePath2. xlsm** is opened, which contains a query named **LargestCities** that retrieves data from the file **LargestCitiesWorld.xlsx** in the same folder, and a table named **tParameters**. These elements are shown in *Figure 8.35*:

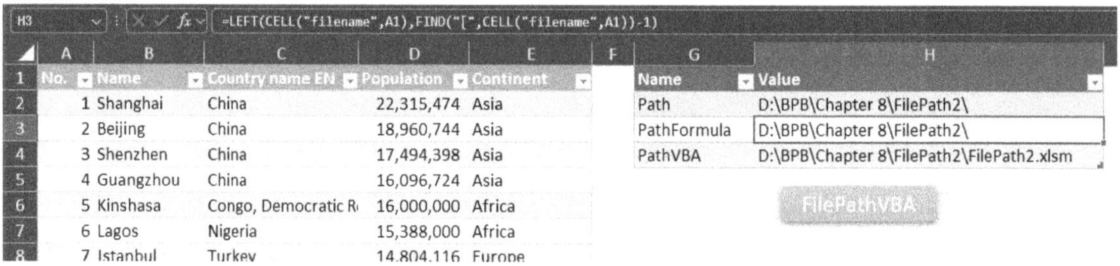

Figure 8.35: Result of the LargestCities query and the tParameters table

The task is to extract the file path from the **tParameters** table and use it in the **LargestCities** query. The **tParameters** table includes rows in which the **Value** column contains the following:

- A manually entered file path.

- A path to the current file, calculated using the following Excel formula:
  ```
  =LEFT(CELL("filename",A1),FIND("[",CELL("filename",A1))-1)
  ```

- A full file path and name generated using VBA code linked to a button labeled **FilePathVBA** (*Figure 8.33*).

It is assumed that the query should extract the path from the first row, meaning that the first row must contain the correct path to the file from which data should be retrieved.

The next step is to load the **tParameters** table using the **From Table/Range** command on the **Data** tab (*Figure 1.1*).

After loading the table into the editor, switch briefly to the **Source** step of the **LargestCities** query. The formula bar shows that the file path has already been split into a folder portion and the file name with the following extension:

```
=       Excel.Workbook(File.Contents("D:\BPB\Chapter       8\FilePath2\"       &
"LargestCitiesWorld.xlsx"), null, true)
```

The objective is to parameterize the folder portion of the path.

Proceed with the following steps:

1. Return to the **tParameters** query.

2. Remove the data type change step, if it was automatically added.

3. Right-click the first cell in the **Value** column and select the **Drill Down** option from the context menu, as was done in *Chapter 7, Logical Operations and Conditional Columns* (*Figure 7.48*).

4. In the new step, the editor opens the **Transform** tab under **Text Tools**. This happens because the query now returns a single text value.

5. Power Query extracts the single text value from the selected cell using the following code:

    ```
    = Source{0}[Value].
    ```

    Modify this code so that the extracted value is based on the key (value from the **Name** column) rather than the row position. Make the change as demonstrated in previous examples from this chapter (e.g., *Figure 8.9*):

    ```
    = Source{[Name="Path"]}[Value]
    ```

Once the query **tParameters** returns the correct file path, return to the **Source** step of the **LargestCities** query and modify the formula bar code by replacing the static folder path with a reference to the query as follows:

```
= Excel.Workbook(File.Contents(tParameters & "LargestCitiesWorld.xlsx"), null, true)
```

Unfortunately, in most cases, such a code modification results in an error, as shown in *Figure 8.36*:

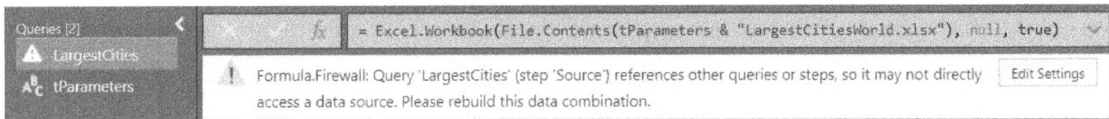

Figure 8.36: Access error when referencing a value from another query

One way to resolve this error is by modifying Power Query's privacy settings using the following steps:

1. Click the **File** menu.

2. Expand **Options and settings** and select **Query options**.

3. In the window that appears, navigate to the **Privacy** tab under the **Global** section.

4. Change the **Privacy Levels** setting to **Always ignore Privacy Level settings**, as shown in *Figure 8.37*:

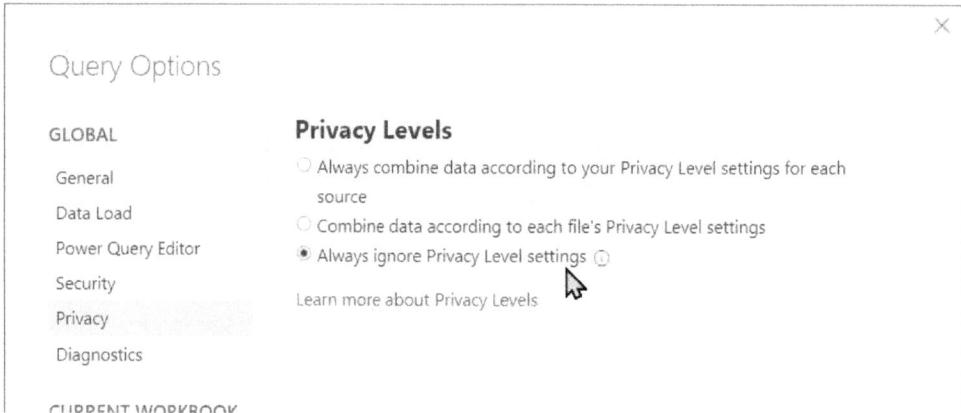

Figure 8.37: Query privacy settings

5. Confirm the changes by clicking **OK**, then refresh the query by clicking **Refresh Preview** from the **Home** tab (*Figure 8.24*).

An alternative approach that does not change the global privacy settings is to modify the output of the **tParameters** query so that it returns a data table rather than a single value. Before doing so, revert the privacy settings to their original configuration by repeating the steps above and changing the setting in *Step 4* to **Combine data according to each file's Privacy Level settings**.

Next, follow these steps to ensure that the **tParameters** query returns the same result as the **Source** step from the **LargestCities** query:

1. Copy the formula bar code from the **Source** step of the **LargestCities** query.

2. Return to the last step of the **tParameters** query.

3. Click the **fx** (Add Step) icon next to the formula bar.

4. The editor adds a step referencing the previous step with the code: = **Value**

   Fun fact: **Although the step name Navigation appears for both the second step in the tParameters and LargestCities queries, this is not their actual name. The editor assigns the correct name to the third step: Value for tParameters and tLargestCities_Table for LargestCities. The actual step names can be confirmed in the full M code.**

5. In this new step, paste the previously copied code from the **LargestCities** query, updating the query reference from **tParameters** to the previous step name:

   ```
   = Excel.Workbook(File.Contents(Value & "LargestCitiesWorld.xlsx"), null,
   true)
   ```

6. Go to the **Source** step of the **LargestCities** query and replace the code with a simple assignment, as follows:

    ```
    = tParameters
    ```

This should eliminate any errors. Finalize the query by completing the following steps:

1. Rename the **tParameters** query to **SourceTable**. The editor should automatically update this reference in all steps where the query is used.
2. Click **Close & Load To** (*Figure 1.13*).
3. Load the **SourceTable** query using the **Only Create Connection** option (*Figure 1.14*).

Parameterized directly in M code

In this example, the work is done using queries from the file **FilePathWithM.xlsm** located in the **FilePath2** folder. It contains the same data as the previous example (*Figure 8.33*). It also includes a query named **Path** that retrieves the file path from the **tParameters** table, similarly to how it was done in the middle of the previous example.

This time, the goal is to combine the **Path** and **LargestCities** queries directly in the M code. In other words, all steps and transformations will be included within a single query (**LargestCities**), and the second query (which will no longer be needed) will be deleted. This means that one query will retrieve data from two different sources outside of Power Query.

Begin by opening the **Path** query for editing. To return to editing an existing query, select the **Edit** option from the query's context menu (*Figure 1.26*) or click the **Edit** command on the **Query** tab (*Figure 1.15*).

To prevent the earlier error (*Figure 8.36*) from appearing at the start, the privacy settings can be adjusted, but this is not necessary for the final version of the query.

Once in the editor, click the **Advanced Editor** command (*Figure 8.31*) while the **Path** query is active. This opens the **Advanced Editor** window for the **Path** query, as shown in *Figure 8.38*:

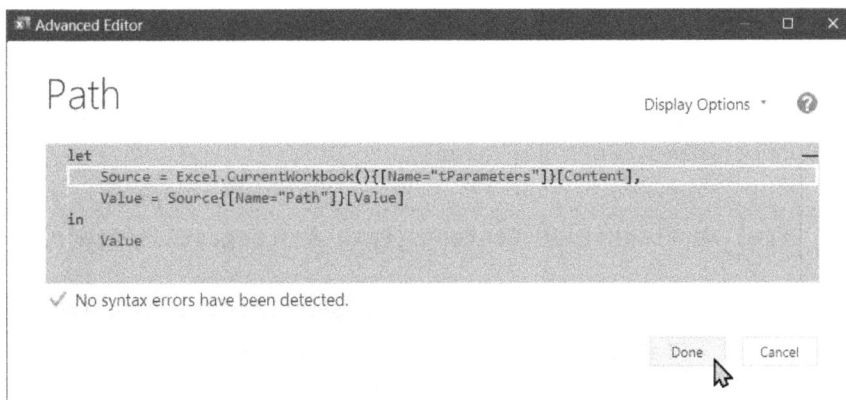

Figure 8.38: The Advanced Editor window for the Path query

The M code in this query is slightly more complex than the earlier nearly blank query example (*Figure 8.34*). The full code is as follows:

```
let
    Source = Excel.CurrentWorkbook(){[Name="tParameters"]}[Content],
    Value = Source{[Name="Path"]}[Value]
in
    Value
```

This code includes two steps: **Source** and **Value**. The **Value** step references the table from the **Source** step. Similar relationships were previously seen in the M code shown in the formula bars.

There is one notable difference from the blank query code. The Source step ends with a comma. This is required in M, where every step, except the one immediately preceding the **in** keyword, must end with a comma.

The next step is to transfer the steps from the **Path** query into the **LargestCities** query. Since the **Advanced Editor** functions like a basic code editor, proceed as follows:

1. Highlight the rows containing the **Source** and **Value** steps.

2. Copy the code using *Ctrl + C*.

3. Close the **Advanced Editor** window for the **Path** query.

4. Open the **Advanced Editor** window for the **LargestCities** query.

5. Paste (*Ctrl + V*) the previously copied steps above the existing Source step in the **LargestCities** query.

6. Add a comma at the end of the **Value** step and insert two forward slashes **//** on a new row to separate the inserted code.

The full M code after these changes should look as follows:

```
let
    //
    Source = Excel.CurrentWorkbook(){[Name="tParameters"]}[Content],
    Value = Source{[Name="Path"]}[Value],
    //
    Source = Excel.Workbook(File.Contents(Path & "LargestCitiesWorld.xlsx"),
null, true),
    tLargestCities_Table = Source{[Item="tLargestCities",Kind="Table"]}[Data],
    #"Changed Type" = Table.TransformColumnTypes(tLargestCities_Table,{{"No.",
Int64.Type}, {"Name", type text}, {"ASCII Name", type text}, {"Country Code",
type text}, {"Country name EN", type text}, {"Population", Int64.Type},
```

```
{"Continent", type text}, {"Timezone", type text}, {"Modification date", type
date}, {"Latitude", type number}, {"Longitude", type number}}),
    #"Removed Columns" = Table.RemoveColumns(#"Changed Type",{"ASCII Name",
"Country Code", "Timezone", "Modification date", "Latitude", "Longitude"})
in
    #"Removed Columns"
```

The current presence of two steps named Source in the **Advanced Editor** triggers the error message: **The variable named 'Source' is already defined in this scope**. A link labeled **Show error** appears beside this message, and clicking it highlights the part of the code causing the conflict.

Before renaming the steps, comments were added to illustrate both single-row and multi-row comment styles in M code as follows:

- The **//** symbol begins a comment that runs until the end of the row. It can appear at the end of a row of code or on its own row to describe a step. In this example, let us change the first two slash characters to a full comment as follows:

  ```
  // This is a single-row comment
  ```

- A block comment starts with **/*** and ends with ***/**, and may span multiple rows. It can also be embedded inside a row of code, provided it does not disrupt function syntax or M language rules. In this example, let us change the second pair of two slash characters to a multi-row comment as follows:

  ```
  /* This is
      a comment in
      many rows */
  ```

If a step name contains spaces or special characters, it must be enclosed in double quotes and prefixed with a hash symbol, for example: **#"Changed Type"**.

Tip: **Clicking inside a function name in newer versions of Power Query will highlight all occurrences of that function in the Advanced Editor window.**

The following step names were changed for clarity and to resolve naming conflicts:

- The first **Source** step was renamed to **PathSource** (to distinguish it from the second **Source** step).

- The **Value** step was renamed to **FilePath** (to clarify the purpose of the step).

- All references to these steps in the M code were updated accordingly.

The entire code after all changes should look like the following:

```
let
    // This is a single-row comment
```

```
    PathSource = Excel.CurrentWorkbook(){[Name="tParameters"]}[Content],
    FilePath = PathSource{[Name="Path"]}[Value],
    /* This is
        a comment in
    many rows */
        Source = Excel.Workbook(File.Contents(FilePath & "LargestCitiesWorld.
xlsx"), null, true),
    tLargestCities_Table = Source{[Item="tLargestCities",Kind="Table"]}[Data],
    #"Changed Type" = Table.TransformColumnTypes(tLargestCities_Table,{{"No.",
Int64.Type}, {"Name", type text}, {"ASCII Name", type text}, {"Country Code",
type text}, {"Country name EN", type text}, {"Population", Int64.Type},
{"Continent", type text}, {"Timezone", type text}, {"Modification date", type
date}, {"Latitude", type number}, {"Longitude", type number}}),
    #"Removed Columns" = Table.RemoveColumns(#"Changed Type",{"ASCII Name",
"Country Code", "Timezone", "Modification date", "Latitude", "Longitude"})
in
    #"Removed Columns"
```

Once the corrected code is confirmed by clicking the **Done** button, two new steps are added. If no mistakes have been made, the final output of the **LargestCities** query remains unchanged. At this point, the **Path** query can be deleted, as its functionality has been fully incorporated into the other query.

Fun fact: After adding comments in the M code, either on their row or at the end of a step (after a comma), those comments become visible in the Applied Steps list under an information icon.

The comments are displayed in the Applied Steps list, as shown in *Figure 8.39*:

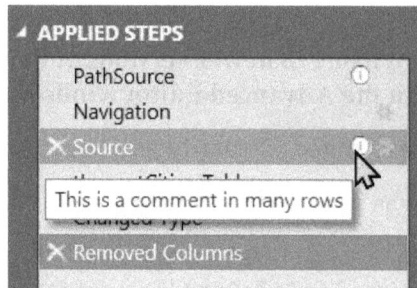

Figure 8.39: Comments displayed in the Applied Steps list

The last step is to close the editor by clicking the **Close & Load** command on the **Home** tab (*Figure 1.13*).

Conclusion

In this chapter, we explored how parameters enhance the flexibility and reusability of Power Query transformations. We learned how to extract specific values using drill down techniques, apply parameters for dynamic filtering, and replace hardcoded file paths with parameterized inputs. We also examined how to create parameters from lists, queries, or worksheet cells, and how to manage them both through the interface and directly in M code.

In the next chapter, we will expand on this foundation by learning how to create custom functions, enabling you to encapsulate logic and reuse it across multiple queries.

Multiple choice questions

1. **What does the drill down feature in Power Query allow you to do?**

   a. Automatically refresh all queries

   b. Extract specific values from a cell, row, or column

   c. Convert tables into charts

   d. Filter rows by color

2. **Which of the following symbols can be used to insert comments in M code?**

   a. // for single-row comments

   b. # for comment rows

   c. /* and */ for multi-row comments

   d. for end-of-row comments

3. **What is the result of using drill down on a column in Power Query?**

   a. A record

   b. A list of values

   c. A binary object

   d. A function

4. **Which statements about the Excel.CurrentWorkbook() function are true?**

   a. It returns all named tables and ranges in the current workbook

   b. It does not return worksheet objects

   c. It returns files from all open workbooks

   d. It is commonly used to retrieve local reference tables

5. **What happens if you use a key in drill down that appears multiple times in a column?**

   a. The first match is returned

   b. Power Query ignores duplicates

   c. All matching rows are returned

   d. An error is generated

6. **What must a query return to be used as a source for a parameter with the Query option?**

   a. A record

   b. A list

   c. A table

   d. A binary file

7. **What may cause Power Query to return an error when referencing a row by key?**

   a. The key value is not unique

   b. The key value does not exist in column

   c. The key column is sorted

   d. The column does not have an assign key

Answers

Question number	Answer option letter
1.	b.
2.	a., c.
3.	b.
4.	a., b., d.
5.	d.
6.	b.
7.	a., b.

CHAPTER 9

Creating Custom Functions

Introduction

In the previous chapter, we examined various methods of introducing parameters into Power Query, including extracting values from worksheet cells and dynamically controlling query logic. These techniques made it possible to adapt transformations to changing input values and user selections.

In this chapter, we focus on creating custom functions. Custom functions allow repetitive transformations to be encapsulated and reused across datasets. Whether importing multiple files with similar layouts, standardizing text formatting, or dynamically constructing queries based on parameters, custom functions streamline the process and reduce duplication.

You will learn how Power Query automatically generates functions when importing from folders, how to transform parameterized queries into reusable functions, and how to construct functions manually using M code. Along the way, we will address common challenges such as handling optional parameters, managing query dependencies, and resolving locale-based data issues.

Structure

This chapter covers the following topics:

- Function auto-created on folder import
- Function based on parameterized query
- Creating a custom function

Objectives

By the end of this chapter, you will be able to create and apply custom functions in Power Query to automate and standardize repetitive data transformations. You will learn how to build functions manually or from parameterized queries, understand how Power Query generates functions during folder imports, and apply them across multiple files or datasets. You will also gain practical skills in handling optional parameters, resolving locale issues, and managing query dependencies, which are essential for scalable and efficient data processing.

Function auto-created on folder import

In this example, data will be imported from files located in a single folder, similar to the example in *Chapter 2, Advanced Data Connections and Imports*, in the subsection *Importing data from folders*. However, this time the focus is on a more detailed explanation of the mechanism that is automatically generated to retrieve and combine data from multiple files.

The folder from which data is being imported is named **`Sales`**. For this example, it contains three files: **`Poland.xlsx`**, **`Italy.xlsx`**, and **`Finland.xlsx`**. All of these files share the same structure, as illustrated in *Figure 9.1*:

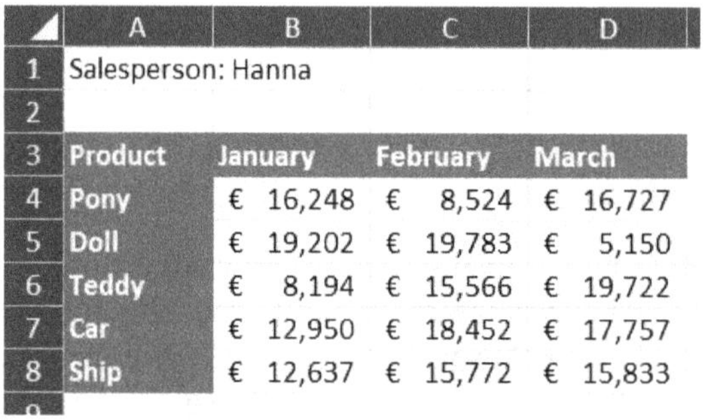

	A	B	C	D
1	Salesperson: Hanna			
2				
3	Product	January	February	March
4	Pony	€ 16,248	€ 8,524	€ 16,727
5	Doll	€ 19,202	€ 19,783	€ 5,150
6	Teddy	€ 8,194	€ 15,566	€ 19,722
7	Car	€ 12,950	€ 18,452	€ 17,757
8	Ship	€ 12,637	€ 15,772	€ 15,833

***Figure 9.1**: Source data layout in Excel files*

The data is located in the first (and assumed only) worksheet within each Excel file. The data is not formatted as an official Excel table but rather resides in regular worksheet cells. Additionally, the salesperson's information is stored only in cell **A1**. The country name where the sales occurred is not embedded in the file content but appears in the file name. Furthermore, the month of sale is not located in a dedicated column but instead appears as column headers. This data structure requires several preparatory transformations on each file before it can be combined.

This task is simplified by the automatic structure of queries, parameters, and functions that Power Query creates when importing data from a folder.

Initial import and combination of data from a folder

The transformation process begins with the following steps:

1. Open the **FromFolder.xlsx** file located in the main folder used for this chapter's files, or create a new blank workbook.

2. On the **Data** tab, expand the **Get Data** command, then expand **From File**, and select **From Folder** (*Figure 2.8*).

3. Locate the desired **Sales** folder on the drive and confirm the selection by clicking the **Open** button (similar to the previously discussed example in *Figure 2.22*).

4. This action opens a window listing the files found in the selected folder and any subfolders, as shown in *Figure 9.2*:

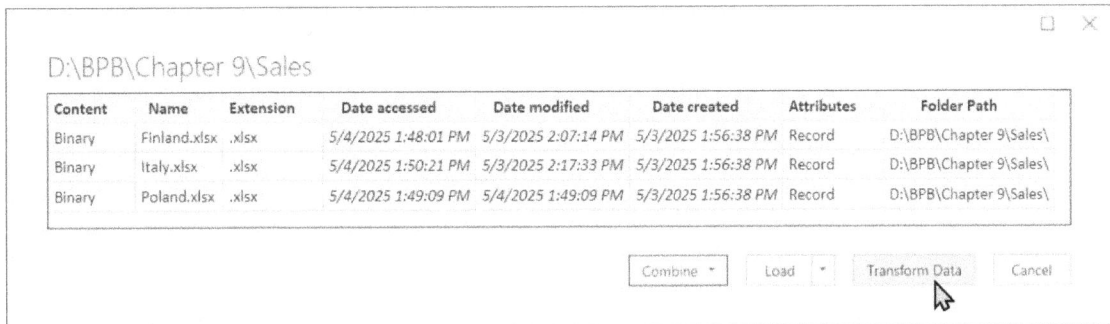

D:\BPB\Chapter 9\Sales

Content	Name	Extension	Date accessed	Date modified	Date created	Attributes	Folder Path
Binary	Finland.xlsx	.xlsx	5/4/2025 1:48:01 PM	5/3/2025 2:07:14 PM	5/3/2025 1:56:38 PM	Record	D:\BPB\Chapter 9\Sales\
Binary	Italy.xlsx	.xlsx	5/4/2025 1:50:21 PM	5/3/2025 2:17:33 PM	5/3/2025 1:56:38 PM	Record	D:\BPB\Chapter 9\Sales\
Binary	Poland.xlsx	.xlsx	5/4/2025 1:49:09 PM	5/4/2025 1:49:09 PM	5/3/2025 1:56:38 PM	Record	D:\BPB\Chapter 9\Sales\

Figure 9.2: List of files in the specified folder

5. In the window that appears, click the **Transform Data** button to import the files into the Power Query Editor.

Compared to the earlier example, this folder does not contain any subfolders, files with unsupported extensions, hidden files, or other problematic items, so no additional filters or cleanup are needed at this stage. However, performing such checks is generally good practice.

In this case, only a filter on the **Extension** column will be applied to demonstrate how to filter on a single expected value while excluding any potential future variations. To do so:

1. Expand the filter menu in the **Extension** column.

2. Expand the **Text Filters** submenu and select **Equals** (*Figure 2.15*).

3. Enter or select the value **.xlsx** and confirm by clicking **OK** (similar to *Figure 2.16*).

A correctly applied filter will generate the following M code step:

```
= Table.SelectRows(Source, each [Extension] = ".xlsx")
```

Assuming the unnecessary data has been removed, the contents of the files can now be expanded. This is done by clicking the icon with two downward-pointing arrows located in the **Content** column header (*Figure 2.26*).

This opens the **Combine Files** window, as shown in *Figure 9.3*:

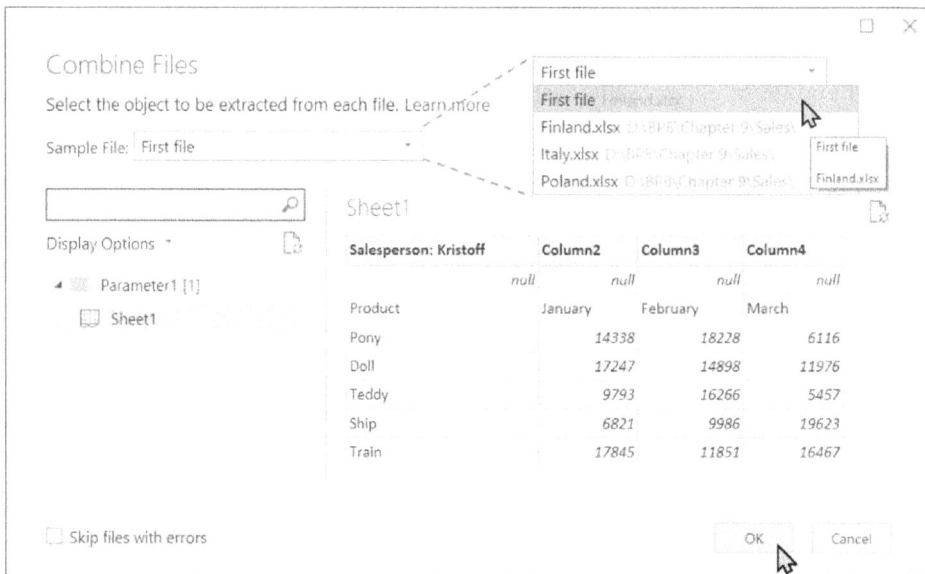

Figure 9.3: Combine Files window

In this window, it is possible to choose which file will be used as the source for subsequent transformations. One may select either the first file or any specific file from the list. Both options come with their respective advantages and disadvantages, as follows:

- If the first file is selected, the corresponding M code will follow the structure:

  ```
  = #"Filtered Rows"{0}[Content]
  ```

  This means that if a new file is added with a name that is alphabetically earlier than the current first file, Power Query will use the newly added file in the transformations. Similarly, if the position of the first file changes in any way, a different file will be processed. However, this approach is less likely to return an error if the original first file is deleted or renamed.

- If a specific file, such as **Poland.xlsx,** is selected, the generated M code will have the following structure:

```
= #"Filtered Rows"{[#"Folder Path"="D:\BPB\Chapter 9\Sales\", Name="Italy.xlsx"]}[Content]
```

This ensures that the same file will always be used as the transformation source, regardless of the number or order of files in the folder. However, an error will occur if that specific file is deleted or renamed.

In this example, the first file will be selected, as it is a safer choice when all files share the same structure but their names (including letter casing) might change in the future.

Since the data will be retrieved only from the first worksheet, it is sufficient to select this worksheet from the left side of the **Combine Files** window (*Figure 9.3*) and confirm the selection by clicking the **OK** button.

The first query to be reviewed after the files have been combined is the primary query that was automatically generated. By default, its name matches the folder from which the files were imported. In this case, **Sales**. All related queries, along with the result and steps of the **Sales** query, are shown in *Figure 9.4*:

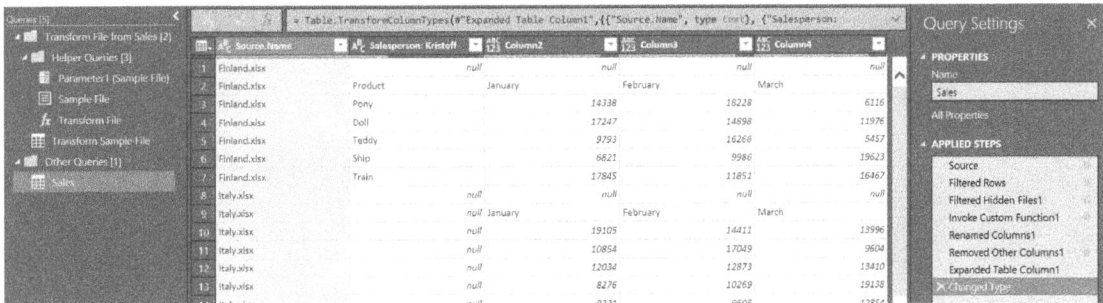

Figure 9.4: Result of file combination with default transformations

First, attention should be paid to the results of the **Sales** query. The first column displays the name of the file from which the data was retrieved.

The second column contains product names, but only for the first file. For the remaining files, the cells are filled with null values. This behavior is due to the column name being **Salesperson:Kristoff**. Power Query automatically used the first row of the worksheet as column headers, which is incorrect in this case because only cell **A1** is populated in that row. Moreover, that cell contains the salesperson's name, not an actual header.

Since each file contains data for a different salesperson, the resulting column names vary. In the **Expanded Table Column1** step, the M code expands the columns found in the first or sample file using the following structure:

```
= Table.ExpandTableColumn(#"Removed Other Columns1", "Transform File", Table.
ColumnNames(#"Transform File"(#"Sample File")))
```

The arguments of the **Table.ExpandTableColumn** function is as follows:

- **#"Removed Other Columns1"**: A reference to the previous step containing the table.

- **"Transform File"**: The name of the column being expanded.

- **Table.ColumnNames(#"Transform File"(#"Sample File"))**: The list of column names to be extracted from the **Transform File** column.

The **Table.ColumnNames** function returns all column names from the specified table. The table is the result of invoking the automatically created function **Transform File**, which takes the file provided by the automatically generated **Sample File** query as its argument.

The remaining columns contain sales values for the sample months.

Query dependencies

Before proceeding with the transformation of individual queries, it is beneficial to understand the dependencies between them. Specifically, the flow of information and which queries rely on the results of others. To view these relationships, one should go to the **View** tab and click the **Query Dependencies** command, as shown in *Figure 9.5*:

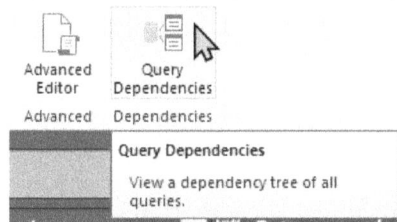

Figure 9.5: Query Dependencies command

This opens the **Query Dependencies** window, which displays dependencies not only between queries but also between queries and their data sources (in this example, the folder). The **Query Dependencies** window is shown in *Figure 9.6*:

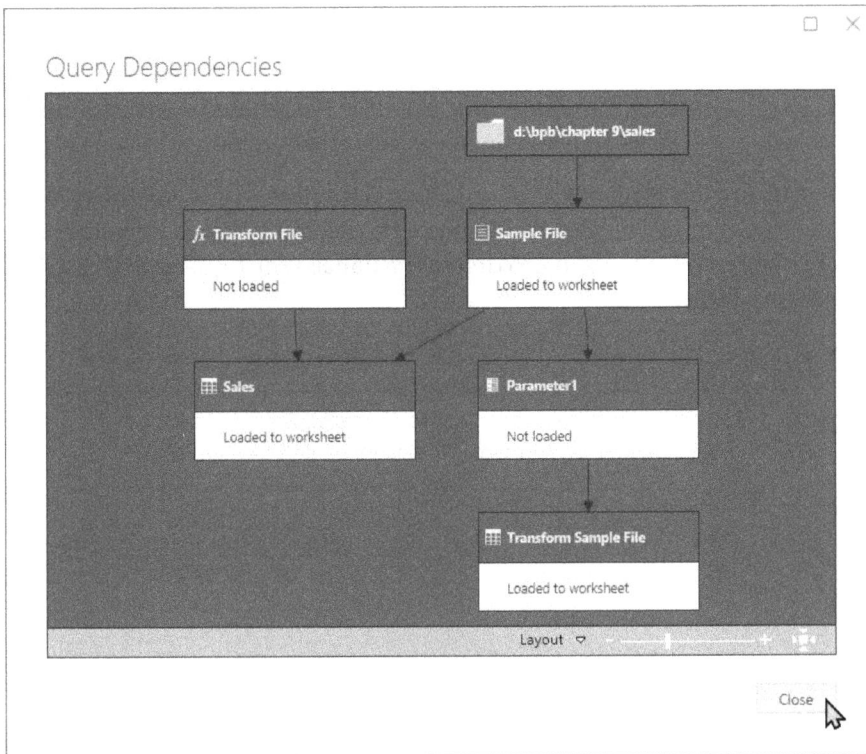

Figure 9.6: Query Dependencies window

Fun fact: Although the Query Dependencies window (Figure 9.6) may initially indicate that the Sample File and the Transform Sample File query will be loaded into Excel, this is not accurate. Clicking the Close & Load command will result in only the Sales query being loaded into Excel. After the results are loaded and the editor is reopened, the Query Dependencies window will reflect the actual data loading status.

This window presents the following elements, each marked with appropriate icons:

- The source folder from which the files are retrieved (**d\bpb\chapter 9\sales**).

- The **Sample File** query, which returns a file as a Binary value.

- The **Parameter1** query/parameter, which references a file (also a Binary value). In the **Manage Parameters** window (*Figure 8.15*), the data type is set to Binary; this is the only data type that adds a fourth option (Binary) to the **Suggested Values** list, allowing the selection of queries returning Binary values as **Default Value** and **Current Value**. In this example, this applies only to the **Sample File** query.

- The **Transform Sample File** query, which currently contains default transformations applied to the **Sample File** via a reference to **Parameter1.**

- The **Transform File** function, containing M code derived from transformations in the **Transform Sample File** query.

- The **Sales** query, which combines files from the designated source folder based on the transformations defined in the related queries and functions.

The direction of the arrows (*Figure 9.6*) shows how data flows between the queries. This also means that a query higher in the hierarchy cannot be deleted before a dependent query below it is removed. For instance, attempting to delete the **Parameter1** query will display a warning message as shown in *Figure 9.7*:

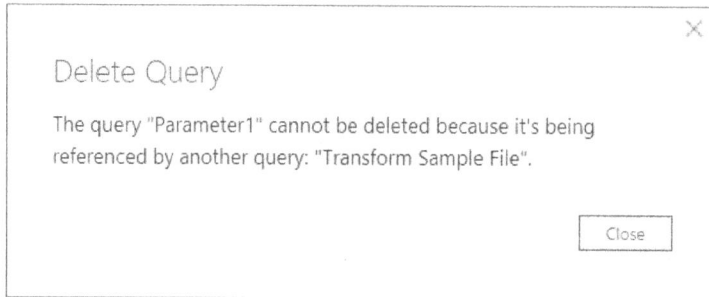

Figure 9.7: *Warning message about query dependencies*

Based on the hierarchy displayed in the **Query Dependencies** window (*Figure 9.6*), the **Transform Sample File** query could be deleted without affecting the overall transformations. However, this is not entirely accurate, as this query is additionally linked to the **Transform File** function. Any transformations added to the **Transform Sample File** query will be reflected in the **Transform File** function.

This can be verified by clicking the **Advanced Editor** command on the **Home** tab (*Figure 8.31*). A message box will appear, confirming this relationship, as shown in *Figure 9.8*:

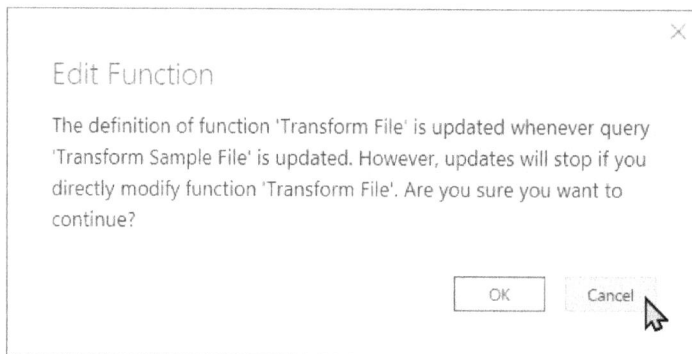

Figure 9.8: *Message showing link between queries*

The **Transform File** function is used in the **Sales** query to extract and modify data from each file in the folder. In order to produce correct results, this function needs to be properly modified. Thanks to the link between the function and the **Transform Sample File** query, the simplest way to adjust the **Transform File** function is to add and modify steps directly in the **Transform Sample File** query.

Modification of query associated with the function

For the first (and only visible) step of the **Transform File** function, the following M code can be observed in the formula bar:

```
= (Parameter1) => let
Source = Excel.Workbook(Parameter1, null, true),
Sheet1_Sheet = Source{[Item="Sheet1",Kind="Sheet"]}[Data],
#"PromotedHeaders"=Table.PromoteHeaders(Sheet1_Sheet,[PromoteAllScalars=true])
in
#"Promoted Headers"
```

The first line contains the function declaration. It is simply the argument name provided in parentheses, followed by the **=>** symbol indicating the start of the **let** keyword. The beginning of the M code, which has already been discussed earlier (*Figure 8.34* and *Figure 8.38*). The remainder follows the standard structure of steps in Power Query, derived from the **Transform Sample File** query.

In the first step (**Source**), the **Excel.Workbook** function uses the argument **Parameter1** (a sample file). Subsequent steps apply transformations to the data, which are returned as the result of the custom function. The name of the function corresponds to the name of the query.

The following steps describe how to modify this function through its associated query (**Transform Sample File**):

1. Remove the **Promoted Headers** step. This will return the raw data imported from the worksheet. These data are shown in *Figure 9.9*:

ABC 123 Column1	ABC 123 Column2	ABC 123 Column3	ABC 123 Column4
1 Salesperson: Kristoff	null	null	null
2 null	null	null	null
3 Product	January	February	March
4 Pony	14338	18228	6116
5 Doll	17247	14898	11976
6 Teddy	9793	16266	5457
7 Ship	6821	9986	19623
8 Train	17845	11851	16467

Figure 9.9: Data imported from the worksheet into Power Query

2. Create a conditional column by clicking the **Conditional Column** command on the **Add Column** tab (*Figure 7.2*).

   a. In the **Add Conditional Column** window, rename the new column to **Salesperson**.

   b. Set the checked column to **Column1**.

   c. Set the operator to **begins with**.

   d. Enter the value **Salesperson** in the **Value** field.

   e. For the **Output** section, change the entry type to column and select **Column1**.

   f. In the **Else** field, enter **null** and confirm by clicking **OK**.

The completed **Add Conditional Column** window is shown in *Figure 9.10*:

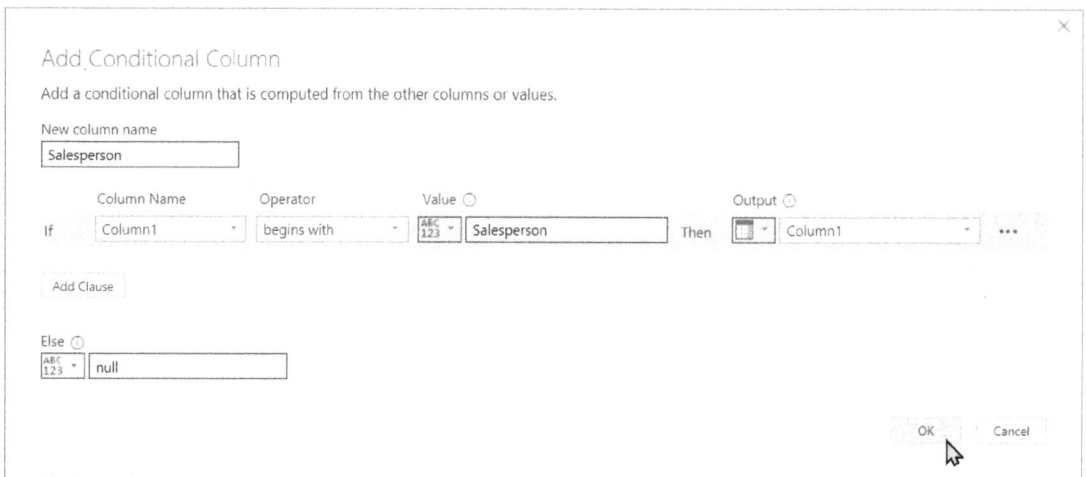

Figure 9.10: *Completed Add Conditional Column window*

3. As a result, a **Salesperson** column will be created. Only the first row will contain the relevant information. The second row will display an error, as the Power Query function fails to process a **null** value. The remaining cells in the **Salesperson** column will contain only **null** values. This is shown in *Figure 9.11*:

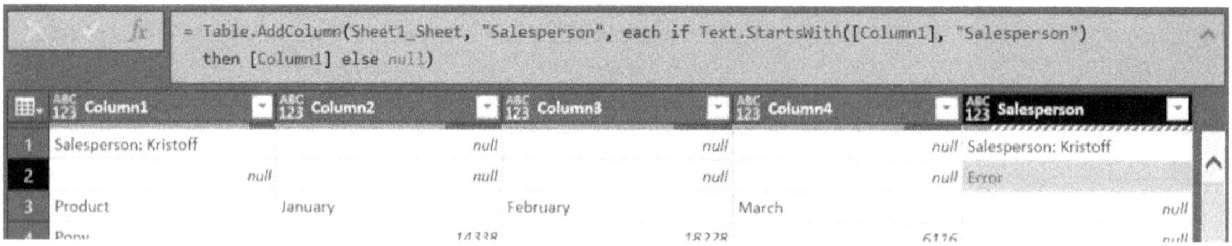

Figure 9.11: *Query after adding the Salesperson column*

Before proceeding with further transformations, it is important to highlight the occasional differences between using Power Query functions through the user interface and writing them directly in M code or within custom column formulas. At this stage, the goal is to extract the text following the delimiter (a space) in the **Salesperson** column (*Figure 9.11*). The extracted value will be the name of the salesperson.

On the **Transform** tab, under the **Extract** options, there is a command called **Text After Delimiter** (*Figure 2.32*). If this command is used through the interface, all **null** values in the **Salesperson** column will be replaced with empty cells. However, if the **Text. AfterDelimiter** function is added manually to the M code within the current step, the **null** values will remain unchanged.

Since the **null** values will be required for further transformations, the M code in the formula bar will be modified accordingly.

4. To extract the name of the salesperson (which appears after the space character), the **Text.AfterDelimiter** function will be added directly to the M code to preserve **null** values. The updated formula bar code should be:

```
=   Table.AddColumn(Sheet1_Sheet,   "Salesperson",   each   if   Text.
StartsWith([Column1], "Salesperson") then Text.AfterDelimiter([Column1],
" ") else null, type text)
```

The appearance of the data after modifying the formula is shown in *Figure 9.12*:

	ABC 123 Column1		ABC 123 Column2		ABC 123 Column3		ABC 123 Column4		A^B_C Salesperson	
1	Salesperson: Kristoff				null		null		null Kristoff	
2			null		null		null		null Error	
3	Product		January		February		March		null	
4	Pony				14338		18228		6116	null
5	Doll				17247		14898		11976	null

Figure 9.12: Query after extracting only Salesperson from Column1

5. In the Salesperson column, rows containing errors are removed by expanding the **Remove Rows** command on the **Home** tab and selecting the **Remove Errors** option (*Figure 1.30*). Alternatively, this can be done by right-clicking the column header and selecting **Remove Errors** from the context menu.

6. The salesperson's name is copied to the remaining cells in the **Salesperson** column by expanding the **Fill** command on the **Transform** tab and selecting the **Down** option (*Figure 5.11*). This option is also available from the context menu after right-clicking the column header.

7. Column names are manually renamed based on the second row of data, except for the **Salesperson** column. The **Promote Headers** command cannot be used because

it applies to all columns in the table, and the last column already has the correct name, while the second row contains the salesperson's name rather than a column label.

8. The first two data rows are removed by expanding the **Remove Rows** command on the **Home** tab and selecting the **Remove Top Rows** option (*Figure 1.30*). In the **Remove Top Rows** window, the value 2 is entered, and the selection is confirmed by clicking **OK**.

9. Since it is sometimes helpful to verify how transformations affect the results of dependent queries, the query **Sales** is opened, and its final step (**Changed Type**) is deleted. The data now appears significantly cleaner than before the transformations. The current result of the **Sales** query is shown in *Figure 9.13*:

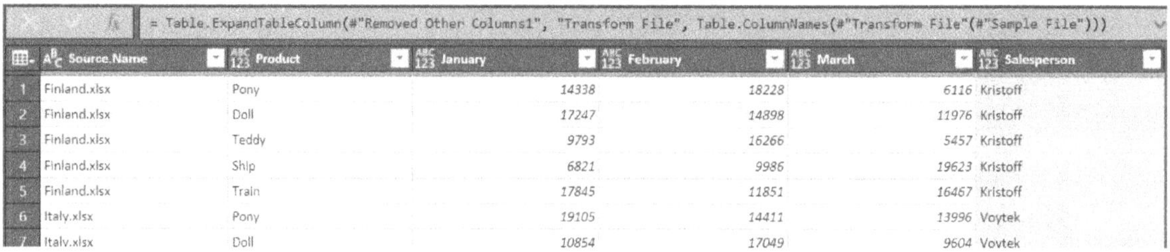

	Source.Name	Product	January	February	March	Salesperson
1	Finland.xlsx	Pony	14338	18228	6116	Kristoff
2	Finland.xlsx	Doll	17247	14898	11976	Kristoff
3	Finland.xlsx	Teddy	9793	16266	5457	Kristoff
4	Finland.xlsx	Ship	6821	9986	19623	Kristoff
5	Finland.xlsx	Train	17845	11851	16467	Kristoff
6	Italy.xlsx	Pony	19105	14411	13996	Voytek
7	Italy.xlsx	Doll	10854	17049	9604	Vovtek

The formula bar reads: `= Table.ExpandTableColumn(#"Removed Other Columns1", "Transform File", Table.ColumnNames(#"Transform File"(#"Sample File")))`

Figure 9.13: Result of combining files after the most recent transformations

10. Return to the `Transform Sample File` query, select the **Product** and **Salesperson** columns, then right-click on one of their headers and choose **Unpivot Other Columns** from the context menu (*Figure 5.17*).

11. In the M code for the new step (**Unpivoted Other Columns**), rename the newly created columns to **Month** and **Profit**. The full code should be as follows:

```
=    Table.UnpivotOtherColumns(#"Removed    Top    Rows",    {"Product",
"Salesperson"}, "Month", "Profit")
```

All necessary transformations for the `Transform Sample File` query have now been completed. Optionally, the function may be briefly reviewed to confirm that all added steps are reflected within it.

The process can now proceed to the final transformations in the **Sales** query, which combines data from multiple Excel files.

Transformations in the query that combines data

The last step, **Changed Type**, has already been removed from this query because column names were modified in the query used to transform files after loading them into Power Query, but before combining them. Therefore, the **Changed Type** step contained column names present immediately after file combination (*Figure 9.4*).

Most of the steps added in the **Sales** query correspond to those in the **Sales** query from the **Importing data from folders** example discussed in *Chapter 2, Advanced Data Connections and Imports*. In this case, there is only one additional step, **Renamed Columns1**, which renames the **Name** column. However, the new name is generated automatically and does not reflect the actual content of that column. Thus, the **Sales** query transformations begin with this step:

1. In the **Renamed Columns1** step, the column name is changed to **Country**, which corresponds to the following M code:

   ```
   = Table.RenameColumns(#"Invoke Custom Function1", {"Name", "Country"})
   ```

2. Renaming the column in the **Renamed Columns1** step causes an error in the **Removed Other Columns1** step. To fix this, the correct (new) column name must be inserted into the M code for that step:

   ```
   = Table.SelectColumns(#"Renamed Columns1", {"Country", "Transform File"})
   ```

3. Proceed to the last step, and then:

   a. Select the **Country** column.

   b. On the **Transform** tab, expand the **Extract** command and choose **Text Before Delimiter** (*Figure 2.32*).

   c. In the **Text Before Delimiter** window, enter a period in the **Delimiter** field and confirm by clicking **OK**.

The final expected result is now obtained, as shown in *Figure 9.14*:

Country	Product	Salesperson	Month	Profit
Finland	Pony	Kristoff	January	14338
Finland	Pony	Kristoff	February	18228
Finland	Pony	Kristoff	March	6116
Finland	Doll	Kristoff	January	17247
Finland	Doll	Kristoff	February	14898
Finland	Doll	Kristoff	March	11976
Finland	Teddy	Kristoff	January	9793

Figure 9.14: Final result of the query

At this point, specific data types may be assigned to the columns extracted from individual sheets. However, since the data will be loaded into Excel, this step is not necessary here. The only remaining action is to expand the **Close & Load** command on the **Home** tab and select **Close & Load To** (*Figure 1.13*), then specify the destination for loading the combined data in the **Import Data** window (*Figure 1.14*). Only the **Sales** query will be loaded into Excel.

Function based on parameterized query

In this example, data will be retrieved from the file **`Crypto_Archive.xlsx`** located in the **PDFs** folder. Cell **B1** in that file contains a formula used to extract the full file path of the Excel workbook it resides in. This is the same formula that was discussed in the Extracting parameters from a cell example in *Chapter 8, Parameters and Query Parameterization*.

Using this formula and the date contained in the **tFiles** table, full file paths to PDF documents are calculated. These documents will be used for retrieving and consolidating data. The information from this table has already been loaded into Power Query as a connection only.

The data in the **`Crypto_Archive.xlsx`** file is shown in *Figure 9.15*:

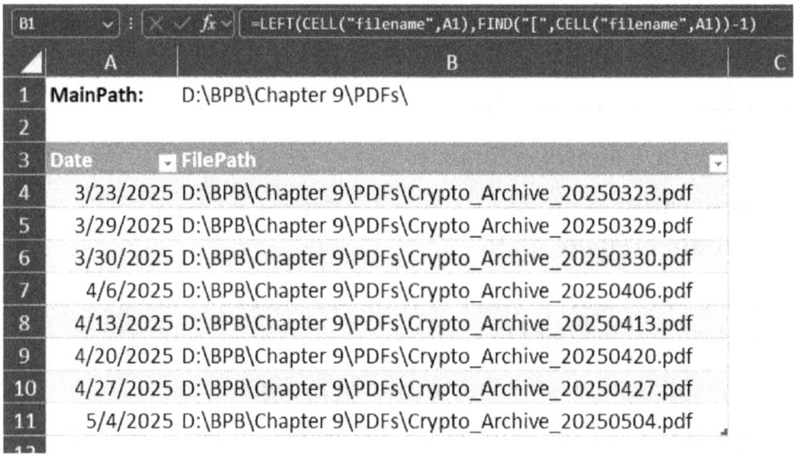
B1 =LEFT(CELL("filename",A1),FIND("[",CELL("filename",A1))-1)

	A	B
1	MainPath:	D:\BPB\Chapter 9\PDFs\
2		
3	Date	FilePath
4	3/23/2025	D:\BPB\Chapter 9\PDFs\Crypto_Archive_20250323.pdf
5	3/29/2025	D:\BPB\Chapter 9\PDFs\Crypto_Archive_20250329.pdf
6	3/30/2025	D:\BPB\Chapter 9\PDFs\Crypto_Archive_20250330.pdf
7	4/6/2025	D:\BPB\Chapter 9\PDFs\Crypto_Archive_20250406.pdf
8	4/13/2025	D:\BPB\Chapter 9\PDFs\Crypto_Archive_20250413.pdf
9	4/20/2025	D:\BPB\Chapter 9\PDFs\Crypto_Archive_20250420.pdf
10	4/27/2025	D:\BPB\Chapter 9\PDFs\Crypto_Archive_20250427.pdf
11	5/4/2025	D:\BPB\Chapter 9\PDFs\Crypto_Archive_20250504.pdf

***Figure 9.15**: Data in the Crypto_Archive.xlsx file*

Some of these file paths are invalid. Specifically, not all of the referenced files exist in the specified folder. Error handling for such cases will be addressed later in the example.

In this case, all files are located in the same folder. However, they could just as easily be distributed across different directories or sourced from other internal systems. The objective of this example is to demonstrate the process of creating a function based on a parameterized query and using that function within another query to transform and consolidate multiple similar datasets.

The process begins with retrieving data from a single PDF file, specifically **`Crypto_Archive_20250330.pdf`**. A portion of the first page of this file is shown in *Figure 9.16*:

Rank	Name	Symbol	Market Cap	Price	Circulating Supply	volume (24h)	% 1h	% 24h	% 7d
1	BTCBitcoin	BTC	$1,633,867,346,035.49	$82,334.52	19,844,256 BTC	$14,763,760,943.16	-0,01%	-0,32%	-4,32%
2	ETHEthereum	ETH	$217,928,323,739.49	$1,806.22	120,654,454 ETH *	$9,854,857,162.01	0,15%	-1,15%	-9,93%
3	USDTTether USDt	USDT	$144,163,645,339.19	$0.9999	144,182,349,121 USDT *	$38,085,432,411.64	0,01%	0,03%	-0,01%
4	XRPXRP	XRP	$124,335,698,808.51	$2.1361	58,205,697,378 XRP *	$2,826,918,737.14	-0,31%	-0,18%	-12,29%
5	BNBBNB	BNB	$85,743,907,513.01	$601.83	142,471,925 BNB *	$1,204,098,084.71	0,08%	-0,23%	-3,45%
6	SOLSolana	SOL	$63,853,468,055.14	$124.64	512,292,346 SOL *	$1,639,017,443.61	-0,31%	0,04%	-6,00%
7	USDCUSDC	USDC	$60,191,852,697.35	$1.0001	60,188,245,014 USDC *	$5,545,589,305.20	<0,01%	0,01%	<0,01%
8	DOGEDogecoin	DOGE	$24,723,280,131.74	$0.1663	148,649,826,384 DOGE	$831,596,448.71	-0,70%	-1,91%	-3,44%
9	ADACardano	ADA	$23,301,871,863.09	$0.6607	35,268,011,575 ADA *	$489,882,248.66	-0,35%	-1,96%	-6,88%
10	TRXTRON	TRX	$21,076,047,507.10	$0.2212	94,994,593,055 TRX *	$979,193,760.51	0,25%	0,25%	0,60%

Figure 9.16: Part of the data from the first page of Crypto_Archive_20250330.pdf

These PDF files were generated based on historical data retrieved from the website **https://coinmarketcap.com/historical**.

Importing and preparing the source data

Before creating a reusable function, it is necessary to begin by importing a single PDF file and preparing its contents for further transformations. The process starts by loading data from the `Crypto_Archive_20250330.pdf` file using the built-in **From PDF** option, as follows:

1. Select the **Get Data** command from the **Data** tab, expand **From File**, and then select **From PDF** (*Figure 2.8*).

2. Locate and select the desired file for import, following the same steps as when importing data from an Excel file (*Figure 2.9*).

3. In the **Navigator** window, choose the content to load into Power Query. This window resembles the Navigator window used when importing from Excel (*Figure 2.10*), but here, the selectable items are either full pages or tables from the PDF file. It is important to note that a single table in a PDF file cannot span multiple pages. Therefore, in the Navigator window, each table is labeled with the page on which it appears. In this example, only the first table (**Table001**) will be selected, as shown in *Figure 9.17*:

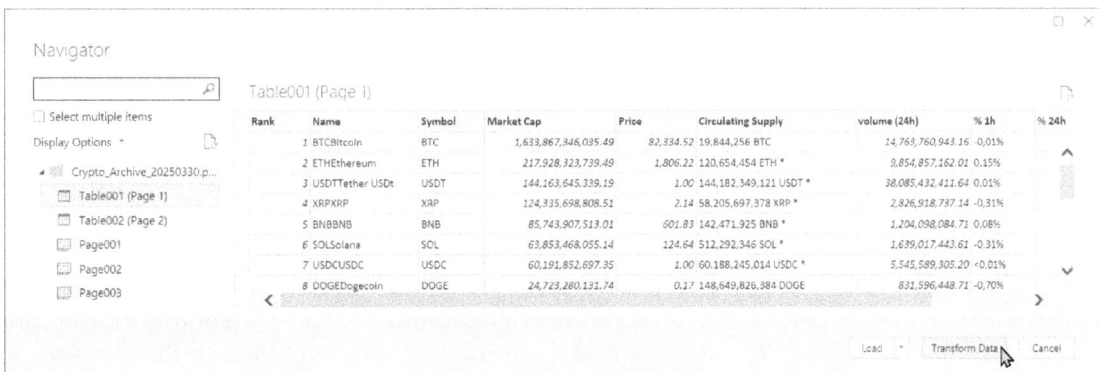

Figure 9.17: Navigator window for importing data from a PDF file

4. Confirm the selection by clicking **Transform Data** to load the content into the Power Query Editor.

After loading the data into the editor, four default steps should be visible, consistent with those generated in previous queries:

- The **Source** step, indicating the origin of the data.
- The **Navigation** step (**Table001**), extracting the relevant table or page content.
- The **Promoted Headers** step, which promotes the first row to column headers.
- The default **Changed Type** step, which automatically assigns data types to each column.

If the **Changed Type** step was not added, all columns should be selected (for example, using the shortcut *Ctrl + A*), and the **Detect Data Type** command on the **Transform** tab should be used (*Figure 2.21*).

Handling locale issues and incorrect data types

Some of the imported columns use incorrect data types due to inconsistencies between file formatting and the regional settings applied.

This issue affects the last three columns, which display the percentage change in value over the periods of 1 hour, 24 hours, and 7 days. For the **Crypto_Archive_20250330.pdf** file, the **% 1h** and **% 7d** columns were assigned a data type of **text**. In contrast, the **% 24h** column was assigned a **percentage** data type, but the values appear incorrect, as the decreases exceed 100%. Such a drop would imply negative asset prices, which is not possible for cryptocurrencies or other financial instruments such as stocks or bonds. These incorrect values are shown in *Figure 9.18*:

% 1h	% 24h	% 7d
-0,01%	-32.00%	-4,32%
0,15%	-115.00%	-9,93%
0,01%	3.00%	-0,01%
-0,31%	-18.00%	-12,29%

Figure 9.18: Incorrect data in the last three columns

The issue in the **% 24h** column arises because the file is being processed using United States regional settings, where a comma is used as a thousand separator. However, when examining the data in the PDF file (*Figure 9.16*), it is clear that the comma is used as a decimal separator, as is common in countries such as Poland, France, or Italy. Similarly, the **% 1h** and **% 7d** columns contain commas, but Power Query assigned them the **text** data type due to the presence of a less-than symbol (<) in the seventh row (visible in *Figures 9.16* and *9.17*). Other numeric columns use number formats compatible with the U.S. regional settings.

Since each **Changed Type** step can only use one locale setting at a time, the following sequence of transformations must be applied to correct the last three columns:

1. Change the data type of the **% 24h** column to **text**. This can be done by clicking the data type icon next to the column header (*Figure 1.7*) and selecting the **text** type.

   Alternatively, the type assignments for the last three columns could be removed entirely, as the **Promoted Headers** step assigns all columns a **text** data type by default. In that case, the **Changed Type** step, instead of the code:

   ```
   = Table.TransformColumnTypes(#"Promoted Headers",{{"Rank", Int64.Type},
   {"Name", type text}, {"Symbol", type text}, {"Market Cap", Currency.Type},
   {"Price", Currency.Type}, {"Circulating Supply", type text}, {"volume
   (24h)", Currency.Type}, {"% 1h", type text}, {"% 24h", Percentage.Type},
   {"% 7d", type text}})
   ```

   It should be replaced with the following:

   ```
   = Table.TransformColumnTypes(#"Promoted Headers",{{"Rank", Int64.Type},
   {"Name", type text}, {"Symbol", type text}, {"Market Cap", Currency.Type},
   {"Price", Currency.Type}, {"Circulating Supply", type text}, {"volume
   (24h)", Currency.Type}})
   ```

2. Select the last three columns, then use the **Replace Values** command from either the **Home** or **Transform** tab (*Figure 5.19*).

3. In the **Replace Values** dialog box, enter the less-than symbol (<) in the **Value To Find** field, and leave the **Replace With** field empty (as shown in *Figure 6.14*).

4. Confirm the changes by clicking **OK**.

   Next, the data type of the last three columns must be changed using locale settings that are different from those applied to the current Excel file. To adjust the regional settings of the workbook:

   a. Click the **File** menu.

   b. Expand **Options and settings**, then select **Query** options.

   c. In the **Query Options** window, go to the **Regional Settings** tab under **Current Workbook**.

   d. From the **Locale** dropdown menu, choose the locale that matches the formatting used in the file, as shown in *Figure 9.19*:

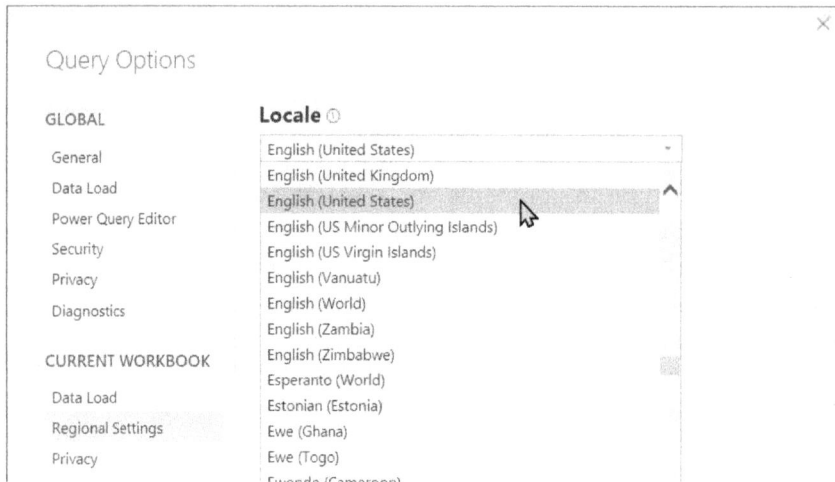

Figure 9.19: *Regional settings assigned to the Excel workbook from the Power Query interface*

Unfortunately, it is not possible to assign a data type that differs from the workbook's regional settings (*Figure 9.19*) using the **Data type** dropdown available on the **Home** tab.

There is a **Using Locale** option at the bottom of the list after clicking the data type icon for a column (*Figure 1.7*); this option only works for a single column at a time.

Therefore, to change the data type for all three columns in a single step, a different approach must be used.

5. Select the last three columns and right-click any of the selected headers.

6. From the context menu, expand **Change Type** and select **Using Locale**, as shown in *Figure 9.20*:

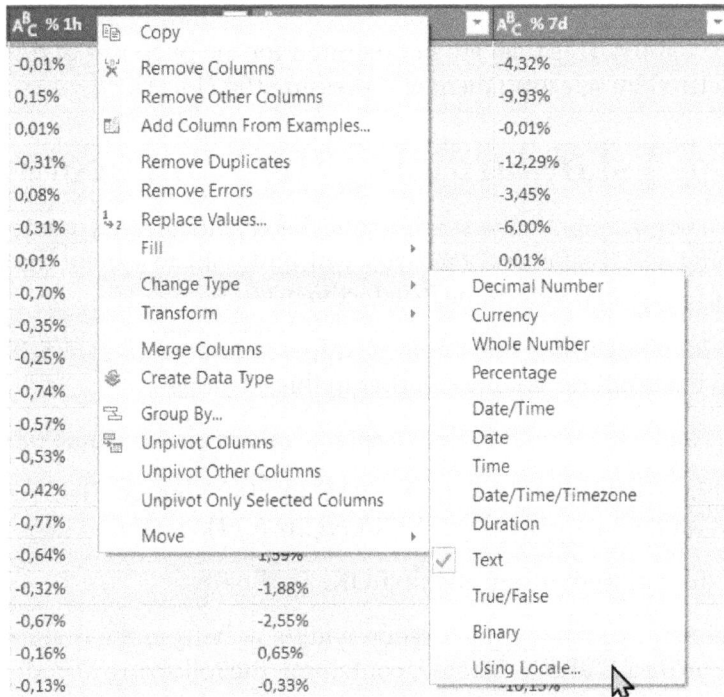

Figure 9.20: *Changing data types for multiple columns using the context menu*

7. In the **Change Type with Locale** window, select **Percentage** from the **Data Type** dropdown and choose **Polish (Poland)** from the **Locale** list, as shown in *Figure 9.21*:

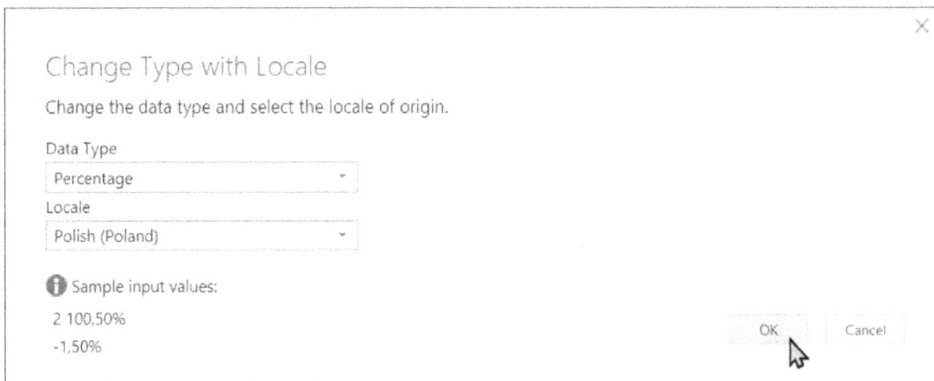

Figure 9.21: *Change Type with Locale window*

8. Confirm the changes by clicking **OK**.

At this stage, the values in the last three columns should be correctly parsed and interpreted.

Before proceeding to the next transformation steps, the **Circulating Supply** and **volume (24h)** columns should be removed, as they are not required for the purposes of this example. These columns can be deleted by selecting them and pressing the *Delete* key.

Cleaning and standardizing the Name column

The **Name** column contains both the symbol and the cryptocurrency name in a single field (*Figure 9.16* and *Figure 9.17*). Several methods will be tested to isolate the name, and each approach will be examined to determine its effectiveness.

The first attempt involves using the **Replace Value** command (*Figure 5.19*), similar to the process applied to the last three columns earlier in this example:

1. Select the **Name** column, then click **Replace Values** on the **Home** tab (*Figure 5.19*).

2. In the **Replace Values** window, enter **BTC** in the **Value To Find** field and leave the **Replace With** field empty (as shown in *Figure 6.14*).

3. Confirm the replacement by clicking **OK**.

    These steps remove the cryptocurrency symbol only from the first row. A step named **Replaced Value1** is also generated, containing the following M code:

    ```
    =        Table.ReplaceValue(#"Removed        Columns","BTC","",Replacer.
    ReplaceText,{"Name"})
    ```

    To correctly reference the **Symbol** column instead of a fixed text, the keyword **each** must be added.

4. Therefore, the M code is modified as follows:

    ```
    = Table.ReplaceValue(#"Removed  Columns",each  [Symbol],  "",  Replacer.
    ReplaceText, {"Name"})
    ```

    The result is shown in *Figure 9.22*:

⊞. 1²₃ Rank	Aᴮ_C Name	Aᴮ_C Symbol
1	1 Bitcoin	BTC
2	2 Ethereum	ETH
3	3 Tether USDt	USDT
4	4	XRP
5	5	BNB
6	6 Solana	SOL

Figure 9.22: Name column after the transformations

However, rows 4 and 5 contain blank cells. This occurs because **Table.ReplaceValue** replaces every instance of the specified value in each cell, and its behavior cannot be changed. As a result, this approach is deemed ineffective, and the **Replaced Value1** step must be deleted.

The second approach involves extracting text after a delimiter from the **Name** column using the following steps:

1. Select the **Name** column, go to the **Transform** tab, expand the **Extract** dropdown, and choose **Text After Delimiter** (*Figure 2.32*).

2. In the **Text After Delimiter** window, enter **BTC** as the delimiter (as in *Figure 2.33*) and confirm by clicking **OK**.

3. Review the resulting step (**Extracted Text After Delimiter**) with the following M code:

    ```
    = Table.TransformColumns(#"Removed Columns", {{"Name", each Text.
    AfterDelimiter(_, "BTC"), type text}})
    ```

    Since the string **BTC** appears only in the first row, only that row will contain the extracted text. Other rows will return blank cells, as the delimiter was not found. To make the transformation dynamic, the fixed text should be replaced with a reference to the **Symbol** column.

4. Modify the M code to:

    ```
    = Table.TransformColumns(#"Removed Columns", {{"Name", each Text.
    AfterDelimiter(_, each [Symbol]), type text}})
    ```

This modification results in an error for each cell. The editor displays the error:

We cannot convert a value of type Function to type Text. This message may be unclear to many Power Query users.

If the **each** keyword is removed, a different error appears: **We cannot apply field access to the type Text**, which is also not intuitive.

These errors occur due to the way the `Table.TransformColumns` function operates. It is designed to apply a transformation function only to the value of a single column and cannot reference other columns in the row. The placeholder _ used in the function refers only to the current column's value, not the entire row.

Due to this limitation, the **Extracted Text After Delimiter** step must be deleted. However, this step demonstrates that the editor uses the `Text.AfterDelimiter` function for such transformations.

This function can be used effectively in a custom column, which allows referencing multiple columns. Alternatively, using the **Extract** command from the **Add Column** tab automatically applies the function in a context where other columns are accessible. This second method is more straightforward. The final, successful attempt follows these steps:

1. Select the **Name** column.

2. On the **Add Column** tab, expand the **Extract** command and choose **Text After Delimiter** (as in *Figure 2.32*).

3. In the **Text After Delimiter** window, enter **BTC** as the delimiter (as in *Figure 2.33*) and click **OK**.

4. In the newly created **Inserted Text After Delimiter** step, modify the M code from:

   ```
   = Table.AddColumn(#"Removed Columns", "Text After Delimiter", each Text.
   AfterDelimiter([Name], "BTC"), type text)
   ```

   To the following:

   ```
   =  Table.AddColumn(#"Removed  Columns",  "Name   only",   each   Text.
   AfterDelimiter([Name], [Symbol]), type text)
   ```

   This replaces the fixed delimiter **BTC** with a dynamic reference to the **Symbol** column and renames the new column to **Name only**.

5. Delete the original **Name** column.

6. Move the **Name only** column into the position previously occupied by the **Name** column.

At this point, all necessary transformations for importing data from the PDF file have been completed.

Parameterizing the PDF file path

Once the data has been cleaned, the next step is to make the query dynamic by converting the fixed file path into a parameter. This is done in the same way as demonstrated in the examples from *Chapter 8, Parameters and Query Parameterization*:

1. Click the gear icon next to the **Source** step.

2. In the PDF window, which defines the data source for the current query, copy the path from the File path field.

3. Expand the dropdown menu next to the **File path** field and select **New parameter** (similarly to the process shown in *Figure 8.14*).

4. In the **Manage Parameters** window, adjust the settings as follows:

   a. Change the parameter name in the **Name** field to `PathToPDF`.

   b. Set the **Type** to `Text`.

   c. Paste the previously copied file path into the **Current Value** field.

The completed parameter settings are shown in *Figure 9.23*:

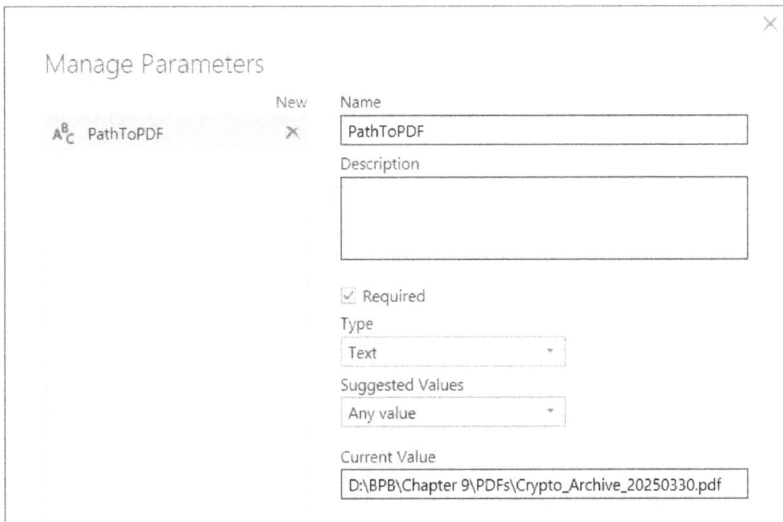

Figure 9.23: Properties of the new parameter

5. Confirm the creation of the parameter by clicking **OK** in both the **Manage Parameters** and **PDF** windows.

The configured PDF data source window with the parameter applied is shown in *Figure 9.24*:

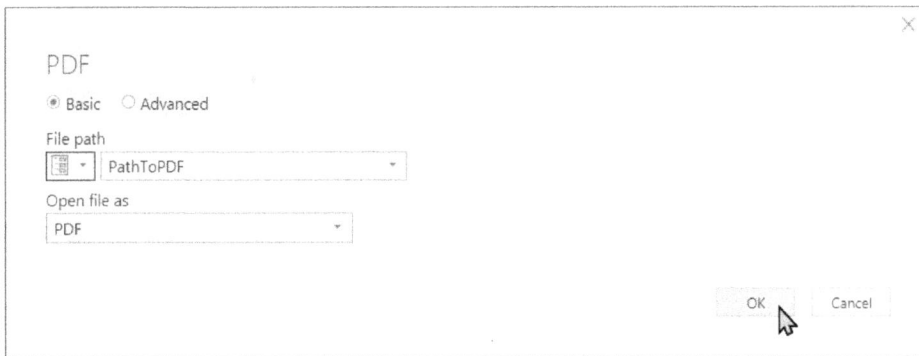

Figure 9.24: PDF data source window with the parameter applied

Creating a reusable function

With the file path parameterized, the next step is to convert the query into a reusable function. To achieve this, the following steps are performed:

1. Rename the query to **SinglePDF**.

2. Right-click the renamed query and select the **Create Function** option from the context menu (*Figure 7.32*).

3. In the **Create Function** window that opens, enter `SinglePDFImport` as the function name, as shown in *Figure 9.25*:

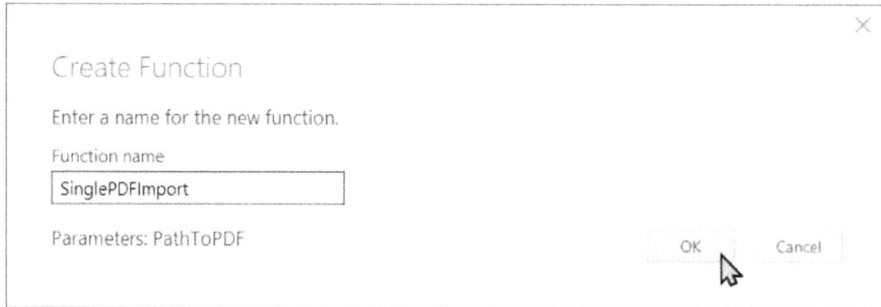

Figure 9.25: Create Function window

4. Confirm the creation of the function by clicking **OK**. This action generates a folder structure as illustrated in *Figure 9.26*:

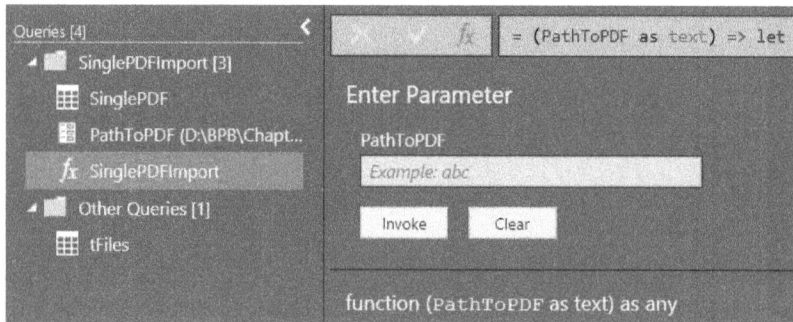

Figure 9.26: Generated query structure

All queries associated with the `SinglePDFImport` function are placed in the `SinglePDFImport` folder, while unrelated queries (in this case, only one) are grouped under **Other Queries**.

If needed, the function can be executed manually by entering the full PDF file path in the **PathToPDF** field (*Figure 9.26*) and clicking the **Invoke** button. This will create a new query, by default named **Invoked Function**, with a single **Source** step containing M code similar to:

```
= SinglePDFImport("D:\BPB\Chapter 9\PDFs\Crypto_Archive_20250427.pdf")
```

Tip: **As in the previous example, if the function is opened using Advanced Editor, Power Query will display a message indicating that the function is bound to a query and should be modified by editing the related query.**

This additional query is not required. Instead, the created function will be used in the previously imported **tFiles** query.

Using the function to process multiple files

The function created earlier can now be applied to all PDF files listed in the **tFiles** table. This process involves invoking the function for each valid file path and combining the results:

1. On the **Add Column** tab, click the **Invoke Custom Function** command, as shown in *Figure 9.27*:

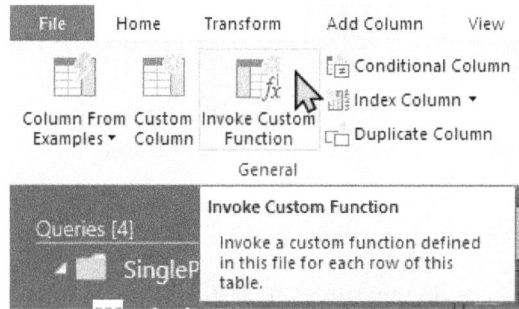

Figure 9.27: Invoke Custom Function command

2. In the **Invoke Custom Function** window, select **SinglePDFImport** from the **Function query** dropdown. In the **New column name** field, enter **SinglePDF**, and for the function argument, select the **FilePath** column.

The completed window is shown in *Figure 9.28*:

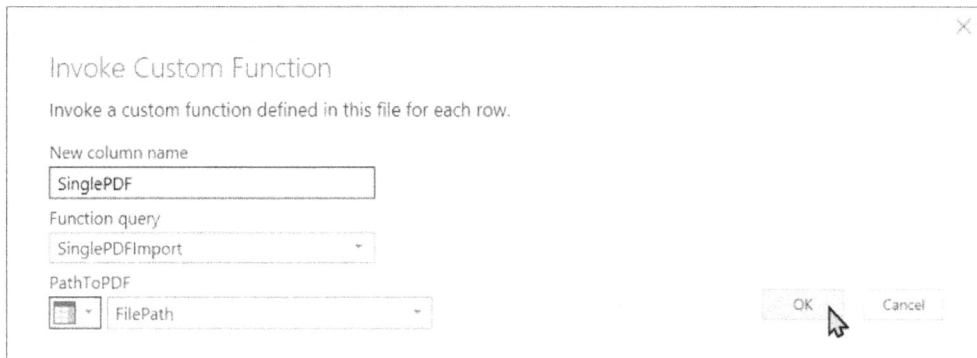

Figure 9.28: Invoke Custom Function window

3. Confirm the configuration by clicking the **OK** button.

4. A new column will be added, which may contain errors for rows where Power Query is unable to locate the PDF file using the given path. This outcome is illustrated in *Figure 9.29*:

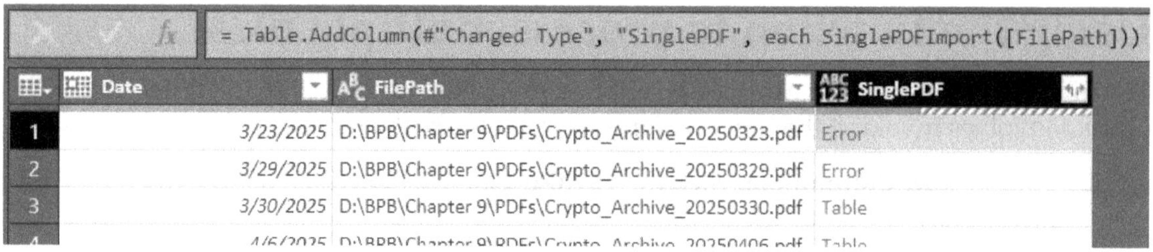

Figure 9.29: Returned errors and tables based on file paths

5. Remove the rows containing errors by expanding the **Remove Rows** command on the **Home** tab and selecting **Remove Errors** (*Figure 1.30*).

6. Expand the **SinglePDF** column by clicking the expand icon in its header and unchecking **Use original column name as prefix**, as demonstrated in *Figure 2.19* and *Figure 3.14*.

7. Optionally, assign appropriate data types to the expanded columns using the **Detect Data Type** command from the **Transform** tab (*Figure 2.21*). This step is optional since the data will be immediately loaded into Excel and will not affect further steps. Moreover, Excel does not distinguish detailed numeric types from Power Query.

8. Rename the query **tFiles** to **CryptoArchives**.

9. Load the final data to Excel by clicking **Close & Load To** on the **Home** tab (*Figure 1.13*).

10. In the **Import Data** window that appears, choose **Only Create Connection** (*Figure 1.14*), as this setting pertains only to the **SinglePDF** query, which is not intended to be loaded directly into Excel.

11. If the **Queries & Connections** pane is not already open, display it by clicking **Queries & Connections** on the **Data** tab (*Figure 1.1*).

12. In the **Queries & Connections** pane, right-click the **CryptoArchives** query and select **Load To** from the context menu (*Figure 1.26*).

13. In the **Import Data** window (*Figure 1.14*), choose to load the data into a table on a new worksheet.

14. Confirm the selection by clicking **OK**.

Creating a custom function

In this example, a custom function will be created that replicates the behavior of the **TRIM** function in Excel. This is necessary because the **Trim** option available under the **Extract** command on the **Transform** tab (*Figure 1.40*) only removes extra spaces from the beginning and end of a string but does not reduce multiple spaces between words to a single space.

Since there are many scenarios in which replicating the exact behavior of the **TRIM** function is needed in Power Query, *Ken Puls* created such a function in 2015. That function will be used here. Its original version, available at **https://excelguru.ca/clean-whitespace-in-powerquery/**, has been slightly modified and is presented as follows:

```
(text_to_trim as text, optional char_to_trim as text) as text =>
let
    delimiter = if char_to_trim = null then " " else char_to_trim,
    split = Text.Split(text_to_trim, delimiter),
    removeblanks = List.Select(split, each _ <> ""),
    result = Text.Combine(removeblanks, char)
in
    result
```

As mentioned in previous examples in this chapter, the structure of a function often resembles a standard step-by-step query. Therefore, the easiest way to create a function is to first construct a query that performs the needed transformations and then convert it into a function. The primary difference between a function and a regular query in Power Query is the first line of M code, which defines the function syntax. The simplest function declaration looks like this:

```
() =>
```

However, such a function rarely has practical use, as it takes no arguments. In the function shown earlier in this example, two arguments are defined inside parentheses:

- The first argument is the required argument **text_to_trim**, which is declared as a text value.

- The second argument is the optional argument **char_to_trim**, also declared as a text value. Optional arguments are defined using the **optional** keyword.

> Tip: **It is important to assign explicit data types to both function arguments and the return value of the function (after the closing parenthesis). If no type is specified, Power Query assigns any type by default, which can impact performance since any is the broadest and slowest type.**

After declaring the arguments and the return type, use the equals sign followed by the greater-than symbol (**=>**) to begin the function. After this, the **let** keyword is used to start the query portion of the function, which contains the individual steps, operations, or conditions required to produce the desired final result.

The behavior and construction of this function will be explained using data stored in the **PowerTrim.xlsx** file. That file contains a table named **tTexts** with example text entries, as shown in *Figure 9.30*:

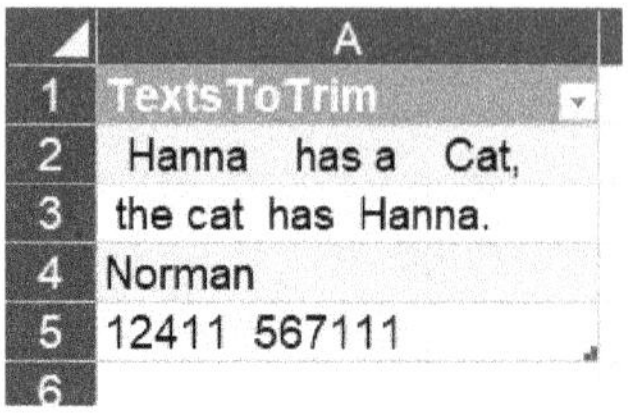

Figure 9.30: Table *tTexts*

Both the table and the function code provided earlier have already been imported into Power Query. They appear as the query **Texts To Trim** and the function **PowerTrim**, respectively. The following section explains the process of building a custom function from copied M code.

The first step is to create a blank query. In the Parameterized query using file path example in *Chapter 8, Parameters and Query Parameterization*, a blank query was created directly from within the Power Query editor by navigating to **Home | New Source | Other Sources | Blank Query** (*Figure 8.33*). This time, the blank query will be created from the Excel interface. On the **Data** tab, expand the **Get Data** menu, go to **From Other Sources**, and select **Blank Query**, as shown in *Figure 9.31*:

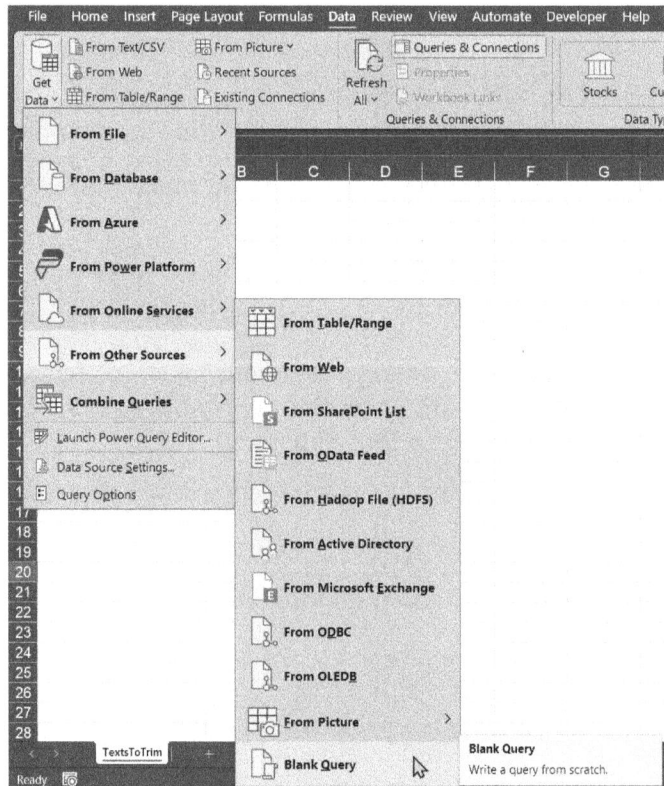

Figure 9.31: *Accessing Blank Query from the Excel interface*

This opens the editor and creates a new blank query named **Query1** by default. Into this blank query, the previously found function code can be pasted. Simply click the **Advanced Editor** command on the **Home** tab (*Figure 8.31*), select all the text in the window that appears, and replace it with the copied code.

However, if the goal is to write a new function from scratch, there are at least two viable approaches. For users already comfortable with M code and familiar with Power Query functions, the function can be written directly in the **Advanced Editor** window (*Figure 8.34* and *Figure 8.38*). For less experienced users, it is possible to rely on commands from the graphical interface to build individual transformation steps. Once the resulting query produces the desired output, it can be converted to a function in the **Advanced Editor**.

Building the function step by step

We begin by loading a sample text string and applying operations that split, filter, and recombine the content:

1. In the blank query **Query1**, enter the sample text "   Hanna   has a   Cat,   " into the formula bar. This value can be copied from the first row of the **Texts To Trim** query. This sample input provides a working example for the transformations to be performed in the following steps.

2. On the **Transform** tab, under the **Text Tools** section, click the **Split Text** command, as shown in *Figure 9.32*:

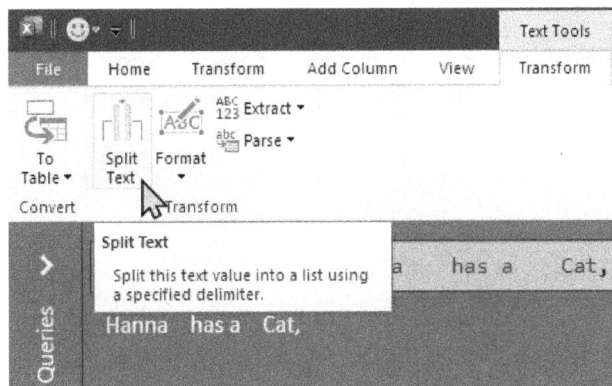

Figure 9.32: Split Text command on the Transform tab under Text Tools

3. In the **Split** window that opens, enter a space character in the **Value** field and confirm the operation by clicking **OK**, as shown in *Figure 9.33*:

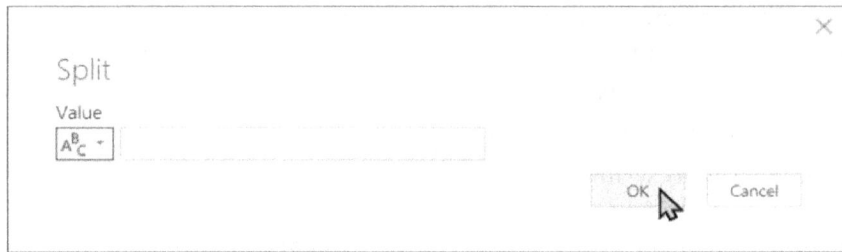

Figure 9.33: Split window

4. The editor converts the single text string into a list of values, creating a new step named **Split Text**. Since this step returns a list and not a text value, the **Text Tools** tab changes to **List Tools** (*Figure 8.5*). The resulting list is shown in *Figure 9.34*:

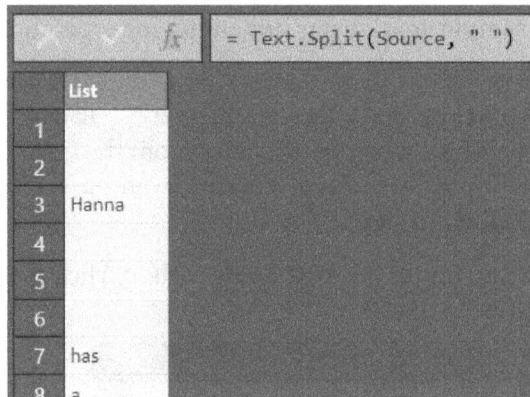

Figure 9.34: Text split into a list

Since there are no commands on the **Transform List Tools** tab for filtering out empty list items, we need to add a function manually:

5. Click the **fx** icon next to the formula bar to add a new custom step.

6. In the formula bar, apply the **List.Select** function from the previous step (**#"Split Text"**) to retain only non-empty list elements. Enter the following M code:

```
= List.Select(#"Split Text", each _ <> "")
```

7. The editor creates a new step with the default name **Custom1**. Rename this step to **without_empty** (for example, by selecting it and pressing *F2*).

Now, we need to combine the filtered list elements into a single text string, using a space as the delimiter. To define this step in code:

a. On the **Home** tab, click the **Advanced Editor** command (*Figure 8.31*).

b. Modify the existing code to add a new step named **Result**, which joins the list items using **Text.Combine**. Ensure to include a comma at the end of the **without_empty** step and change the output step after the **in** keyword.

So, the current code is changed as follows:

```
let
    Source = "  Hanna    has a    Cat,  ",
    #"Split Text" = Text.Split(Source, " "),
    without_empty = List.Select(#"Split Text", each _ <> "")
in
    without_empty
```

To:

```
let
    Source = "  Hanna    has a    Cat,  ",
    #"Split Text" = Text.Split(Source, " "),
    without_empty = List.Select(#"Split Text", each _ <> ""),
    Result = Text.Combine(without_empty, " ")
in
    Result
```

Tip: While typing in the formula bar or the Advanced Editor, newer versions of Power Query offer autocomplete suggestions for functions and existing step names.

After confirming the changes in the **Advanced Editor** by clicking **Done**, the query will return the text string with all unnecessary spaces removed, functioning as the **TRIM** function does in Excel.

Transforming the query into a function

After verifying that the query returns the expected result, it is time to convert it into a reusable function by declaring arguments and introducing logic to handle an optional delimiter parameter as follows:

1. In the **Advanced Editor** window, begin by inserting the first line to declare the function signature:

   ```
   (text_to_trim as text, optional char_to_trim as text) as text =>
   ```

2. The next step is to remove the following line:

   ```
   Source = "  Hanna    has a    Cat,  ",
   ```

   Since the input will now come from the **text_to_trim** argument, update the reference in the step **#"Split Text"** to use this argument instead of the former **Source** step.

3. Add a step to handle the optional parameter. If the **char_to_trim** argument is not provided, Power Query assigns it a value of **null**. Unlike some programming languages, Power Query does not support assigning default values directly in the function declaration. Therefore, this logic must be implemented as a separate step using an **if** expression:

```
Delimiter = if char_to_trim = null then " " else char_to_trim,
```

4. Replace the hardcoded space character previously used in the split and combine operations with a reference to the **delimiter** step. The final version of the function code should appear as follows:

```
(text_to_trim as text, optional char_to_trim as text) as text =>
let
    delimiter = if char_to_trim = null then " " else char_to_trim,
    #"Split Text" = Text.Split(text_to_trim, delimiter),
    without_empty = List.Select(#"Split Text", each _ <> ""),
    Result = Text.Combine(without_empty, delimiter)
in
    Result
```

5. Finally, rename the query to **FullTrim** so it can be invoked as a custom function from other queries.

Applying the function to a dataset

Once the function is ready, it can be applied to the dataset from the **Texts To Trim** query using the **Invoke Custom Function** command. This will allow the function to process multiple text values simultaneously:

1. Navigate to the **Texts To Trim** query and on the **Add Column** tab, click the **Invoke Custom Function** command.

2. In the **Invoke Custom Function** window that opens:

    a. In the **New column name** field, enter **Text after trim**.

    b. From the **Function query** dropdown, select the **FullTrim** function.

    c. For the **text_to_trim** argument, select the **TextsToTrim** column.

    d. Leave the **char_to_trim** argument blank.

The correctly configured **Invoke Custom Function** window is shown in *Figure 9.35*:

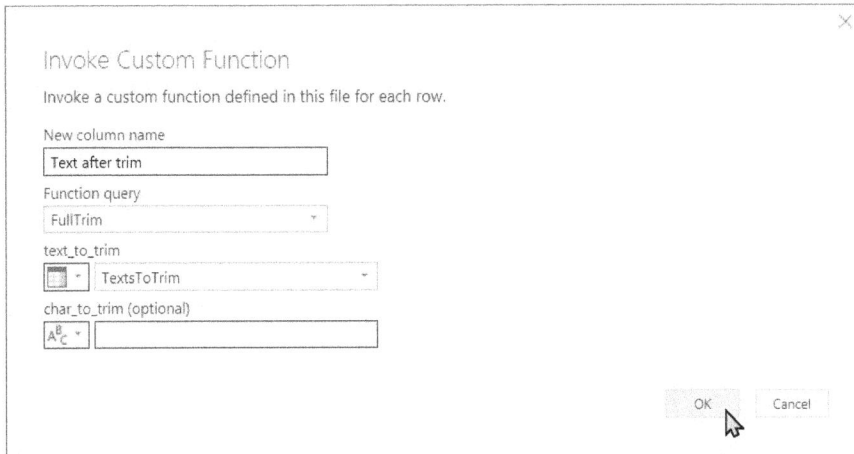

Figure 9.35: Properly configured Invoke Custom Function window

3. Confirm the function arguments by clicking the **OK** button.

4. Power Query will add a new column containing the trimmed and standardized text values.

This completes the creation and application of the custom function. Optionally, it may be tested with the `char_to_trim` argument set to a specific value, such as **1**, to observe how the function behaves with a custom delimiter.

To finalize the process, close the editor by selecting **Close & Load** on the **Home** tab. Since the blank query was converted into a function, the editor will not prompt for a load destination because Power Query functions are always loaded as connections only.

Alternatively, as demonstrated in the previous example, the load behavior of the `Texts To Trim` query may be adjusted from **Connection Only** to loading the data as a table in Excel.

Conclusion

In this chapter, we focused on building and applying custom functions in Power Query. We learned how functions are auto-generated during folder imports, how to convert parameterized queries into reusable logic, and how to write your M-based functions from scratch. We also covered error handling, dynamic file path referencing, and techniques for cleaning and standardizing data at scale.

In the next chapter, we will see practical examples of using Power Query together with the M language to solve complex transformation scenarios.

Multiple choice questions

1. **What is the main advantage of using the first file as a transformation template when importing data from a folder in Power Query?**

   a. It ensures a fixed file is always used for transformations

   b. It works even if filenames change in the future

   c. It avoids the need for any parameterization

   d. It works even if the previously used file is deleted

2. **What components are automatically created by the Combine Files feature when importing from a folder in Power Query?**

   a. A parameter for the file input

   b. A sample query used for preview and transformation

   c. A transformation function to apply to each file

   d. A custom column for file names

3. **Which Power Query window visualizes dependencies and data flow between queries?**

   a. Query Settings

   b. Navigation

   c. Query Dependencies

   d. Manage Parameters

4. **What is the purpose of using the function Text.AfterDelimiter manually in M code rather than through the interface?**

   a. To avoid using dynamic delimiters

   b. To preserve null values during transformation

   c. To convert data to currency format

   d. To extract full row values

5. **What is the default data type assigned to function parameters if no type is declared?**

   a. text

   b. binary

   c. any

   d. number

6. **What is the correct syntax for declaring a Power Query function with an optional argument?**

   a. (text_to_trim as text, optional char_to_trim as text) as text =>

   b. (text, optional char = " ") =>

   c. function(text_to_trim, char_to_trim = " ") =>

   d. let function = (text, optional char)

Answers

Question number	Answer option letter
1.	b., d.
2.	a., b., c.
3.	c.
4.	b.
5.	c.
6.	a.

Join our Discord space

Join our Discord workspace for latest updates, offers, tech happenings around the world, new releases, and sessions with the authors:

https://discord.bpbonline.com

CHAPTER 10

Examples Using M Language

Introduction

In the previous chapter, we explored how to create and apply custom functions, focusing on parameterization and dynamic query building. This chapter builds on those concepts by presenting real-world examples that demonstrate how to solve practical data transformation challenges using the M language in Power Query.

You will learn how to calculate running totals, sort data using custom-defined lists, compare individual averages to global metrics, and dynamically remove unwanted rows or columns based on file structure. These examples go beyond standard interface options and require a deeper understanding of Power Query's formula language, particularly its list functions.

The chapter also introduces recursion through the implementation of a factorial function, highlighting a powerful technique rarely covered in basic Power Query use. Each scenario addresses a common data preparation task, helping you develop more flexible and scalable transformation logic.

Structure

This chapter covers the following topics:

- Running total

- Sorting by custom lists
- Seller average to overall average
- Removing a dynamic number of top rows
- Remove the last two columns
- Generating pairs
- Introduction to recursion through factorial
- Tips for efficient M language scripting
- Guidelines for structuring queries

Objectives

By the end of this chapter, you will be able to apply advanced M language techniques to solve common data transformation challenges in Power Query. You will learn how to calculate running totals using list functions, sort data based on custom-defined orders, and compare group-level metrics to global averages. You will also discover how to dynamically remove a variable number of rows or columns based on content, and how to generate combinations of data, such as unique player pairings. Finally, you will understand the concept of recursion in Power Query and how to implement it through a custom factorial function.

Running total

In this example, the work is performed using the table **tTotal** located in the file **`RunningTotal.xlsx`**. The data is shown in *Figure 10.1*:

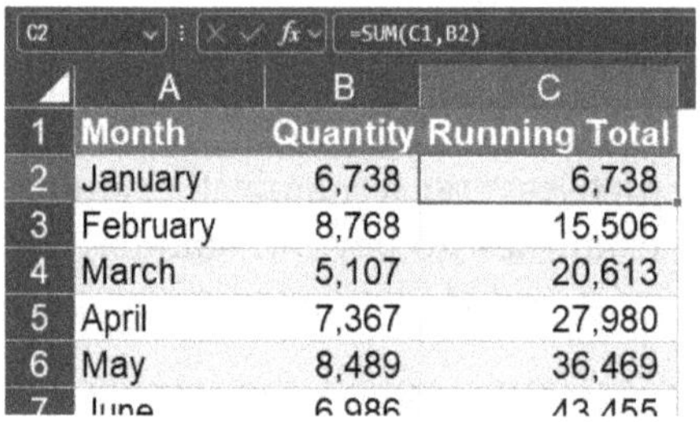

	A	B	C
1	Month	Quantity	Running Total
2	January	6,738	6,738
3	February	8,768	15,506
4	March	5,107	20,613
5	April	7,367	27,980
6	May	8,489	36,469
7	June	6,986	43,455

***Figure 10.1**: Data in the tTotal table*

This table contains a running total calculated using an Excel formula. The task will be to replicate this logic in Power Query. As usual, begin by importing the data into the editor using the **From Table/Range** command from the Excel **Data** tab (*Figure 1.1*).

After the data has been loaded, an index column can be added immediately by expanding the **Index Column** command on the **Add Column** tab and selecting the **From 1** option (*Figure 4.15*). This column will serve as an indicator of how many values from the beginning of the dataset must be summed for each row.

The next step involves using the **List.Range** function, which returns a subset of elements from a list based on a specified range. Its syntax is as follows:

```
List.Range(list as list, offset as number, optional count as nullable number)
as list
```

The arguments of the **List.Range** function are as follows:

- **List**: The list from which the subset of elements is to be extracted.

- **Offset**: The number representing the position of the first element to be returned. It is important to remember that indexing in Power Query starts at zero.

- **Count**: An optional argument specifying how many elements should be returned from the specified starting point. If omitted, **List.Range** returns all elements from the offset to the end of the list.

The greatest challenge will be with the first argument, because currently, there is no list (in terms of data types) available in the query. However, such a list can be quickly created. To better understand the process of creating a list, examine the description of the **List.Range** function within the editor by performing the following steps:

1. Click the **fx** icon next to the formula bar. This will add a new step referencing the previous table step (**#"Added Index"**).

2. Replace the default reference in the formula bar with **=List.Range**.

This action displays the function's description, as shown in *Figure 10.2*:

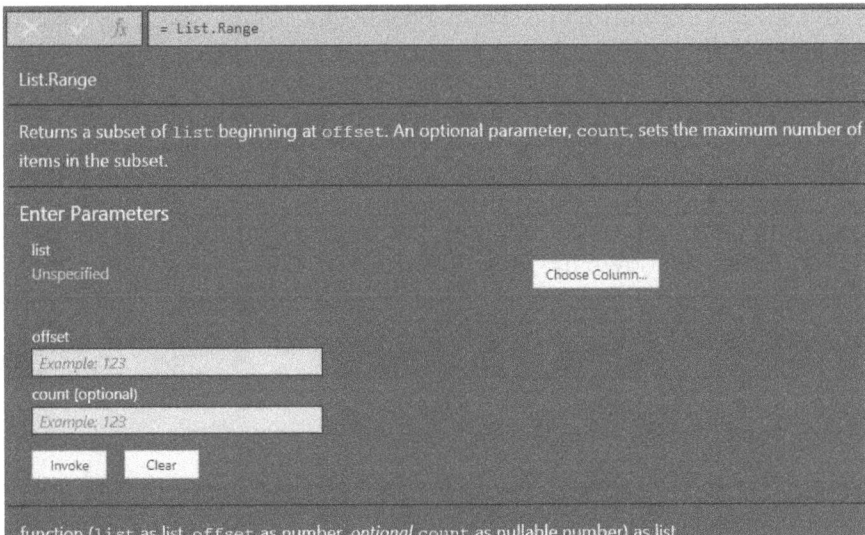

Figure 10.2: Description of the List.Range function in the editor

In this window, after entering the function arguments, the **Invoke** button can be used to execute the function. In this example, the important element is the **Choose Column** button, which indicates that the first argument of the **List.Range** function can be a column reference. Clicking this button directly will not help produce a valid function call in this case, but it serves as an important hint.

Another hint comes from the column extraction operations demonstrated in *Chapter 8, Parameters and Query Parameterization*, where it was shown that extracting a single column from a table causes Power Query to treat it as a list (*Figure 8.5*).

Tip: **In many functions that require a list as an argument, a reference to a specific column from a table can be used. The syntax must follow the pattern TableName[ColumnName], as this transforms the column into a list in Power Query.**

Now, the step containing the placeholder **List.Range** function can be removed, and the knowledge just gained can be applied to use the function properly:

1. Click the **Custom Column** command on the **Add Column** tab (*Figure 3.6*).
2. In the **Custom Column** window:
    a. Enter Total in the **New Column Name** field.
    b. Enter the following formula:
        ```
        List.Range(#"Added Index"[Quantity],0,[Index])
        ```

It is important in this formula not to refer directly to the **Quantity** column, because that would cause the formula to reference individual cells in successive rows rather than the entire column. Instead, the reference must begin with the previous step. In this case, **#"Added Index"**. Then followed by the specific column name. From Power Query's perspective, this converts the column into a list.

Since a running total is required, the calculation must always start from the first element in the list, which is element number 0. In each successive row, more elements should be retrieved. This dynamic behavior is ensured by the Index column.

After confirming this formula, a new column will be created in which each row contains a progressively longer list, as shown in *Figure 10.3*:

	A^BC Month	1²3 Quantity	1²3 Running Total	1²3 Index	ABC 123 Total
1	January	6738	6738	1	List
2	February	8768	15506	2	List
3	March	5107	20613	3	List
4	April	7367	27980	4	List

List
6738
8768
5107

Figure 10.3: Lists created using the List.Range function

The task is to sum all the elements within each of the generated lists. This requires applying the `List.Sum` function and changing the data type of the column to whole numbers.

A simpler approach would involve the following steps:

1. Modify the formula in the Added Custom step by clicking the gear icon and appending the `List.Sum` function so that the complete formula is:

   ```
   List.Sum(List.Range(#"Added Index"[Quantity],0,[Index]))
   ```

2. Confirm the formula update by clicking **OK**.

3. Change the data type of the Total column to Whole Number, for example, by clicking the icon in the column header and selecting Whole Number.

A more optimized approach would involve editing the entire formula directly in the formula bar so that a single query step produces the same result as the two-step method described. Instead of this formula:

```
=   Table.AddColumn(#"Added   Index",   "Total",   each   List.Range(#"Added
Index"[Quantity],0,[Index]))
```

The following should be used:

```
= Table.AddColumn(#"Added  Index",  "Total",  each  List.Sum(List.Range(#"Added
Index"[Quantity],0,[Index])), Int64.Type)
```

After correcting the formula in the Total column, the results should exactly match those in the Running Total column. Only the final steps remain:

1. Remove the Index column.

2. Rename the query to RunningTotal.

3. Load the query into Excel by clicking the **Close & Load To** command (*Figure 1.13*).

4. Choose the location for the resulting table in the Import Data window.

Sorting by custom lists

In this example, the work is performed using the table **tSort** located in the file **CustomSort. xlsx**. The table is shown in *Figure 10.4*:

# No.	Year	Month	Quantity
5	2025	March	5107
8	2026	april	5315
6	2026	march	5424
1	2025	january	6738
12	2026	June	6972
11	2025	June	6986

Figure 10.4: Data in the tSort table

The task in this example is to correctly sort the data, first by month name (which is the more important criterion in this case), and then by year. The correct row order is indicated in the # **No.** column. In Excel, this is a straightforward task because custom lists are available and sorting by them is supported. In Power Query, sorting by custom lists is more complex.

An additional challenge in this example is that some of the month names are written in lowercase letters, while others begin with an uppercase letter.

Before presenting a possible solution to the problem, it should be noted that the approach was developed based on information from the following source:

https://stackoverflow.com/questions/26364388/power-query-sort-by-custom-list

The main point here is that, in many cases, it is worth checking whether someone has already solved the problem at hand, rather than attempting to develop a solution from scratch.

Now, two simple steps can be taken to proceed with data analysis:

1. Load the data into Power Query by selecting any cell in the **tSort** table and then clicking the **From Table/Range** command on the Excel **Data** tab (*Figure 1.1*).

2. Once the table is loaded into the editor, sort the data first by the **Month** column and then by the **Year** column. In Power Query, the significance of columns during sorting depends strictly on the order in which they are sorted.

The data, sorted by default from A to Z, is shown in *Figure 10.5*:

fx	= Table.Sort(#"Changed Type",{{"Month", Order.Ascending}, {"Year", Order.Ascending}})

▦	1^2_3 # No.	1^2_3 Year	A^b_C Month	1^2_3 Quantity	
1		7	2025 April	7367	
2		3	2025 February	8768	
3		11	2025 June	6986	
4		12	2026 June	6972	
5		5	2025 March	5107	
6		9	2025 May	8489	
7		8	2026 april	5315	
8		4	2026 february	7658	

Figure 10.5: Data sorted in Power Query by the Month and Year columns

The first point to notice is the order of the months. When sorting, Power Query places uppercase letters before any lowercase letters. Therefore, april written in lowercase appears after May (uppercase), and not immediately after April (uppercase). This order does not meet the intended requirements and will need to be corrected through appropriate transformations or by using a suitable function.

The next item for analysis is the **Table.Sort** function, which is visible in the formula bar:

```
= Table.Sort(#"Changed  Type",{{"Month",  Order.Ascending},  {"Year",  Order.
Ascending}})
```

In the formula, it is evident that the column name is specified first as a text value, followed by the sort order. These options appear to be insufficient for this example. Furthermore, the function description does not provide any additional parameters or configurations.

Tip: **Sometimes, the function descriptions available directly in the editor differ from those published on Microsoft's official documentation website.**

However, when reviewing the previously referenced website from which the solution was derived, an additional method for sorting columns is revealed. This method uses custom sorting logic. It employs a function to determine the sort order (by assigning each row an alternative or transformed value).

Tip: **An increasingly popular way to obtain a precise explanation of a function is to query an artificial intelligence tool. This approach often proves faster than searching directly on the internet. Unfortunately, the drawback is that AI models can sometimes hallucinate and return inaccurate information.**

To compute the custom logic, the **List.PositionOf** function is used. As in the previous example, the following steps can be performed:

1. Click the **fx** icon next to the formula bar. This adds a step that references the previous table step (**#"Sorted Rows"**).

2. In the formula bar, replace the default reference with: **= List.PositionOf**

This reveals that the optional **occurrence** argument can be selected from a dropdown list, as shown in *Figure 10.6*:

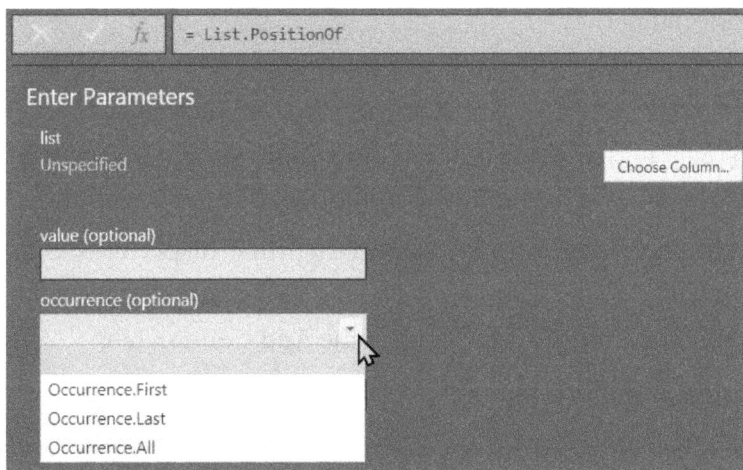

Figure 10.6: Description of the List.PositionOf function with a dropdown for the occurrence argument

Unfortunately, this behavior is currently not documented on Microsoft's official site, nor is it mentioned in the editor's built-in help. Therefore, a detailed explanation of the `List.PositionOf` function is provided as follows, to ensure it is used correctly in the following steps. The description begins with its syntax:

`List.PositionOf(list as list, value as any, optional occurrence as nullable number, optional equationCriteria as any) as any`

The function returns the position (number) of the **value** argument within the list provided in the **list** argument. Indexing starts at zero. If the **value** argument does not appear in the **list** argument, the function returns **-1**. The **occurrence** argument can be used to modify how the **value** is searched. The **equationCriteria** argument can be used to define how the comparison between **value** and **list** elements is performed.

Detailed description of the arguments is as follows:

- **list:** The list of values in which the desired value is to be located.

- **value:** The value whose position is to be found.

- **occurrence:** An optional argument determining which occurrence of the value should be found. Available options include:

  - **Occurrence.First**: Finds the first occurrence of the value. This is the default value. The number 1 can be used as a shorthand.

  - **Occurrence.Last**: Finds the last occurrence of the value.

  - **Occurrence.All**: Finds all occurrences of value. In this case, `List.PositionOf` returns a list of positions.

  - **An integer**: Allows specifying a particular occurrence of a value, for example, the second one.

- **equationCriteria**: An optional argument defining the comparison method. In this example, the relevant method is `Comparer.OrdinalIgnoreCase`.

Before using `List.PositionOf` to determine sorting order, the function will first be added in a simplified form (with only the two required arguments) in a new column:

1. Remove the previously added **Custom1** step that displayed the `List.PositionOf` function description.

2. Click the **Custom Column** command on the **Add Column** tab.

3. In the **Custom Column** window:

   a. Leave the new column name unchanged (this step is temporary and the column will be removed in later transformations).

   b. Enter the exact formula:

```
List.PositionOf({"January", "february", "March", "April", "May",
"June"},[Month])
```

Note that the second element in the list (february) is written in lowercase.

The resulting positions returned by the function are shown in *Figure 10.7*:

▦ ▾	1²₃ # No.	1²₃ Year	Aᵇ꜀ Month	1²₃ Quantity	ᴬᴮꟲ 1 2 3 Custom	▾
1	7	2025	April	7367	3	
2	3	2025	February	8768	-1	
3	11	2025	June	6986	5	
4	12	2026	June	6972	5	
5	5	2025	March	5107	2	

Figure 10.7: *Results of the List.PositionOf function with mismatched letter casing*

It can be observed that in the second row, the **List.PositionOf** function returns -1, because it fails to locate the value February on the hardcoded list. Power Query, by default, performs case-sensitive matching. Therefore, February and february are considered distinct values. For all other entries where the letter casing matches exactly, the correct list position is returned (indexing starts at zero).

To improve the formula so that all month names are correctly matched, there are at least two solutions:

1. Use the **Text.Proper** function, which is applied when using the **Capitalize Each Word** option available under the **Format** command on the **Transform** tab (*Figure 1.12*), before referencing the Month column. Alternatively, use one of the other letter-case conversion functions on the Month column and adjust the casing of the list items accordingly.

2. Supply the fourth argument of the **List.PositionOf** function with **Comparer. OrdinalIgnoreCase**. When entering the fourth argument, the third argument must also be provided. To avoid typing the full phrase **Occurrence.First**, the number **1** may be used. The result will be identical.

Note: **In Power Query, if a later optional argument is used, all preceding optional arguments must also be provided. Unlike Excel, commas cannot be used to skip over optional parameters; each must be assigned a value.**

In this example, the second solution will be applied. First, modify the formula in the added **Custom** column to the following form:

```
List.PositionOf({"January", "february", "March", "April", "May",
"June"},[Month],1,Comparer.OrdinalIgnoreCase)
```

Even though the casing of the word february was not changed, the **List.PositionOf** function successfully finds the position for each month, as shown in *Figure 10.8*:

```
= Table.AddColumn(#"Sorted Rows", "Custom", each List.PositionOf({"January", "february", "March", "April",
    "May", "June"},[Month],1,Comparer.OrdinalIgnoreCase))
```

1²₃ # No.	1²₃ Year	AᵇC Month	1²₃ Quantity	ᴬᴮᶜ Custom
1	7	2025 April	7367	3
2	3	2025 February	8768	1
3	11	2025 June	6986	5
4	12	2026 June	6972	5
5	5	2025 March	5107	2
6	9	2025 May	8489	4
7	8	2026 april	5315	3
8	4	2026 february	7658	1
9	1	2025 january	6738	0

Figure 10.8: Results of the List.PositionOf function with case-insensitive comparison

Tip: **You can also create a mapping table that assigns each month name to its corresponding number, then merge it with the main table to retrieve the correct month number directly.**

Now the **Added Custom** step can be removed, and the sorting formula modified. Instead of a column name specified as text (*Figure 10.5*), the **List.PositionOf** function used in the removed **Added Custom** step should be inserted. It is important to include the **each** keyword so that the function is applied to each row of the **Month** column individually:

```
= Table.Sort(#"Changed  Type",{{each  List.PositionOf({"January",  "february",
"March", "April", "May", "June"},[Month],1,Comparer.OrdinalIgnoreCase), Order.
Ascending}, {"Year", Order.Ascending}})
```

The result of sorting with custom logic (using a function) is shown in *Figure 10.9*:

```
= Table.Sort(#"Changed Type",{{each List.PositionOf({"January", "february", "March", "April", "May",
    "June"},[Month],1,Comparer.OrdinalIgnoreCase), Order.Ascending}, {"Year", Order.Ascending}})
```

1²₃ # No.	1²₃ Year	AᵇC Month	1²₃ Quantity
1	1	2025 January	6738
2	2	2026 january	7612
3	3	2025 February	8768
4	4	2026 february	7658
5	5	2025 March	5107
6	6	2026 march	5424
7	7	2025 April	7367

Figure 10.9: Sorting results using custom logic, i.e., with a function

Fun fact: **When custom logic is used during sorting, the editor does not display column numbers in the headers.**

Custom list sorting has now been performed in Power Query. Before closing this query, it is worth considering when such an operation is truly justified, given that sorting by custom lists (especially for months) is much simpler in Excel. Example reasons include:

- When the sort order affects subsequent steps or calculations, such as indexing, `Table.FirstN`, or row-to-row comparisons.

- For task automation, so that no manual operations are required in Excel.

- In Power Query used within Power BI, where supporting columns for sorting may not exist.

- For consistency across different machines, especially since not every computer may have the same custom lists configured.

The final steps to complete this example are:

1. Rename the query to **CustomSort**.

2. Load the query into Excel by clicking the **Close & Load To** command (*Figure 1.13*).

3. Choose the location for the output table in the **Import Data** window.

Seller average to overall average

In this example, the work is performed using the **tAvg** table located in the file **Averages.xlsx**. In addition to the **tAvg** table, the file contains Excel formula-based calculations used to determine the average revenue for each merchant and the percentage average relative to the overall average of all sales. The data in **Averages.xlsx** is shown in *Figure 10.10*:

	A	B	C	D	E	F	G	H	I
F2			=AVERAGEIF(tAvg[Merchant],E2,tAvg[Sales])						
1	Month	Merchant	Sales		Merchant	Avg. Sales	% Avg.		Average
2	January	Lily	$46,381		Barney	$29,479	80.99%		$36,398.81
3	January	Tracy	$31,899		Lily	$34,308	94.25%		
4	January	Lily	$26,561		Marshall	$36,093	99.16%		
5	January	Tracy	$47,176		Robin	$36,502	100.28%		
6	February	Tracy	$36,870		Ted	$41,350	113.60%		
7	February	Ted	$41,342		Tracy	$37,118	101.98%		
8	February	Robin	$32,453						

Figure 10.10: Data in the file Averages.xlsx

The task will be to obtain equivalent percentage averages using only Power Query.

As usual, begin by loading the data from the **tAvg** table into Power Query by selecting any cell in the table and then clicking the **From Table/Range** command on the Excel **Data** tab (*Figure 1.1*).

After loading the data into the editor, the first step is to sum the values from the **Sales** column by merchant. To perform this:

1. Select only the **Merchant** column.

2. Click the **Group By** command located on the **Home** tab (*Figure 4.4*).

3. In the **Group By** window that opens:

    a. Leave the **Basic** option selected.

    b. Choose the **Sum** operation for the **Sales** column.

    c. Assign the name **Avg. Sales** to the new column.

4. Confirm the grouping by clicking **OK**.

The correctly filled **Group By** window is shown in *Figure 10.11*:

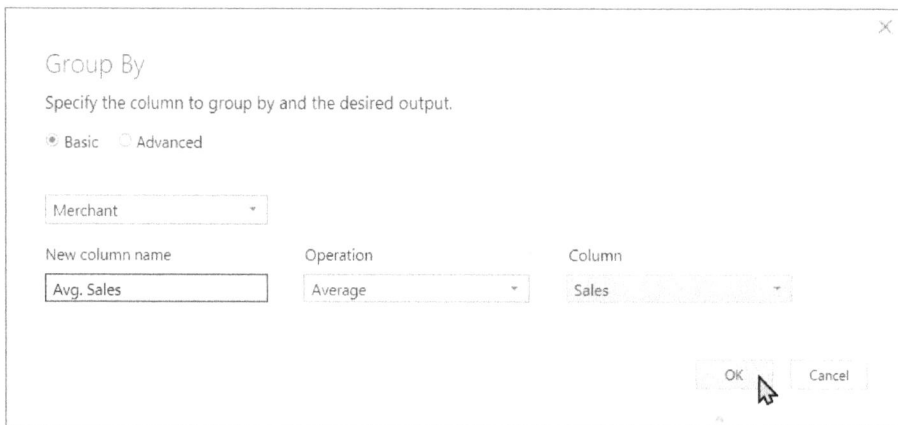

Figure 10.11: The Group By window calculating the average sales value for merchants

After confirming the grouping, the new **Grouped Rows** step will return averages similar to those calculated in Excel (*Figure 10.10*). The following formula should appear in the formula bar for this step:

```
= Table.Group(#"Changed Type", {"Merchant"}, {{"Avg. Sales", each List.
Average([Sales]), type nullable number}})
```

However, the goal is not only to calculate the average sales for each merchant but also to compute the percentage of each merchant's average relative to the overall average of all sales. To calculate the overall average of the **Sales** values, follow these steps:

1. Go back to the previous step. By default, this should be the step named **Changed Type**.

2. Select the **Sales** column.

3. On the **Transform** tab, expand the **Statistics** command and choose **Average**, as shown in *Figure 10.12*:

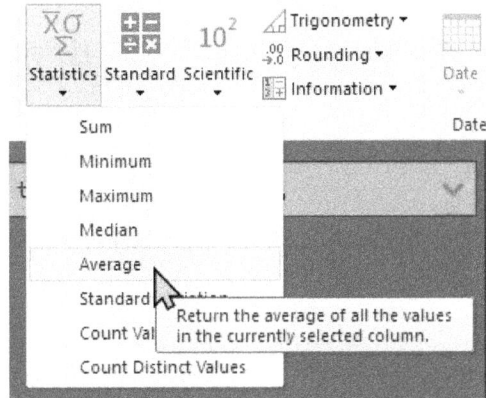

Figure 10.12: Expanded Statistics command

4. Confirm the insertion of the new step between existing steps (*Figure 5.20*).

The editor will add a step named **Calculated Average**, which returns only a single value, that is the average of the **Sales** column. Since the result is a number, the editor will display the **Transform Number Tools** tab for this step. The result and this tab are shown in *Figure 10.13*:

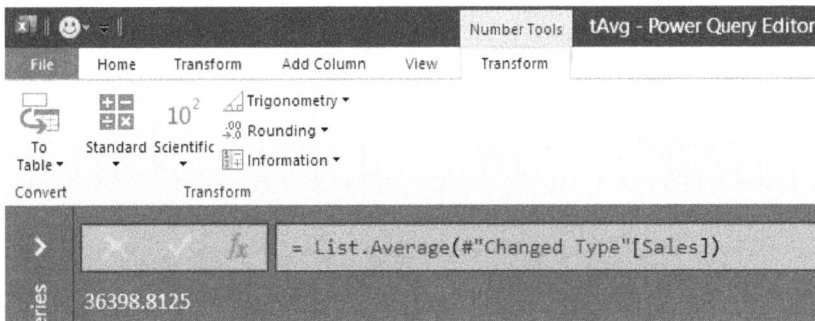

Figure 10.13: Number Tools Transform tab after using the Statistics command

Since a step was inserted before the previously created **Grouped Rows** step, the latter will begin to return an error. This happens because the editor has updated the formula in that step to reference **Calculated Average** instead of **Changed Type**, as follows:

```
= Table.Group(#"Calculated Average", {"Merchant"}, {{"Avg. Sales", each List.
Average([Sales]), type nullable number}})
```

In Power Query, it is possible to reference the same step multiple times across different steps. Therefore, the step name in this formula should be reverted back to **Changed Type**.

To verify the current M code structure, click the **Advanced Editor** command on the **Home** tab (*Figure 8.31*). This allows viewing the complete M code, where it becomes clear that both the **Calculated Average** and **Grouped Rows** steps correctly reference the **Changed Type** step, as shown in the M code:

```
let
    Source = Excel.CurrentWorkbook(){[Name="tAvg"]}[Content],
    #"Changed Type" = Table.TransformColumnTypes(Source,{{"Month", type text},
{"Merchant", type text}, {"Sales", Int64.Type}}),
    #"Calculated Average" = List.Average(#"Changed Type"[Sales]),
    #"Grouped Rows" = Table.Group(#"Changed Type", {"Merchant"}, {{"Avg. Sales",
each List.Average([Sales]), type nullable number}})
in
    #"Grouped Rows"
```

The final step is to divide the results from the **Grouped Rows** step by the value calculated in the **Calculated Average** step. To perform this:

1. Click the **Custom Column** command on the **Add Column** tab (*Figure 3.6*) while the **Grouped Rows** step is selected.

2. In the **Custom Column** window:

    a. Enter % **Avg.** in the **New column name** field.

    b. For now, enter only the reference to the previous step in the **Custom column formula** field: **#"Calculated Average"**.

3. Confirm the calculation by clicking **OK**.

In the newly created **Added Custom** step, Power Query will insert the same value (the result from the **Calculated Average** step) in every row of the % **Avg.** column. This is shown in *Figure 10.14*:

		f_x	= Table.AddColumn(#"Grouped Rows", "% Avg.", each #"Calculated Average")	

▦	A^B_C Merchant	1.2 Avg. Sales	$^{ABC}_{123}$ % Avg.
1	Lily	34307.66667	36398.8125
2	Tracy	37118	36398.8125
3	Ted	41349.5	36398.8125
4	Robin	36501.66667	36398.8125
5	Marshall	36092.5	36398.8125
6	Barney	29479	36398.8125

Figure 10.14: Overall sales average repeated in every row

When a **Custom Column** is assigned a constant value, regardless of whether it is a number, text (*Figure 5.15*), or a reference to another step, Power Query will repeat that value in every cell of the new column.

Now, the formula can be modified to perform the division and simultaneously assign a percentage data type. In the formula bar, update the M code from:

```
= Table.AddColumn(#"Grouped Rows", "% Avg.", each #"Calculated Average")
```

To:

```
= Table.AddColumn(#"Grouped Rows", "% Avg.", each [Avg. Sales]/#"Calculated
Average", Percentage.Type)
```

The transformations are now complete. The final steps are:

1. Rename the query to **PercentAverage**.
2. Sort the data in ascending order (A to Z) by the **Merchant** column.
3. Load the query into Excel by clicking the **Close & Load To** command (*Figure 1.13*).
4. Choose the destination for the resulting table in the **Import Data** window.
5. Apply the appropriate number formats to the **Avg. Sales** and **% Avg.** columns.

Removing a dynamic number of top rows

In this example, the task is to combine data from the **FirstRows** folder. This folder contains two **.csv** files: **GreatBritain.csv** and **Poland.csv**. This number of files is sufficient for demonstration purposes. The method demonstrated here can be used to combine a much larger number of files. The data structure in the files is shown in *Figure 10.15*:

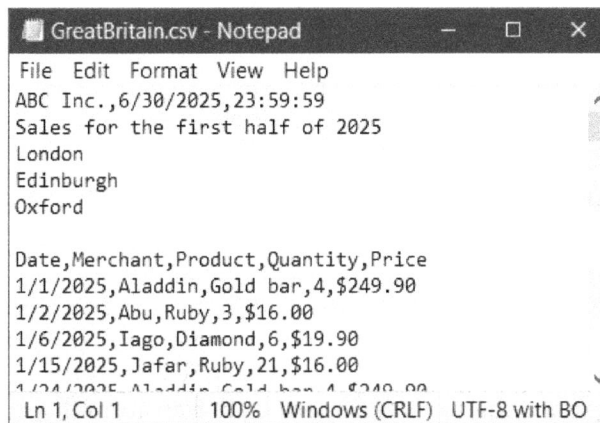

Figure 10.15: *Data structure in the .csv files, using GreatBritain.csv as an example*

The challenge when combining these files lies in the presence of descriptive data at the beginning of each file, with a varying number of rows. This means that the row to be used as the column header is not known in advance. It must be dynamically determined for each file.

The first step is to retrieve and combine the data from the folder:

1. Open the **FirstRows.xlsx** file or create a new blank workbook.
2. On the **Data** tab, expand the **Get Data** command, then choose **From File**, and select **From Folder** (*Figure 2.8*).

3. In the **Browse** window, locate the **FirstRows** folder from which the data will be retrieved and combined (as shown in *Figure 2.22*), and confirm the selection by clicking **Open**.

4. In the **Navigator** window (with the folder path displayed in the header, similar to *Figure 2.23*), click the **Transform Data** button.

    For this example, no additional transformations are required to filter the files. However, in general, basic filters should be applied. These preliminary transformations are discussed in the example *Importing data from folders* in *Chapter 2, Advanced Data Connections and Imports*.

5. Click the icon with two downward-pointing arrows in the **Content** column header.

6. In the **Combine Files** window that appears, choose the options as shown in *Figure 2.27*.

7. Confirm the combination of files from the folder by clicking **OK**.

After this operation, the query and data structure will appear as shown in *Figure 10.16*:

Figure 10.16: Query structure after retrieving and combining files from the folder

It is evident that nearly all columns have default names, while the correct column headers appear in a later row. Only the **Source.Name** column retains a name based on the original header. For the purpose of this example, this column is not needed. While it could simply be removed, that would result in an additional query step, which is not optimal. Therefore, it is better to identify and remove the steps that specifically transform this column.

There are two main ways to investigate this: reviewing each step sequentially from the beginning of the query, or opening the **Advanced Editor** (*Figure 8.31*) to view the full M code. The Advanced Editor does not offer a search function, but in newer versions of Power Query, the code is syntax-highlighted, and placing the cursor inside a word highlights all occurrences of that word.

In this example, the first approach will be used, as it avoids reviewing large blocks of code at once and does not require renaming steps. The first step related to the **Source.Name** column is **Renamed Columns1**, where the column name `Name` is changed to `Source.Name`. This can be seen in the formula bar:

```
= Table.RenameColumns(#"Invoke Custom Function1",{{"Name", "Source.Name"}})
```

This step is unnecessary and can be deleted. To do this, select the step and click the **Delete** button, or click the **x** next to the step name. Since this step is located in the middle of the query, a **Delete Step** confirmation dialog will appear (*Figure 5.8*).

After removing the **Renamed Columns1** step, the **Source.Name** column will no longer exist, and any steps that refer to it will generate errors. These can then be more easily identified and corrected. It is important to correct these steps one by one to prevent errors from propagating.

For instance, after deleting the **Renamed Columns1** step, selecting the **Changed Type** step may display an error message. However, the error might actually be caused by an earlier step. This can be confirmed by the presence of the **Go To Error** button in the top-right corner of the error message, as shown in *Figure 10.17*:

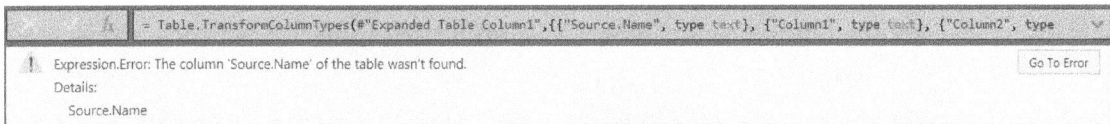

Figure 10.17: Query structure after loading and combining files from the folder

Clicking the **Go To Error** button causes the editor to jump to the step that triggered the error. In this case, the error originates from the **Removed Other Columns1** step. This step attempts to retain the **Source.Name** and **Transform File** columns, as seen in the formula bar:

```
= Table.SelectColumns(#"Invoke Custom Function1", {"Source.Name", "Transform
File"})
```

The editor displays a clear error message for this step: **The column 'Source.Name' of the table was not found**. This indicates that the specified column no longer exists. Therefore, the portion of the formula referencing it should be removed, leaving only:

```
= Table.SelectColumns(#"Invoke Custom Function1", "Transform File")
```

Since only one column is being retained, the curly braces can also be removed, as the function no longer receives a list of text values, but a single text value.

After correcting the **Removed Other Columns1** step, the next (and final) step that triggers an error is **Changed Type**. Since column names will be modified in the upcoming transformations, this step should be deleted. Since it is the final step of the query, no confirmation prompt will appear when removing it.

The main query (**FirstRows**) has now been cleaned. The next task is to move to the **Transform Sample File** query to identify the row containing the column headers. Since this query processes a single file, and it is known that the header row always contains the word Date in the first column (**Column1**, as shown in *Figure 10.15* and *Figure 10.16*), the goal is to locate the row index where this word appears (with zero-based indexing).

The steps are as follows:

1. Add an index column starting from zero by expanding the **Index Column** command on the **Add Column** tab and selecting **From 0** (*Figure 4.15*).

2. Add a conditional column by clicking the **Conditional Column** command on the **Add Column** tab (*Figure 7.2*).

3. In the **Add Conditional Column** window, complete the fields as follows:

   a. In the **New column name** field, enter Row.

   b. From the **Column Name** dropdown, select the first column (**Column1**).

   c. As the operator, choose **equals**.

   d. In the **Value** field, enter **Date**.

   e. For the **Output**, select **Select a column** from the list, then choose the **Index** column.

   f. In the **Else** field, enter **null**.

   The correctly completed **Add Conditional Column** window is shown in *Figure 10.18*:

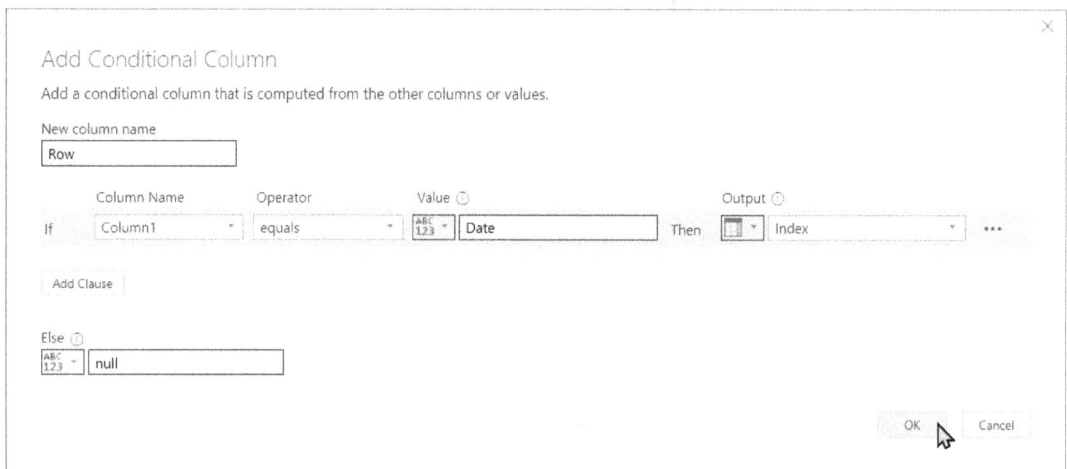

Figure 10.18: Correctly configured Add Conditional Column window

In the newly added **Row** column, a number should appear in only one row. To return that number as the result of a query step, follow these steps:

1. Select the **Row** column.

2. Then, go to the **Transform** tab.

3. Expand the **Statistics** command and choose **Minimum** (*Figure 10.12*).

This action will create a step that returns a single number (similar to the earlier example in *Figure 10.13*). This value will be used in a later step to remove the top rows of the table.

To add that removal step:

1. Select the first step of the query (**Source**).

2. On the **Home** tab, expand the **Remove Rows** command and choose **Remove Top Rows** (*Figure 1.30*).

3. Confirm insertion of the step within the query by clicking **Insert** in the **Insert Step** window (*Figure 5.20*).

4. In the **Remove Top Rows** window, enter a sample number of rows to remove, such as 3 (*Figure 1.31*).

5. Take note of the code generated:

   ```
   = Table.Skip(Source,3)
   ```

6. Drag the **Removed Top Rows** step to the end of the query using the mouse.

7. Modify the formula bar to:

   ```
   = Table.Skip(Source,#"Calculated Minimum")
   ```

Alternatively, if the function needed to skip rows was known in advance, the process could be shortened as follows:

1. Select the last step (**Calculated Minimum**).

2. Click the **fx** icon next to the formula bar.

3. Enter the formula: `= Table.Skip(Source, #"Calculated Minimum")`

This step dynamically removes the top rows of data, depending on the position of the word Date.

Now, only the following steps remain:

1. In the **Transform Sample File** query, expand the table icon next to the first column and select **Use First Row as Headers** (*Figure 1.8*).

2. Optionally, switch to the **FirstRows** query, select all columns (which should now have the correct names), and on the **Transform** tab, click **Detect Data Type** (*Figure 2.21*).

3. Load the combined data into Excel.

Remove the last two columns

In this example, the task is to retrieve data from a single worksheet in the file `RemoveLastColumns.xlsx`. A sample of the data from the **Report1** worksheet is shown in *Figure 10.19*:

◢	A	B	C	D	E	F	G
1	Salesman	Product	January	February	March		Report1
2	Richard	Doll	$3,544	$12,672	$12,101		3
3	Richard	Teddy	$2,871	$9,562	$6,462		
4	Richard	Train	$8,206	$2,463	$6,142		
5	Richard	Car	$3,103	$4,636	$5,931		
6	Mary	Doll	$9,843	$11,735	$1,513		
7	Mary	Teddy	$4,588	$3,914	$9,902		

Figure 10.19: Data structure in worksheets of the RemoveLastColumns.xlsx file

The worksheets all share the same structure, differing only in the number of columns representing months. There are always two additional columns with irrelevant data. These columns do not have consistent names, so they cannot be removed by name. Instead, they must be removed based on their position.

Although this example involves retrieving data from only a single worksheet, the method demonstrated here can also be applied when retrieving data from multiple sheets simultaneously, as described in the *Importing data from an Excel file* example in *Chapter 2, Advanced Data Connections and Imports*.

To begin, load the data from the selected worksheet (Report1) into Power Query:

1. Open the RemoveLastColumns.xlsx file or optionally create a new blank workbook.

2. On the **Data** tab, expand the **Get Data** command, navigate to **From File**, and select **From Excel Workbook** (*Figure 2.8*).

3. In the **Import Data** window, locate the **RemoveLastColumns.xlsx** file on disk and click the **Import** button (as shown in *Figure 2.9*).

4. In the **Navigator** window, select the **Report1** worksheet and click **Transform Data**, as shown in *Figure 10.20*:

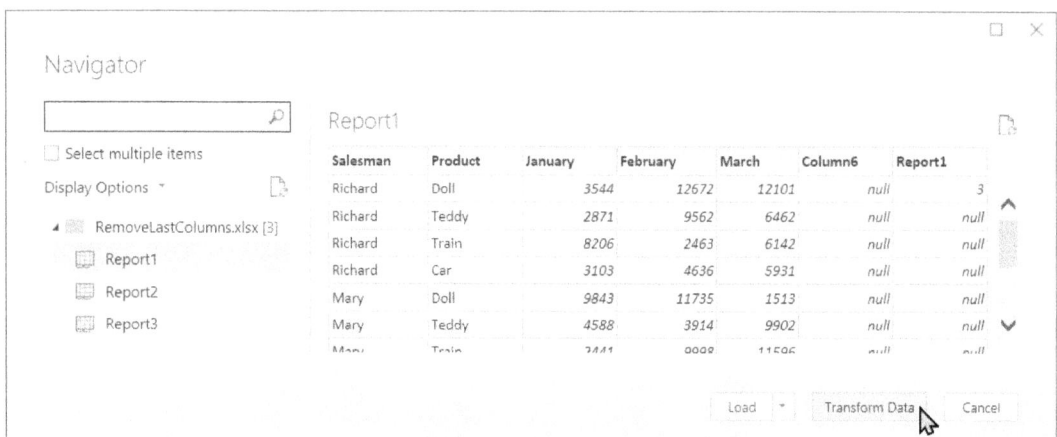

Figure 10.20: Selecting a single worksheet in the Navigator window

5. If the query automatically includes a **Changed Type** step, remove it. The goal is to create a dynamic solution. If the source worksheet changes and the column names differ, this step would result in an error.

The query should now contain three steps: **Source**, **Navigation**, and **Promoted Headers**.

Now it is time to dynamically remove the last two columns. When using the **Remove Other Columns** option from the context menu (*Figure 2.18*), Power Query generates a new step with the `Table.SelectColumns` function containing a list of column names to keep, removing the rest. The goal now is to build such a list of column names, excluding the last two.

To achieve this:

1. Click the **fx** icon next to the formula bar to add a new step.

2. In the formula bar, enter the following formula:

   `= Table.ColumnNames(#"Promoted Headers")`

   This function returns a list of column names for the specified table. In most cases, the reference to the table is the name of the previous query step. In this example, the relevant step is **Promoted Headers**.

   The result will be a list of column names in their original order from left to right.

3. From this list, the last two items need to be removed. To do this, on the **Transform** tab (while working with a list), expand the **Remove Items** command under **List Tools** and select **Remove Bottom Items**, as shown in *Figure 10.21*:

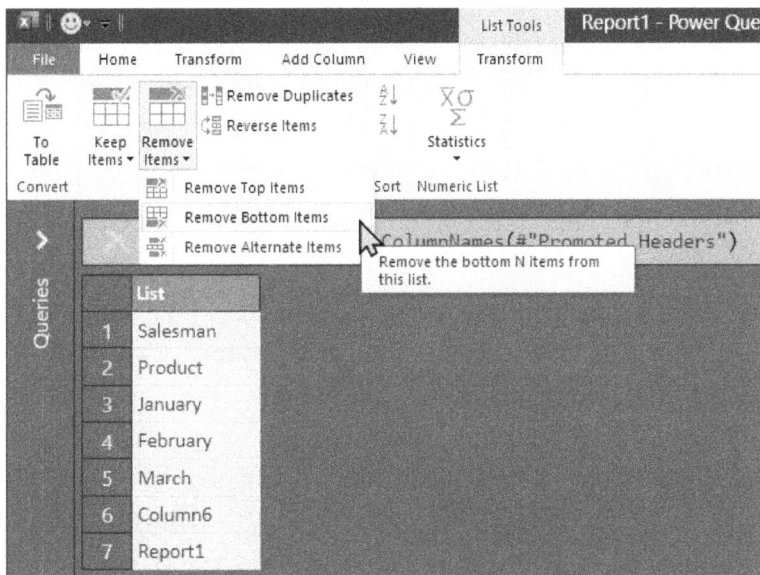

Figure 10.21: *Remove Bottom Items option*

4. In the **Remove Bottom Items** window, enter the number **2** in the **Number of Items** field and confirm the operation by clicking **OK**, as shown in *Figure 10.22*:

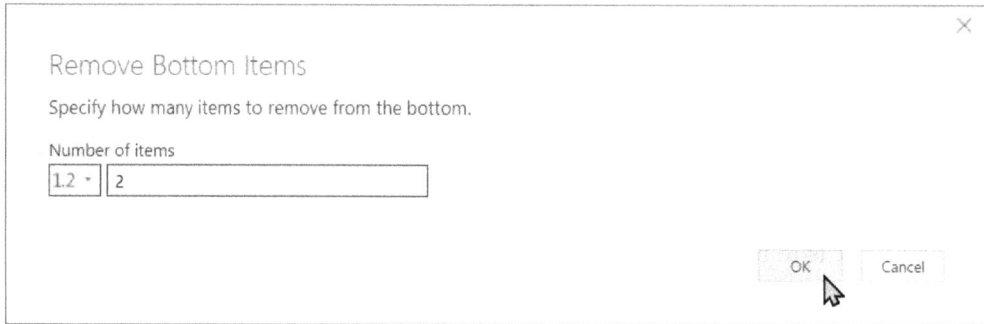

Figure 10.22: Remove Bottom Items window

At this point, a list of column names to retain has been generated. It now needs to be used in the next step. Since the required function is known, a new step can be added directly:

1. Click the **fx** icon next to the formula bar.

2. In the formula bar, enter the following formula:

```
= Table.SelectColumns(#"Promoted Headers", #"Removed Bottom Items")
```

In the **Table.SelectColumns** function used; the first argument refers to the **Promoted Headers** step, which contains the table from which columns should be selected. The second argument points to the **Removed Bottom Items** step, which contains the list of column names to retain.

The core objective of this example has now been accomplished. However, a few final transformations are needed due to the fact that month names appear as column headers rather than as values within a single column. Therefore, an **Unpivot** operation will be performed, which was previously discussed in *Chapter 5, Pivot and Unpivot,* as follows:

1. Select the **Salesman** and **Product** columns.

2. Right-click one of the selected column headers and choose **Unpivot Other Columns** from the context menu (as shown in *Figure 5.17*).

3. In the formula bar, rename the generated columns by modifying the code from:

```
= Table.UnpivotOtherColumns(Custom2, {"Salesman", "Product"}, "Attribute",
"Value")
```

To:

```
= Table.UnpivotOtherColumns(Custom2, {"Salesman", "Product"}, "Month",
"Sales")
```

4. Select all columns and, on the **Transform** tab, click the **Detect Data Type** command (*Figure 2.21*).

```
= Source{[Item="Report1",Kind="Sheet"]}[Data]
```

If everything functions correctly, the final step is to rename the query to **WithoutLastTwo** and load the data into a new worksheet in Excel.

Generating pairs

In this example, the task is to work with a list of players contained in the **tPlayers** table in the file **BuildPairs.xlsx**. Based on this list, the goal is to generate pairs of players. Three pairing methods will be discussed:

- Each with each, where an element from the list may appear twice in a pair, that means a player can be paired with themselves.

- Each with each, where an element from the list may not appear twice in a pair, that means a player cannot be paired with themselves.

- Unique pairings, where each player is paired with every other player exactly once. For example, the pair *(Timon, Pumbaa)* is considered the same as *(Pumbaa, Timon)*.

The player list and the number of resulting pairs for each pairing method are shown in *Figure 10.23*:

	A	B	C	D	E	F
1	Name		All pairs:	n^2	25	
2	Timon		Not the same:	$n * (n - 1)$	20	
3	Pumbaa		No repetitions:	$n * (n - 1)/2$	10	$\binom{n}{2}$
4	Simba					
5	Kiara					
6	Rafiki					
7						

Figure 10.23: List of players and number of pairs for each pairing method

The main focus will be on the last method (unique pairings), but the first two will also be covered, as they are easy to implement in Power Query.

Since the data is stored in a table, it is sufficient to select any cell within the table and then click the **From Table/Range** command on the **Data** tab (*Figure 1.1*) to load the data into the Power Query Editor.

After loading the **tPlayers** table into the editor, the **Name** column should be renamed to **Players1** to clarify that this column contains the first player. A new column will later be created to represent the second player.

All vs. all pairing

To generate all possible pairs (each with each), including self-pairings, follow these steps:

1. Click the **Custom Column** command on the **Add Column** tab (*Figure 3.6*).

2. In the **Custom Column** window:

   a. Enter **Player2** in the **New column name** field.

   b. In the **Custom column formula** field, enter: `= Source`

This creates a new column named **Player2**, where for each row in **Player1**, a full list of players is assigned. The result is shown in *Figure 10.24*:

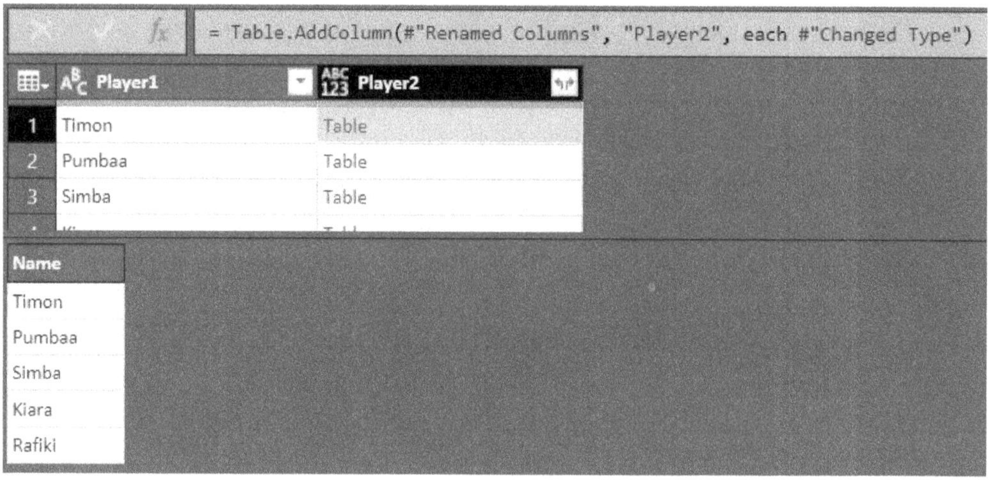

Figure 10.24: Each player is assigned a list of all other players

To complete the pairing logic and display both players in separate columns, follow these steps to expand the nested data and rename the resulting column appropriately:

1. Click the double-arrow icon (**Expand** icon) in the **Player2** column header, and expand the **Name** column without any prefix (similar to *Figure 3.14*).

2. Since Power Query automatically names the resulting column using the original column name, the formula in the formula bar will be:

   `= Table.ExpandTableColumn(#"Added Custom", "Player2", {"Name"}, {"Name"})`

   Change the second **Name** to **Player2** to clearly reflect the pairing:

   `=   Table.ExpandTableColumn(#"Added   Custom",   "Player2",   {"Name"}, {"Player2"})`

This operation successfully pairs each player with every player, including themselves. The resulting table should contain 25 rows (5 players × 5 players).

Excluding self-matches

The next task is to remove rows where **Player1** and **Player2** represent the same person. To preserve both pairing methods, the query should first be duplicated. The steps to remove self-matching pairs are as follows:

1. Right-click on the **tPlayers** query and choose the **Duplicate** option from the context menu (*Figure 3.36*).

2. In the duplicated query, open the filter dropdown from the **Player2** column header, navigate to **Text Filters**, and select **Does Not Equal** (*Figure 2.15*).

3. Since the **Filter Rows** window (*Figure 2.16*) does not allow selection of another column as a comparison value, enter any placeholder value, such as 1, and confirm with **OK**.

4. In the formula bar, modify the code:

```
= Table.SelectRows(#"Expanded Player2", each [Player2] <> "1")
```

To dynamically reference the **Player1** column instead of text 1:

```
= Table.SelectRows(#"Expanded Player2", each [Player2] <> [Player1])
```

This completes the transformation. Rows where a player is paired with themselves have been removed. The resulting table should now contain **20 rows**.

Scheduling matches to ensure all players compete against one another

To generate the third type of pairing, an iterative approach over each element in the list will be used. The first step is to convert the table containing the players into a list. This is done by following these steps:

1. Right-click on the **tPlayers** query and select **Duplicate** from the context menu (*Figure 3.36*).

2. Remove all steps except for the first one (**Source**). Steps can be removed one by one by clicking the x next to the step name, or by right-clicking the second step and selecting **Delete Until End** from the context menu (similar to *Figure 5.7*).

To convert the column into a list, either:

- Select the column and click **Convert to List** on the **Transform** tab (*Figure 8.21*), or
- Right-click the column header and choose **Drill Down** from the context menu (*Figure 8.4*).

Both actions generate the same code:

```
= Source[Name]
```

However, since this scenario allows for easy code simplification, the transformation will be merged into the **Source** step. The original code:

```
= Excel.CurrentWorkbook(){[Name="tPlayers"]}[Content]
```

Will be modified by appending the column reference:

```
= Excel.CurrentWorkbook(){[Name="tPlayers"]}[Content][Name]
```

3. This modification should be made directly within the **Source** step instead of adding a new step.

As a result, the single-column table has now been converted into a list, which will facilitate subsequent transformations. Before proceeding, the step name **Source** will be changed to better reflect its content. To do this, click **Advanced Editor** on the **Home** tab (*Figure 8.31*) and update all instances of Source to Players in the M code:

```
let
    Source = Excel.CurrentWorkbook(){[Name="tPlayers"]}[Content][Name]
in
    Source
```

We are changing to:

```
let
    Players = Excel.CurrentWorkbook(){[Name="tPlayers"]}[Content][Name]
in
    Players
```

Tip: **It is not possible to rename the Source and Navigation steps directly from the APPLIED STEPS pane. These step names can only be changed in the Advanced Editor.**

In the next transformation phase, the goal is to add a step that returns the indices of all elements in the list, that is, a sequence of numbers starting from zero and containing the same number of elements as the list of players. This is done using the following steps:

1. Click **fx** next to the formula bar.

2. In the formula bar of the newly added step, enter the following code:

    = **List.Positions(Players)**

3. Rename the new step in the **APPLIED STEPS** pane to **Indexes**.

Now, the transformation moves on to the most complex step of this query. In this step, based on the **Indexes** step, the objective is to pair the players so that each one plays exactly one match with every other player. Based on the indexes of elements in the **Players** list, each subsequent player will be assigned an increasingly shorter list of opponents.

To better understand the structure of the written code, functions will be added progressively.

The following operations are executed:

1. Click **fx** next to the formula bar.

2. Rename the new step in the **APPLIED STEPS** pane to **Matches**.

3. Enter the following code into the formula bar:
```
= List.Transform(Indexes, (i) => i + 1)
```

The purpose of the **List.Transform** function is to transform the list (step **Indexes**) using a custom function. Currently, the function is simple: **(i) =>**. The letter **i** is the function's argument and represents each element of the list in turn. At this stage, the transformation merely adds one to each element (**i + 1**). It can be viewed as a loop over all elements of the list. The result of this first transformation is shown in *Figure 10.25*:

Figure 10.25: Result of the first transformation of the Indexes list

4. In the next code version, a more complex transformation of the **Indexes** list is applied:
```
= List.Transform(Indexes, (i) => List.Range(Indexes, i + 1, List.Count(Indexes) - i - 1))
```

Instead of generating a single value, this time, each element in the **Indexes** list generates a list of subsequent elements using the **List.Range** function. This function was previously discussed in the *Running Total* example in this chapter. With each iteration, the number of returned elements decreases so that the last element results in an empty list. The resulting list represents the second players in the pairings. The list returned for the second element of the **Indexes** list is shown in *Figure 10.26*:

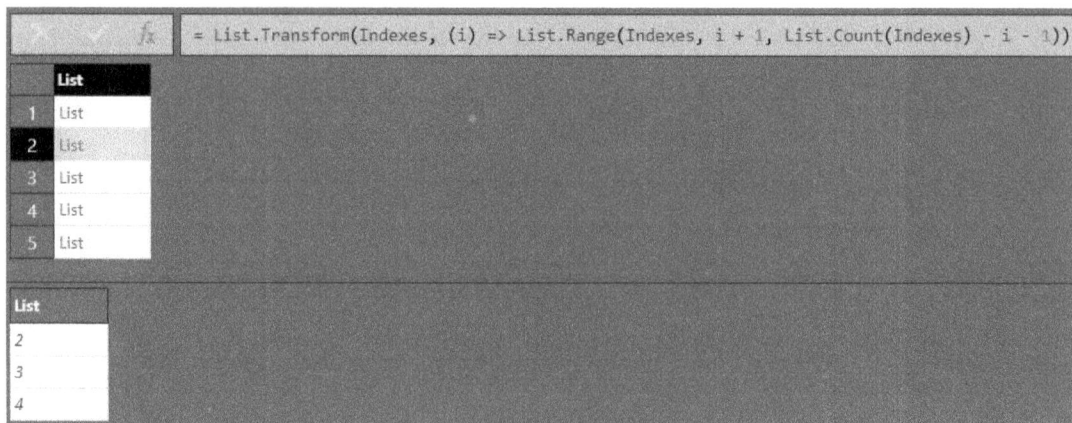

Figure 10.26: Result of the second transformation of the Indexes list

5. In the next code revision, a second **List.Transform** function will be added to obtain both players in each pairing. The second function will use the argument j as:

```
= List.Transform(Indexes, (i) => List.Transform( List.Range(Indexes, i +
1, List.Count(Indexes) - i - 1),(j) => Text.From(i) & "_" & Text.From(j)))
```

This transformation yields the list of match pairings that were being sought. In this transformation, the previously generated lists (player indexes) are processed to pair them with the index of the opponent. Therefore, it is necessary to add the argument **j**, which represents the second player in the pair. The argument **i** continues to represent the first player. For now, a temporary transformation is applied for the argument **j**, allowing both the first and second player indexes to be viewed side by side. The list of pairings for the second player is shown in *Figure 10.27*:

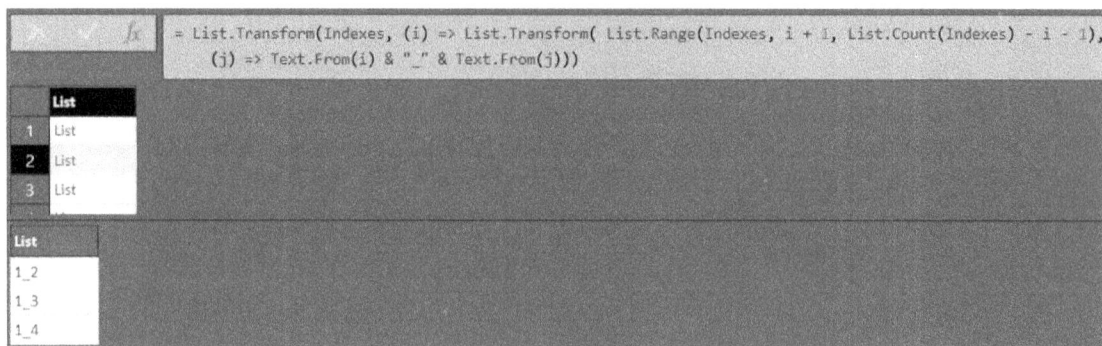

Figure 10.27: Result of the third transformation of the Indexes list

6. The temporary transformation is now replaced so that each result contains both players as a record. This is done by defining the record using square brackets and assigning column names to specific list positions:

```
[Player1=Players{i}, Player2=Players{j}]
```

The full code after this edit should appear as follows:

```
= List.Transform(Indexes, (i) => List.Transform( List.Range(Indexes,
i + 1, List.Count(Indexes) - i - 1),(j) => [Player1=Players{i},
Player2=Players{j}]))
```

Since the elements of the list are now records, their content cannot be directly previewed without expanding the list. This is illustrated in *Figure 10.28*:

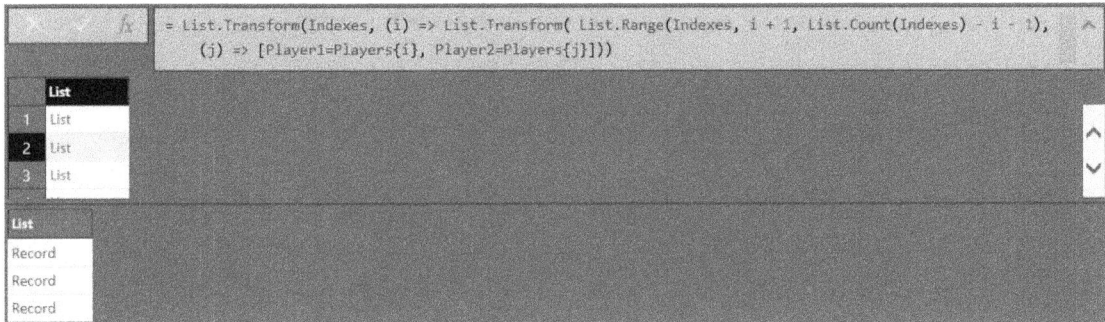

Figure 10.28: Result of the fourth transformation of the Indexes list

Additional functions could be appended in the same **Matches** step, but to simplify the code for further analysis, a new step is introduced:

1. Click **fx** next to the formula bar.
2. Rename the new step in the **APPLIED STEPS** pane to **AllMatches**.
3. In the formula bar, enter the following code:

```
= List.Combine(Matches)
```

This step yields 10 elements in the list, which is the correct number of matches according to the Excel-based calculation (*Figure 10.23*). A preview of the second record is shown in *Figure 10.29*:

Figure 10.29: Record with players in the second match

4. In the next (final) edit, the `Table.FromRecords` function is added in the formula bar to convert the list of records into a table of paired players. After the edit, the code becomes:

```
= Table.FromRecords(List.Combine(Matches))
```

The final table of player pairings is shown in *Figure 10.30:*

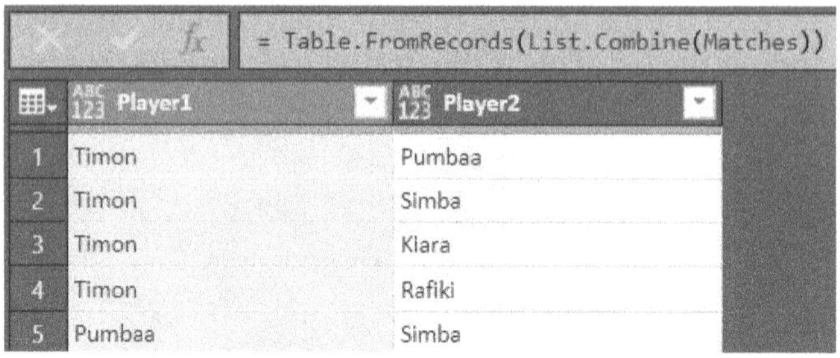

Figure 10.30: Paired matches

Three pairing sets have now been created. Appropriate names should be assigned to them in sequence: **AllPairs**, **ExcludingSelfMatches**, and **DistinctMatches**. Finally, select the **Close & Load** command from the **Home** tab (*Figure 1.13*). Since three queries were created simultaneously and the **Close & Load** command was not expanded, they should each appear on separate (new) worksheets. If it is preferred to place them on the same worksheet, select the full tables (e.g., using *Ctrl + A*), cut them (*Ctrl + X*), and paste them (*Ctrl + V*) in the desired location.

Introduction to recursion through factorial

In this example, the objective is to create a sample **factorial** function in order to demonstrate how recursion works in Power Query. A factorial, in simple terms, is the product of all natural numbers from a given natural number down to one. Mathematically, this is represented as:

$$n! = n * (n-1) * (n-2) * \ldots * 2 * 1$$

For example: $5! = 5 * 4 * 3 * 2 * 1$

Recursion, on the other hand, is when a function calls itself, typically with a reduced input. In the general mathematical formula for computing factorials, the function involves a series of decreasing multiplicative factors. Each factor is one less than the previous, continuing this way until reaching one. The value of one is the base case (termination condition), which every recursive function must include. The base case is the specific input value for which the recursive function returns a fixed result. In the case of a factorial function, the return value is defined to be one when `n = 1`, or even for smaller values.

To create a factorial function in Power Query, the following steps are performed:

1. Open the file **Factorial.xlsx**, or create a new blank Excel workbook.

2. On the **Data** tab, expand the **Get Data** command, navigate to **From Other Sources**, and select **Blank Query** (*Figure 9.31*).

3. Rename the query to **Factorial**.

4. Click the **Advanced Editor** command on the **Home** tab (*Figure 8.31*) to open the **Advanced Editor** window and enter the following code:

```
(n as number) as number =>
let
        result = if n <= 1 then 1 else n * Factorial(n-1)
in
        result
```

In the first line of this code, a function is declared that takes **n** as an argument and returns a number as its result.

The most crucial part is the third line, which defines the **result** step. This line contains an **if** conditional statement that checks whether the input number is less than or equal to 1. If so, the function returns **1**. This is the **base case** (termination condition) of the recursion. If the number passed to the function is greater than one, the function returns the product of that number and the result of calling itself recursively with the input decreased by 1. **Factorial** is the name of the initially created blank query, which becomes a function through the above code, although the name remains the same.

The remaining lines include the **let** keyword (which begins the query), the **in** keyword (which ends the query), and the return value, which is explicitly the **result** step following the **in** keyword.

Let us now go through a step-by-step explanation of how the custom **Factorial** function operates for the input value of **3**:

1. **3** is not less than or equal to **1**, so the initial call to **Factorial** triggers a second call to **Factorial**, this time for the value **2** (**3 - 1**), which will later be multiplied by **3**.

2. In the second instance, **2** is still not less than or equal to **1**, so a third call to **Factorial** is made for **1** (**2 - 1**), whose result will later be multiplied by **2**.

3. In the third instance, **1** is equal to **1**, so the function returns **1** and exits.

4. The result **1** from the third instance is returned to the second instance and multiplied by **2**, yielding **2**. The second instance concludes and passes the result to the first instance.

5. The result **2** is returned to the first instance and multiplied by **3**, resulting in **6**.

6. The final result **6** is returned as the output of **Factorial(3)**.

The custom **Factorial** function can be saved by clicking the **Close & Load** command on the **Home** tab (*Figure 1.13*). The function will be loaded as a connection only. However, saving it is not strictly necessary, as Power Query provides a built-in function `Number.Factorial`, which performs the same calculation.

This example primarily serves to illustrate the basic mechanism of recursion in Power Query.

Tips for efficient M language scripting

The following techniques, drawn from the examples in this chapter, can help improve the performance, clarity, and flexibility of your M code when working in Power Query:

- Combine multiple steps into one. Use nested functions (e.g., `List.Sum(List.Range(...))`) instead of creating intermediate columns and steps when possible.

- Use column references as lists. Many list-based functions accept a column reference written as `PreviousStep[ColumnName]` to treat it as a list.

- Apply dynamic logic using index columns. Generating an index column can help implement running totals, remove specific rows, or create row-wise operations.

- Leverage built-in functions. Explore functions such as `List.PositionOf`, `List.Transform`, `Table.ColumnNames` or others to simplify logic that may otherwise require complex manual steps.

- Use optional arguments for better flexibility. For example, provide `Comparer.OrdinalIgnoreCase` to make matching case-insensitive.

- Explore function behavior with the formula bar and fx icon. Use the editor's formula bar to inspect syntax, and use the fx button to insert new steps that reference earlier ones.

Guidelines for structuring queries

To keep your Power Query solutions clear, efficient, and easy to maintain over time, consider the following best practices drawn from the techniques used throughout this chapter:

- **Use meaningful step names**: Rename each query step (e.g., `#"Grouped Rows"`, `#"Promoted Headers"`) to reflect its purpose clearly. Avoid keeping default names like `Changed Type1`.

- **Minimize the number of applied steps**: Avoid redundant steps such as unnecessary renaming, type changes, or column reordering unless needed for logic.

- **Group related transformations**: Keep logically related transformations close together. For instance, when filtering rows and sorting data for reporting purposes, it is best to perform both operations within the same section of the query to keep related transformations organized.

- **Keep queries dynamic**: Design logic that adapts to changes in source data (e.g., changing column names, number of rows, or file structure). Use `Table.ColumnNames`, `List.Count`, or conditional logic, to support such scenarios.

- **Avoid direct column name references when not stable**: If the source is expected to change, avoid hardcoded column names in functions like `Table.SelectColumns`. Instead, generate column lists dynamically.

- **Comment your M code when needed**: Use double slashes `//` to add short comments explaining complex logic in the Advanced Editor.

- **Separate complex logic into helper queries or custom functions**: This modular approach makes debugging and reuse easier.

- **Validate step dependencies**: Use the Advanced Editor to verify that earlier steps are not accidentally overwritten or referenced incorrectly after changes.

Conclusion

In this chapter, we focused on practical examples that demonstrate the power of the M language in solving real-world data transformation problems. You learned how to calculate running totals using list operations, sort data based on custom-defined logic, and compare group averages to global values. We also covered techniques for dynamically removing rows and columns, handling inconsistent file structures, and generating unique pairings from a list. Finally, the concept of recursion was introduced through a custom factorial function, providing insight into more advanced scripting possibilities. These examples bridge the gap between interface-based transformations and full M code flexibility.

In the next chapter, we will cover query optimization and Power Query extensions.

Multiple choice questions

1. **How is a column in a table referenced as a list in Power Query?**
   a. ColumnName only
   b. TableName[ColumnName]
   c. Column{Table}
   d. Table(ColumnName)

2. **What value does List.PositionOf return if the item is not found in the list?**
   a. 0
   b. -1
   c. Null
   d. Error

3. **What are the common reasons to perform sorting by custom list in Power Query rather than Excel?**

    a. To ensure consistent results across computers

    b. To affect subsequent calculations like indexing or ranking

    c. To enable better chart visuals

    d. Since Excel does not support custom lists

4. **What does the function Table.ColumnNames return?**

    a. A record of field names

    b. A list of column names from a table

    c. A list of values in the first column

    d. A text string of headers

5. **Which of the following is true about recursion?**

    a. A function calls itself with a smaller input

    b. It is only used for loops

    c. It replaces all conditions with constants

    d. It cannot be implemented in M

6. **Which options are valid in the List.PositionOf function's occurrence argument?**

    a. Occurrence.First

    b. 1

    c. Comparer.OrdinalIgnoreCase

    d. Occurrence.All

Answers

Question number	Answer option letter
1.	b.
2.	b.
3.	a., b., d.
4.	b.
5.	a.
6.	a., b., d.

CHAPTER 11
Optimization and Extensions

Introduction

In the previous chapter, we explored practical examples of using the M language to solve complex data transformation challenges. This chapter focuses on enhancing the performance and efficiency of your Power Query solutions.

It introduces key optimization techniques, such as minimizing applied steps, using appropriate data types, and avoiding costly operations like merges or grouping when possible. We will also explore tools for measuring query runtime, including **Visual Basic for Applications (VBA)** macros and Power BI diagnostics.

We will also introduce Power Query extensions in Visual Studio Code, providing a more flexible environment for developing and formatting M code.

Structure

This chapter covers the following topics:

- View and statistics options
- Optimization
- Runtime
- Power Query extensions

Objectives

By the end of this chapter, you will be able to evaluate and optimize Power Query performance using practical techniques and built-in tools. You will learn how to reduce unnecessary steps, choose efficient data types, and avoid costly operations. You will also discover how to measure query execution time using Power Query functions, VBA macros, and Power BI Desktop diagnostics. Additionally, you will be introduced to the basics of using Visual Studio Code for writing and formatting M code more effectively.

View and statistics options

Based on the data in this example, several options in the Power Query editor related to data display and statistics will be discussed (statistical options are available in newer versions of Power Query).

The work is conducted with the **Sales** query from the **Sales.xlsx** file. The data has been specifically prepared so that the first few rows include special characters, some empty cells, and a few errors. This is shown in *Figure 11.1*:

	A	B	C	D	E	F
1	**Date**	**Merchant**	**Product**	**Quantity**	**Income**	**Price**
2	1/4/2025	Aladdin	Sapphire	21	$294.00	$14.00
3	1/8/2025		Gold bar	3	$749.70	$249.90
4	1/15/2025	Jasmine	Goldcoin	2	$20.00	$10.00
5	1/16/2025	Genie	Copper coin	1		$0.00
6	1/18/2025	Genie		8	$40.00	$5.00
7	1/24/2025	Genie		2	$29.60	$14.80
8	1/27/2025	Jasmine	Diamond		$378.10	#DIV/0!
9	1/27/2025	Iago	Copper◻coin	2	$2.00	$1.00
10	1/28/2025	Jafar	Ruby	10	$160.00	$16.00

Figure 11.1: Data in the tSales table used in the Sales query

To access the query, on the **Data** tab, expand the **Get Data** command and select **Launch Power Query Editor** (*Figure 2.8*). Even though there is only one query in this file, it is not opened automatically, and a blank editor is displayed. To display the query, expand the **Queries** list on the left side of the editor and select the **Sales** query. This will load the data, the appearance of which in the editor is shown in *Figure 11.2*:

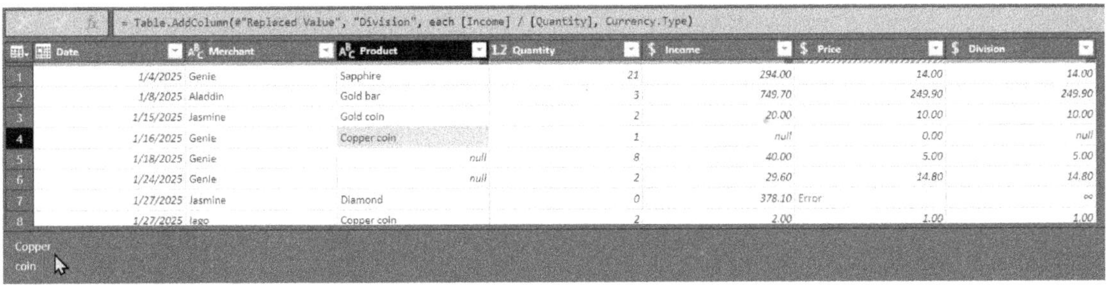

Figure 11.2: *View of the final step of the Sales query*

The focus will be on analyzing the changes in data display and the presentation of statistics related to the checkboxes located on the **View** tab. These checkboxes are shown in *Figure 11.3*:

Figure 11.3: *Data Preview checkbox group*

View options

The first checkbox is **Monospaced**. It means that each character has exactly the same width. This can improve data readability, especially for numbers and codes of identical length (character count). The appearance of the data after selecting the **Monospaced** checkbox is shown in *Figure 11.4*:

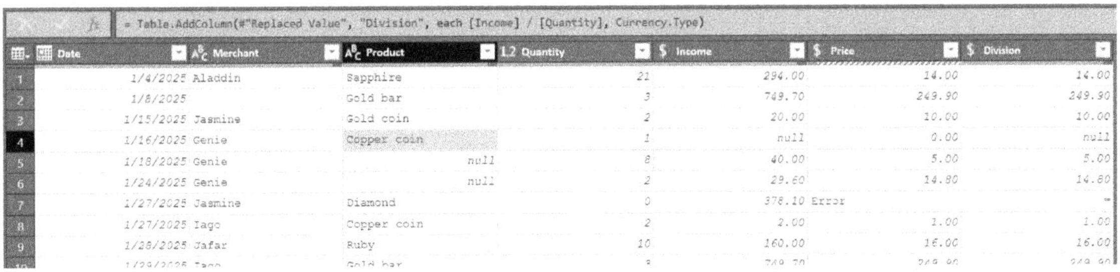

Figure 11.4: *Data after selecting the Monospaced checkbox*

Tip: **The Monospaced checkbox does not affect the font in the formula bar or in the Advanced Editor window. It only influences how the data is displayed. In Power Query, the editor font cannot be changed in any other way. There is no option to choose a specific font, such as Cambria or Times New Roman, for displaying the code.**

The next checkbox is **Show whitespace**. It allows the display of whitespace and newline signs. In practice, it enables the identification of characters such as line breaks or tab characters (if present within text). By default, the Power Query editor displays these characters as spaces in the data preview (*Figure 11.2* and *Figure 11.4*). The appearance of the data after selecting the **Show whitespace** checkbox is shown in *Figure 11.5*:

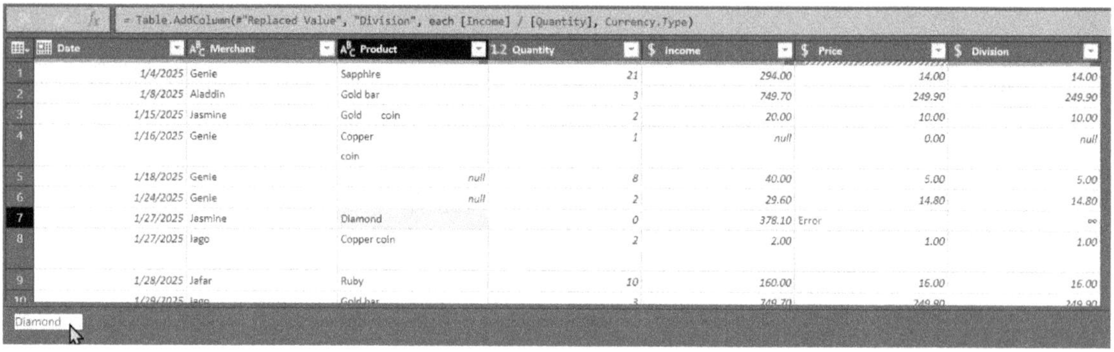

Figure 11.5: Data after selecting the Show whitespace checkbox

As shown in the preceding figure, the editor does not visually differentiate between tab characters, other special characters, or spaces at the end of the data. For example, in row 7 of the data in the **Product** column, a tab character appears after the word **Diamond**. It is not visible in the cell itself. Only by selecting the cell directly and then examining its value can it be seen that additional characters follow the word **Diamond**. Therefore, this checkbox only facilitates the identification of cells containing newline and tab characters.

Examples of special characters and their symbolic notations are shown in *Table 11.1*:

Character name	Code in PQ	ASCII	HTML	Word
Tab	#(tab)	9	\t	→
Paragraph break	#(cr)	13	\r	¶
Line break	#(lf)	10	\n	↵
Non-breaking space	#(00A0)	160		°

Table 11.1: Example special characters

Tip: **After selecting the Show whitespace checkbox, the special characters remain displayed as spaces in filters and statistics. This means that in this example, the Copper coin will appear three times in the list of items in the Product column. They will look identical to the user, but they are considered three different values by data analysis tools due to the presence of different separating characters.**

Statistic options

Before discussing the next checkboxes, it is necessary to examine the lines located beneath the column headers (these are available in newer versions of Power Query). They present a general overview of the data condition in a column. In general, if all data entries are valid, the entire bar below the header is green. If some cells are empty or contain **null** values, the width of this bar adjusts proportionally to the number of such values. If the column contains errors, the bar begins to be filled with red.

When the cursor is hovered over this bar, a summary window appears after a short delay, showing data quality statistics for the selected column. The editor displays information on how many cells contain valid values, how many are empty, and how many contain errors. In the lower-right corner of this summary, there is an ellipsis which, when clicked, reveals additional options, as shown in *Figure 11.6*:

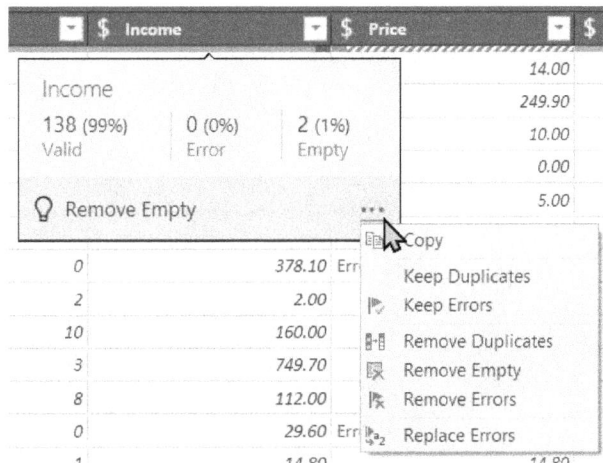

Figure 11.6: Context window with data quality summary for the Income column

The **Copy** option copies the statistical data, that is, the number and percentage of valid, error-containing, and empty cells. If errors are present in the column, the editor does not display statistics about valid and empty cells. The default option shown next to the lightbulb icon (*Figure 11.6*) also changes from **Remove Empty** to **Remove Errors**. If the column contains neither errors nor empty cells, no default option is displayed.

Tip: **All statistical options analyze a maximum of the first 1000 rows.**

It is now possible to immediately select the checkboxes **Column quality** and **Column distribution**. This causes the display of statistical data beneath the column headers, which corresponds to the information previously shown in the window (*Figure 11.6*), as well as distribution statistics, meaning the count of distinct and unique values. Additionally, a visual distribution of values is shown as bars whose width is proportional to the frequency of the values. The number of displayed bars depends on the number of unique elements in the column and on the column width, but the editor never displays more than fifty distribution bars. The data after selecting the **Column quality** and **Column distribution** checkboxes is shown in *Figure 11.7*:

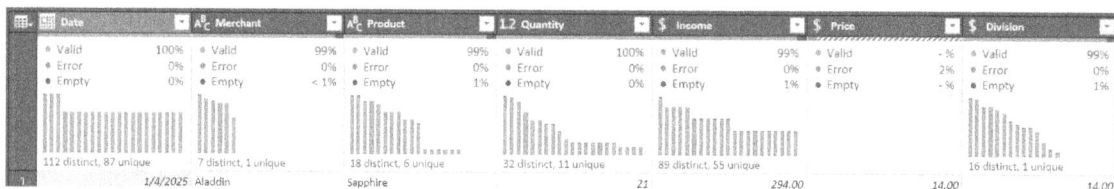

Figure 11.7: Context window with data quality summary for the Income column

To view more detailed statistical data about a column, the **Column profile** checkbox must be selected. Then, after clicking the column header, two areas appear below the data pane (**Column statistics** and **Value distribution**) as shown in *Figure 11.8*:

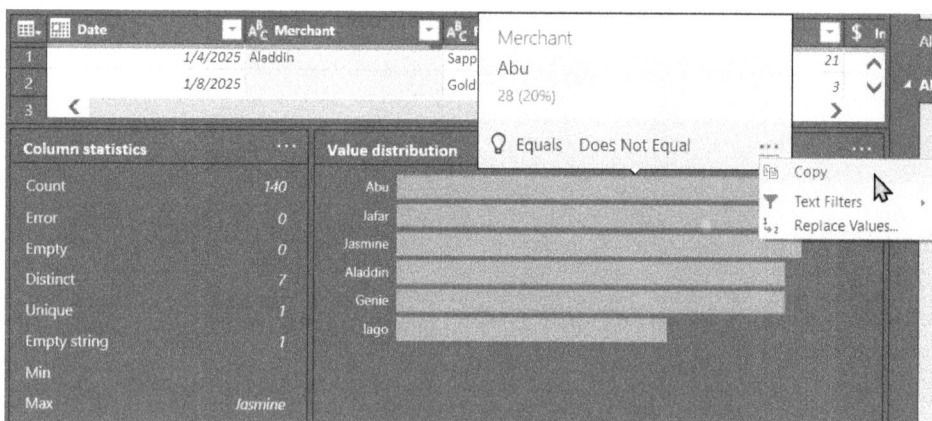

Figure 11.8: Data summary for the Merchant column

Hovering over a bar or column related to a specific element within the **Value distribution** area opens a window showing the distribution details for that element. These include the column name, element name, the number of occurrences of that element, and its percentage share in the total (*Figure 11.8*). At the bottom of this window, there are options for quickly applying filters. Filters can be applied so that values in the column are either equal to or different from the selected element. Additionally, clicking the ellipsis in the bottom-right corner of this window reveals more options:

- **Copy**: Copies the name of the selected element.

- **Filters**: Displays filters tailored to the data type of the analyzed column.

- **Replace Values**: Opens the **Replace Values** window (*Figure 5.21*), with the **Value To Find** field already populated with the name of the selected element.

The statistics shown in the **Column statistics** area depend on the data type assigned to the column. If the column contains errors or is assigned the **any** data type, the editor does not analyze the data distribution within the column and only provides the most basic statistical calculations.

> Fun fact: **The Value distribution area does not analyze empty cells or cells containing null values. However, these values are included in calculations within the Column statistics area.**

Clicking the ellipsis in the top-right corner of the **Column statistics** area only reveals the **Copy** option, which allows all statistical calculations to be copied. Clicking the ellipsis in the top-right corner of the **Value distribution** area opens a context menu with two options, as shown for the **Date** column in *Figure 11.9*:

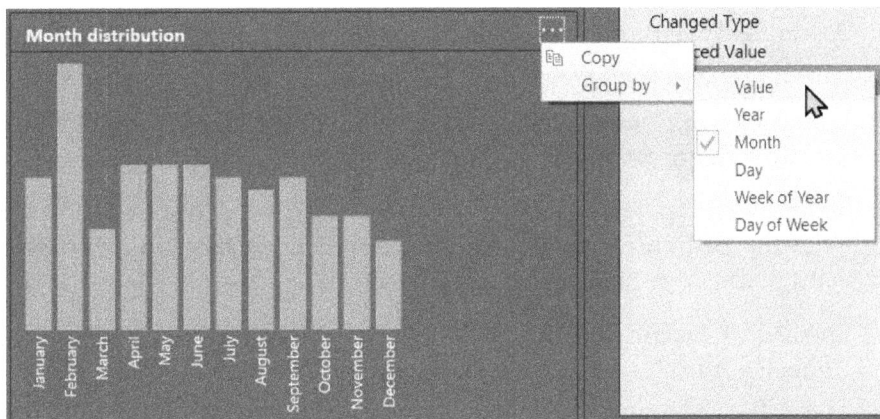

Figure 11.9: Data distribution in the Date column grouped by Month

The first option allows copying the visible distribution information, that is, the element name and its occurrence count. The second option enables grouping data. Grouping options for a date-type column are shown in *Figure 11.9*. By default, the distribution is displayed by values in the column, and then the grouping options can be adjusted. For the **Percentage** and **Currency** data types, no grouping options are available, and for numeric types, the only grouping option is by sign (including zero).

All view and statistics options have now been discussed, so the editor can be closed without saving changes.

Optimization

A number of Power Query query examples have already been discussed. In some of them, optimization techniques were mentioned. Some of these optimizations focus on improving query performance, while others aim to reduce the number of errors in the code. This section organizes the discussed methods and introduces additional optimization possibilities.

The most important optimization techniques aimed at improving performance include:

1. Remove unnecessary data (columns and rows) before it reaches Power Query. If the data source can be controlled, it is best to limit the amount of information imported before it is loaded into the editor. The fewer the data rows and columns Power Query has to process, the faster the query will execute.

   a. **Example**: When exporting information from an external program to a .csv file, it is advisable to limit the number of columns and rows at the export stage.

2. If the first step is not possible, remove unnecessary columns and filter unnecessary rows and files as early as possible. If the data source cannot be limited (e.g., a folder containing `.csv` files), filtering and column removal should be performed at the beginning of the query.

   a. **Example**: When combining files from a folder (e.g., `200` `.csv` files), apply a filter to exclude files from previous years.

3. Use the most appropriate and smallest possible data type. Unnecessarily *heavy* data types slow down queries and may lead to inefficient memory usage.

   a. **Example**: Instead of using the Date/Time data type, use Date if the time is not relevant for transformations. Similarly, if Power Query incorrectly interpreted values, consider changing the type.

   Instead of **Decimal Number**, use **Whole Number**, which represents `Int64.` `Type`. If applicable, use smaller integer types, as shown in *Table 11.2*:

Type	Description	Range
Int8.type	8-bit integer	−128 to 127
Int16.type	16-bit integer	−32,768 to 32,767
Int32.type	32-bit integer	Approximately ±2 billion
Int64.type	64-bit integer	Approximately ±9 billion billions

Table 11.2: Example special characters

4. Minimize the number of steps when possible, and when it does not overcomplicate the code. Each step is a potential recalculation and increased memory usage. When a simple combination of steps is possible, it should be implemented.

   a. **Example**: Steps that add a new column assign it a name. In some cases, it is possible to change the name directly in the user interface; in others, it is necessary to edit the name directly in the formula bar. This is more optimal than adding a separate step to rename the column.

   Similarly, some user interface operations do not assign a data type, even though it may be required later. It is often possible to provide the type as an argument directly in the applied function.

5. Replace multiple interface steps with a single M function. Performing a transformation through the user interface may require multiple steps, whereas equivalent transformations can often be completed using one or two M functions.

    a. **Example**: Data shown in *Figure 10.28* is transformed into the structure shown in *Figure 10.30* using the following formula:

    ```
    = Table.FromRecords(List.Combine(Matches))
    ```

    While this result could be achieved using commands from the user interface, it would require at least three steps (or four if null values were to be filtered out).

6. Avoid merge and Group By operations, as they are computationally expensive. Although these operations are sometimes necessary, they should be avoided if simpler alternatives exist.

    a. **Example**: Instead of joining a table that contains a discount threshold, a logical condition can be used in a new column:

    ```
    if [Amount] > 1000 then "High" else "Low"
    ```

7. Test the performance of different methods that yield the same result. The same result can often be achieved using several approaches. It is worth testing which one is faster, especially with large datasets.

    This concept is discussed in greater detail later in the chapter.

Methods aimed at reducing errors include the following:

1. Do not refer to columns by their positions, and try to limit references to column names.

    Column positions may easily change in the data source. Referring to columns based on their default position-dependent names increases the risk of referencing incorrect data.

    Similarly, column names can also change. Therefore, for example, when removing a large number of unnecessary columns, it is better to use the `Table.SelectColumns` function, which allows for specifying a smaller set of columns by name.

2. When importing data from a folder, do not rely on exact file names, and remember to filter out unnecessary files.

    During folder import, file names are typically not examined individually. However, it is often possible to identify files to be included based on a code in the filename, such as a region name. Unnecessary files (with incorrect extensions or temporary files) should be filtered out. It is also possible to filter by file attributes such as creation or modification date.

3. Replace values in a case-insensitive manner.

   Power Query is case-sensitive. Functions such as **Text.Replace** or **List.PositionOf** are case-sensitive by default. Therefore, it is advisable to use transformations such as **Text.Lower** to neutralize case sensitivity, or to provide the appropriate comparer argument, e.g. **Comparer.OrdinalIgnoreCase**, when available.

4. Avoid hardcoding values in filters or conditions across multiple places or locations where they are difficult to update.

   Changing hardcoded values is slow, especially if the changes must be made in multiple places or by someone unfamiliar with Power Query or the M language. It is therefore recommended to use parameters or reference values from Excel tables, which are much easier for an average Excel user to modify.

5. Avoid referencing specific indexes.

   Using expressions such as **Source{4}[Column]** may result in retrieving incorrect data if the dataset becomes sorted differently. A better practice is to retrieve row information based on a unique key, for example:

   = Source{[Product="Train"]}[Column]

Runtime

The best query optimization requires measuring query execution time. This book discusses three methods in the following sections.

Power Query

The first method, often found while browsing the internet, involves using the internal Power Query function **DateTime.LocalNow()** at the beginning and end of a query. At first glance, this seems like a valid approach, as Power Query processes steps sequentially. However, **DateTime.LocalNow()** is evaluated at the beginning of the processing, which means that both recorded timestamps can be nearly identical. Therefore, this method is unreliable in practice.

Visual basic for applications

The second solution uses VBA code, such as:

```
Sub MeasureRefreshTime()
    Dim t0 As Double
    t0 = Timer
    Selection.ListObject.QueryTable.Refresh BackgroundQuery:=False
    MsgBox "Elapsed time: " & Timer - t0 & " seconds"
End Sub
```

At the beginning of the macro, a variable named **t0** is declared and assigned the current time, representing the macro's start. The macro then refreshes the query. It is important that the VBA code disables background query refresh, as otherwise, the next line of code would begin executing before the query has completed. This would result in an inaccurate measurement.

At the end of the macro, the current time (via the **Timer** function) is subtracted from the value stored in **t0** to calculate the elapsed time, which can then optionally be displayed.

When running this VBA code, it is necessary to ensure that the active cell is located within the table returned by the query to Excel. This method does not allow measuring execution time for queries that exist only as connections.

To refresh the query by its internal name, the following line of code:

```
Selection.ListObject.QueryTable.Refresh BackgroundQuery:=False
```

Should be replaced with:

```
ActiveWorkbook.Connections("Query - tFiles").Refresh
```

After this change, it is essential to disable background refresh in the query options (*Figure 2.44*) and to correctly reference the query's internal name in the VBA code.

Power BI Desktop diagnostics

The third solution involves using the built-in diagnostic features in Power BI Desktop. Since this book focuses on Power Query, only the essential aspects of this solution will be discussed. If Power BI Desktop is installed, it is possible to follow along using the **Diagnostics.pbix** file.

First, it is necessary to ensure that diagnostic tracing is enabled. To do so, follow these steps:

1. Click the **File** menu.
2. Locate **Options and settings** at the bottom left.
3. In the **Options and settings** window that opens, click **Options**.
4. In the **Options** window, navigate to the **Diagnostics** tab and check the **Enable tracing** checkbox, as shown in *Figure 11.10*:

Options   □ ×

Tracing will affect all currently open files. Tracing will be automatically disabled when you close the last file.

GLOBAL

Data Load

Power Query Editor

DirectQuery

R scripting

Python scripting

Security

Privacy

Regional Settings

Updates

Usage Data

Diagnostics

Preview features

Save and Recover

Report settings

Copilot (preview)

CURRENT FILE

Data Load

Regional Settings

Privacy

Auto recovery

Published semantic model settings

Query reduction

Report settings

Diagnostic Options ⊙

☑ Enable tracing

☐ Bypass geocoding cache

Crash Dump Collection

Crash dump collection for the Mashup Engine process is currently not enabled.

🛡 Enable Now

Open crash dump/traces folder

Clear Traces folder

[Collect diagnostic information]

Version

2.143.878.0 64-bit (May 2025)

Query Diagnostics

○ Enable in Report and Query Editor (may require running as admin)

⦿ Enable in Query Editor (does not require running as admin)

Diagnostics Level

☑ Aggregated ⊙

☑ Detailed ⊙

Additional Diagnostics

☑ Performance counters ⊙

☑ Data privacy partitions ⊙

[OK] Cancel

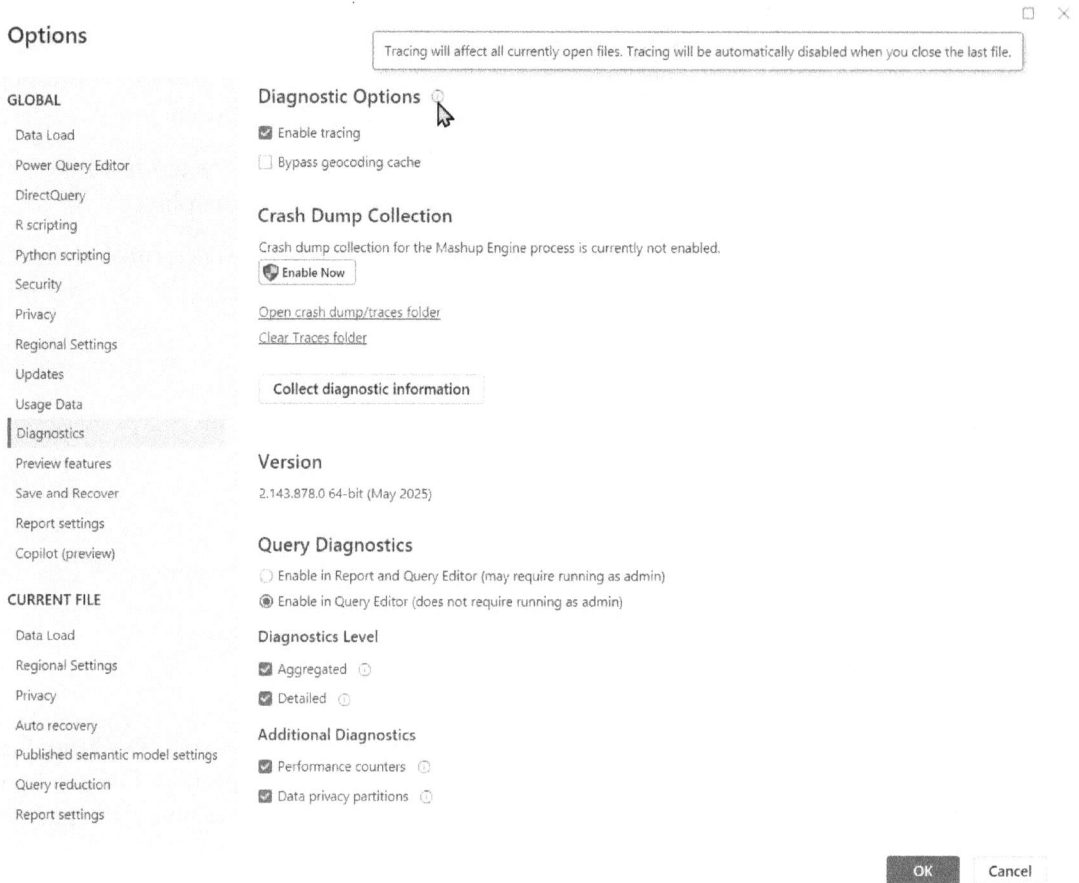

Figure 11.10: *Diagnostics options properties*

It is important to note that this checkbox will be automatically cleared once all instances of Power BI Desktop are closed.

Depending on the desired level of detail in the diagnostic reports (queries), enable or disable the four checkboxes at the bottom of the **Diagnostics** tab (*Figure 11.10*):

- Aggregated
- Detailed
- Performance counters
- Data privacy partitions

5. Confirm changes by clicking the **OK** button.

Queries between Power Query and Power BI Desktop can be transferred by following these steps:

1. Copying the query code between the Advanced Editors of Power Query in Excel and Power Query in Power BI Desktop.

2. Importing a query into Power BI Desktop using the following steps:

   a. Click the **File** menu.

   b. Select the **Import** option.

   c. In the **Import** window, select **Power Query, Power Pivot, Power View**, as shown in *Figure 11.11*:

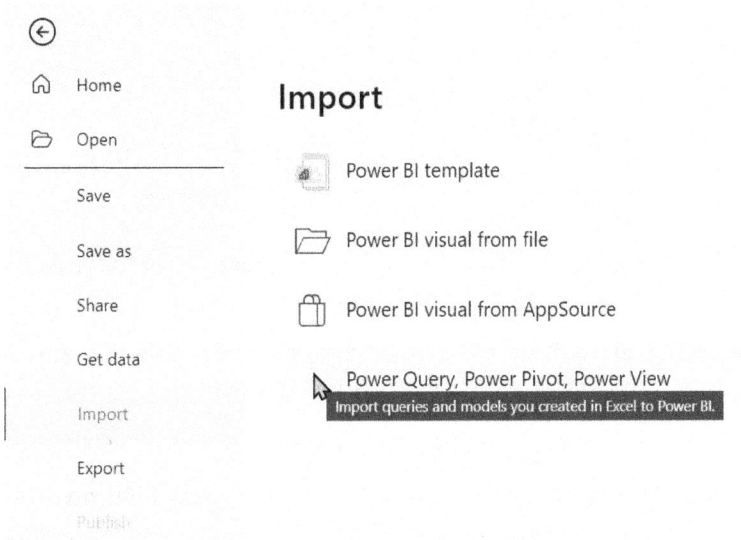

Figure 11.11: *Import options in Power BI Desktop*

   d. Locate and open the Excel file from which the queries will be imported, then confirm the import.

3. Once tracing is enabled and the desired query has been loaded into the **.pbix** file, proceed to Power Query by clicking **Transform Data** on the **Home** tab. In the Power Query Editor, the **Tools** tab will appear, containing commands related to query diagnostics.

4. The **Diagnose Step** command allows diagnosing a specific selected step of the query, as shown in *Figure 11.12*:

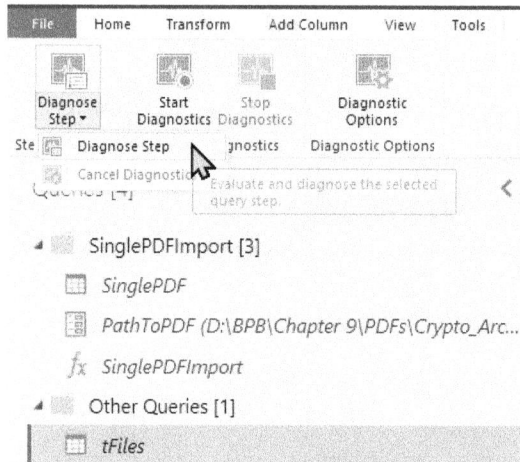

Figure 11.12: Diagnostic commands in the Tools tab

5. The **Start Diagnostics** command enables diagnostics for all executed operations, usually related to the refresh of a particular query.

6. After completing all actions to be analyzed, click the **Stop Diagnostics** command, which becomes active after selecting **Start Diagnostics**.

7. The **Diagnostic Options** command opens the same window as shown in *Figure 11.10*.

Assuming diagnostics have been started using the **Start Diagnostics** command, the query **tFiles** has been refreshed, and diagnostics have been stopped using the **Stop Diagnostics** command. Since all four checkboxes at the bottom of the diagnostics options window (*Figure 11.10*) were selected, Power Query generated four additional queries (diagnostic outputs), as shown in *Figure 11.13*:

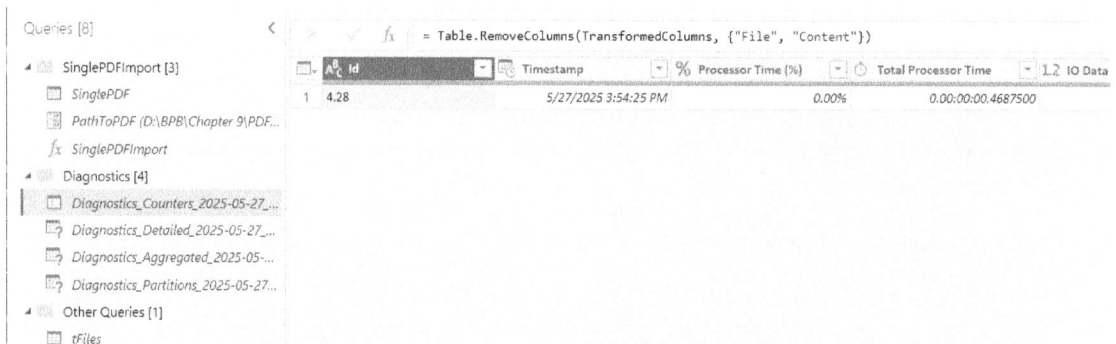

Figure 11.13: Diagnostic queries created for refreshing the tFiles query

Each query contains various details about operations performed at each step of the refreshed query. In addition to execution time, an important insight is that a single query step typically corresponds to the execution of multiple operations.

8. If the generated diagnostic queries are no longer needed, they can be deleted. Simply select them and click the **Delete** button.

9. Once diagnostics for the target query are complete, the Power Query Editor and Power BI Desktop application can be closed.

Power Query extensions

At the end of this book, we will mention extensions related to Power Query. Visual Studio Code will be used for this purpose, which can be downloaded from the following website:

https://code.visualstudio.com/docs/setup/windows

Once the program has been installed and launched, follow these steps:

1. Click the **Extensions** icon on the left side and type Power Query into the search bar, as shown in *Figure 11.14*:

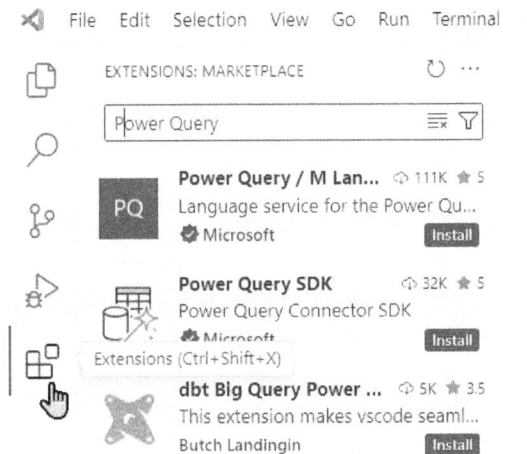

Figure 11.14: Searching for extensions in Visual Studio Code

The first extension from the search results list (*Power Query / M Language*) should be installed.

2. The second extension, *Power Query SDK,* allows for the creation of custom connectors, and its discussion goes beyond the scope of this book. To install an extension in **Visual Studio Code**, simply click the **Install** button located next to the listed extension. Clicking the name of the extension will display additional information about it.

3. Clicking the **Extensions** icon again on the left will close the search window. The keyboard shortcut *Ctrl + Shift + X* opens this window but does not close it.

4. After closing the **Extensions** window, a new project or file can be created by pressing *Ctrl + N*. By default, the created file will be a plain text file, meaning that the code pasted into it will not be color-coded, nor will there be any function name suggestions. It is recommended to change the **Language Mode** for the file so that the M code is formatted properly. To do this, click the current language mode (**Plain Text**) in the bottom-right corner of the **Visual Studio Code** window, as shown in *Figure 11.15*:

Figure 11.15: Changing the Language Mode

5. After clicking **Language Mode**, a search field will appear where the desired language mode can be entered. Select the appropriate item from the search results to confirm the change, as shown in *Figure 11.16*:

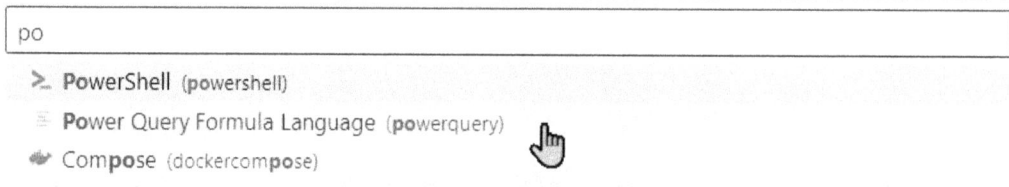

Figure 11.16: Searching for Language Mode

6. Now, a sample M code can be pasted into the file (taken from the `DistinctMatches` query in *Chapter 10, Examples Using M Language*):

```
let
    Players = Excel.CurrentWorkbook(){[Name="tPlayers"]}[Content][Name],
    Indexes = List.Positions(Players),
    Matches = List.Transform(Indexes, (i) => List.Transform(
List.Range(Indexes, i + 1, List.Count(Indexes) - i - 1),(j) =>
[Player1=Players{i}, Player2=Players{j}])),
    AllMatches = Table.FromRecords(List.Combine(Matches))
in
    AllMatches
```

7. After pasting, the keyboard shortcut *Shift + Alt + F* can be used to format the document automatically. Alternatively, right-click on the code and select the appropriate option from the context menu. The formatted code is shown in *Figure 11.17*:

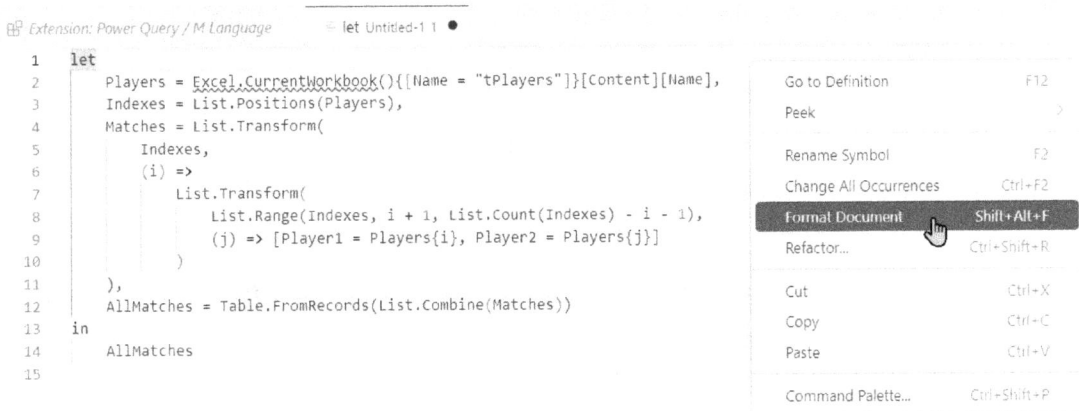

Figure 11.17: *Pasted code after formatting*

Properly formatted code is easier to understand. Additionally, the editor in Visual Studio Code provides more informative suggestions and descriptions for functions while editing the code. It is also possible to install additional extensions that further improve the developer experience, as well as change the font and many other settings unavailable in the Advanced Editor of Power Query.

If needed, the formatted code can be copied and pasted back into Power Query.

Conclusion

This chapter focused on improving performance and extending capabilities in Power Query. We learned how to analyze data quality and structure using built-in view and statistics options, helping identify issues such as null values, errors, or inconsistent formatting. Practical optimization techniques were introduced, from reducing step count and using appropriate data types to avoiding inefficient operations like merges and unnecessary references. Finally, we explored basic usage of Visual Studio Code as a supplementary editor for writing and formatting M code.

Multiple choice questions

1. **What does the Monospaced checkbox in Power Query affect?**

    a. The font used in the formula bar

    b. The font used in the Advanced Editor

    c. The way data is displayed in the preview grid

    d. The font type in exported reports

2. **What is the main reason to disable background refresh in VBA when measuring query time?**

    a. To prevent Power Query from refreshing

    b. To allow simultaneous macro execution

    c. To avoid errors with table selection

    d. To ensure the macro waits for the query to complete

3. **What options are available in the Power Query column statistics context menu?**

    a. Copy statistics

    b. Replace column name

    c. Group data

    d. Add data labels

4. **What is the purpose of the Column quality window?**

    a. Displays syntax errors in the code

    b. Shows invalid values in formulas

    c. Shows valid, error, and empty values per column

    d. Groups values by type

5. **Which of the following are valid ways to optimize Power Query performance?**

    a. Remove unnecessary columns early

    b. Use the most detailed available data types

    c. Combine steps when possible

    d. Filter files before importing

Answers

Question number	Answer option letter
1.	c.
2.	d.
3.	a., c.
4.	c.
5.	a., c., d.

Index

www.ingramcontent.com/pod-product-compliance
Lightning Source LLC
Chambersburg PA
CBHW061745210326
41599CB00034B/6791